Margaret Morris

D1614816

THE EUROPEAN MULTINATIONALS

A Renewed Challenge to American and British Big Business

Lawrence G. Franko

Centre d'Etudes Industrielles, Geneva
and
Congressional Budget Office, Washington, D.C.

Harper & Row
Publishers

London   New York   Hagerstown   San Francisco

Copyright © 1976 Lawrence G. Franko
All rights reserved

First published 1976
Harper & Row Ltd
28 Tavistock Street,
London WC2E 7PN

No part of this book may be used or reproduced in any
manner whatsoever without written permission except in
the case of brief quotations embodied in critical
articles and reviews.

Designed by Millions
Typeset by T. H. Brickell & Son Ltd at The Blackmore Press,
Gillingham, Dorset
Printed by A. Wheaton & Company, Exeter

Standard Book Number 06-318049-9

Contents

Introduction

This book tells the story of the international operations of the 85 largest industrial firms of the Western part of Continental Europe. It is concerned primarily with the manufacturing and extractive operations which Continental enterprises have owned outside of their home countries, for it is the conduct of these activities which distinguishes multinational enterprise from the less complicated, less controversial, national or export-oriented company.

This book is not, however, the story of the international activity of *all* large Western European enterprises. We are concerned with the international networks of the major enterprises based on the European Continent: the firms headquartered in Belgium, France, Germany, Italy, Luxemburg, the Netherlands, Sweden and Switzerland. Except by way of occasional contrast and comparison, British enterprises and their international operations are not the subject of this work.

A number of reasons for undertaking a special study of the evolution of the international activities of Continental enterprises emerged early on in the course of our research. The distinctive character of the Continental condition is discussed many times in the present work, but crudely put, the international history of Continental enterprises was radically different from that of British firms for three reasons. First, no industrialized Continental country, not even France, ever possessed an Empire akin to that once held by the United Kingdom. Secondly, no Western Continental country ever had the militarily secure sources of raw materials assured to Great Britain by its control of the oceans (or to the United States by its gigantic territory and its natural endowment). Thirdly, no Continental country had enterprises which could dominate natural resource-based industries in the manner of British firms (helped occasionally by American cousins). In sum, General de Gaulle's famous division of the world into 'les Anglo-Saxons et les autres' turned out to be more than a political shibboleth, and the British newspaper headline 'Fog in Channel, Continent Isolated' was more than a joke.

There was also a fourth reason for telling the story of Continental Multi-national Enterprise: few Continental enterprises had told their own in the leading international language – English. Indeed, perhaps because of the habits of secrecy naturally acquired by those living in countries which had frequently been under siege, few Continental firms had told the story of their international operations in any language.

While this book tells a story, it nevertheless differs from many histories. The reader will find not only events and dates, but also a search for patterns, causes and explanations which betrays both the author's biases and his affiliation with the Comparative Multinational Enterprise Project co-ordinated by Raymond Vernon, of Harvard University. As part of this search for patterns and causes, the experience of Continental European enterprise is often compared to the much more widely known evolution of American multinational enterprise. Hypotheses and theories useful in understanding the development of American companies' foreign manufacturing and extractive operations are examined for their usefulness in explaining the behavior of Continental enterprise.

An author inevitably owes an enormous debt to others when he attempts to summarize the international experience of enterprises which in 1971 employed some 5,900,000 people, had sales totalling some $132 billion, and which conducted their business operations in six different languages.

Thanks are due first and foremost to the many managers of the 80 Continental enterprises who provided the materials necessary for a reconstruction of the international histories of their enterprises. This work could never have been undertaken without their contribution. The managers of large Continental enterprises gave generously of their time and company records, both at their companies' headquarters and in informal conversation when they attended courses and seminars at the *Centre d'Etudes Industrielles* (CEI).

Thanks are also due to the many scholars and managers who commented on drafts of various parts of this book. So many have contributed at various stages of the work that it is almost unfair to single out individuals for special comment. A number of people had a direct impact on portions of this work, however. Particularly helpful comments and contributions were made by Michel Delapierre, Patrick Fridenson, Montgomery Graham, L F Haber, Max Hall, Gary Hufbauer, Charles P Kindleberger, Noritake Kobayashi, Charles-Albert Michalet, Zuhayr Mikdashi, Lars Otterbeck, Glenn Porter, Jan Tumlir, Victor Umbricht, Constantine Vaitsos, Louis T Wells, Jr, Mira Wilkins, and by my colleagues at the CEI. An early version of Chapter II was published by the *Business History Review* in September 1974.

This book could not have been written without the help of research assistants who went to companies and scoured libraries for data and sources on the international spread of Continental firms. Susanne Brun, Urs Schneider, Michael Tiger and William Davidson left few, if any, stones unturned, and the help of Ninon Lagrange and Henri de Bodinat was also appreciated. American library sources were examined by a team directed by Mrs Joan Curhan, and she, along with James Vaupel assembled the data bank on US and non-US multinational enterprise which underpins our comparisons of Continental behavior with the behavior of enterprises of other nationalities.

A special word of thanks is in order to the library staff of the CEI, and especially to its librarian, Dr Thérèse Seiler. Locating and obtaining the references used for this book were time-consuming tasks. Continental Europe has many good national libraries, but references were often dispersed among them. Dr Seiler's efforts enabled me to consult many more works than otherwise would have been possible.

Books are not only written, they also need to be typed, and I would like to thank Sakuntala Imhof-Lewis for her patience while first deciphering my horrible handwriting, and then preparing drafts and re-drafts.

The greatest debts of gratitude I owe, however, are due to Professor Raymond Vernon and to my wife, Marjorie. Professor Vernon provided me with a constant stream of encouragement, suggestions and criticism which helped to sustain my spirits and stretch my thinking during the three and a half years this book was in preparation. My wife Marjorie not only provided moral support, marvellous cooking, and companionship, she also had a major impact on the content and style of this work: her passion for history was matched only by her industriousness in unscrambling some of my more tortured sentences. She was superb.

My family, too, contributed to this work. Derek and Tania serenaded me with music and were patient indeed when Papa had to work. Although their raids into my desk meant that I never could find my scissors, scotch-tape or pencils, their conversion of my discarded drafts into drawings of flowers and models of viking ships entertained me immensely. My parents also helped, both morally and substantively: they found many references, particularly on European companies' US operations, that helped me greatly.

Research, of course, costs money. And the research on which this book is based cost rather a lot. I am more than thankful for the financial support given to this work by the *Centre d'Etudes Industrielles*, the Ford Foundation and the Harvard Business School.

Geneva, Switzerland
March 1975

Chapter I

The Largest Continental European Enterprises

During the 1960's, the phenomenon called multinational enterprise bore the indelible stamp: 'made in USA'.[1] Signposts in Europe, Latin America, and most of the rest of the non-socialist world were increasingly advertising the presence of IBM, Du Pont, Kodak, Esso, Gillette, Xerox, Coca-Cola, Ford, ITT and other representatives of American Big Business. Faced with this phenomenon, governments and political élites feared for their economic sovereignty and cultural identity. Their fear was all the greater since the American presence was not confined to American goods, but included a multitude of American-owned manufacturing and extractive operations embedded in the lives of nation-states.[2]

A few British, or jointly British and Dutch-owned enterprises were noticed as also having manufacturing or extractive operations in numerous countries, thus fitting the first and simplest definition of what constituted a multinational enterprise.[3] British Petroleum was extracting and refining in numerous countries, much like the five American oil majors.[4] Anglo-Dutch Unilever, and Anglo-Dutch Royal Dutch-Shell were also conspicuously present in several dozen nations. Several British enterprises had rather large numbers of manufacturing or extractive outposts in the former British Empire.[5] And Imperial Chemical Industries was observed to be adding European manu-facturing operations to its Empire activities.[6]

When the international activity of large enterprises based in Western Con-tinental Europe attracted attention, however, it was on account of the export activities of these firms. An American could hardly have remained unaware of the prodigious number of Volkswagens being shipped into his country. Europeans, too, saw an increasing number of foreign cars and household appliances crossing Continental borders. Moreover, the growing deficit in the United States balance of trade, and the successive revaluations of the Deutschmark, Dutch guilder, and Swiss franc, made the world suspect that Continental enterprises had other, less obvious distinctive competitive advantages in world trade. Nevertheless, to most observers, this Continental export activity still did not look like multinational enterprise.

Except for the tiny handful of enterprises undertaking transnational mergers, thus linking production facilities in more than one European country by common ownership, it was sometimes even thought that enterprises on the Continent were becoming increasingly *national*. Continental governments, it seemed, were encouraging or obliging large industrial enterprises to become instruments of national policy. Mergers and acquisitions were announced in every Continental nation, and in some industrial sectors they left in operation only one or two large 'national champion' enterprises.[7] The task conceived

---

[1] Servan-Schreiber, 1967: p 20; Behrman, 1969: p 13.
[2] Vernon, 1971; Behrman, 1971: Chapter 3.
[3] See, Aharoni, 1972 for a discussion of definitions of what constitutes a multinational enterprise.
[4] Longhurst, 1959.
[5] Hobsbawm, 1968; Stopford, 1974.
[6] Servan-Schreiber, 1967: p 20.
[7] European Communities, 1972, 1973, and 1974; Jacquemin and Cardon, 1973; Vernon, et al, 1974; Siekman, 1970.

by national governments for such champions was scarcely camouflaged: they were to serve as a counterforce to the real or imagined threats to sovereignty posed by multinational – meaning American or British – enterprises.

The Multinational Spread of Continental European Enterprise

A close examination of the historical record shows, however, that multi-nationality of manufacturing or extractive operations has never been an exclusive characteristic of American and British enterprises. More than a century and a half has elapsed since Cockerill of Belgium put up its first foreign manufacturing plant in Prussia in 1815, thus antedating the first American foreign manufacturing investment by 37 years.[8] Since the time of Cockerill's pioneering venture in textile machinery, almost all of Europe's large industrial enterprises have come to produce outside their home countries.

In 1970, there were 85 manufacturing enterprises headquartered in Western, Continental European nations whose sales of manufactured goods exceeded 400 million US dollars. The names and nationalities of these enterprises are listed in Chart 1. Eighty of these firms were included on Fortune's list of the largest 200 non-American industrial companies for 1970; the other five were family enterprises or financial holding companies not cited by Fortune but which nevertheless had manufacturing sales exceeding Fortune's 400 million dollar cut-off point. The headquarters' nationalities of the 85 large Continental enterprises were distributed as follows: six were Belgian (although one of these was 50% German-owned), five Dutch (if one included 60% Dutch-owned Royal Dutch-Shell, but not 50% Dutch—50% British Unilever), 21 French, 29 German, 7 Italian, 1 Luxemburg, 9 Swedish, and 7 Swiss.

On January 1, 1971, all but three of these 85 enterprises owned at least 25% of one or more foreign manufacturing ventures. Even 'national' steel and coal producers, like Buderus'che and Salzgitter of Germany, and *Charbonnages de France* and Vallourec of France had at least one foreign manufacturing sub-sidiary. And no fewer than 64 of the 85 largest Continental industrial firms had ownership interests exceeding 25% in manufacturing operations in six or more foreign nations. Thirty-four of the 85 largest Continental European industrial enterprises also owned a 25% or greater share in one or more foreign extractive subsidiaries.

During 1970 some 60 of the 71 large Continental enterprises for which information is available derived more than 25% (and, in the case of a handful of Swiss and Swedish enterprises, as much as 95%) of their total sales from exports and foreign production. Moreover, 26 of the 48 firms for which data

---

[8] Vanhemelryck, 1970: p 38; Wilkins, 1970: p 30. As the name of the enterprise suggests, however, neither the Cockerill family, nor the technology on which their investments were based were of Belgian origin. They came to the Continent from Great Britain. Belgium did not exist as a country until the Belgian province of the Kingdom of the Netherlands seceded in 1830. Between 1792 and 1814, Liège, the city near which the Cockerills established them-selves, had been French. In 1815, Liège was in the process of being attached to the Nether-lands as a result of the diplomatic negotiations following the Napoleonic wars.

Chart 1.1　Large Continental European Manufacturing Enterprises:
Company Names, Main Industries and Sales, 1970

Country of Headquarters & Name of Firm	Main Industry of Firm	Interlocking Ownership	Total Sales, 1970 ($Billion)
Belgium & Luxemburg:			
Arbed	Metals	Société Générale de Bélgique (15 %)	1·3
Agfa-Gevaert	Chemicals	Bayer of Germany (50 %)	0·5
Cockerill-Ougrée	Metals	Société Générale de Bélgique (13 %)	0·8
Metallurgie-Hoboken-Overpelt	Metals	Société Générale de Bélgique (15 % + indirect)	0·6
Petrofina, SA	Petroleum		1·3
Solvay & Cie	Chemicals		0·8
Société Générale	Various		
France:			
Aerospatiale	Transportation equipment	French Government (92·6 %)	0·6
L'Air Liquide	Chemicals		0·4
Boussois Souchon Neuvesel (BSN)	Glass		0·6
Charbonnages de France	Coal	French Government (100 %)	0·9
Citröen	Transporation equipment	Fiat (27 %) Michelin (55 %)	1·4
Compagnie Francaises des Pétroles	Petroleum	French Government (35 %)	1·9
Compagnie Générale d'Eléctricité	Electrical equipment		1·5
Librairie Hachette	Printing		0·5
Michelin	Rubber		1·2
Compagnie Péchiney, SA	Metals		1·6
Peugeot, SA	Transportation equipment		1·4
Renault	Transportation equipment	French Government (100 %)	2·5
Rhone-Poulenc, SA	Chemicals		1·9
Saint-Gobain-Pont-à-Mousson	Glass		1·6
Schneider, SA	Metals		0·6
Thomson-Brandt	Electrical equipment		1·0
Ugine Kuhlmann	Chemicals		1·5
Usinor	Metals		0·9
Vallourec	Metals	Michelin	0·5
Wendel-Sidelor, SA	Metals		1·1
Elf-Erap	Petroleum	French Government (100 %)	1·5

Germany:

AEG-Telefunken	Electrical machinery		2·3
BASF, AG	Chemicals		2·8
Bayer	Chemicals		2·5
BMW, AG	Transport equipment	Quandt Family	0·5
Bosch, GmbH	Electrical machinery		1·5
Buderus'sche-Eisenwerke	Metals	Flick Family (96 %)	0·6
Continental Gummi Werke	Rubber	Bayer (30 %)	0·4
Daimler-Benz, AG	Transport equipment	Quandt Family, Flick Family	3·1
Degussa	Chemicals	Owns Norddeutsche Affinerie (40 %), Owned by Henkel (30%)	0·5
Feldmuhle, AG	Pulp and paper	Flick Family	0·6
Friedrich Flick, KG	Iron and steel	Flick Family	
Gelsenberg, AG	Petroleum		0·7
Gutehoffnungshutte	Non-electrical machinery		1·3
Henkel	Chemicals	Owns 30 % Degussa	
Hoesch	Metals	Hoogovens (14.5 %)	1·4
Hoechst AG	Chemicals		3·0
Klöckner-Humboldt-Deutz AG	Non-electrical machinery	Klöckner Family	3·0
Klöckner-Werke AG	Metals	Klöckner Family	0·6
Fried. Krupp AG	Metals		1·6
Mannesmann AG	Non-electrical machinery		1·8
Metallgesellschaft AG	Metals		1·4
Norddeutsche Affinerie	Metals	Degussa (40 %) Metallgesellschaft (40 %)	0·4
Rheinstahl AG	Metals		1·3
Salzgitter AG	Metals	German Government (100 %)	0·8
Siemens AG	Electrical machinery		3·2
A Thyssen-Hutte AG	Metals		2·9
Varta AG	Electrical equipment	Quandt Family (65 %)	0·4
Veba AG	Petroleum	German Government (40 %)	
Volkswagenwerke (VW)	Transportation equipment	German Government (16 %); State of Lower Saxony (20 %)	

Italy:

ENI	Petroleum	Italian Government (100 %)	1·8
Fiat SpA	Transportation equipment		2·7
Montedison SpA	Chemicals	Italian Government (6 % as of 1971)	2·8
Ing C Olivetti SpA	Office machinery		0·7
Pirelli SpA	Rubber	In 1971 Dunlop (UK) and Pirelli took jointly-owned holdings (49 % or 51 %) in the subsidiaries of the two groups	1·2
Snia Viscosa	Chemicals		0·5
IRI	Various	Italian Government	

Chart 1.1—*continued*

Country of Headquarters & Name of Firm	Main Industry Of Firm	Interlocking Ownership	Total Sales, 1970 ($Billion)
Netherlands:			
Akzo	Chemicals		2·0
DSM	Chemicals	Dutch Government (100 %)	0·5
Hoogovens	Metals	Dutch Government (29 %)	0·6
NV Philips	Electrical machinery		4·2
Royal Dutch-Shell	Petroleum		10.7
Sweden:			
Asea	Electrical machinery	Wallenberg Family	0·7
L M Ericsson	Electrical machinery	Wallenberg Family	0·6
Gränges	Metals		0·6
Saab-Scania	Transportation	Wallenberg Family	0·7
SKF	Non-electrical machinery	Wallenberg Family	0·9
Swedish Match Co Ltd	Wood	Wallenberg Family	0·4
Volvo	Transportation equipment		1·0
A Johnson & Co	Various		
Kooperativa Forbundet	Food		1·3
Switzerland			
Alusuisse Ltd	Metals		0·5
Brown, Boveri & Cie	Electrical machinery		1·3
Ciba-Geigy	Chemicals	Merger 1971	1·5
Hoffmann-La Roche & Co	Chemicals		1·1
Nestlé Alimentana SA	Food		2·3
Sandoz AG	Chemicals		0·6
Sulzer AG	Non-electrical machinery		0·5

is available each had more than one-fifth of their employees in foreign manufacturing and extractive operations. Nine enterprises indicated that more than half of their employees worked abroad. Five of these companies were Swiss, three Swedish, two Dutch, and one each French and Italian.[9]

When World War I broke out, seven Continental enterprises were already manufacturing in seven or more countries (including their homelands). On the eve of World War II, there had been 14 Continental enterprises which had (or whose direct predecessors had) such a degree of multinationality. By 1960, 34 of the largest Continental firms were manufacturing in seven or more countries.

[9] Companies did not count employees of minority-owned subsidiaries as 'their' employees in these data. The 48 companies supplying data on employment had 3,677,000 employees on January 1, 1971, of whom 1,295,200 were located in foreign countries.

It was thus not a national, but a multinational picture of Continental European industrial enterprises which gradually emerged from a study embarked upon in 1971 by the *Centre d'Etudes Industrielles* (CEI) and the Harvard Business School with the support of the Ford Foundation. The first aim of this study was to reconstruct the international histories of the largest Belgian, Dutch, Luxemburg, French, German, Italian, Swiss and Swedish manufacturing firms. This study of Continental European enterprise was undertaken in collaboration with a broader survey of the international operations of large industrial enterprises known as the Comparative Multinational Enterprise Project.

The Comparative Multinational Enterprise Project

Toward the end of the 1960's, observers of large business enterprises began to suspect that the popular image of the American Challenge was largely a function of the availability of American statistics.[10] International organizations such as the OECD had attempted to make some estimates of the size of the foreign production activity of non-American manufacturing companies, but the dearth of government data still left the multinationality of those firms, if any, a matter for speculation.[11] The data concerning non-US foreign investments, such as it was, chiefly concerned the British and Japanese-based enterprises. Some aggregate data was available on German, French and Swedish foreign investment, but it was almost impossible to find information concerning the international manufacturing and extractive activity of Swiss, Dutch, Belgian, Luxemburg and Italian enterprise.[12]

A major aim of the Comparative Multinational Enterprise Project was to clear up some of the mystery surrounding the international activity (or lack thereof) of non-American enterprise. Under the overall co-ordination of Professor Raymond Vernon, the project began in 1971 to undertake an exhaustive search of the literature and company-interview survey of the history of the foreign operations of all non-US enterprises of sufficient size to qualify for inclusion in the Fortune '200' list for 1970. The data-gathering effort in Continental European countries was based at the CEI and supervised by the author.[13]

This census of the international activity of non-American enterprises constituted a sequel to the data-gathering phase of a study of American multinational

---

[10] Rolfe, 1969: p 20.
[11] OECD, 1972; Robock and Simmonds, 1970.
[12] For early efforts to synthesize the official statistics on foreign investments on non-American firms, see Behrman, 1969; Rolfe, 1969.
[13] The reconstruction of the international histories of the 67 largest Japanese enterprises was undertaken from the Harvard Business School and supervised by Professors Yoshihiro Tsurumi and Michael Yoshino: the survey of the foreign operations of the 47 largest British enterprises was directed by Professor John Stopford of the London Business School. The co-ordination of this multinational data-gathering enterprise was undertaken by Mrs Joan Curhan of the Harvard Business School. Mrs Curhan also supervised the preliminary literature search undertaken in libraries located in the United States. Mrs Curhan and Professor James Vaupel of Duke University also compiled the information on non-American enterprise into the Comparative Multinational Enterprise Data Bank. Aggregate tabulations from this data bank, as well as a detailed description of the data-gathering process are to be found in Vaupel and Curhan, 1973.

enterprise co-ordinated by the Harvard Business School between 1966 and 1970.[14] Data-gathering and analysis concerning US multinational enterprise had essentially (although not exclusively) focused on the 187 enterprises which manufactured in seven or more nations on Fortune's 1968 list of the 500 largest US industrial companies.[15] In the case of non-US enterprises, it was not possible to apply such an *a priori* rule of inclusion: too little was known about their foreign operations. The paucity of data available on the scope of foreign operations of non-US enterprise thus made it desirable to include all large non-American companies in the census, even at the cost of a loss in strict comparability of the samples.[16]

Data available from company annual reports, histories, and other published sources were supplemented by interviews with company officials. Co-operation from officials of large Continental European enterprises was particularly generous. Officials of 80 of the 85 Continental companies surveyed contributed between one and three days of their time to the initial data-gathering effort during 1971 and 1972. Considerably more time was often contributed to follow-up interviews and questionnaires.[17] Three of the five enterprises which chose not to co-operate in the initial interview program subsequently provided company histories and documentation which previously had not been widely circulated. The data collected prior to mid-1972, and therefore included in the Comparative Multinational Project Data Bank, has been partially tabulated and published in a separate volume by the Harvard Business School and the CEI.[18] Inevitably, however, numerous sources on Continental enterprises have become available since 1972; these are cited separately when promises of confidentiality would not be violated.

A Century of Subsidiary Proliferation

The large Continental European enterprises turn out to have been active in international manufacturing for a very long time. Sixty-one of them were founded (or had direct predecessors which were founded) before World War I, and no fewer than 37 of them owned one or more foreign manufacturing subsidiaries by 1914. Enterprises active in chemicals and electrical equipment had achieved a particularly impressive spread of foreign manufacturing activities. The earliest pioneers are cited in Table 1.1. German companies were particularly prominent in this early outward movement; indeed, according to some estimates, German foreign manufacturing investments alone considerably exceeded those of American enterprises on the

---

[14] Vaupel and Curhan, 1969.

[15] Vaupel, 1971; Vernon, 1971: Chapter 1.

[16] For a detailed discussion of the American and non-American samples, see Vaupel and Curhan, 1973.

[17] The efforts of Mr Urs Schneider of the CEI in obtaining this cooperation from enterprises were particularly noteworthy: he undertook 54 of the 80 interviews involved in the survey of the Continental firms.

[18] Vaupel and Curhan, 1973.

Table 1.1 Location of Foreign Manufacturing of Selected Continental European Companies, about 1914

Parent firm and country	Main industry	Location of Foreign Manufacturing Operations:									
		Russia	France	Germany	US	UK	Spain	Austria	Italy	Holland	Elsewhere
Switzerland:											
Ciba	Chemicals	X	X	X		X					
Geigy	Chemicals	X	X	X	X	X		X	X		Norway
Brown-Boveri	Electrical		X	X				X	X		Norway
Nestlé	Food			X	X	X	X		X	X	Norway, Australia
Germany:											
Siemens	Electrical	X	Xf		Xf	X		X			Belgium f
AEG	Electrical	X					X	X	X		Belgium
Degussa	Chemicals		X		X	X	X				
Bosch	Electrical	X			X	X	X				Japan
BASF	Chemicals	X	X			X					Norway
Hoechst	Chemicals	X	X								
Bayer	Chemicals	X	X		X						
Agfa	Chemicals	X	X								
Metallgesellschaft	Non-ferrous metals		Xf		X	X		X	X	X	Belgium, Mexico
Daimler-Benz	Automobiles					X		X			
France:											
Cie De St Gobain	Glass			X			X	X	X		Belgium
Netherlands:											
Margarine Uni (later Unilever)	Food		X	X	Xw	X		X			Belgium, Denmark
Belgium:											
Solvay	Chemicals	X	X	X	X	X	X	X	X		
Sweden:											
SKF	Machinery	Xw	X	X	Xw	X					

Notes: f = failed or abandoned prior to World War I.
w = entered between the years 1914 and 1918.
Sources: List follows chapter.

eve of World War I.[19] In any event, it seems very probable that before the Great War the total number of foreign manufacturing subsidiaries owned by all large enterprises based on the Continent exceeded the number of those established by American firms outside the United States. This conclusion emerges from the comparative histories of subsidiary proliferation by American, British, Continental, and Japanese enterprises summarized in Table 1.2. Continental European multinational enterprise thus emerged at least as early as the American variety, and considerably earlier than the British or Japanese. During the inter-war period, the Continental pioneers were joined by other venturers into international manufacturing. Dutch, Swiss and Swedish newcomers, such as Philips, AKU (later merged into AKZO), Alusuisse, and Ivar

Table 1.2 Entry into Foreign Manufacturing: Comparative Histories of US, British, Continental European and Japanese Enterprise

| Period | Numbers of Foreign Manufacturing Subsidiaries Established or Acquired by Parents from: | | | |
	US	UK	Continental Europe	Japan
Pre –1914	122	60	167	0
1914–1919	71	27	51	0
1920–1929	299	118	249	1
1930–1938	315	99	112	3
1939–1945	172	34	44	40
1946–1952	386	202	129	2
1953–1955	283	55	117	5
1956–1958	439	94	131	14
1959–1961	901	333	232	44
1962–1964	959	319	229	90
1965–1967	889	459	532	113
1968–1970	n.a.	729	1,030	209
Total	**4,836**	**2,529**	**3,023**	**521**

Notes: Data on subsidiaries of 47 UK, 85 Continental European, and 67 Japanese-based firms were collected for all parent firms on the 1971 Fortune '200' list of non-US industrial enterprises, as well as for a few financial holding companies and family groups that had more than $400 million sales in 1970 coming from manufacturing operations. Data on subsidiaries of US-based parents were collected for 187 US firms on the 1968 Fortune '500' list with an equity interest of at least 25% in manufacturing subsidiaries in at least six foreign countries as of January 1, 1968. Some 50 of these US firms were smaller than the non-US companies surveyed. About 50 non-US firms did *not* manufacture in six or more foreign countries. Data incomparabilities thus exist. They do not, however, seem to alter critically the orders of magnitude indicated by the above comparisons. For a fuller explanation of the data in the Comparative Multinational Enterprise Data Bank, see the Vaupel and Curham book.
Source: Vaupel and Curhan, 1973 and 1974: Tables 1.17.2, 1.17.3, 1.17.4, and 1.17.5, pp 72–103.

[19] Staley, 1935: pp 5, 9, Appendix A. More exactly Staley states the long-term foreign investment of German companies and investors exceeded that of American interests by a factor of three. Staley's sources lump together both financial (or portfolio) foreign investments and direct foreign investments in controlled business enterprises. Moreover, foreign direct investment itself is a concept which not only includes investments in manufacturing, but also in controlled or managerially-influenced sales, service and extractive companies. From other sources, however it is known that almost all early German foreign investment was in manufacturing: see Feis, 1930.

Kreuger's Swedish Match Company were perhaps the most prominent. But Italy's Pirelli and Luxemburg's ARBED also established or acquired numerous foreign outposts.

All of these enterprises manufactured in at least five foreign nations by 1939.[20] German enterprises, of course, had seen many of their foreign operations confiscated during World War I. Nevertheless, one found I G Farben, the temporary successor to Hoechst, Bayer, BASF and Agfa, producing in at least 13 countries by World War II, and Siemens, Bosch and AEG were all stubbornly reconstituting lost foreign outposts.[21]

The major expansion in the numbers of European companies with significant multinational operations has, to be sure, occurred since World War II. Dutch, Swiss and Swedish enterprises continued their multinational expansion; the German pioneers rebuilt their foreign production networks for a second time by the late 1950's, and then vastly augmented them; and the large Italian, French and Belgian enterprises established or acquired foreign manufacturing outposts. In the sectors of the earliest Continental multinational spread, chemicals and electrical machinery, the pioneers were joined by firms like France's Rhône-Poulenc, Air Liquide, and Compagnie Générale d'Eléctricité, and Italy's Snia Viscosa and Olivetti. In other sectors substantial foreign production activity appeared for the first time. France's Renault had established two vehicle assembly plants in Russia prior to the Revolution, and Mercedes produced in the United States prior to World War I, but despite these early efforts, Europe's automobile enterprises were to expand abroad significantly only after 1946.[22] Anglo-Dutch Shell excepted, Continental European petroleum companies with extensive international refining and extractive operations emerged only after the Second World War.[23] Nevertheless, it is clear that even in the mid-1950's, neither the condition nor the process of multinationality were unusual for European enterprises.

The spread of foreign manufacturing by the large firms of Continental Europe has, however, alternately exploded or stagnated.[24] A look at the number of parent firms with international operations conveys an impression of a smooth European expansion into multinationality, but a different picture is painted by the record of foreign subsidiaries set up or acquired. Table 1.2 shows that the numbers of foreign manufacturing outposts of Continental firms proliferated at a high rate just before and just after World War I; the next great

---

[20] Bouman, 1958; Avram, 1927: p 575 *et seq*; Alusuisse, 1960; Shaplen, 1960; Pirelli, MCMXLVI pp 62–65; ARBED, 1920, 1922, 1923.
[21] I G Farben, 1927, 1933; Stocking and Watkins, 1946: especially pp 323–324, 468; Siemens, 1957.
[22] Fridenson, 1972; Wells, 1974.
[23] See Chapter III below.
[24] Table 1.2 exaggerates the 1968–1970 subsidiary explosion, however. When company managers were not sure of the date of start-up or acquisition of a recent subsidiary they would respond: 'before 1970.' The Comparative Multinational Enterprise Computer Code arbitrarily allocated such responses to the 1968–1970 period. Table 1.2 may also understate the number of subsidiaries established by Continental enterprises between 1920 and 1929. Sources which became available to the author after the data underlying Table 1.2 was collected suggested that several subsidiaries in Eastern Europe (subsequently confiscated by Nazi or Communist regimes) escaped inclusion. See: Berov, 1965; Teichova, 1974.

spurt was only in the late 1960's. This was quite a different evolution than the continually increasing expansion of US company subsidiaries also shown in Table 1.2.

By 1971, it was almost certain that the rate of expansion of foreign manufacturing operations of large Continental European enterprises taken as a whole exceeded that of large American enterprises. This conclusion is suggested by the data on subsidiary acquisition and formation presented in Table 1.2, even if account is taken of discrepancies in sample sizes and dates. Not only was the rate of growth of the Continental multinational spread apparently greater than that of the American multinationals, but more foreign production outposts were being added to Continental systems than were being added to American multinational networks. Between 1962 and 1970, the rate of growth in numbers of foreign manufacturing subsidiaries of Continental enterprises also very substantially exceeded the rate of growth of Japanese multinational production: Table 1.2 shows that during the three year period extending from 1962 through 1964, Continental enterprises added two and a half times as many foreign manufacturing subsidiaries to their holdings as did large Japanese enterprises; between 1968 and 1970 Continental enterprises added almost five times as many as did the Japanese!

The long growth and recent rapid expansion of the foreign manufacturing operations of large Continental enterprises still left these companies with fewer foreign outposts than large American enterprises. Table 1.3 points out that as of 1971, the total active foreign manufacturing subsidiaries of Continental enterprises came to 2,627. This was some 16% greater than the number of British foreign manufacturing subsidiaries, but still equal to only three-fifths of the number of foreign production subsidiaries of the 187 American multinational enterprises in 1968. In 1971, foreign manufacturing

Table 1.3 Foreign Manufacturing Subsidiaries of Large Industrial Enterprises, Classified by Country of Parent Company, January 1, 1971 (187 US Multinational Companies as of January 1, 1968)

Parent Country	Number of Subsidiaries in Operation	Percentage Share
United States	4,246	42·8 %
United Kingdom	2,269	22·9
Bel Lux	276	2·8
France	429	4·3
West Germany	792	8·0
Italy	133	1·3
Netherlands	429	4·3
Sweden	171	1·7
Switzerland	397	4·0
Sub-Total: Continental Europe	2,627	26·4 %
Japan	483	4·9
Canada	201	2·0
Other	100	1·0
Grand Total	**9,926**	**100·0**

Source: Comparative Multinational Enterprise Project.

subsidiaries of Continental enterprises accounted for a little more than 26% of all foreign manufacturing subsidiaries in the Comparative Multinational Enterprise Project census.

The orders of magnitude uncovered by the Comparative Multinational Enterprise Project for the foreign manufacturing activity of large enterprises based in different nations turn out to correspond rather well to estimates of foreign direct investment compiled by the United Nations in 1973.[25] The UN data for 1967 and 1971 shown in Table 1.4 are based on national statistics, such as they are, and include the value not only of foreign manufacturing investments but also of sales, service and extractive operations. In addition, the UN data attempt to cover activities of all enterprises, and not just the large ones surveyed by the Comparative Multinational Enterprise Project. The UN estimates suggested that Continental foreign investment corresponded to roughly 18% of the total in 1967 and 23% of the total in 1971.[26]

Table 1.4 Stock of Foreign Direct Investment, Various Parent Countries (Book Value), 1967, 1971
(Millions of Dollars and Percentages)

	1967		1971	
Country	Millions of Dollars	Percentage Share	Millions of Dollars	Percentage Share
United States	59,486	55·0%	86,001	52·0%
United Kingdom	17,521	16·2	24,019	14·5
France	6,000	5·5	9,540	5·8
West Germany	3,015	2·8	7,276	4·4
Switzerland	4,250	3·9	6,760	4·1
Canada	3,728	3·4	5,930	3·6
Japan	1,458	1·3	4,480	2·7
Netherlands	2,250	2·1	3,580	2·2
Sweden	1,514	1·4	3,450	2·1
Italy	2,110	1·9	3,350	2·0
Belgium	2,040	0·4	3,250	2·0
Australia	380	1·9	610	0·4
Portugal	200	0·2	320	0·2
Denmark	190	0·2	310	0·2
Norway	60	0·0	90	0·0
Austria	30	0·0	40	0·0
Other	4,000	3·7	6,000	3·6
Total	108,200	100·0%	165,000	100·0%

Sources: Centre for Development Planning: Table 11; OECD, 1972;
US Department of Commerce, various issues;
Bundesministerium für Wirtschaft, various issues;
Handelskammer Hamburg, 1969; Bank of England, various issues;
Scharrer, 1972; Toyo Keizai, 1972; Canadian Department of Industry, 1971;
Skandinaviska Enskilda Banken, 1972.

---

[25] UN, 1974: p 139.
[26] The most careful examination of foreign direct investment data thus far seen by the author is that of Von Saldern (1973). Von Saldern's comparisons lead to a similar order of magnitude estimate, although she is unwilling to make any statement whatever concerning Italy, Luxemburg and Belgium. She finds German official statistics to be understated by about 20% because of their failure to include reinvested earnings.

The Largest Continental Enterprises

The Continental enterprises responsible for the bulk of the proliferation of foreign manufacturing subsidiaries turn out to have some very special characteristics, much in the manner of their US multinational counterparts.[27] A particular parent nationality, however, was not a prominent characteristic.

Continental enterprises with a multinational spread were based in all the developed Continental European countries. Although Continental multinational enterprises were predominantly German before 1914, and predominantly Northern European before 1939, no country or group of developed European countries has dominated since. One sees from Table 1.5 that more than two-thirds of large companies based in each of the developed, Western Continental countries manufactured in seven or more countries in 1971. The fact that all large Swiss companies were manufacturing in more than 11 nations lent some credence to the notion that companies based in small countries were especially prone to establish foreign subsidiaries. Nevertheless, there were a half-dozen large Swedish, Belgian and Dutch enterprises with a limited multinational spread, thus demonstrating that large enterprises based in small countries could sometimes produce at home and export. Germany, the country with the largest internal market, had the largest number of enterprises with few foreign manufacturing outposts (see Table 1.5); but Germany was also the home of the largest number of enterprises producing in more than 11 countries, including one manufacturing in 43 nations in 1971. France, a country whose governmental pronouncements had given its industry perhaps the most 'national' image in Europe, was the home of 15 enterprises manufacturing in more than seven nations.

Table 1.5 Large Continental Enterprises Classified by Parent Country and Number of Countries of Manufacturing Operations January 1, 1971

	Continental Enterprises Manufacturing in:			
Headquarters country	Fewer than 7 countries	7 to 11 countries	12 or more countries	Total number of firms
Bel & Lux	2	2	3	7*
France	6	7	8	21
Germany	9	9	11	29
Italy	—	2	5	7
Netherlands	1	1	3	5**
Sweden	3	2	4	9
Switzerland	—	—	7	7
Total	**21**	**23**	**41**	**85**

Notes: *Includes Agfa-Gevaert, a 50% German-owned enterprise.
          **Includes Royal Dutch-Shell but not Unilever. Unilever manufactures in many more than 12 countries.

Source: Comparative Multinational Enterprise Project.

[27] Vernon, 1971: Chapter I; Vaupel, 1971.

Principal Industries

Although Continental multinational enterprises were fairly evenly distributed across parent-country nationalities, multinationality of manufacturing varied widely among the industries in which Continental firms were active. All 27 of the large Continental enterprises having chemicals or electrical products as their main industry were manufacturing in seven or more countries by 1971, regardless of parent nationality. Enterprises manufacturing mainly iron and steel products were notably less likely to be spawning foreign manufacturing offspring, however. Ten of the 21 large Continental enterprises manufacturing in fewer than seven nations were based in the ferrous metals sector (see Table 1.6). Even so, six of Europe's large iron and steel firms *did* have a significant multinational spread.

The propensity of Continental enterprises to have different degrees of multinationality when based in different industries thus resembled that of their American counterparts. Table 1.6 shows that American multinationals, too, made an especially frequent appearance in chemical and electrical sectors. Quite unlike Continental enterprises, however, many American multinationals were also to be found in the food, fabricated metals products and non-electrical machinery industries.

Table 1.6 Industry Distribution of Large Continental Enterprises, 1971, Compared with Industry Distribution of 187 US Enterprises Manufacturing in Seven or More Countries in 1968

Main industry of parent enterprise	85 Continental Enterprises:		187 US Enterprises manufacturing in 7 or more countries
	Enterprises manufacturing in 7 or more countries	Enterprises manufacturing in 6 or fewer countries	
Food	1	1	29
Tobacco	0	0	1
Textiles	0	0	4
Wood, paper & printing	2	1	9
Chemicals & pharmaceuticals	17	0	40
Petroleum	6	1	9
Coal	0	1	0
Rubber	3	0	5
Leather	0	0	1
Stone, clay, glass	2	0	7
Iron, steel	6	10	1
Non-ferrous metals	3	2	7
Fabricated metal products	0	0	10
Non-electrical machinery, including office equipment	5	1	20
Electrical machinery, including scientific instruments	10	0	24
Transport equipment	7	3	18
Miscellaneous or conglomate	2	1	2
Total	**64**	**21**	**187**

Source: Comparative Multinational Enterprise Project.

Ownership Links

Although the relationship between the industry of Continental enterprises and their degree of multinationality was similar to that found in the case of American multinational enterprise, there was a strong reason for expecting a different pattern for Continental European enterprise. There were a considerable number of family, bank and government ownership links at the parent-company level among Europe's largest companies in 1971, and almost all of these were national links. Had national shareholder influence been the prime determinant of enterprise strategy, enterprises belonging to the same 'macrogroup' might have shown similar degrees of multinational expansion, despite their being based in different industries. Yet, such was not the case: widely differing degrees of multinational spread were to be found among enterprises of such macro-groups.

The most important ownership links among European enterprises are described in Chart 1. Suffice it to mention a few of the outstanding ones here. Five of the 21 French enterprises on the list of 85 were wholly or partly owned by the French government; one of these enterprises had no foreign production, another was manufacturing in 18 countries; both were 100% state-owned. The *Société Générale de Bélgique*, in addition to constituting one of the 85 in its own right, also owned significant minority positions in four of the other six largest Belgian and Luxemburg enterprises: one manufactured in 13 nations, another only in five. Sweden's Wallenberg family owned important blocks of shares in five of the nine largest Swedish companies through its bank, the Stockholm Enskilda Bank. The multinational spread of these firms ranged from 5 to 19 countries. The Dutch government owned all of one and 29% of another of the largest Dutch firms; the first manufactured in nine, the second in only four countries. The German Federal Government had ownership participations in three large German firms, the Flick family in four, the Klockner family in two and the Quandt family in three. Moreover, Germany's Henkel owned 30% of Degussa, and Degussa and *Metallgesellschaft* each owned 40% of another enterprise among the largest 85, *Norddeutsche Affinerie*. Again, wide variations in the multinational spread of manufacturing were to be found among the enterprises making up most of these macro-groups.

Although national ownership interlocks had little relationship to whether European enterprises spread manufacturing operations to many countries, multinational ownership link-ups and multinational production activities did go together. Six large Continental enterprises had (or were planning) so-called transnational mergers by 1971. Germany's Agfa and Belgium's Gevaert had entered a 50–50 link-up in 1964.[28] Fiat of Italy had taken a 15% stake in France's Citroën in 1968, which was increased in 1970 (the Fiat–Citroën link was to break up, however, in 1973).[29] And Hoogovens of Holland owned 40% of Hoesch of Germany – a prelude to their 50–50 transnational merger into Estel in 1972.[30] Nevertheless, in these instances transnational ownership links looked like the consequence of previous multinational operations (and

---

[28] Whitehead, 1971: p. 315.

[29] Aszkenazy, 1971: pp 67–71; *Business Week*, June 30, 1973: p 20.

[30] *Financial Times*, January 19, 1972: p 18.

multinational competition) by the companies involved; not like a cause of multinational manufacturing. The transnational mergers had been too recent for transnational ownership itself to have demonstrated any noticeable effect on multinational spread. Transnational ownership was neither a necessary nor a sufficient condition for multinational production operations.

Size and Concentration

Although the Continental enterprises with important multinational production operations were a heterogeneous lot with respect to ownership and nationality, they were less so with respect to their size. Continental enterprises resembled their American counterparts in that the largest tended to have the greatest multinational spread.[31] To be sure, all 85 of the largest Continental enterprises are industrial giants by any standards. But the biggest of these companies had a tendency, albeit slight, to have the greatest multinational spread – as one observes from Table 1.7. The average 1970 sales volume of the Continental enterprises manufacturing in more than seven countries reached $1·639 billion; the average size of all 85 enterprises was $1·125 billion. Nevertheless, the relationship between size and multinationality is a somewhat ambiguous one for Continental enterprises, in that a significant number of the smaller Continental firms had an impressive spread of foreign manufacturing activity.[32]

Table 1.7 Large Continental Enterprises, Classified by Worldwide Sales Volume and Number of Countries of Manufacturing Operations

| Sales volume worldwide, 1970 | Number of countries in which enterprise manufactured, January 1, 1971 | | | Total number of firms |
	1–6	7–11	12 or more	
$2 Billion to $10·7 Billion	2	4	12	18
$1·0 to $1·9 Billion	4	9	16	29
$0·4 to $0·9 Billion	15	10	13	38
Total	**21**	**23**	**41**	

Source: Comparative Multinational Enterprise Project.

Big firms are usually found in concentrated oligopolistic industries, and Continental enterprises were no exception to the rule. Despite massive efforts by the European Economic Community, data on industrial concentration on the Continent are still somewhat fragmentary. Nevertheless, the indicators of concentration presented for German and French industries in Table 1.8 seem representative enough, and these data suggest another similarity in the pictures of Continental European and American multinational enterprises. The Continental firms with manufacturing in many foreign

---

[31] Vernon, 1971: Chapter 1; Vaupel, 1971.
[32] Unfortunately, the difference in sample between the present study and those of Vernon (1971) and Vaupel (1971) does not make it possible to say whether the association of size and multinationality is greater or less for Continental than American enterprise. Table 1.7 does not suggest a particularly powerful statistical relationship in the Continental case.

countries are all found in oligopolistic industries. However, there is clearly
no correlation between the degree of concentration in the main industries of
Continental firms and their foreign spread. There is a high degree of concentration in the iron and steel industry in Continental countries, but the steel
firms have shown the lowest propensity to spread foreign manufacturing
subsidiaries over many nations. And the highly multinational, Continental
chemicals and electrical enterprises are found in industries with a medium
degree of concentration.

Table 1.8   Measures of Oligopolistic Concentration in Germany and
France, Various Industries

Industry	Germany: Market share, ten largest enterprises, 1960	France: Percentage share of working population employed in eight largest enterprises, 1963
Food and drink	12·0 %	18·0 %[1]
Tobacco	84·5	na
Textiles	7·2	6·6
Wood, paper, printing	41·5	14·6
Chemicals	40·6	42·0[2]
Drugs		20·8
Oil	91·5	90·5
Rubber	59·7	50·6
Leather and footwear	37·3	10·6
Stone, clay, glass	51·7[3]	46·8[3]
Iron and steel	57·8	63·1
Non-ferrous metals	44·7	66·4
Fabricated metals	9·3	8·3
Non-electrical machinery	13·4	7·8
Electrical machinery	38·4	35·5[4]
Transport	67·0[5]	52·9[5]

Notes: [1] Dairy products.
       [2] Organic chemicals.
       [3] Glass only.
       [4] Household appliances.
       [5] Automobiles only.

Sources: For Germany: *La Documentation Francaise*, 1970: pp 61–62;
For France: Morvan, 1972: pp 148–150.

Technological Prowess

Most of the Continental enterprises with a multinational spread of foreign
manufacturing subsidiaries turned out to be undertaking a large effort in
Research and Development (R & D), as shown in Table 1.9. Continental multinational enterprises fit the high-technology image that had long been
associated with the American multinationals. The special skills, proprietary
know-how and patent advantages of high technology appear to be at least
as closely related to the spread of Continental multinational enterprise as
to that of American business abroad.

Table 1.9   Large Continental Enterprises, Classified by Number of
Countries of Manufacturing Operations and Research and Development
(R & D) Expenditures as a Percentage of Sales

R&D as a percentage of sales, 1970	Number of countries in which enterprise manufactured, January 1, 1971			Total number of firms
	1–6	7–11	12 or more	
Greater than 3 %	2	2	13	17
Between 1 % and 3 %	0	5	3	8
Less than 1 %	2	6	9	17
Unknown	17	10	16	43
Total	21	23	41	85

Source: Comparative Multinational Enterprise Project.

A majority of the large European enterprises do not report or even calculate a measure of their R&D activity. Thirty-eight enterprises which did offer a measure of the amount of money spent on R&D share were, however, among the firms with production in seven or more countries. The average percentage of sales revenue spent on R&D by these 38 reached the impressive height of 3·2%. Ninety of the 187 US multinationals examined by the Comparative Multinational Enterprise Project had provided similar data in 1967, and their average R&D expenditure was 2·4%.[33]

The distribution of the Continental multinationals by their main industry shown in Table 1.6 also demonstrates the high-technology lustre of these firms, albeit indirectly. American data on corporate-funded R&D as a percentage of sales, and on scientists and engineers as a percentage of employees, clearly single out electrical machinery (including instruments), transport, and chemicals (including pharmaceuticals) as being the three most R&D-intensive industries.[34] Assuming that European data were available and would show the same pattern, Table 1.6 would indicate that 53% of the 85 Continental enterprises manufacturing in seven or more countries were in the three most R&D-intensive industries, compared to 44% of the 187 American multinationals. Only three (or 5%) of the 21 Continental enterprises manufacturing in fewer than seven countries were based in these high-technology industries.

There were, thus, several points of similarity between the American and the Continental multinationals: large size, industry distribution, and R&D orientation. Nevertheless, there was no comparison between American and Continental firms when it came to exporting from their home countries. The popular image of Continental enterprise as exporters was very right indeed. While the average American enterprise on the Fortune '500' list of 1963 exported some 6·5% of its sales, and the average of the 187 US multinationals exported 6·9% of its sales, the average Continental firm exported 26% of its sales volume in 1970. *All* large Continental firms exported more than 7% of

---

[33] Vernon, 1971: p 8.
[34] Gruber, Mehta and Vernon, 1967: p 24.

their production from their home countries.[35] These figures even looked low relative to other historical periods. Germany's Robert Bosch, for example, exported 28% of its sales in 1970; but 88% of its sales in 1913![36] Siemens exported 26% of its sales in 1970, compared to 40% in 1913.[37] Whereas the average dollar volume of exports of the 187 US multinationals was $29 million in 1963, that of the 85 largest Continental enterprises was an enormous $450 million in 1970.[38]

Table 1.10   Large Continental Enterprises, Classified by Export Orientation and Number of Countries of Manufacturing Operations

Exports from home country (as a % of total company sales, 1970)	Number of countries in which enterprise manufactured, January 1, 1971 (59 enterprises for which export data was available):			Total number of firms
	1–6	7–11	12 or more	
30% or more	7	8	8	23
10% to 29%	9	5	15	29
Less than 10%	1	1	5	7
Total	**17**	**14**	**28**	**59**

Source: Comparative Multinational Enterprise Project.

The exporting propensity of Continental European enterprises with few foreign manufacturing operations was actually considerably greater than that of Continental firms manufacturing in seven or more countries. Despite the larger average size of the 64 Continental firms with many foreign manufacturing subsidiaries, their average 1970 dollar volume of exports ($453·9 million) was barely different than that of Continental firms with a less multinational spread ($441·5 million). Moreover, exports as a percentage of total company sales showed no particular tendency to increase with the extent of the multinational spread of Continental firms, as shown in Table 1.10. Such behavior was in evident contrast to that of American enterprises: in the American case, with but few exceptions, high absolute export sales, a high propensity to export relative to total production, and a multinational net of manufacturing subsidiaries went hand in hand.[39]

Product Diversity

The largest Continental enterprises were not only prodigious exporters, but they were also more prone to diversify their product lines than were the American firms. It was rare to find a Continental enterprise confining all its domestic and foreign productive activities to a single industry (as defined at

---

[35] Data was available for 59 of the Continental enterprises. US comparisons are from Vernon, 1971: p 16 m.

[36] Bosch, 1961: p 122.

[37] Siemens, *Annual Report*, 1970; Kocka, 1969: p 326.

[38] This contrast between Continental and American behavior is consistent with the United Nations' (1973: p 159) estimates of ratios of exports to foreign production for firms based in various countries.

[39] Vaupel, 1971: p 30, Table 12.

Table 1.11 Continental European and American Enterprises Classified by Domestic and Foreign Product Diversity, 1970

		Foreign product diversity:		
Domestic product diversity	Total number of firms	None	Low	High
85 Largest Continental enterprises:				
None	10	4	3	3
Low	44	9	16	19
High	31	6	5	20
Total	85	19	24	42
64 Continental multinationals manufacturing in seven or more countries, 1970:				
None	7	2	3	2
Low	35	7	12	16
High	22	1	5	16
Total	64	10	20	34
162 American multinationals manufacturing in seven or more countries, 1967:				
None	26	26	0	0
Low	65	28	37	0
High	71	3	31	37
Total	162	57	68	37

Note: See Appendix B for definitions.
Sources: For Continental enterprises, Comparative Multinational Enterprise Project.
For American enterprises, Stopford and Wells, 1972: p 37.

the two-digit level of the US Standard Industrial Classification – SIC). Table 1.11 demonstrates that there were very few Continental equivalents of the US enterprises that had developed one product or product-line and then covered the world with it: there were hardly any Continental counterparts to America's IBM, Caterpillar or Kellogg.

Another striking characteristic of Continental enterprises was their tendency to be sometimes more diversified in their foreign production than they were at home. For example, five Continental enterprises with a substantial multi-national spread were diversified in foreign, but not in domestic, production (see Table 1.11). Much of this foreign diversity was found in these enterprises' US manufacturing operations. The phenomenon of high foreign diversity and no domestic diversity was totally unknown in the experience of American multinational enterprise. The diversity of Continental enterprises often played a role in causing their behavior to differ from that of American multi-nationals.

The Distinctive Personality of Continental European Multinational Enterprise

Despite some apparent similarities between the characteristics of the American and Continental enterprises which expanded abroad, Continental multinational enterprise had its own special personality and history. One began to wonder why Continental enterprises had their special export and product-diversity characteristics. The striking absence of Continental enterprises – multinational or otherwise – from certain sectors of intense American multinational activity was also a puzzle. So was the fact that the multinational spread of Continental European enterprises was rarely, if ever, associated with advantages in marketing and advertising like those which underlay the foreign expansion of numerous American companies, in both consumer and capital goods.[40] Why were Continental enterprises not particularly active in non-electrical machinery, a sector with connotations of the substitution of capital for labor in numerous production processes? Why, with their evident experience and capability for exporting, had Continental enterprises gone to the bother of establishing so many foreign manufacturing operations? And why, if the reality of Continental enterprise was so multinational, had Continental firms so long managed to avoid the political storms swirling around American, British and Japanese multinational companies?

This book is about the distinctive characteristics of those Other Multinationals of Continental Europe. One place to begin the story is with the comparative innovative and cost advantages which led Continental enterprises to have their first export contacts with foreign lands.

Sources for Table 1.1

Firm	Source
Ciba	Haber, 1958 and 1971.
Geigy	Haber, 1958 and 1971.
Brown-Boveri	Brown-Boveri, 1966.
Nestlé	Heer, 1966.
Siemens	Siemens, 1957.
AEG	AEG, 1956.
Degussa	Degussa, 1973; Haber, 1958 and 1971.
Bosch	Bosch, 1961.
BASF	Haber, 1958 and 1971.
Hoechst	Haber, 1958 and 1971.
Bayer	Haber, 1958 and 1971.
Agfa	Haber, 1958 and 1971.
Metallgesellschaft	Dabritz, 1931.
Cie de St Gobain	Choffel, 1960.
Margarine Uni (Unilever)	Wilson, 1954: Vol II.
Solvay	Haber, 1958 and 1971; Bolle, 1963.
SKF	SKF, 1957.

[40] Statistical measures of marketing and advertising intensity by American enterprises have been shown to be closely related to their propensity to undertake foreign manufacturing. (Vaupel, 1971; Vernon, 1971.) Continental enterprises were requested to provide similar data. In the event, only five of the 85 largest Continental enterprises were able to provide a measure of marketing intensity such as advertising expenditures as a percentage of sales. In the opinion of the author the inability to obtain such information was not the result of secrecy by Continental European firms. Rather, it was a logical consequence of the lesser importance of advertising and marketing expenditures in the industries and products of Continental enterprise activity. As emphasized below, customer demand for the products of European enterprises was much more sensitive to price than has been the case for American products.

Chapter II

The Origins of Continental European Multinational Enterprise

Technological Innovation and Exports

Continental European manufacturing firms, like their American counterparts, almost always began the process of becoming multinational by exporting on the basis of oligopolistic advantages in technological innovation.[1] The kinds of innovations developed by Europe's nascent multinationals tended, however, to be quite unlike those first commercialized in the US market.

European exports which later led to multinational production, like American exports which did the same, stemmed from innovation, that is, from first commercial introduction of a product or process. European invention, that is to say, discovery, often led neither to home nor export sales. Frequently, European inventions were uprooted to the US and first commercialized there.[2] The examples of penicillin, the computer, and the integrated circuit are three among many.[3] Even within Europe invention in one country was followed by innovation elsewhere: invention of margarine in France was followed by first commercial introduction in Holland.[4]

Examples of the connection between Continental European innovation, exports and subsequent foreign production are numerous and convincing, despite the fact that a rigorous test of the link is lacking. The history of synthetic dyestuffs is a case in point. Dyestuffs firms such as Ciba, Geigy, BASF, Hoechst, Bayer, and Agfa established numerous foreign manufacturing operations between 1880 and 1914. Several authors have chronicled how, prior to this multinational spread, the invention of synthetic dyestuffs in England and France was followed not by English and French exports, but rather by large-scale commercialization, and process and product development in Germany and Switzerland. Massive exports, and then industrial implantation back into the countries of invention later emanated from the innovating German and Swiss enterprises.[5] Something of the export phase of

Table 2.1   Growth of the Synthetic Dyestuff Industry

Five year periods ending	Dyestuff patents granted in England to:		Number of employees of the *Badische Anilin und Sodafabrik* (BASF)	Exports in metric tons:	
	German inventors	British inventors		By Germany:	By Switzerland:
1860	8	20			
1880	47	13	1,534	8,294	
1900	427	52	6,711	46,858	3,116
1910	561	30	7,610	84,110	6,975

Source: Encyclopaedia of the Social Sciences, Vol V, p 302, as cited in Friedlaender and Oser, 1953: p 243.

[1] The role of oligopolistic competitive advantage in explaining the rise of multinational enterprise has been emphasized in: Hymer, 1960; Vernon, 1966; Caves, 1971; Wells (ed), 1972; Harmann, 1970.
[2] Hufbauer, 1965: pp 86–87; Landes, 1969; OECD, 1971; Jewkes, 1969.
[3] Jewkes, 1969; OECD, 1971.
[4] Wilson, 1954: pp 25 and 26.
[5] Haber, 1958; Friedlaender and Oser, 1953: p 243; Aldcroft, 1968: p 278.

this sequence prior to World War I can be glimpsed from Table 2.1. One's impression of the connection between innovation and exports becomes yet stronger upon noting that Germany and Switzerland were almost the only countries exporting synthetic dyestuffs.[6] German firms alone accounted for about nine-tenths of world production of synthetic dyes on the eve of World War I.[7]

Advantages based on technological innovations were also intimately linked with the extraordinary export successes of Germany's Siemens and AEG. Some of their innovative advantages were indigenous, others originated with US company licences which gave European companies exclusive rights to produce and market on the Continent in electric lights, automatic telephone exchanges and the like. On the eve of World War I, Germany accounted for over 48% of total world electrical exports.[8] Indeed, until World War II, Germany remained the largest single exporter of electrical equipment in the world.[9] Exports of unique goods, or goods produced with unique processes preceded essentially all of the substantial pre-World War II expansion of Siemens and AEG into foreign manufacturing. Only one exception of note appears: Siemens quite exceptionally commenced production in England in the 1850's with telegraph cables and water meters – products the firm did not then manufacture at home.[10]

A link between innovation and export is also to be found in the histories of virtually all the Continental enterprises which established foreign manufacturing operations before World War II. The formation of Ivar Kreuger's Swedish Match empire in the 1920's followed a half century of Swedish exports based on innovations in safety matches.[11] Alusuisse had been the first firm formed to exploit the Herault process for producing aluminum. It exported long prior to beginning significant foreign production.[12] I G Farben earned much foreign exchange for Weimar, and later Nazi Germany by first spending up to 12·7% of its sales revenue (in 1927) on Research and Development.[13] By 1908, Philips of Holland had ceased simply imitating carbon filament electric lamps and exporting only on the basis of a price advantage due to relatively low cost labor. Development efforts underlay increasing product process distinctiveness which in turn preceded Philips' major moves into foreign manufacturing in the 1930's.[14]

After World War II much the same sort of sequence seemed again in motion. The distinctive post-1945 European innovations in autos, pharmaceuticals, plastics, and metalworking processes, cited in Table 2.2 led first to exports, and only later to foreign production. Continental European companies sometimes exported when they only had a comparative advantage in labor costs or in economies of scale, but such exports were rarely followed by

---

[6] Haber, 1958.
[7] Henderson, 1963: p 40.
[8] Friedlaender and Oser, 1953: p 247.
[9] Siemens, 1957: Vol II.
[10] Siemens, 1957: Vol II, pp 32 *et seq*; AEG, 1956.
[11] Friedlaender and Oser, 1953: p 417.
[12] Wallace, 1937: pp 6, 33, 34.
[13] Gross, 1950: p 12.
[14] Philips, 1970: pp 3–8; Bouman, 1958: pp 48 *et seq*.

foreign production. There were, however, some exceptions to this rule, as we shall see in the following chapters. Perhaps the most notable of these exceptions deserves mention here: these were the petroleum-refining operations of the oil companies started and owned by governments in France and Italy.

Table 2.2   Some European Innovations Leading to the Rise of Multinational Enterprise

Product or process	Year	Firm	Apparent market stimulus
Ammonia-Soda process	1864	Solvay (Belgium)	High cost of fuel & sulphuric acid inputs, profit from recovery of nitrogen-rich ammonia.
Alizarin	1870	BASF (Germany)	Cut-off of imports from France by Franco-Prussian war of natural dyes needed for military uniforms.
Ammonia synthesis for fertilizer	1913	BASF (Germany)	Scarcity of arable land; intolerable strategic dependence on Chilean nitrates; guaranteed military demand for explosives.
Margarine	1872	Jurgens/Unilever (Netherlands)	Working-class mass demand, high price of butter.
Anti-syphilitic drugs (Salvarsin)	1910	Hoechst (Germany)	Mass demand guaranteed by government health insurance.
Synthetic rubber	1930's	Bayer/I G Farben (Germany)	Military fear of cut-off from natural rubber supplies.
Low power utilization for aluminum electrolysis	1950's & 1960's	Péchiney (France)	High cost of French electricity.
Volkswagen beetle	1939	VW (Germany)	Military market, mass demand.
Polypropylene	1957	Montecatini (Italy)	Desire to use waste products.
Synthetic menthol flavoring	1971	Bayer (Germany)	High price, declining supply of natural peppermint oil.

Sources: Haber, 1958 and 1971; OECD, 1971; Jewkes, 1969; Bäumler, 1966; Eco and Zorzoli, 1961; Sheahan, 1963; Fishlock, 1974: p 24; Sandoz, 1961; ASEA, 1972; SKF, 1957; Heer, 1966; Hufbauer, 1965; BASF, 1965; Bosch, 1961.

Western Europe, as it again abruptly came to realize in the 1970's, never had had the indigenous resources of petroleum that allowed American firms to develop rapidly innovative advantages in refining, let alone exploration. Of the Continental countries, only Holland had oil-producing colonies during the first half of the century. After the Russian Revolution had eliminated foreign-owned firms from the Caucasus, Western European governments felt dependent for their oil supply on either Anglo-Saxon companies (including partly British Royal Dutch-Shell) or the Soviet state. Some Western European governments were content with neither choice. One result was what the historian of *Compagnie Francaise des Pétroles* (CFP) refers to, in jest, as the 'immaculate conception' of that firm out of the post-1918 debris of German ambitions.[15] The company was formed at the initiative of the French government to administer the part of the Turkish Petroleum Company (later the Iraq Petroleum Company, IPC) awarded to France as part of the spoils of World War I at the San Remo Diplomatic Conference.[16] After oil was struck, CFP's British and American partners in IPC built a refinery in Iraq. Thus, politics (and a cash contribution) put CFP into both foreign manufacturing (ie oil refining) and into exporting refined petroleum products. With experience thus gained, and later a protected home market as well, CFP could subsequently apply the lessons it learned to operations in foreign countries. Indeed, even if such a firm never developed marked *technological* advantages by this process, it could, and often did, offer a differentiated, non-Anglo-Saxon political product.[17]

The Role of Home Market Conditioning

More than 'immaculate conceptions' have, however, set apart the story of the spread of Continental European multinational enterprise: early home-market conditioning played a considerable role. It is clear that the economic

Table 2.3 Some American Innovations Leading to the Rise of Multinational Enterprise

Product or process	Year	Firm	Apparent market stimulus
Sewing machine	1851	Singer	Shortage of seamstresses.
Telephone	1878	Bell Telephone (later Western Electric & ITT)	Long distances in USA, high cost of travel.
Strowger bar telephone switch	1892	Strowger (later Western Electric & ITT)	Shortage of telephone operators leading to unreliable service.
Moving assembly line for automobile production*	1914	Ford	Shortage of skilled labor; middle-income market.
Automatic transmission	1939	General Motors	Relatively high-income, convenience demand.
Vat fermentation for penicillin*	1945	Pfizer, Lederle	Shortage of skilled labor, military demand.
The computer*	1951	Sperry-Rand	Military demand; shortage of clerical labour.
Planar process for integrated circuit production*	1961	Fairchild	Shortage of labor to assemble transistor circuits; military demand.

* Indicates that the innovated product had been invented in Europe.
Sources: Jewkes, 1969; OECD, 1971; Siemens, 1957: Vol I; Eco and Zorzoli, 1961; McKern, 1972.

---

[15] Rondot, 1962: p 5. Also Chapter III below.
[16] Rondot, 1962: p 11.
[17] See Chapter III below; Tiger and Franko, 1973; Frankel, 1966; Chiado-Fiorio, 1973.

Table 2.4   Nature of Major Innovations in the USA and Continental European Countries, 1945–1973

Nature and stimulus of innovation	Country or Region of Origin			
	USA		Continental Europe	
	No	(%)	No	(%)
New Products				
No apparent prior need	29	(48%)	22	(37%)
Material substitute or material-saving	23	(38)	35	(58)
Labor-saving	8	(13)	3	(5)
Sub-total	60	(100%)	60	(100%)
Product Adaptations				
To save labor	4	(31%)	1	(2%)
To save materials	2	(15)	19	(42)
To save space	1	(8)	7	(16)
To increase safety	1	(8)	9	(20)
Other adaptations	5	(38)	9	(20)
Sub-total	13	(100%)	45	(100%
Process Innovations				
Labor-saving	24	(62%)	8	(8%)
Capital-saving	7	(18)	26	(25)
Material-saving	8	(20)	69	(67)
Sub-total	39	(100%)	103	(100%)
Grand Total	112		208	

Notes: Pharmaceutical innovations are not included in these compilations. Some of these innovations may not have been put into foreign production. Due to rounding percentage totals may not add to 100.

Sources: Comparative Multinational Enterprise Project, as compiled by Mr William Davidson. See notes at end of chapter for detailed listing.

Table 2.5   Product Innovations of Large European Enterprises before 1945

Characteristic of product innovation	1850–1913		1914–1944	
	No	(%)	No	(%)
No apparent prior need	4	(6%)	5	(14%)
Material substitute or material-saving	28	(40)	16	(43)
Labor-saving	25	(36)	4	(11)
New pharmaceutical	13	(19)	12	(32)
Total	70	(100%)	37	(100%)

Notes: All of these innovations were eventually taken into foreign production. Due to rounding percentages may not add to 100.

Sources: Published company histories and studies of innovations, including: Jewkes, 1969; BASF, 1965; Hufbauer, 1965; Bosch, 1961; Brown-Boveri, 1966; ASEA, 1972; SKF, 1957; Heer, 1966; Sandoz, 1961; Eco and Zorzoli, 1961.

characteristics of home markets in Continental Europe have differed from those facing innovators in the United States. Distinctive home markets left their mark on Europe's nascent multinationals primarily in terms of the kinds of product and process innovations they developed.

The distribution of European innovations that were eventually put into foreign production appears to have long been biased toward material-saving processes, *ersatz* material substitutes, and goods oriented toward low-income consumers. This tendency is illustrated by the Continental innovations cited in Table 2.2. By way of contrast, the examples presented in Table 2.3 argue that American innovations were typically skewed towards goods and processes that had an appeal to the unique high-income, labor-short American market.[18] Quantitative corroboration of these examples of transatlantic contrasts is far from perfect, since few studies of innovation have examined the market stimuli to which enterprises responded. Nevertheless, a compilation of major post-1945 innovations done by the Comparative Multinational Enterprise Project, and

Table 2.6 Income *Per Capita* of Various Countries in 1914

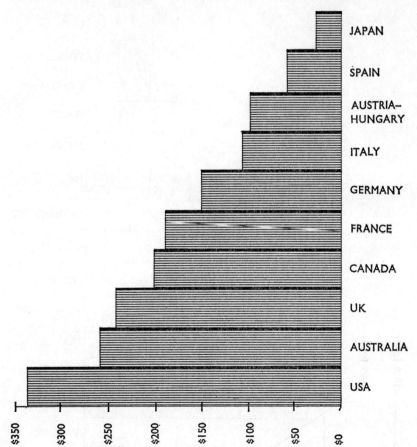

Source: Income in the United States: Its Amount and Distribution, 1909-1919, The Staff of the National Bureau of Economic Research, Vol I, Harcourt, Brace and Co, New York, 1921.

---

[18] Vernon, 1971: Chapter III.

Table 2.7
Income *Per Capita* of Various Countries in
1959 and 1969

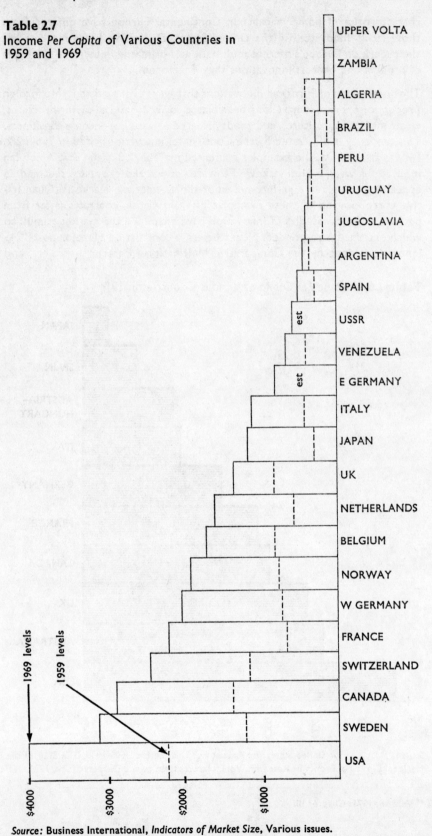

Source: Business International, *Indicators of Market Size*, Various issues.

reported in Table 2.4, shows differences in orientation which are hardly random. Also, a survey of the pre-World War II product innovations mentioned in published histories of the largest Continental enterprises with multinational operations added further credence to the notion that Continental innovations were distinctive. Table 2.5 summarizes the results of this examination of pre-war product innovations by large Continental enterprises. The Continental penchant for saving materials is particularly marked in the case of process innovations and product adaptation.

Conditioning by Different Income Levels

Part of the explanation for differences between European and American patterns of innovation undoubtedly lies in differences in absolute levels of income *per capita*. Average national income *per capita* data is presented in Table 2.6 for the ten countries for which it is available as of 1914. Table 2.7 presents similar data for 24 of the world's 186 nations for 1959 and 1969. In both tables, countries are ordered from those with the highest to those with the lowest income levels. These tables show that the United States was highest on the list for both 1914 and 1969. Moreover, the relative rankings of income levels for the United States, France, Germany and Italy did not change over this 55 year span. Even changes in proportional differences were not great. US *per capita* income throughout the first half of the twentieth century was nearly twice that of France and Germany, and roughly three times that of Italy. Some nations changed their relative positions for the better (Japan) or the worse (the UK), but the relationship between the United States and the largest Continental countries remained stable.

These international differences in income levels are important for innovative activity since consumers appear to behave as if they had a hierarchy of needs varying with their income levels.[19] Evidence suggests, for example, that the order in which consumers acquire household appliances is primarily a function of income, rather than of culture.[20] Barring obvious differences due to resource endowments, it also appears that there is an order of acquisition of industrial goods that is followed predictably as a result of economic growth.[21] By extension one expects new needs to emerge as incomes grow to previously unreached levels. If scientific and technical skills are available, would-be innovators will presumably respond to such new needs. Moreover, would-be innovators located in the first market for new products seem to have an enormous advantage over those located outside it. It is they who will be most conscious of the emergent market opportunity; it is they who can most rapidly respond to customer requests to define concretely a product that at first may be only a hazy idea.[22]

Given the historical constants shown in Tables 2.6 and 2.7, it is understandable that the US market has long acted as midwife to the development by US companies of the time-saving, convenience products that substitute for high-income, high-cost labor.[23] The link between such product innovation and

---

[19] Duesenberry, 1949.
[20] Parush, 1964.
[21] Lee, 1968.
[22] Hirsch, 1967; Vernon, 1966: pp 191–192.
[23] Vernon, 1966: p 193; Vernon, 1971: Chapter III.

exporting is also rather clear: such products tended to be demanded in ever-increasing quantities in Europe as income levels continually moved up toward the level prevailing previously in the US. But what kind of innovation might one expect in Continental European countries, where potential innovators have long had a level of scientific and technical ability similar to that found in the highest income, US market?[24]

A certain amount of innovation directed toward needs to save labor, or satisfy high incomes did occur on the European Continent. Nestlé's mothers' milk substitute which allowed women to begin breaking away from *Kinder, Kirche, Kuche* in the 1890's looks like the sort of product that one would expect to be a US innovation, but it was Swiss.[25] And, in at least one case, that of the *Compagnie de Saint-Gobain*, a European firm obtained an innovative lead in mirrors and glass, two products for which demand was income-elastic, in the early 1700's, well before the US existed as a nation.[26]

Sometimes a guaranteed military demand drew forth new labor-saving product innovations from Continental European enterprise, as in Germany before 1945. According to the member of the Siemens family who chronicled the history of that enterprise, much of the stimulus to several Siemens' innovations in X-ray and electronic medical equipment came from the customer who:

'called for portable apparatus, as far as possible proof against bad roads and rough handling, and in large quantities. This customer came not only from Germany, but also from other "civilized" countries, as he is always among the first to be attracted by new technical developments, and "money is no object." Above all, he works into the hands of the doctors.'[27]

Military demand also assured Siemens a leadership position in teleprinter production. The telex was apparently invented almost simultaneously in America and Germany, but the totalitarian character of the Nazi state created a special, guaranteed use for such a product:

'The ideal type of "yes-man" was furthered by the teleprinter in a way hitherto undreampt of. Over the telephone it was still possible to register doubt or protest, but not on the teleprinter. The message closed with the words: "report compliance." '[28]

Nevertheless, most innovative activity undertaken on the Continent was not oriented to the development of time and labor-saving products. Indeed, a good deal of Continental European innovation was not directed to new products at all, but rather toward applying new processes to American-type, high-income products. Some observers have commented on the seeming tendency of American companies to innovate new products, whereas European firms tended to introduce new processes.[29] The most current available

---

[24] OECD, 1971.
[25] Heer, 1966.
[26] Choffel, 1960.
[27] Siemens, 1957: Vol I, p 282.
[28] Siemens, 1957: Vol II.
[29] Miller: p 152.

data, summarized in Table 2.4, do not provide much support for such a neat dichotomy between US and European innovation. Nevertheless, both Table 2.4 and examples found in company histories suggest that process innovation was a major European theme. Philips of Holland and AEG of Germany even began life as independent entities in the 1890's by innovating processes for the production of Edison's product: the electric lamp.[30]

Whether process or product, however, most Continental innovation was conditioned by distinctive patterns of distribution of income *around* average *per capita* levels and by patterns of relative labor and raw-materials costs which long diverged from those prevailing in the United States. These factors more than others appear to underlie the recurring emphasis in the history of European innovation on material-saving processes, and material-saving and low-income versions of existing products.

Income Distribution and Innovation

Over long periods of time the pattern of distribution of personal income in most European countries has been notably unlike that prevailing in the United States. Sociological, historical and business writers have often referred to the United States as a uniquely middle-class society.[31] European countries, and particularly the large Continental countries have often been sketched as having aristocratic élites on the one hand and peasants and workers on the other – with few people in between.[32] If such characterization were true, one would expect European innovators to be attracted to fulfilling luxury or low-income needs, rather than those of a less numerous, less visible middle class.

Table 2.8 suggests that generalizations about European income distributions must be made with considerable care, and with attention to variations among European countries and among historical periods. In 1936, the middle classes in Nazi Germany were receiving a somewhat higher percentage of total personal income than the middle classes in the United States, although contrasts were still in evidence at high and low-income levels. In the 1960's, Sweden, the Netherlands, and the United States (and also the United Kingdom), came to have rather similar distribution patterns: in these countries similar percentages of total income went to the lowest forty, upper-middle forty, and top twenty percent of their populations. Nevertheless, clear contrasts between the United States and the largest European countries do emerge from Table 2.8.[33] Moreover, one is struck by the persistence of certain patterns. The resemblance between the German and US distributions of 1964 with those of 1913 is a case in point.[34] To the extent that one may judge from the imperfect (and not very recent) data made available by European governments, there is empirical justification for the notion that the United States market has been peculiarly middle class.

---

[30] Philips, 1970: pp 4–8.
[31] Fayerweather, 1965: p 32; Krech *et al*, 1962: pp 304–316.
[32] Landes, 1969: pp 48, 129 and 131; Dahrendorf, 1968: Chapter 6.
[33] See United Nations Economic Commission for Europe, 1967: Chapter 6, for a discussion of the imperfections in the data summarized in Table 2.8. The little after-tax data available suggests surprising similarity to pre-tax data.
[34] See, however, Dotti and Fontela, 1970, for arguments as to why European distributions may have been converging to the US pattern during the 1960's.

Table 2.8   Distribution of Family Personal Income in Europe and the US

Percentage of total income before tax received by indicated fraction of families

Country & year	Lowest tenth	Lowest two fifths	Fortieth to eightieth percentile	Highest fifth	Highest tenth
About the time of World War I					
US 1918	2 %	18 %	36%	46 %	34 %
Germany 1913	3·5	18	27	55	41
During the inter-war period					
US 1935–6	na	12·7	34·1	53·2	36
UK 1929	3	18	31	51	41
Germany 1936	1	11	36	53	39
Sweden 1935	na	na	na	58·1	39·5
Netherlands 1938	na	na	na	52·5	38·7
Around 1950					
US 1950		15·8	38·5	45·7	30·3
UK 1949	na	17	35·5	47·5	33
Germany 1950	1	12·5	39·5	48	34
Sweden 1948	na	12·8	40·6	46·6	30·3
Netherlands 1950	1·3	13·8	37·2	49	35
During the 1960's					
US 1969	1	15	40	45	27
UK 1964	2	15·3	40·5	44·2	29·3
Germany 1964	2·1	15·4	31·7	52·9	41·4
France 1962	0·5	9·5	36·8	53·7	36·8
Sweden 1963	1·6	14	42	44	27·9
Netherlands 1962	1·3	14	37·6	48·4	33·8

Sources: List follows chapter.

Note: The percentages for the fortieth to eightieth percentiles are highlighted to call attention to the fraction of incomes received by what most observers might be inclined to refer to as the 'middle-class'.

These contrasts in income distributions were the basis of important differences between the home environments of European and American multinationals. Where markets diverged, the nature of innovation diverged, and distinctive oligopolistic strengths were developed. As the history of the auto industry was to show, European companies tended either to introduce luxury products or near-necessities for the masses. American firms were pulled toward satisfying middle and upper-middle income needs.[35]

Daimler and Benz marketed the first workable automobiles in Germany in 1888 and 1886. Conditioned then and later by their home-market demand, 'the German manufacturers concentrated on luxury cars, since the German middle class was not large enough to support the scale needed for the innovation and manufacture of an inexpensive automobile.'[36] For French auto

---

[35] McKern, in Vernon (ed), 1972; Wells, in Vernon (ed), 1974.
[36] Wells, in Vernon (ed), 1974: p 4.

manufacturers before World War I, the market demand was much the same. One examination of the market for automobiles between 1899 and 1928 in the French *Département* of Indre-et-Loire led to the conclusion that 'the demand for private automobiles comes principally from people of independent means, noblemen, and large landowners.'[37] A government report in 1917 went even further.

It was argued that past successes meant that the orientation of the French industry to luxury demands ought to be elevated to the level of doctrine:

> It is the luxury article that has given birth to our worldwide reputation – we must defend this patrimony – it is this that has led to the development of our automobile industry – purity and harmony of form, even more than luxury manufacture, must be one of the primordial elements of the maintenance of our supremacy.'[38]

The automobile, like the jet engine, the computer, penicillin, the aerosol can, the continuous strip mill, and other European inventions, found an important market in the US only after it had been uprooted from Europe. By accident rather than design, the low-price (then) middle-class US market was discovered when one of the factories of Ransom Olds burned down. The only car he could produce was the least expensive of his line. The demand turned out to be enormous. When Olds was unable to finance the expansion of Oldsmobile, Ford stepped in with the mass-produced Model T in 1908 and the moving assembly line in 1914.[39] It was during these years that US production and exports outstripped that of Germany and France.[40] But France and Germany were outstripped in products that had little else but the name 'automobile' in common.

Much later, in 1970, Continental European auto production was once again to equal that of American.[41] And Europe's exports in the 1950's, 1960's and 1970's were to be vastly more important than those of America.[42] The oligopolistic advantages that underlay these developments, however, had much to do with mass markets consisting largely of customers with incomes still lower than those of any mass markets that had ever tempted American producers. In 1946, a year after nationalization, the French company Renault introduced its low price 4-CV. Then came Citroën's 2-CV.[43] Almost immediately thereafter came the market introduction of Germany's Volkswagen.[44] Automobiles all, but of a very different sort than the middle-class models which set US manufacturers on the path to multinationality. Indeed, it was not until the late 1960's that the introduction of Citroën's GX and Volkswagen's Audi gave hints that middle-class market segments were becoming so significant on the Continent that Continental firms were no longer willing

---

[37] Fridenson, 1972: p 21.
[38] Fridenson, 1972: p 37.
[39] McKern, in Vernon (ed), 1972: p 433.
[40] McKern in Vernon (ed), 1972: p 435.
[41] UN Statistical Yearbook, 1971.
[42] McKern, in Vernon (ed), 1972: p 443.
[43] Sheahan, 1960; Wells, in Vernon (ed), 1974: p 13; Sheahan, 1963: p 109.
[44] Wells, 1974: p 13.

to leave middle-class markets in their home countries to the European subsidiaries of General Motors, Ford and Chrysler.[45]

Developments in other industries were often to parallel European-US contrasts in automobiles. The favorable income position of the lowest classes in Germany, compared to that in other countries, plus the introduction of social insurance legislation as early as the 1880's meant that German and Swiss-German companies were to lead in basic pharmaceuticals.

'Germany was not alone in having the technology to translate a laboratory synthesis into a full-scale operating production operation. Both England and France had strong chemical industries, capable of producing what was discovered in Germany. The missing ingredient (in these former countries) was demand.'[46]

By 1939, Germany accounted for 43% of world exports of pharmaceutical products.[47] Important US pharmaceutical companies were to emerge only after World War II, when they made their distinctive contribution in antibiotics and psychopharmaceuticals. These US innovations reduced hospitalization time, but they were probably less 'essential' than aspirin or novocaine – both introduced in Europe by Bayer, Hoechst and Ciba before World War I.[48]

The phenomenon of European, and especially Italian, specialization in small household appliances, and American dominance in more expensive models seems related to differences in income distribution, as well as in income levels.[49] Although the companies that produce timepieces are too small to have been systematically included in our study, the split in the world watch industry between Swiss producers of luxury goods and US middle-class, mass-merchandizers, seems another variation on the auto-industry theme.[50]

Relative Factor Costs and Innovation

Perhaps, however, the distinctive histories of European and American commercial innovation were most conditioned by persistent international differences in the relationship between labor costs and costs of other production inputs. The most obvious transatlantic contrast has been in comparative ratios of labor to raw-material costs. Except for partial exceptions such as resource-endowed Sweden and free-trading Switzerland, European entrepreneurs have faced the cost consequences of scarcity of land and raw materials. US entrepreneurs confronted an environment in which labour commanded a relative premium due to its scarcity.

Table 2.9 presents quantitative estimates of the differences in relative costs of raw materials and labor for the years 1913, 1929, 1950, 1963 and 1971. These estimates were made because historical information concerning prices paid

---

[45] Analysis of the models produced in Continental markets by European and American firms clearly shows Continental autos clustered in luxury and low-price categories while the autos produced by American subsidiaries are aimed at medium-price market segments. See: Channon, 1973: p 29.
[46] Wortzel, 1971: p 11.
[47] DAFSA, 1974: p 8.
[48] Haber, 1971.
[49] Wells, 1969.
[50] Harvard Business School, 1972; Retornaz, 1974.

Table 2.9 International Comparisons of Ratios of Raw Materials to Labor Costs, 1914–1971.

(Approximate cost of one arbitrary unit of raw materials relative to the cost of one hour of labor, with the US ratio of materials to labour costs taken as 100.)

	1913	1929	1950	1963	1971
USA	100	100	100	100	100
Belgium		136	176	330	263
France	194	180	448	460	364
Germany	294	356	290	290	190
Italy		524	502	460	345
Netherlands		224	420	370	251
Sweden	158	144	113	180	139
Switzerland		144	181	210	182

Sources: Derived from UN, *Statistical Yearbook*, various issues, for 1929–1971 data on hourly earnings and raw material costs; International Labor Organization, *Year Book of Labor Statistics*, various issues. See text for method of calculation.

for raw materials by entrepreneurs within national markets was difficult or impossible to obtain. National indices of raw-materials prices, however, were readily available, as were indices and values for wage rates. If one assumed that in any given year, a relatively open, one-price international market in raw materials prevailed, it then became possible to derive indicators of earlier or subsequent divergences in relative factor-costs ratios based on domestic price indices. In this table, it is assumed that 1963 was such a year, and that raw-materials prices were identical in all markets. No special exchange-rate adjustments were made, the rationale being that if 1963 exchange rates were equilibrium rates (an admittedly debatable assumption), the influence of prior and subsequent rate changes would be reflected in the local index of the cost of raw-materials index to the extent that raw materials were imported. First, wage and price series were put on a comparable 1963 = 100 basis. Wage indices were then adjusted to reflect differences in wage levels among countries in 1963, eg, since the Swedish average wage rate was equal to 57% of that in the US in that year, the whole Swedish series was adjusted in proportion to this difference. This meant that the Swedish index was shifted 43% lower to reflect absolute US-Swedish differences. It did *not* mean that the margin between Swedish and US revised indices was ever at 100 : 57 in any year other than 1963. Once this adjustment was made, wage and raw-materials price indices could be treated as if they were money-price series. One arbitrary unit of raw materials could be said to cost whatever one average hour of labor cost in the US in 1963. National materials-cost series were divided by the adjusted labor-cost series and the resulting ratios proportioned to the base of US = 100 as shown in Table 2.9. The estimates are crude. Nevertheless, the orders of magnitude shown accord well with what qualitative sources tell us of differences among countries and in different periods of time.

Throughout the twentieth century, and even from its earliest days as a nation, the US had comparatively little labour relative to its abundant land

and material resources.[51] Prior to World War I neither the slave trade nor successive waves of immigration seemed to make much of a dent in this fact of life facing the US entrepreneur, and the passage of restrictive immigration laws in 1917, 1921, and 1924 only aggravated the problem.[52]

In Europe, and particularly on the Continent, labor was long in substantial surplus. From the mid-1800's to the 1960's, most of Europe worried about what to do with its reserve army of the unemployed. The scarce resources in Europe were not hands nor brains: they were raw materials. This scarcity was sometimes relieved by trade or colonial expansion. Yet, the autarkic reflexes first nurtured by Colbert under Louis XIV in the 1600's continually re-asserted themselves as successive European governments declared their dependence on foreign supply to be militarily intolerable. The result was a concern for substitution and saving of raw materials that recurs repeatedly in European history. Innovation of synthetic nitrogenous fertilizers, dyestuffs, rubber, and rayon, constituted one sort of response to the stimuli provided in such markets. Products and processes that saved fuel were another. One finds European firms pioneering in high efficiency auto engines, electric furnaces, and fuel-injection apparatus, as well as in industrial processes such as that of Solvay for soda-ash, and that of Péchiney for producing aluminum with high-cost electricity.

Hitler's policy of systematically reducing foreign exchange allocations for imports of raw materials while encouraging *ersatz* innovations during the 1930's, is often taken as the apotheosis of this tendency.[53] His policies of suppressing trade unionism, imposing a ceiling on wages, and encouraging population growth made the effect on relative factor costs all the more pronounced.[54] Nevertheless, Nazi Germany provided only an extreme variation on a common theme. This concern in Germany had been in evidence well before Hitler's time. Table 2.9 suggests that the material/labor costs ratio in the German market was in the order of three times that in the United States in 1913. As early as 1870 we find instances of material-saving innovation being triggered by raw-material price increases. The interruption of supplies of natural dyestuffs from France into Germany by the Franco-Prussian War gave enormous stimulus to the synthetic alizarin dyes developed by BASF in that year.[55]

The recurrent fear or reality of naval blockades constituted a particularly powerful incentive to material substitution. English sea-power long controlled Germany's access to natural resources. In the words of Walther Rathenau, German Foreign Secretary and son of the founder of one of Germany's great electrical firms, the first World War meant that:

'When on 4 August of last year England declared war our country became a beleaguered fortress. Cut off by land and cut off by sea it was made wholly self-dependent; we were facing a war the duration, cost, danger, and sacrifices of which no one could foresee . . . Materials difficult

---

[51] Habakkuk, 1962: Chapter 3.
[52] *Encyclopaedia Britannica*, 1973: Vol II, pp 106 *et seq.*
[53] Friedlaender and Oser, 1953: p 444ff.
[54] Friedlaender and Oser, 1953: p 411; Shirer, 1960: pp 388, 362, 364.
[55] Haber, 1958: pp 83–204.

to obtain must be replaced by others more easily procurable. It is not ordained that this or that object must be made of copper or of aluminium; it may be made of some other material. Substitutes must be found. Instead of using the time-honoured materials for our household goods, etc., we must use new substances, and articles must be manufactured that do not require so much raw material. . . .'[56]

Chilean nitrates were among the critical raw materials no longer available to Germany. This shortage led that country's chemists to work furiously on developing the Haber-Bosch process for synthetic nigrogen fixation, a process first discovered on the eve of the War in 1913. That process itself was only one important result of a series of investigations sponsored from 1897 onward by BASF, a firm based in a land-hungry and militarily conscious state. Nitrogen was needed for both fertilizers and explosives, and fear of the blockage to come had long stimulated even the research that preceded innovation.[57]

Not only the state of war, but also its aftermath sometimes stimulated innovations of a material-saving nature in Germany. A scarcity of coal after World War I led many German households to turn to electrical heating and cooking appliances. Siemen's entry into the appliance business was a direct result of this shift in demand.[58]

The interest of the German government and of German industry in material saving and substitution sometimes stemmed from economic, as well as military and strategic concerns. American, or Anglo-Saxon oligopolies or cartels occasionally determined prices and quantities of natural resources supplied to Germany, even in peacetime. Before World War I the Deutsche Bank unsuccessfully attempted to break the dominance of the US Standard Oil Company and of Royal Dutch-Shell in the German market. The result of the bank's failure to obtain crude oil in meaningful quantities was a redoubled support for Germany's electric industry. In 1912, bank officials argued that hydro-power offered the only means of 'fighting the oil cartel.'[59]

German fears for supplies of raw materials were accompanied by abundant, even overabundant supplies of labor In the pre-Hitler period. Labor-saving innovations and imitations were known in Imperial Germany. But the home-market conditions for their utilization were not propitious – compared to the US. Desai notes that:

'We have evidence that throughout the period (1871–1913) labour for industry was abundant in Germany. The increase in the industrial working population between 1882 and 1895 was about 3·2 million; in the same period there was a net emigration of nearly 1·5 million of whom perhaps 80 per cent would have been working if they had stayed. Thus, more than a quarter of the increase in the labour force emigrated in this period. Emigration in the 1870s, though less heavy, was nevertheless substantial. After 1892 or so there was a decline in emigration, and there

---

[56] Rathenau, cited in Pollard and Holmes, 1972.
[57] Haber, 1958: pp 84–91.
[58] Siemens, 1957: Vol II, p 66. Siemens does not mention the causes of the shortage. One surmises that it was related to the French occupation of the Ruhr between 1921 and 1925. (*Encyclopaedia Britannica*, 1973: Vol 19, p 719.)
[59] See Lenin, 1960, and sources cited therein.

was even a little net immigration after 1895; but the statistics of urban labour exchanges, which start in 1896, show a large excess of registered male seekers of work over vacancies. Labour exchange statistics are subject to serious pitfalls and the conclusions they suggest are not final. But their evidence is generally borne out by literary sources: while particular industries (for instance, sugar and brick-making) suffered shortages of labour and particular skills were often scarce, this was due to local circumstances and not to a general labour shortage.'[60]

In France, relative factor cost conditions before World War II appear to have lain somewhere between those in Germany and those in the US. France had long had relatively resource rich colonies. Germany had not. Yet French history is replete with complaints concerning the scarcity or the price of coal, petroleum and copper.[61] Descriptions of the early twentieth-century days of French firms like Renault, show that industrial entrepreneurs felt that the profits obtainable from introducing labor-saving innovations were likely to be considerably less than those that could be secured from cheaper material inputs.[62] Government policies in France perhaps underlay the relatively high cost of imported raw materials even more so than they did in Germany. At a time when the French population and labor supply was notoriously stable, the Méline tariff of 1892 included 'tariffs for all, including, absurdly, tariffs on raw materials.'[63] In the post-World War I era, and then again after World War II, repeated devaluation of the franc compounded yet further the effect of tariffs.[64] With the loss of the colonies in the fifties and sixties, France's materials/labor cost ratio came to be over four times that of the US in 1963.

The innovative response in France to this relative factor cost situation differed from that in Germany. Market differences might explain the divergence of responses. For example, France had long been virtually self-sufficient in agriculture and had access to substantial phosphate deposits in its North African colonies.[65] Thus, a race to synthetic nitrogen for fertilizers was unlikely to be as interesting for French firms as for BASF. Nevertheless, historians have argued that protective and autarkic policies, rather than stimulating French industry, provoked France 'to turn inward, to allow its markets to be dominated by "Malthusianism", under which coalitions of interests maintain(ed) production at relatively low levels and high prices.'[66] In making their case they frequently cite the fact that French inventive successes often were merely preludes to Swiss and German innovations in industries such as chemicals.[67] French legal, patent and educational structures are all said to have blocked innovation – regardless of market or factor-price conditions.[68]

[60] Desai, 1968: p 43.
[61] Kindleberger, 1964.
[62] Fridenson, 1972.
[63] Kindleberger, 1964: p 280.
[64] Rondot, 1962.
[65] Clapham, 1951.
[66] Kindleberger, 1964: p 279.
[67] Haber, 1958.
[68] Haber, 1958.

'Malthusianism' notwithstanding, innovative responses were often forth-coming. A French enterprise developed rayon in 1892 when a silkworm disease and protective tariffs had raised French prices of natural silk.[69] France, along with the United States in the same year, was one of the twin birthplaces of aluminum in 1886. Because of strategic fears, tariffs, a booming electrical industry, and an auto industry that led the world, there was a major market demand awaiting aluminum, which was a substitute for copper and other imported non-ferrous metals. Before World War I France was second only to Switzerland in European production of aluminum, and much Swiss produc-tion went to supply French needs.[70] Germany had copper; France had very little.[71] Production of aluminum in France and Switzerland exceeded that in the US and Canada from the turn of the century to 1913.[72] More recently, French enterprises have innovated in long-lasting radial tires, high-efficiency, fuel-saving automobile engines, electricity-saving processes for aluminum smelting, and in the substitution of clays and shale for bauxite in the pro-duction of alumina.[73]

Italian relative factor cost conditions were even more propitious for the introduction of innovations oriented toward the economizing of materials. Italy faced both a labor surplus and a shortage of indigenous raw materials. The drastic fall in the real wages of agricultural workers following the open-ing of the Suez Canal in 1869 is said to have started Italy's chronic labor surplus. Italian rice production became hopelessly uneconomic in the face of cheaper imports from the Far East. Almost overnight much of the population of Southern Italy became unemployed and the migration to the North and the United States began.[74] Italy's lack of natural resources and fuel was her second major problem.[75] Free trade would have been a solution. But free trade implied dependence on British lines of supply in the Mediterranean. After World War I, Britain was seen as having betrayed Italy by breaking territorial promises made while Italy was hovering between neutralism and interventionism during the war. Britain was considered unreliable, and dependence on her became unthinkable. In 1922, Mussolini began fascist Italy's attempt at autarky. Table 2.9 suggests that by 1929 Italian material/labor cost ratios were more than five times higher than the American ratios. Palatial electric generating stations, replete with sculptures destined to inspire patriotic feeling, were built to provide a substitute for imported fuels. Montecatini's ventures into aluminum enjoyed direct state support, as well as tariffs against imported copper.[76] And, although imitation and importation of material-saving innovations previously developed by firms from other Continental countries ruled the day, Italy's educational and institutional bottlenecks did not totally prevent innovative creativity by Italian-owned

---

[69] Kindleberger, 1964: p 280.
[70] Pitaval, 1946: p 71.
[71] *Oxford Economic Atlas*, 1972: p 45.
[72] Pitaval, 1946: p 71.
[73] *Enterprise*, 1973; Sheahan, 1960; Sheahan, 1963; David, 1974: p 24.
[74] Wells (1893: pp 29–35) cited in Pollard and Homes, 1972: p 142.
[75] Grindrad, 1955: p 40.
[76] Pitaval, 1946: p 139.

firms. Snia Viscosa, for example, pioneered the production of rayon staple fibre as a wool substitute in 1924.[77]

From time to time, entrepreneurs and firms in the small countries of Europe shared the same factor-price fate as their larger brethren. Wartime constituted the period of greatest similarity. Between 1914 and 1918, and then again in the 1940's, all of Continental Europe faced prohibitively priced or rationed raw materials. British and American blockades were part of the cause. But in the First War, control of Swiss and Dutch raw-material imports by the Central Powers and the near-annexation of Belgium by Germany had their parts to play. Prices 'rose steeply and rapidly, leaving wages far behind.'[78] The Second World War saw Switzerland subordinated to Axis control, and the occupation of what later became Benelux.

Even during peacetime, domestic factor endowments in the smaller Continental countries were occasionally such that entrepreneurs feared scarcities of raw materials. The Netherlands had few material resources (until North Sea Oil), and has long had one of the highest population densities in the world.[79] Table 2.9 suggests that internal factor prices amply reflected this endowment. Except for abundant hydro-electric power, Switzerland has always been dependent on the good will of her larger neighbors for the passage of raw materials. Belgium had coal and iron-ore but little else.[80]

Perhaps it is partly because of the fears engendered by a sense of insecurity concerning materials supplies that Switzerland, Holland and Belgium each gave the world some of its most famous material-saving innovations; to wit, epoxy plastic resins, margarine substitutes for butter, and the Solvay ammonia-soda process for soda ash.[81] Wartime problems in obtaining coal supplies combined with the availability of hydro-electric power, certainly spurred the development of the Swiss and Scandinavian electrical industries.[82]

The small countries of Europe, however, knew that they could never aspire to the self-sufficiency dreamt of by the large. They never put tariffs on raw materials as did the French, or force-fed material-saving innovations as did Germany and Italy. All sought low raw-materials prices through trade. Belgium and the Netherlands supplemented this effort with conquest and exploitation of colonies rich in resources. To the extent they were successful in affecting relative factor cost patterns, their firms faced materials/labor cost ratios similar to those faced by American enterprise. It is in these countries that emphasis on process innovations for the production of American-type products appears to have been the highest. The R&D orientation of Hoboken-Overpelt, Belgium's largest non-ferrous metals group has been explicitly oriented to such process development.[83] Philips of Holland has long appeared to be a past master of 'imitation and development' as well as of

---

[77] US Tariff Commission, *The Rayon Industry*, 1944.
[78] Bonjour, Offler and Potter, 1952: p 349.
[79] Encyclopaedia Britannica, *Book of the Year*, 1973: p 553.
[80] Société Générale de Belgique, 1972: p 54.
[81] Discussion with Ciba executives; OECD, 1970: p 192; Haber, 1958: pp 100–101; Wilson, 1954: Vol 2, Chapter 2.
[82] Siemens, 1957: Vol II, p 65.
[83] De Geest, 1972: p 369.

research and development.[84] Perhaps because of their free-trade orientation, small countries also gave birth to numerous exceptions to the rule of first innovation of labor-saving, middle-class products in the US. Philips' tape cassettes and Sulzer of Switzerland's automatic looms are two cases in point. Nevertheless, it was in Sweden that the factor cost ratios faced by entrepreneurs became most similar to that in the US.

From 1870 to nearly the First World War, factor cost ratios in Sweden were similar to those on the Continent. Sweden passed through an agricultural crisis as improved transport brought Russian and American grain to its shores.[85] That crisis resulted in the impoverishment and subsequent emigration of a large percentage of the population. Between 1867 and 1886, 500,000 people left the country, largely to go to the United States.[86] Emigration continued to 1914, though at a rapidly declining pace.[87] During the World Wars, blockades, unrestricted submarine warfare and the like had the same effect on many raw materials' prices in Sweden as elsewhere in Europe.[88]

Nevertheless, quite unlike the rest of Western Europe, Sweden had natural resources in abundance. Despite her dependence on imports for coal, textiles, leather products, chemicals, rubber and foods, 'the greatest impetus toward industrialization in Sweden was derived from the exploitation of her own material resources for the export market.'[89] Sweden had timber, iron-ore, copper and water power.[90] After the emigration wave, the rate of population growth declined markedly and her territory (after that of Finland and Iceland), came to be the third most thinly populated in Western Europe.[91]

Such an environment proved receptive to labor and time-saving innovations to a degree that was unique in Europe. True, Swedish industry responded to raw-material scarcity in wartime with *ersatz* products.[92] But these innovations are hardly ever heard of again. The exports, and later the multinational manufacturing activity of Swedish firms, sprang from singularly 'American' roots. Perhaps Sündberg was right when he wrote that Swedes were so good at technical activities because of 'their lack of interest in people.'[93] Skills, certain natural resources and some attitudes were preconditions of Swedish pre-eminence in matches, bearings, trucks, electrical transmission equipment and telecommunications. Still, the type of pre-eminence; the emphasis on time and labor-saving products would appear to have been intimately conditioned by their birth in a resource-rich, thinly populated land, where real wages were generally increasing. Before World War I wages increased rapidly relative to prices.[94] It was in this climate that Sven Wingquist, the textile

---

[84] Bouman, 1958; Pavitt, 1971: p 144.
[85] Andersson, 1955: pp 371 and 381; Thomas, 1941: p 89.
[86] Andersson, 1955: pp 418–423 and 448–449.
[87] Thomas, 1941.
[88] Heckscher, 1954: p 274.
[89] Thomas, 1941, p 155.
[90] Friedlaender and Oser, 1953: p 144.
[91] Heckscher, 1954: p 275; Encyclopaedia Britannica, *Book of the Year*, 1973: p 553.
[92] Thomas, 1941: p 156.
[92] Thomas, 1941: p 156.
[93] Thomas, 1941: p 388.
[94] Thomas, 1941: p 97.

company maintenance engineer who founded SKF, innovated a ball-bearing that required less maintenance than traditional bearings.[95] After an interlude between 1913 and 1923 during which wages stagnated and prices increased, labor-saving needs once again predominated in the industrial marketplace.[96] The 45% increase in industrial output with but a nine percent increase in the Swedish labor force between 1923 and 1933 indicate that a 'sharp upward trend toward replacing men by machines' was underway.[97] During that decade SKF introduced spherical ball-bearings and the Volvo car (Volvo was then a subsidiary of SKF).[98] Depression and war gave Sweden one last push toward traditional Continental factor price patterns. But by 1947, she imported her first Italian laborers. Ever since, relative factor cost ratios have converged toward the US patterns.[99]

Sources for Table 2.4:

Books:
Allen, 1967; Batelle Institute, 1970; Dennis, 1963; Enos, 1962; Hogan, 1971; ITT Research Institute, 1969; Jewkes and Stillerman, 1969; Langrish et al, 1972. Simonds, 1963: Vols I and II; Winnacker and Kucher, 1959.

Periodicals, Journals and Reference Works:
Encyclopaedia of Chemical Technology; Japanese Industry; Metal Finishing Abstracts; Technike der Zkunft; World Textile Abstracts.
Numerous individual articles and corporate research publications.

Institutes and Agencies:
Bundesministerium for Research and Technology, Bonn; German Museum of Technology, Munich; National Research and Development Corporation, London; Science Policy Research Unit, University of Sussex, Brighton, UK; OECD, Directorate of Scientific Affairs, Paris; Siemens Institute, Munich; TNO, Appeldorn; Vienna Technisches Museum, Vienna; various industrial associations.

Industrial Corporations:
Interviews with over 20 large European firms.

Sources for Table 2.8:

For the US in 1918:
Mitchell and others: Vol I, p 141.

For Germany in 1913, the UK in 1929, and the US in 1935–36:
Woytinsky and Woytinsky, 1953: pp 409–407.

For Germany, Sweden and the Netherlands in the 1930's, and for the UK, Germany, Sweden and the Netherlands in the 1940's and in 1950:
United Nations, 1957: Chapter IX, p 6.

For the US in 1950 and 1969:
United States, 1972: Table 504, p 317.

For European countries in the 1960's:
United Nations, 1967: Chapter 6, p 15.

---

[95] SKF, 1957.
[96] Thomas, 1941: p 155; Heckscher, 1954: p 277.
[97] Thomas, 1941: p 155.
[98] SKF, 1957.
[99] SKF, 1957: page headed '1947'.

Chapter III

The Search for Raw Materials: Adaptation to Colonies, Nationalism, and Interdependence

Innovation of materials-saving processes and synthetics was one response of European enterprise to the lack of natural resources in the Western part of the Continent. Searching for raw materials in foreign lands was another.

Since the 1870's, 34 of the 85 largest Continental firms started or acquired more than 290 foreign extractive operations.[1] More than half of these mining, petroleum, or plantation operations were begun during the quarter century that has elapsed since World War II, as one observes from Table 3.1. About 6% of these 290 operations were detached from their European parents, due to confiscations of German properties after each of the wars. Another 10% disappeared because of Communist takeovers in Russia and Eastern Europe, nationalizations in developing countries, commercially unsuccessful results and other miscellaneous causes. Nearly 240 were still in operation in 1971.[2]

These data suggest that Continental firms were engaged in foreign extractive activities on a scale close to that of American multinationals.[3] This conclusion will appear extreme to readers familiar with the figures of book values of foreign direct investment in extraction currently available. These figures show the stakes of American, British and Japanese enterprises in foreign mining and petroleum each far overshadowing that of German companies, for example. Table 3.2 reproduces the available data covering American, German, and Japanese and British foreign investment in extractive industries. These value-of-investment data reflect undeniable facts, such as the American domicile of five of the seven most important petroleum companies. Yet, the volume of German investment alone in mining and petroleum hardly reflects the behavior of enterprises based elsewhere on the European continent. Fifty-two, or nearly one-sixth of the foreign extractive start-ups or acquisitions shown in Table 3.1, were made by enterprises headquartered in Belgium or Luxemburg. No value data are available for these firms' activities. Similarly, Holland shares ownership (along with Britain) of one of the major oil firms, but it too publishes no value figures. France is the site of the head-quarters of two large international petroleum firms, one of which is the eighth biggest in the industry. French firms are also heavily involved in foreign extraction of non-ferrous ores. Again, no value figures are published. In addition, no value statistics are available for the foreign oil, gas, and iron-ore interests of Italian firms, or the foreign mining operations of Swiss and Swedish firms. One must therefore qualify the prevailing picture of an overwhelming American and British ascendancy in industrial raw materials. Furthermore, if there is Anglo-Saxon dominance, it does not seem to be for lack of effort on the part of Continental enterprise. Up to 1968, 53 (or 28%) out of 187 American industrial multinational firms were active in extractive operations outside of the United States, compared to the 34 (or 39%) of 87 Continental enterprises. US multinationals had established or acquired 320 foreign extractive subsidiaries by 1968 of which 172 were operating in that year.[4] These were numbers smaller than those concerning the extractive operations of a considerably lesser number of Continental European industrial firms.

---

[1] Anglo-Dutch Unilever is not included as a Continental firm in this count. It, of course, has numerous plantations abroad. Wilson, 1954: Vols I and II; Wilson, 1968.
[2] Comparative Multinational Enterprise Project.
[3] Vaupel and Curhan, 1969: pp 128 and 129.
[4] Vaupel and Curhan, 1969: pp 16, 128 and 129.

Table 3.1 The Spread of Extractive Operations of Continental European Enterprise: Number of Subsidiaries Established or Acquired, by Region and Period

	Europe	Middle East & Africa	N America	S America	Other	Total
Iron-ore and Coal						
Prior to WWI	11	3	—	—	4	18
1914–1945	17	6	—	5	—	29
1946–1971	15	12	8	8	—	46
Unknown	5	—	3	2	—	7
Non-ferrous Metals						
Prior to WWI	4	1	—	—	—	7
1914–1945	8	4	1	—	—	14
1946–1971	5	20	4	2	1	32
Unknown	1	—	—	—	—	1
Oil and Gas						
Prior to WWI	5	1	3	6	6	21
1914–1945	3	8	4	6	2	23
1946–1971	8	35	14	4	3	64
Other or Unknown						
Prior to WWI	2	—	—	—	—	2
1914–1945	8	—	—	—	—	8
1946–1971	9	6	1	3	3	22
Total	**101**	**96**	**38**	**38**	**21**	**294**

*Includes Royal Dutch Shell but not Unilever. Prior to the 1929 Margarine-Uni Lever merger, all the plantation or extractive operations of Unilever's predecessors had been entered by the British company, Lever Brothers.

Source: Comparative Multinational Enterprise Project.

Table 3.2 Selected Developed Market Economies: Stock of Foreign Direct Investment by Sector (Value and Percentage)

Distribution by sector	United States (end 1970)		United Kingdom (end 1965)		Federal Republic of Germany (end 1970)		Japan (end 1970)	
	Millions of dollars	Percentage	Millions of dollars	Percentage	Millions of dollars	Percentage	Millions of dollars	Percentage
Mining	6,137	8%	760	5%	260	5%	} 1,127	31%
Petroleum	21,790	28	3,853	23	164	3		
Others	17,932	23	6,290	37	908	14	1,506	42
Manufacturing	32,231	41	5,894	35	4,443	77	963	27
All Sectors Total	**78,090**	**100%**	**16,797**	**100%**	**5,775**	**100%**	**3,596**	**100%**

Source: United Nations, *Multinational Corporations in World Development*, New York, 1973, page 151, compiled from: Centre for Development Planning, Projections and Policies of the Department of Economic and Social Affairs of the United Nations Secretariat, based on Bundesministerium für Wirtschaft, *Runderlass Aussenwirtschaft*, 1 April 1971; Hans-Eckart Scharrer, ed, *Förderung privater Direktinvestitionen* (Hamburg, 1972); Japanese Ministry of International Trade and Industry, *White Paper on Foreign Trade*, 1972; United Kingdom Board of Trade, *Board of Trade Journal*, 26 January 1968; United States Department of Commerce, *Survey of Current Business*, various issues.

Continental Problems

The direction and scale of the search for natural resources by Continental firms was rendered unique by their – and their governments' – sense of their vulnerability to external threats to Western Europe's materials supply. One finds firms and their governments often responding to the reality of fear or wartime blockades of the Continent and to the frequent dominance of Continental markets by large Anglo-Saxon companies in resource-based industries. This sense of vulnerability to external forces was compounded by fears born of a geographical distribution of Western Europe's meagre resources that seemed planned by some malevolent deity to have no relationship whatever to national boundaries.

The Mismatch Between Continental Borders and Resources

Sufficient deposits of iron-ore and coal enabled the Continental countries to ignore the spectre of British dominance of sea-lanes that was long to haunt them in other minerals prior to the end of World War II. The nations of the Continent began to catch up with Britain's industrial revolution in the late 1800's without depending on British or Empire resources. The coal, however, was found in Germany, Belgium, and Holland, and the iron was located in Sweden and France, especially in oft-disputed Alsace and Lorraine.

This patchwork pattern of iron-ore and coal deposits gave rise to trade, but to no significant cross-investment in mining between great power Germany and small Sweden. Throughout the nineteenth century German iron masters acted as if they were confident that Swedish specialty steel makers would never have a demand for Sweden's considerable ore deposits that would tempt them to withhold supplies, charge excessive prices, or seriously compete with German steel. After the outbreak of World War I German companies were simply blocked from acquiring Swedish deposits by the early involvement of Sweden's government in the iron-ore business. The Swedish state participated in ownership of important mines after 1914 and nationalized them altogether in the mid-1950's. In addition,

> '. . . important negative measures were taken during World War I designed to protect the mines from coming under foreign control. Every acquisition of mine property . . . needed explicit approval of some government office.'[5]

German, Belgian, and Luxemburg firms, however, did attempt to secure supplies of French iron-ore through ownership of French mines. Belgian and Luxemburg – and to a smaller extent French – firms attempted to secure supplies of coking coal through investments in mining in Germany.[6] Desire to avoid dependence on German owners of coal fields was the motivation for the latter international vertical integration moves.[7] A number of examples of early investments of this type are shown in Table 3.3. The German investments in France were confiscated after the outbreak of World War I. The Belgian and Luxemburg investments have continued and indeed have been

---

[5] Friedlaender and Oser, 1953: pp 415 and 416.
[6] Feis, 1930: pp 198 and 199.
[7] ARBED, 1913.

Table 3.3   Illustrative Extractive Investments of Large Continental European Companies Undertaken Prior to World War I

Company	Country of origin	Materials extracted	Country of investment
Cockerill	Belgium	Coal Iron ore	Russia Germany France
Arbed	Luxemburg	Coal	Germany
Alusuisse	Switzerland	Bauxite	France
Krupp	Germany	Iron ore Nickel Various ores	France New Caledonia Australia, India
Thyssen	Germany	Iron ore	France Russia Norway Morocco Algeria India
Metallgesellschaft	Germany	Copper Copper, lead, zinc Zinc Non-ferrous ores	Spain Australia Mexico Algeria
Royal Dutch-Shell	Holland/UK	Oil	Indonesia Russia Roumania Mexico USA Others

Sources: McKay, 1970: pp 143–145; ARBED *Annual Reports*, especially 1925; Wallace, 1937: p 34; Manchester, 1969: p 300; Treue and Webbing, 1969: Vol I, p 156; Dabritz, 1931; Elliott, 1937: p 411; Wilkins, 1974.

expanded since. The German motivation to buy French mines apparently had to do with the failure of German annexation of Alsace-Lorraine in 1870 to 'solve' nature's mischief in placing coal and iron-ore in different countries. Germany had thought she had assured herself of territorial possession of both resources; part of the German motive for annexing French territories after the Franco-Prussian war was to deny French steel companies their indigenous ore. The French promptly discovered even more ore on their remaining Lorraine territory, however. Other than renewed warfare, the only way for German firms to limit this resurgent competitive advantage of French steel firms was to attempt to buy as many mines as possible.[8] The Belgian and Luxemburg mines appear to have served the more prosaic function of acting as a brake on price pressure that could have resulted from a French iron-ore cartel.

[8]ARBED, *Annual Report*, 1913.

World War II, and then the emergence of the European Coal and Steel Community in the 1950's, made cross-border ownership ties in coal and iron-ore within Western Europe irrelevant, at least in theory. Once freer trade was about to emerge, however, European coal and iron-ore soon became increasingly scarce relative to the demand placed on these materials by the rapidly growing post-war European economies.

Once the cost of labor in Western Europe began its ascent in the late 1950's, toward American heights, many European mines for both coking coal and iron-ore rapidly became uneconomic. New sources were being discovered elsewhere in the world, and European collieries began to be closed or phased out.[9] For coal, the competition of low cost oil was vastly more important than were alternative sources of coking coal or alternative processes like the so-called direct reduction of steel, but these latter compounded the injury.[10] In 1938, the six Continental countries that later formed the European Coal and Steel Community (ECSC) had been producing nearly one-third of the world's production of 800 million metric tons of coal. By 1969, the ECSC was producing less than 15% of a total of 1·2 billion metric tons, and much of that production was heavily subsidized.[11] In 1937, Western Continental Europe (including Sweden) produced over one-third of the world's iron-ore needs. By 1950, Western Europe accounted for less than one quarter of total ore production and had but 13% of total reserves then known.[12] In 1966, the EEC countries plus Sweden had but 4% of estimated total ore reserves, although Sweden and France still accounted for about 14% of world ore production. Sweden remained a substantial exporter, but the six countries of the EEC supplied less than two-fifths of their own needs.[13] Even in its own traditional industrial resources Western Europe was thus coming by the 1970's to look more and more like the unendowed island it had already long been in oil, most non-ferrous metals, and many other raw materials. The fear of vulnerability to overpricing and supply cutoffs that had long affected Continental views of resources other than iron-ore and coal was surfacing even for these materials.

Early Anglo-American Dominance

With so few indigenous raw materials, the Western part of the European Continent had depended on ocean transport for supplies ever since the first flowerings of industrialization in the 1700's. Dependence on ocean supplies, however, meant that these supplies could be cut by British sea-power. In the early 1800's Napoleon had wanted to harm Britain's economy by denying it Continental markets. Instead, the riposte to his blockade of the British Orders in Council ended up denying the Continent 'imports of Sicilian sulphur for vineyards, silk works, and powder mills, of Spanish Barilla for soap boilers, of sal-ammoniac from the Levant, and of saltpetre from India . . . .'[14]

---

[9] Manners, 1971: pp 3, 15 and 116.
[10] Manners, 1971: p 45.
[11] Gordon, 1970: p. 21.
[12] UN 1959: p 73. The data concerns so-called 'contained tons', or tons of ore mined corrected to give ferrous content only.
[13] Manners, 1971: pp 240, 348 and 349.
[14] Haber, 1958: p 39.

English sea power and subsequent control of the Suez Canal became a constraint that Continental governments could not ignore.[15] If they forgot the
lesson administered to Napoleon, the severing of shipping links to the
Continent during World War I served as a reminder to belligerents and small
neutral nations alike that ownership of foreign mineral deposits provided no
guarantee of supply unless it was within the lines of potential blockades.
Thus, some 49% (or 68% if Shell's operations are excluded) of the extractive
operations of all Continental firms were located on the Continent itself prior
to 1946.

While the threat of military blockades hung over Europe, the menace of the
determination of price and supply by American or Anglo-Saxon oligopolies
and cartels was omnipresent. The story of the dominance of American and
British firms in the petroleum industry, and of the European government and
enterprise reactions is well known.[16]

Early industrialization and abundant domestic resources in the United States
interacted to cause America to be the world's first major source of oil, and to
give its companies an experience in the industry that others were long hard-
put to match. Economies of scale in refining and distribution led to the
emergence of the Standard Oil near-monopoly in North America. Early
technological advantages in those functions enabled Jersey Standard to achieve
a world-wide market share of well over 70% by 1911.[17]

Oil found in the Dutch colony of the Dutch East Indies (now Indonesia), the
South of Russia, and Rumania provided the only footholds in the industry
for non-American firms. In 1907, most of these firms were consolidated into
Royal Dutch-Shell, a company owned 60% by Dutch and 40% by British
shareholders. The Dutchman, Deterding, controlled the Russian sources,
and the Englishman, Samuels, had access to British Empire markets as well as
transport experience.[18] A German group, headed by the Deutsche Bank, had
attempted to break into the industry by acquiring Rumanian sources in the
early 1900's. By the time the Germans moved, however, Standard Oil and
Shell had already acquired a near-stranglehold on known sources, as well as on
distribution and transport. In 1907, the Deutsche Bank agreed 'not to attempt
anything which might injure American interests'. By 1912, German banking
circles were arguing that the only way to fight the oil trust was to rely on
hydroelectricity.[19] Shortly before World War I, the discovery of oil in Britain's Persian sphere of influence allowed the British government to set up
Anglo-Persian, the forerunner of BP, and the first state-owned instrument in
the industry.[20] This step was taken because the British feared being over-
charged for oil supplied to its navy by an American, or American-Anglo-
Dutch cartel.

---

[15] Shimoni and Levine, 1972: p 80.
[16] Anglo-American cooperation was not without its strains, for the US companies often felt
that British enterprises were trying to exclude American enterprises from the Middle East,
Asia and Africa. By 1923, however, an inter-firm, inter-government entente had been reached.
See: Hogan, 1974. The following discussion of the petroleum industry owes much to: Adelman, 1972; Penrose, 1968; Tugendhat, 1968; Vernon, 1971: Chapter II.
[17] Tugendhat, 1968.
[18] Tugendhat, 1968.
[19] Lenin, 1960: pp 766 and 767.
[20] Penrose, 1968: p 112; Tugendhat, 1968: pp 67 and 68.

When World War I broke out Continental enterprise was a very minor factor in the industry, save for the 60% Dutch holding in Royal Dutch-Shell and small German holdings in Rumania, Russia and Turkey.[21] The communist revolution of 1917 nationalized Shell's holdings in the Caucasus. Had Shell not discovered oil in Venezuela, not far from Holland's Caribbean Colonies in 1922, Continental enterprise might have been virtually eliminated from the industry.

During the inter-war period, the international oil industry became the all-but-exclusive preserve of the Americans, BP, and partly-British Shell. Over 90% of Europe's oil was supplied by these companies between 1914 and 1939. Dominance of nearly this order of magnitude continued into the 1950's.

The Anglo-Saxon military and commercial command over oil was more than some national governments could tolerate. The bulk of Europe's energy needs might be supplied by coal, but liquid fuels were needed to power airplanes, trucks, and tanks. Thus Continental military budgets and strategies were uncomfortably dependent on Anglo-American decisions. The French government aggressively sought, and obtained, the share of the Iraq Petroleum Company concession originally destined for the Deutsche Bank as part of the spoils of World War I: France subsequently formed a partly state-owned firm, *Compagnie Française des Pétroles*, to manage it. Mussolini started up ENI's forerunner AGIP in 1926.[22] I G Farben became Nazi Germany's semi-official arm for the industry.[23]

Anglo-American ascendancy was not limited to the petroleum industry, however. Industry structures were analogous in copper and some other non-ferrous metals. Although Great Britain was the leading producer during the first half of the nineteenth century, on the eve of World War I American firms nearly had a world monopoly in copper. The ancient mines of Germany and Sweden provided little for these countries' own needs;[24] the foreign operations of *Metallgesellschaft* were of only minor importance; and the pre-World War I output in the Congo of the *Union Minière du Haut Katanga*, a subsidiary of Belgium's *Société Générale*, was negligible.[25]

Continental fears of being held to ransom by American cartels were not imaginary in copper, as the cartels of 1918–1924, 1926–1932, and 1935–1941 were to demonstrate. The first copper cartel was an exclusively American grouping.[26] By joining the second cartel, the Belgian group showed that it was not averse to high prices for Congolese ore. And it is possible that *Union Minière*'s participation in the cartel was an indication of a more profound difference in interests of small versus large Continental countries: the earliest prospection undertaken in the Congo's Katanga district for *Union Minière* was performed by Cecil Rhodes' Tanganyika Concessions Limited, and that British enterprise from the first has owned a large block of *Union Minière*'s shares.[27]

[21] Feis, 1930: p 270.
[22] Tiger and Franko, 1973.
[23] Sasuly, 1947.
[24] Skelton in Elliott (ed), 1937: pp 392 *et seq.*
[25] *Société Générale de Belgique*, 1972: pp 83 and 93.
[26] Hexner, 1946: p 224.
[27] D'Ydewalle, 1960: pp 40, 42 and 43; *Union Minière*, 1974.

The third cartel included Americans, the Anglo-Belgian *Union Minière*, and a number of British firms that had made discoveries in Britain's Rhodesian colonies.[28] Because of disagreements among members, new entrants, and a buyers' strike in 1932, the inter-war copper cartels kept breaking down. Notwithstanding these breakdowns, they had some effect on prices.

American dominance in lead and zinc was less strong than in copper or oil.[29] In lead especially, British firms were foremost in international markets. But the Continent, yet again, was isolated. America had its own sources and spawned many of the earliest mining firms. Britain was almost as much of a latecomer to large-scale mining as were Continental nations, but Britain had its Mid-East and African colonies or spheres of influence that were to prove rich in deposits.

Continental Reactions before 1945

Before 1945, the anxiety caused by dependence on American and British goodwill for natural resources often led to the seeking of materials in foreign countries on or near the Continent. Innovation of material-saving processes or synthetics could not completely resolve the Continental problem. Sometimes it was possible to promote and use alternative materials based on resources found in Western Europe: when Anglo-Saxon copper cartels threatened, it became patriotic in France and Germany to use aluminum made with French, Italian and Eastern European bauxite.[30] But in Western Europe only France had much bauxite. And making oil out of coal, as I G Farben succeeded in doing by 1928, was exceedingly costly. State-owned extractive firms could be formed, but they had to find something to extract.

The Search in Eastern Europe

With the foreclosure or pre-emption of American and British Empire sources, one obvious course for Continental companies was to search to the East. Moreover, since there was much British capital invested in Russian oil and mining before World War I, it seemed urgent to obtain ownership of Eastern European deposits quickly.[31] Some of the Continental investments in Russian coal and iron-ore mining mentioned in Table 3.3 were of the 'spillover' variety: they were undertaken not to supply Western markets, but rather to put technology to use in mining the resources of the Czarist Empire for its own needs. In oil, however, Russia was primarily a source for Continental, as well as British, markets.

The Russian revolution nationalized the extractive operations owned by Continental companies in the Soviet Union and closed off the search for resources east of Minsk after 1917. During World War II, Hitler unsuccessfully attempted to undo this foreclosure by replicating the Eastern resource-seeking conquests of the twelfth century Teutonic knights.[32] Before starting the invasion of the Soviet Union with operation Barbarossa in 1941, however, Germany tried to gain access to Russian resources by other means.

---

[28] Hexner, 1946: pp 224 and 225.
[29] Skelton in Elliott (ed), 1937: pp 591 *et seq.*, US Bureau of Mines, 1960: pp 429 and 975.
[30] Wallace in Elliott (ed), 1937: p 453.
[31] Feis, 1930: p 233.
[32] On the German colonization of Prussia, see: Carsten, 1954.

'On May 23, 1941 Hitler sent Stalin a secret memorandum calling for the joint exploitation of Russia's oilfields, and Stalin's refusal was among the immediate factors which led to the invasion of Russia.'[33]

Between the wars, the search for resources in Eastern Europe was intense, especially in post-Hapsburg and post-Hohenzollern Central Europe. Part of the inter-war foreign investment resulted merely from redrawing of borders: the coal-mining activities of German firms in Polish Silesia were now Polish by dint of Polish independence.[34] And part of it was merely expansion of operations started up long before. The Rumanian fields had been an important German source, even before their seizure by the Nazis in 1940.[35]

New operations in Eastern Europe were especially numerous in bauxite, the primary metal for aluminum. French tariffs on copper and the effects on copper prices of several early attempts to cartelize that industry had already insured that the Western European demand for aluminum would be greater than that of the United States during most of the period prior to World War I. French bauxite was sufficient to supply the raw material for this need prior to 1914. It was largely shipped to Germany to be transformed into alumina by the Bayer process, and then transported back to France and Switzerland to be turned into metal by hydro-electricity.[36] During the life of the Heroult patents used by the first few European firms in the industry there was little vertical integration among these stages, either within or across national borders: control of technology sufficed to keep newcomers out of the industry. With the expiration of the patents in 1902, however, new entrants threatened and a race to own bauxite deposits was touched off. In Europe:

'. . . the original companies did not begin aggressive acquisition of ore lands until competitors emerged.'[37]

Before World War I, the race for access to bauxite caused Alusuisse to invest in France. After World War I, the search was in the East. As with copper and oil in the Western hemisphere, the deposits had been pre-empted by large North American companies: Aluminum Company of America and its post-1928 spin-off, Aluminum of Canada. African deposits were unknown, or in British colonies, or in the hands of the French, whose two aluminum producers were still content with their domestic bauxite. The main thrust to the East was made during a few years before World War II by a firm that was too small in 1970 to have appeared on the Fortune '200' list, but which was once the second largest aluminum producer in the world. That firm was Germany's state-owned *Vereinigte Aluminium Werke* (VAW), founded in 1917.[38] After the Nazi takeover, aluminum was to be Germany's means of escaping the Anglo-Belgian-American copper cartel. The metal took on patriotic significance for that country as well as for France. But bauxite was needed, and the French deposits were not for sale. Bauxite was then sought and discovered in Italy, Hungary, Yugoslavia, Rumania, and Greece. VAW acquired deposits in all

---

[33] Tugendhat, 1968: p 115.
[34] Ogger, 1971: pp 70 *et seq.*
[35] The Royal Institute for International Affairs, 1939; Tugendhat, 1968: p 114.
[36] Haber, 1973: Chapter II.
[37] Wallace in Elliott (ed), 1937: p 224.
[38] Hexner, 1946: p 220; Wallace, 1937: pp 83, 84 and 139.

these areas.[39] Alusuisse was obliged to follow if it did not want to run the risk of being undercut by VAW in the German market. So Alusuisse also ventured into Eastern Europe.[40] Even Péchiney, the principal French producer, took the precaution of purchasing ore deposits in Yugoslavia in the inter-war period.[41]

Extraction in the Middle East and Africa

Although acquisition of resources in the East appealed greatly to Continental governments and enterprises, there were those who felt that there was something to be gained by looking South: to the Middle East and Africa. Continental governments, of course, had long sought political adventures in the Islamic and Black African lands. France had taken a special interest in the Christians of the Middle East ever since the twelfth century crusades.[42] Napoleon's expedition to Egypt in 1798 rekindled French ardour for influence around the Mediterranean. And Napoleon III's colonization of Algeria made part of that dream reality.[43] Imperial Germany tried to emulate British and French colonial exploits in Africa with its abortive takeovers of Tanganyika, Southwest Africa, and the Cameroons.[44] And, although Germany never colonized Turkey, Iraq, or Iran, its attempts to add these nations to the German political sphere of influence before World Wars I and II were numerous – and sometimes successful.[45] Mussol'ni tried to reconstitute his new Roman Empire in Libya, Somalia, and Ethiopia.[46] Belgium's King Léopold II held the Congo as a private possession from 1885 until its transformation into a colony in 1908.[47]

As in the case of resource seeking in Eastern Europe, government and enterprise initiatives were occasionally inter-twined. Nevertheless, the correspondence between colonial adventures and business activities seems to have been rather limited. By World War I the *Union Minière* was beginning to extract copper and other non-ferrous metal ores from the Congo. Nevertheless, during the first years of Belgian colonialism, that African land supplied exiguous quantities of raw materials for European industry – and the raw materials it did supply were produced by plantations belonging to the then exclusively British-owned soap firm of William Hesketh Lever.[48] Schneider-Creusot, the French steel and armaments firm, undertook some iron-ore

---

[39] Wallace, 1937: p 139; Wallace in Elliott (ed), 1937: p 239.
[40] Alusuisse had in fact begun to acquire deposits in Eastern Europe during World War I. Because Alusuisse was partly financed by German interests, France had denied the company access to its French bauxite mines, and Alusuisse acquired deposits in Hungary. (Wallace, 1937: p 138). Until Italy refused to export bauxite as part of a move to stimulate local smelting in 1924, however, neither Alusuisse nor VAW moved aggressively to extract in the East. Indeed, Alusuisse had let several options on Italian and Yugoslav deposits lapse in 1921. Aluminium-Industrie-Aktien-Gesellschaft, 1943: Band II, p 14.) The Eastern thrust began in earnest with VAW's moves of 1925. (Wallace, 1937: p 139).
[41] Wallace in Elliott (ed), 1937: p 239.
[42] Shimoni and Levine, 1972: pp 134 *et seq.*
[43] Spillman, 1972: Chapter XII.
[44] Cohen, 1974: pp 28 and 29, and sources cited therein.
[45] Shimoni and Levine, 1972: pp 141 and 142; Mosely, 1973: Chapter 10.
[46] Mack Smith, 1969: p 449.
[47] D'Ydewalle, 1960: pp 119 and 120.
[48] Wilson, 1954: Vol I.

mining in North Africa.[49] *Metallgesellschaft* and the *Norddeutsche Affinerie* explored for copper in Turkey during the inter-war period.[50] But the returns from colonies, if returns there were, were mainly non-industrial and psychic, for enterprise and state strategies were an imperfect match.

Raison d'état was undoubtedly present in some of the Southern moves of European enterprise, but much evidence argues that commercial desires to protect – or to break into – one or another oligopolistic market position back home played an equally important role in determining enterprise behavior. For example, the Swedish investments in North African iron-ore deposits between the wars appear to have been motivated by their desire to maintain their near-monopoly on ocean-going ore, not by any particular desire to show the Swedish flag.

Commercially inspired moves could, of course, have political consequences, as the Moroccan affair of 1911 was to demonstrate. According to most accounts of that crisis, rivalry between German oligopolists seeking to control iron-ore deposits led to the establishment of the French protectorate over Morocco, not collusion between French firms and their government.

'Apart from Krupp, virtually all the large weapons emporia were listed on the world's stock exchanges, and through the cross-pollination of investments, patent inter-changes, and out-and-out cartels their interests often coincided. The Kaiser's growls during the Moroccan crisis of 1911 have often been attributed to Gustav Krupp on the erroneous assumptions that France and Germany were jockeying for commercial privileges there and that Wilhelm dispatched the gunboat *Panther* to scare Frenchmen. Six years earlier, when the Emperor landed at Tangier and demanded an open-door policy, he *had* been egged on by Marga Krupp's directors, who had been using Morocco as a dumping ground for obsolete cannon and were alarmed at the prospect of tariff walls which would favour Schneider. At the time of the *Panther*'s here-comes-the-cavalry ride to Agadir, however, the situation had altered. The country's attraction for steelmakers was no longer as a market but as a source of minerals. And though the Wilhelmstrasse and the Quai d'Orsay were still at odds over who should pull its political strings, Krupp and Schneider had joined their claims, together with those of Thyssen, in a dummy Union des Mines. The firms had agreed to split the sultan's iron ore three ways. The last thing they wanted was a Franco-German diplomatic showdown. One arose because Reinhard Mannesmann, a Remscheid ironmaker, had been excluded from the agreement. Mannesmann had paid the Moroccans a heavy subsidy for mining concessions. If the country became a French Protectorate he would lose everything. He convinced several Reichstag deputies that he was being victimized, and the flag-waving Alldeutsche Verband did the rest. The gunboat sailed, Britain rallied to France's side, Wilhelm's gesture failed. Morocco became French, and Schneider, no longer in need of allies, quit the cartel. All three Germans – Krupp, Thyssen, and Mannesmann – were left to sulk.'[51]

---

[49] Manchester, 1969: p 309.
[50] Elliott, 1937: p 483.
[51] Manchester, 1969: pp 308 and 309; see also Feis, 1930: p 414; Staley, 1935: pp 178–195; Staley, 1937; pp 9 and 10.

Raison d'état was, of course, often present when the enterprises seeking resources were wholly or partly state owned The German aluminum company VAW was state owned. The *Union Miniére de Haut Katanga* was partly owned by the Belgian government.[52] The *Compagnie Française des Pétroles*, 'immaculately conceived' out of diplomatic conference, was also partly state owned.[53] And the moves of these latter two firms in the Congo and the Middle East respectively were directly influenced by (and perhaps influenced in turn) the African and Levantine colonial ambitions of their state masters during the inter-war period. As one might have expected, the 1914–1915 heyday of *raison d'état* was also the heyday of the creation of state-instrument companies. All but one of the seven wholly or partly state-owned enterprises included in the Comparative Multinational Enterprise project that engaged in foreign extraction were born before 1939 – and the one exception was created in 1945.

Curiously, however, it was not while territorial imperialism flowered that these state firms undertook significant extractive operations outside of their mother country's borders. These firms' foreign extractive activities proliferated furiously only when those of most private Continental firms also proliferated; that is to say, during the post-World War II era in which Continental enterprise was obliged to commence adapting to an open, post-colonial world.

The Search for Resources since World War II

World War II and its outcome caused some abrupt changes in the resource-seeking activities of Continental European industrial enterprise. The resources remaining in Eastern Europe after Nazi Germany's frantic wartime exploitation of them became unavailable. The Eastern bauxite, iron-ore, coal, and oil deposits once owned by firms from the Western part of the Continent were expropriated. Nevertheless, a compensation of sorts came with the creation of the North Atlantic Treaty Organization. By choice or by necessity, the ancient conflict between Continental governments and Anglo-Saxon sea power was resolved. Yet, the fact that it was resolved so unambiguously in favor of the latter occasionally rankled on the Continent. The irritation was greatest in Paris, and France eventually withdrew from the NATO joint military command. But some irritation was felt in both Rome and Bonn.

Continental unhappiness with dependence on British and American navies for the defense of supply lines was exacerbated by the realization that the rapidly growing industrial body of Western Europe could only be nourished by resources from abroad. Resources were increasingly scarce on the Western part of the Continent – at prices Western Europeans found consistent with

---

[52] *Union Minière* management. Until the Congo became independent, the Belgian state had an effective two-thirds ownership in *Union Minière* through an entity called the *Comité speciale pour le Haut Katanga*. The Belgian government shareholding was, however, ceded to the Katangese government at the time of independence, and after *Union Minière's* Congolese properties were nationalized in 1966, the enterprise ceased to have any government participation.

[53] Rondot, 1962: pp 5, 11 and 12.

newly increased living standards. Such resources were to be found only in the Middle East and Africa, the Western hemisphere, South East Asia and Oceania, or under the control of the Soviet Union, China and their allies. By 1970, as Table 3.4 shows, Western Europe accounted for an insignificant proportion of the world's output of major minerals and hydrocarbons.

Table 3.4 Percentage Distribution of the Output of Major Metals, Minerals and Hydrocarbons in the World, 1970

	US	Canada	Western Europe (including UK)	Japan	Socialist Countries	Others	Total
Bauxite	3·6%	—%	5·1%	—%	14·2%	77·1%	100%
Cadmium	28·6	5·8	14·6	16·0	18·9	16·1	100
Chromium	—	—	—	—	38·6	61·4	100
Coal (1969)	24·3	—	15·6	2·1	45·1	12·9	100
Cobalt	10·2	7·7	—	—	13·5	68·6	100
Copper	24·5	9·6	—	—	18·6	47·3	100
Germanium	16·0	—	—	32·0	16·5	35·5	100
Iron ore	12·0	6·0	18·7	—	25·9	37·4	100
Lead	15·6	10·7	—	—	24·0	49·7	100
Magnesium	47·8	4·9	18·3	3·0	22·2	3·8	100
Manganese	—	—	—	—	46·6	53·4	100
Nickel	3·0	45·1	—	—	26·8	25·1	100
Oil	21·0	2·8	—	—	17·2	59·0	100
Phosphate rock	41·4	—	—	—	26·4	32·2	100
Platinum	—	—	—	—	57·9	42·1	100
Uranium	54·5	16·2	7·2	—	na	22·1	100

Sources: For all minerals and oil, but excluding coal: US Bureau of Mines, 1973.
For coal (1969): Gordon, 1970: p 21.

Note: (—) equals less than 0·1 %.

The gap between Continental production and consumption was particularly striking in petroleum, as can be observed from Table 3.5. In 1938, not long before the battle of Stalingrad determined that Soviet oil would remain Soviet, Western Europe (including Great Britain) consumed 36 million tons of oil per year. Less than one million tons was actually produced in Western Europe. However, an additional seven to ten million tons was being extracted each year in Rumania, and it is estimated that about 80% of that amount was being lifted by subsidiaries of Shell, Petrofina and other Continental enterprises.[54] By 1960, Western Europe was consuming almost six times as much oil as it had before the war; by 1972, the increase was twenty-fold. Indigenous production had also increased twenty times by 1972, but it provided only three percent of Western Europe's needs. Although the countries on the Western edge of Europe were geographically part of a Continent, in terms of resources they had become islands like Japan.

[54] *Collier's Encyclopaedia*, 1962: Vol 20, p 152; The Royal Institute for International Affairs, 1939; Priouret, 1970: p 366.

Table 3.5   Production and Consumption of Oil, Various Regions, 1938, 1960, 1972 (million tons)

	1938		1960		1972	
	Production	Consumption	Production	Consumption	Production	Consumption
Western Hemisphere	212	174	605	596	646	1,016
USSR, Eastern Europe, China	35	25	167	145	443	396
Western Europe	0·8	36	15	205	22	704
Japan	—	3	—	30	—	237
Middle East and Africa	16	na	276	76	1,178	105
World Total	**274**	**255**	**1,091**	**1,065**	**2,610**	**2,590**

Source: BP Statistical Review of the Oil Industry, various issues.

National Responses

If the old conflict between Continental needs and Anglo-American sea-power had been the only irritant in North Atlantic relations, perhaps the new reliance of the Continent on non-European materials would have only been seen as trade. But some saw it as dependence, however, for in a number of extractive industries the fact remained that the post-war market was dominated by the same firms headquartered in the United States and Great Britain that had been dominant before 1945. This divergence of views was reflected in different responses by Continental European governments to the presence of these Anglo-Saxon oligopolies.

Although West Germany's policy began to show signs of a drastic shift in the mid-1970's, that country was long willing to live with the fact that most of its petroleum was supplied by American and British firms, and that much of its non-ferrous metal ores were also purchased from large foreign firms. After the war her iron-ore supply was commercially assured, as Germany's large steel firms quickly acquired ore properties in Africa and South America.

Sweden, too, showed a willingness to live with the ever-growing American and British presence in petroleum – in spite of a certain ambivalence evidenced by the cordial relationship of the government with the one small internationally integrated oil firm and the two refining and distribution firms owned by Swedes. In iron-ore, Sweden began the post-war era with an oligopolistic position in Continental European markets that approached that of the Anglo-Americans in other minerals. In 1951, Swedish producers accounted for half of world seaborne trade in iron-ore. As new ore bodies were being discovered around the world, the leading Swedish ore company defended its market share by taking positions in a number of mines, just as American or British companies were doing. Even so, the Swedish share of ocean-going trade in iron-ore had fallen to but 15% in 1966.[55]

The Netherlands claimed full-fledged membership in the Anglo-Saxon oil club through their investors' 60% share in Royal Dutch-Shell, made 40% British by Henri Deterding, Royal Dutch's first president. Furthermore, they had long been able to counter American threats to their markets via Shell Oil, US – a firm ranked number 19 on Fortune's '500' list in its own right in 1973.[56] Hoogovens, the Dutch steel and non-ferrous metals concern, undertook foreign extraction in iron-ore, bauxite, and other minerals. But it is probable that the company received no particular political urging to seek foreign resources despite its partial ownership by the Dutch government. Thanks to the deterrent effect of having their own Anglo-American connections, the Dutch seemed relatively unperturbed by the non-European presence at home.

During the post-war era, Belgium became famous for its hospitality to firms, including those based in natural resources, from English-speaking lands. Belgium owners did, of course, possess Petrofina, the only private oil concern of any size based in the Continent besides Royal-Dutch. By virtue of contracts signed shortly after World War II, Petrofina had long constituted a major

---

[55] Mikdashi, 1971: p 98.
[56] Vernon, 1971: pp 30ff.

refining and marketing outlet for British Petroleum, a company which had too few marketing outlets for its crude oil production throughout most of the post-World War II period.[57] Petrofina's symbiotic relationship with BP was supplemented by rapid moves to establish operations in the United States which added to the commonality of Belgian and Anglo-Saxon interests. Belgium's partly British-owned *Union Minière* also gave that country a presence in non-ferrous metal ores that facilitated friendly relations with large American and British mining companies. After *Union Minière*'s Congolese operations were expropriated in 1966 (and with them, any direct governmental participation in the enterprise), *Union Minière* moved rapidly to seek Canadian, Australian and other sources.[58] Above and beyond commercial interests, harmonious relations may have been aided by Belgian memories of two liberations by British and American troops, and American memories of the fact that *Union Minière* had supplied the uranium for the first atomic bombs.[59]

Small landlocked Switzerland could afford few illusions about independence from foreign firms for materials supply. Its concern about foreign control over pricing, output, and supply decisions was nonetheless mitigated in the immediate post-war period by a number of factors. Some reassurance about the likely conduct of North American oil and minerals companies may have come from the fact that several of them temporarily chose Swiss sites for their European regional headquarters after the war. The country also had its own entrant in aluminum, Alusuisse, which was actively exploring for copper by 1973.[60] Iron-ore and coal were of lesser concern, as Switzerland had only the tiniest steel-producing capacity. Abundant hydro-electric power and large oil stockpiles also could be used to discourage excessive price demands of the American and British oil firms. And Migros, a large Swiss consumer goods distributor with close connections with a popular political movement, aggressively sought oil from sources not controlled by the Anglo-American oligopoly.

The French and Italian governments, however, viewed the problem of materials supply by foreign oligopolies with very different eyes. And, by the early 1970's, the German and Swedish governments were showing signs of following the lead of these Latin countries. The problem was felt to be most acute in oil, for in the immediate post-war period, the tightest Anglo-American oligopoly was in that industry. It was here that Italian and French state-owned companies were encouraged to seek resources abroad. While the American majors, and BP and Shell had multiplied extractive subsidiaries in the post-war period in order to defend established market shares, state-owned ENI, *Compagnie Française des Pétroles*, and ERAP became deliberately international in order to get direct access to crude.

The State-Instrument Companies

The moves of the French state oil companies to find resources outside Europe after World War II were in the first instance moves to colonies – especially to

---

[57] Petrofina management.
[58] *Union Minière, Annual Reports:* various issues.
[59] D'Ydewalle, 1960: pp 80 and 81.
[60] Private communication by Professor Louis T Wells, Jr, of the Harvard Business School following his trips to Papua and New Guinea.

Algeria, a territory administered as part of the mother country until independence in 1962. CFP, in which the state owned a minority position, as well as ERAP, the 100% state company founded in 1945, were both urged to seek 'French' oil.

Political reasons underlay much of this effort. French policy makers felt that:

'The fact of buying from others, or the need to buy from others, regardless of the terms at which one buys is itself a dependence.'[61]

French military needs for freedom from any possible Anglo-Saxon pressures may have oriented her search for oil to the colonies. But the perennial French balance of payments problem may have played an even greater role in launching oil exploration and extraction after the war.[62] Until 1958, there was a dollar shortage in Europe. Paying fewer dollars for the economic rents accruing to the Anglo-Saxon majors was one way of reducing the problem. Thus, French governments of many a political complexion found it convenient to seek to pay for petroleum in French francs. This aim in turn meant sourcing first in colonies, and then in franc-zone lands. CFP had learned from its post-1924 share in the Iraq Petroleum Concession that the majors were in no hurry to develop fields that could help competitors.[63] Thus, although the majors might predictably follow French initiatives in the Sahara and colonial Black Africa, they could hardly be expected to lead cheerfully in efforts to help the French balance of payments.

CFP proceeded to put much, and ERAP virtually all, of their exploration efforts into the colonies. After independence these activities became foreign, yet continued membership in the franc-zone was the rule rather than the exception for the newly independent African nations. Guinea withdrew in 1968, but Guinea had no oil. Until Algeria also left the franc zone in 1968 and took the main source of *pétrole-franc* oil into the dollar-denominated world, the foreign extraction activities of French state oil firms met the goal of paying for much of France's oil in francs.

Many Italians, too, felt that the Anglo-American oligopoly price of oil was excessive. One of them, Enrico Mattei, was head of Agip (later to form the nucleus of ENI) between 1945 and 1962. This state firm had been founded in 1926 by Mussolini to search for Italian hydrocarbons.[64] Mattei's first orders were to liquidate Agip. Far from selling off its small distribution network, Mattei reactivated preliberation exploration efforts in Italy's Po valley. In 1949, a little oil and much natural gas were discovered. By pricing just under alternative oil, coal, and hydro-electric energy sources, Mattei was able to finance a burgeoning distribution net for gas, fuel oil and gasoline. Until the mid-1950's, however, ENI-Agip did not undertake foreign exploration. The company depended for crude on long-term contracts with BP (then called Anglo-Persian). In 1952, Iran nationalized Anglo-Persian's concessions. Mattei cooperated with the majors in boycotting the nationalized oil. For his pains,

---

[61] Adelman, 1972: p 137.
[62] Rondot, 1962: Chapters X and XI.
[63] Rondot, 1962: pp 56 and 57.
[64] On ENI's history see: Tiger and Franko, 1973: Frankel, 1966: pp 177–181; Chiado-Fioro, 1973.

Mattei expected to be admitted to the consortium of companies set up to operate the former Anglo-Persian concession after Iran was forced to come to terms with the oligopoly. This would have given ENI access to oil for the sum of the ten to twenty cents per barrel it took to bring crude out of the ground, plus producing-country taxes – rather than for the very much higher price the majors were charging. As a result of pressure from the US State Department, five American independent firms with no Middle East or European experience were admitted to the Iranian Consortium in 1953. ENI was not. Economic considerations became almost a secondary concern as Mattei began a virtual vendetta against the Seven Sisters, as he termed Jersey, Mobil, Socal, Texaco, Gulf, BP and Shell. Whether ENI was carrying out Italian state policy, or whether ENI was formulating policy for the state seemed a moot point in what followed. Mattei did obtain low-priced Russian crude on contract as part of his attempt to chip away at the oligopoly, but ENI also sought to own sources in many countries. To this end, ENI began to enter joint ventures with governments of producing countries at a time when such arrangements were anathema to the majors. Its 1957 joint venture with the Iranian state company was but a forerunner of things to come. Despite poor luck in exploration, ENI was extracting crude in Qatar, Tunisia, Iran and Nigeria by 1973, eleven years after Mattei's death. And it was exploring or preparing to develop fields in the North Sea, Alaska, Libya, Egypt, Canada, Greenland, Australia and Trinidad.

As the government-owned oil companies of the Continent grew, they began to display behavior increasingly like that of the majors. Exploration and extraction were embarked upon in a spirit of sworn emnity with the Anglo-Saxons. But as successes occurred, the objectives actually pursued by European state and Anglo-Saxon private companies began to converge. Success in exploration led to expansion of refining, transport and distribution, an expansion which gradually came to take place increasingly outside of the state firms' home markets. Such downstream expansion provided a tempting rationale for ownership of yet more foreign concessions – even if crude prices on open spot markets were declining in the 1950's and 1960's with the waning of the Seven Sisters' control of the market. Balance of crude production, refining and distribution was pursued as zealously by state-owned firms as it had ever been by the majors. Once positions were obtained in the highly capital-intensive producing, transport and refining stages of the business, the state companies became equally conscious of the short-term temptations, and long-term horrors of price cutting. Indeed, the thought of price cutting may have been even more of a nightmare to managers in state firms financed to a much greater extent than the majors by publicly subscribed debt which required regular payments. Thus, although a state-owned firm like ENI continued to publicize its social responsibilities as a state firm to Italy, it perhaps was nearer to the mark when it advertised in 1969 as 'ENI: A Multinational Company'. Statements appeared in ENI Annual Reports like 'A primary requirement (for ENI) is to have *controlled* adequate supplies of raw materials' (emphasis added).[65] The French state companies, although they made no such revisionist statements, had nonetheless begun to look less concerned with cheap oil or French

---

[65] ENI, *Annual Report*, 1968.

oil and more concerned with balance among crude production, refining capacity, and marketing outlets as the 1960's progressed.[66]

The behavioral metamorphosis of the Italian and French state-owned, international firms was reflected in their relations with governments of the countries in which extraction took place. In the 1950's and early 1960's these state companies were newcomers to the oil business; they were willing to make deals with host countries that were much more generous than those offered by the majors. ENI, ERAP, and CFP were all leaders at one time or another in revolutionary arrangements that traded refineries, technical assistance, host-country participation, or service contracts, for preferential access to oil.[67] These once-revolutionary actions were imitated, however, mostly by American independents who were now the newest newcomers to the industry. This third wave of newcomers eventually began to challenge the established positions of the state-owned companies of Continental Europe. It was now the turn of the one-time challengers to defend the sanctity of contracts and to attempt to shore up the oligopoly. At the time of Algerian independence, technical assistance and favorable tax deals were seen by the Algerian government as being an adequate *quid-pro-quo* for continued 100% ownership of concessions by the French companies.[68] But in 1968, Getty Oil, an American firm, entered an arrangement which gave the Algerian state 51% ownership participation, a commitment to invest over $16 million in exploration, and a much more favorable share of the financial returns.[69] The handwriting was on the wall, and in 1971 51% of the concessions of the French state firms were nationalized. The companies' reactions to these nationalizations were quite like the majors' reactions to similar host-country moves. If anything, the dispute was made more contentious by the direct involvement of the French government in it. After two years it was resolved, largely on Algerian terms, but only after the French government and the French companies had threatened to veto World Bank loans to Algeria and to repatriate Algerians working in France.[70] Despite flare-ups such as these, producing countries long remained more willing to give the benefit of the doubt to the Continental European state instruments than they were to the majors. The majors had nearly always been in the 'forefront of the rearguard action', according to one industry official. Within recent memory, the Continental European companies had pushed for faster development of the Iraqi fields and made package deals of refineries for concessions in Arab and Black Africa. Nonetheless, by the early 1970's, it was increasingly common to hear government officials and intellectuals in the producing countries refer to one or another European state firm as 'just another international oil company.' [71]

The change in behavior of the European state companies was understandable, for their very success in breaching the walls of the old oligopoly had accelerated a movement that by 1971 threatened to bring down the whole vertically

[66] Adelman, 1972.
[67] Tiger and Franko, 1973; Wells, 1969.
[68] Adelman, 1972: p 235.
[69] Petroleum Press Service, 1972.
[70] Chevalier, 1973: pp 158 et seq.
[71] Remark communicated to the author at the seminar on 'Administration of Arab Oil Resources', Tripoli, Libya, April 1974.

integrated international structure of the industry. Adelman, Penrose, Vernon, and others have described how the increasing diffusion of technology and the increasing number of firms in the industry led both to price declines for crude, and to the beginnings of vertical disintegration in the industry.[72] But perhaps it was precisely because the old oligopoly was losing control over oil supplies and prices, that the very concept of internationally integrated state-owned enterprise was far from having universal support in Europe.

Alternatives to State Companies

In an industry like oil, for which the old spectre of Anglo-Saxon domination seemed to be rapidly disappearing, it was debatable whether the public interest in European countries was best served by vertically integrated firms – state owned or otherwise – with foreign extractive operations.[73] Germany, Switzerland and the Scandinavian countries seemed rather pleased at the option given to their independent refiners to seek low-priced oil rather than owned oil during the change in the 1960's to a looser industry structure. Even in Italy, the reliance on state-owned firms in the oil industry was limited by political forces that included independent refining companies. Until its 1974 acquisition of the Shell distribution network, ENI supplied only about 25% of the total hydrocarbon market in Italy – an amount more than equalled by independent non-vertically integrated Italian refiners.[74]

Once oligopolistic control over a particular raw material diminished, it was arguable that ownership of foreign deposits was unnecessary to the maintenance of an uninterrupted flow of inexpensive supplies to the Continent. This seemed to be the lesson of developments in iron-ore. Between the mid-1950's and the early 1960's, Europe's iron and steel companies entered many an iron-ore mining venture in foreign lands. Table 3.1 shows that this movement took Continental firms to Africa, South America, and Canada. American and Swedish firms strained to keep their traditional hold on iron-ore trade, while companies from a number of Continental countries – especially from ore-poor Germany – strove to break or mitigate the oligopoly's effects. A few of these foreign ventures were those of state-owned companies like Italy's Finsider and Germany's Salzgitter. Yet, it soon became clear that when iron-ore deposits were scattered so widely, and so many firms were technically able to undertake mining operations, there was little threat that vertically integrated firms might withhold or overprice supplies to non-integrated concerns. The race to acquire foreign ore bodies did not stop the decline in the percent of deposits owned outside of Europe by firms based on OECD countries from 50% in 1955 to 22% in 1974.[75] The post-war race by Continental firms to own iron-mining concessions died out in about 1965. After that, the role of European governments in the industry was one of tolerating or encouraging national purchasing pools and consumer cartels along the lines of France's *Groupement d'Importation*

---

[72] Adelman, 1972; Penrose, 1968; Vernon, 1971.
[73] Adelman, 1972, argues that the public interest was not served by vertically integrated firms. He bases his argument on the assumption that it was in the European public interest to have low oil prices.
[74] Tiger and Franko, 1973.
[75] *Vision*, 1974: p 40.

et de Répartition des Métaux (GIRM), or Germany's two ore-purchasing companies.[76]

European governments also backed away from intervention of the state-instrument type in copper and bauxite as the structure of these industries became less Anglo-American and less oligopolistic. In 1974 trade in both of these minerals still took place in vertically integrated channels to a much greater extent than was the case with iron-ore. The behavior of European governments and enterprises with respect to non-ferrous metals nevertheless displayed a number of similarities to their behavior concerning iron-ore. In the late 1950's and early 1960's new entrants appeared at the smelting and refining stages of the industry, new deposits were discovered, and members of the old oligopoly quickly moved to insure their existing positions by purchasing concessions. Table 3.1 reflects the European participation in this rush toward non-ferrous metal deposits, especially toward those in Africa. The interests of home governments were clearly not ignored by European players in this game. For example, Péchiney, although privately owned, had cordial relations with the French government that undoubtedly influenced it to seek resources in franc-zone Africa. At the same time, governmental concern about non-ferrous ores was attenuated by the existence both of European-owned firms integrated back to ore deposits and of a continual increase in the number of firms with sources of non-ferrous ores. Only during the late 1960's when it briefly seemed that American firms might gain market share in France at French expense, did the French government support Péchiney as the nucleus of a 'national' champion for non-ferrous metals. In rapid succession, France's largest copper fabricator, *Tréfimétaux*, was 'practically thrown into Péchiney's embrace', the only two aluminum firms in France were merged into one to become Péchiney-Ugine Kuhlmann, and a massive program of government subsidization of exploration was announced.[77] The American gains in copper and bauxite apparently did not occur as feared, however, for in the early 1970's the massive exploration program looked as if it had been quietly shelved. Even for France, flexibility of supply had seemingly taken pride of place over owned resources.[78]

New Threats and New Protagonists

Between the time of their foundation and the 1970's, the behavior of the large extractive enterprises of Continental Europe had become very similar to that of the American and British firms some of them had once so energetically attacked. The pattern had been set by Royal Dutch-Shell. In 1907 it was the challenger of the Americans. But by 1928, it was Shell's Dutch president, Henri Deterding that organized the Scottish grouse shoot at which the famous 'as is' market-sharing agreement was signed to defend the established companies from ungentlemanly competition.[79] Nuances between the behavior of the Continental, American and British firms remained, but similar stimuli had eventually led to similar responses.

---

[76] Mikdashi, 1971: pp 48–50.
[77] Mikdashi in Vernon (ed), 1974: p 175.
[78] *Entreprise*, May 31, 1974: pp 26 and 27.
[79] Tugendhat, 1968: p 99.

The post-World War II Continental challengers, relieved of old fears of British sea-power, went through a similar progression; whether they were private or state-owned was of marginal importance. Because the Continentals were latecomers to the resource-based industries outside of iron-ore and aluminum, they were often much smaller than their Anglo-American counterparts. Since they had a relatively recent history of attacking the Anglo-Americans, they willingly recalled the problem of Anglo-Saxon dominance when it might give a tactical advantage in the fight for balance and market share. They nonetheless had spaced extractive subsidiaries around the world, including North America. They thus had interests that were very much like those of American and British enterprise. The search for resources became less important than the search for industrial stability.

The impression that Continental behavior in seeking resources was increasingly conforming to norms long displayed by the Anglo-Americans strengthened when it was noted that the Continental extractive firms too, were trying to defend themselves against vertical *dis*integration in oil and non-ferrous metals during the 1960's. New entrants had appeared in abundance, and producing nations were increasingly nationalizing resource deposits and setting up their own companies to market the extracted materials. This movement was most advanced in copper and oil, but it seemed likely to affect bauxite in the not-too-distant future.

Suddenly, the problem changed. In 1971, the Teheran negotiations reversed the declining trend of oil prices. In October 1973, the supply of oil to Europe was reduced; by February 1974 the price of crude oil delivered to the Continent had increased fourfold over its mid-1973 level. Copper prices were escalating, and much was heard about a possible increase in the price of bauxite.[80] The ancient fears of Western Europe had become reality. The cause had nothing to do with British sea-power, or the villainy of an Anglo-Saxon cartel, although British and American firms were accused of profiting from the price increases.[81] In a large measure, it was agreed that the main source of discomfiture was a new set of protagonists: the countries in which extractive activities took place. These producing countries had formed co-operative organizations whose aims looked very much like those of the old-time cartels. While the Continent feared what the copper organization, CIPEC, or the bauxite-producing countries in the International Bauxite Association *might* do, they were forced to react to what members of the Organization of Petroleum-Exporting Countries, OPEC, were in fact doing.

The output reductions and the embargoes on Holland, Denmark, and Portugal (as well as the USA) showed that while ownership of foreign extractive deposits might provide a deterrent to over-pricing by Anglo-Saxon competitors, ownership did not mean security of supply in terms of prices or output when producing countries did not play by OECD-country rules. In fact, the increasing pressure of OPEC countries not only for price increases, but also for ownership participation and service contracts, began to suggest that many of the extractive subsidiaries whose establishment was reflected in Table 3.1 might eventually disappear from that compilation.

---

[80] *Journal de Genève*, February 3, 1974.
[81] *Entreprise*, May 24, 1974: p 44.

In oil, where the threat was real, Continental European enterprises and governments reacted immediately. The Continental oil enterprises asserted that the problem was still to 'get access to crude'. By this it was understood that the entity that should get the maximum amount of crude was the enterprise in question. There were few, if any, moves by any of the large Continental firms to help independent refiners gain market share – much less by other European, British or American firms.[82] Some enterprises publicly or tacitly gave support to bilateral deals between their government and producing-country governments willing to channel oil through the transport and distribution net of the firm in question. Companies also urged their governments to support massive exploration efforts in 'politically safe' areas, particularly the North Sea. The cost to the public of such deals, or of exploration efforts in 'safe' areas – especially in comparison to the cost of alternative measures such as EEC, OECD, or NATO joint bargaining with producer countries – was not often mentioned.

While state companies were acting like private firms, European national governments met the new problems with an old solution: more state-owned companies. In Germany, a political compulsion to 'do something' had already arisen while oil prices rose between 1971 and 1973. There was a sudden rebirth of interest in the state's 40% ownership of Veba – a diversified energy and chemicals firm. Gelsenberg, a diversified firm which *inter alia* refined and distributed petroleum and had a concession in Libya, was the object of a takeover bid by Veba, and a German state instrument was born.[83] In Sweden a partly state-owned drilling firm was already exploring on its Baltic island of Gotland. Bills introduced in the Swedish parliament to put all oil finds in the hands of the state looked like a prelude to still another government firm.[84] In Italy, ENI's market share was increased from 28% to 40% when Shell ceded its distribution network to the state firm, after finding that Italy's price controls precluded it from making an adequate profit.[85]

Whether such state companies would in any economic sense help to solve the problem of Continental Europe's lack of energy supplies was an interesting question. Whether a European state company response would be relevant to the threat of 'One, Two, Many OPEC's?' feared in copper, bauxite, uranium and so on, was another.[86] In the short run the proliferation of national companies in Europe looked like an expensive throw-back to the days when nation-states dreamt of being 'self-sufficient'.[87] It seemed highly unlikely that Western Europe's national companies would ever discover under their own soil adequate, reasonable cost supplies of the resources they needed. It seemed all too likely that if they determined national policies, their acquired interests would inhibit supranational co-ordination of consumer-country responses to

---

[82] *The Economist*, November 16, 1974: pp 72 and 73; Mauthner, 1975.

[83] *Entreprise*, May 24, 1973: pp 44 and 45.

[84] *To The Point International*, May 18, 1974: pp 33 and 34.

[85] *The Petroleum Economist*, February 1974: p 65. Britain, too seemed caught up by the fashion of creating new state enterprises. In July 1974, a new 100%-owned state enterprise was announced to participate in the UK's North Sea oil finds. (*The Petroleum Economist*, August 1974: p 284.)

[86] *Foreign Policy*, Spring 1974.

[87] *Entreprise*, May 24, 1974.

producer-country initiatives. The consequence of such a national approach would be to facilitate the playing off of one Continental country or firm against another by any fairly cohesive supplier group. Thus, a state-instrument response might be counterproductive for the consumers of Western Europe. In the short run, it would seem far less expensive for European governments to bargain together with the United States and Japan to keep down producer-country demands.

The long-run consequences of the propagation of resource-seeking firms by European governments need not be negative, however. As long as governments do not guarantee market share at any price for 'their' companies, new entrants could mean new sources, and sufficient new sources could mean a decline in the collusive power of either Anglo-Saxon firms or producer countries. Alternatively, an increase in the number of European companies in resource-based industries could facilitate unconventional moves of the 'If you cannot beat OPEC, join it' variety.[88] In 1974 it was rumored that ENI might soon form a joint firm with the National Iranian Oil Company. The purpose of this joint enterprise would be to carry out refining, transport and chemical operations of the two state firms outside of Italy. The quid pro quo for ENI would be preferential access to crude.[89] Such ventures would reinforce, rather than attack the vertically integrated structures of the oil industry. On partial equilibrium economic grounds it could be argued that such arrangements are disadvantageous to consumers of oil products. Nevertheless, by providing a political bridge between resource-poor Europe and market-poor producing countries, such arrangements might provide an insurance policy against the unforeseeable consequences of adversary, 'us versus them,' bargaining.

The fact that Europe's resource-seeking enterprises face a new variety of protagonists, suggests that new solutions must be sought to the problem of supplying the Continent. The new solutions did not, however, seem to lie in national, or even exclusively 'European' resource policies. Action by Europe's national governments, based on reflexes conditioned by history might be understandable, but of dubious value: why should Europe's governments direct enterprises to fight Anglo-American cartels and British sea power at a time when these spectres had been supplanted by new ones? Barring wholly unforeseen technological breakthroughs, Continental countries can obtain neither national nor Continental self-sufficiency. Moreover, grandiose resource-seeking policies aimed at achieving autonomy for Continental Europe through conquest, have led to equally grand disappointments in the past. Napoleon III's Southern Strategy ended with the Suez fiasco in 1956, the Algerian war and independence for Black Africa and the Middle Eastern countries. Nostalgia for controlled sources in the South lives on in the form of the dream 'Eurafrique' sometimes expressed in the French press.[90] But nostalgia is hardly a realistic basis for public or enterprise policy, and the Eastern Strategy died when the Battle of Stalingrad determined that output and market decisions for Eastern European oil would remain in Russian hands.

[88] Franko, 1975.
[89] Financial Times, August 13, 1974: p 16.
[90] Le Figaro, March 16–17, 1974: p 3.

Even a wholehearted adoption of the Western, or North Atlantic Strategy pursued with ambivalence by the Continental countries after World War II appeared to be an insufficient solution to Europe's resource problems, much as it seemed a necessary component of a solution. Reliance on the wearing down of oligopolistic industry structures by competition for reasonable prices, and on the US Sixth Fleet in the Mediterranean for uninterrupted supply, sufficed only as long as producing-country governments were too weak to change the rules of the game. It seems a poor bet to rely on Western countries for long-term alternatives to LDC supplies. The United States and Great Britain talk and dream of independence in oil by 1980, but it seems unlikely that either will also be able to supply the Continent's needs for petroleum, much less for other industrial raw materials. Moreover, the Continent's enterprises and governments alike are discovering that peripheral Western nations with rich resource deposits, like Canada, Norway and Australia, can easily find their interests more aligned with LDC exporters than with Western industrialized importers.[91] Several of the Continent's resource-seeking enterprises massively expanded exploration and production efforts in the periphery of the West in the 1960's and early 1970's – only to find the same local pressures for ownership, a bigger portion of the 'take', and higher prices that were thought to be specific to the less developed countries to the South and South-East. When Continental enterprise managers and government officials used phrases such as 'blue-eyed Arabs' to describe the Norwegians, the intention was not entirely that of jest.

Proposals for new solutions have, of course, been made in the aftermath of the events of October 1973. European national governments, in addition to attempting to get more of their 'own' raw materials via the promotion of state-instrument companies, have turned out lights on highways, made unilateral cutbacks in foreign exchange available for oil payments, announced enormous schemes for promoting nuclear power (with American technology), and attempted to arrange bilateral trades of technology for resources with OPEC countries.[92] Yet the sum of these measures hardly added up to a politically feasible solution either to the problem of price, or to that of security of supply. European populations gave little sign of willingness to cut their overall consumption sufficiently to enable an immediate real transfer of goods and services to materials-supplying countries, much less to an extent sufficient to finance meaningful investments in energy and materials substitution. Nor did European populations or the supplier-countries accept the alternative of 'inflating away' the transfer problem, even though many of the oil-exporting countries, if not other supplier countries, seemed incapable of absorbing a significant real transfer of goods and services on account of their exiguous size. Paying for natural resources in a debased currency could solve the price problem for certain groups in European societies, but permanent inflation is unacceptable to other groups in Europe. And all but the most naive supplier countries have learned not to confuse money with wealth.[93]

---

[91] On Australia's participation in the meeting organizing the International Bauxite Association, see United Nations General Assembly, September 1974: p 7.
[92] See *International Herald Tribune*, September 28–29, 1974: p 6.
[93] Tumlir, 1974.

National measures had some chance of adding up to a politically feasible solution in countries where payments made to supplying countries (the so-called petro-dollars) were 're-cycled' into more or less offsetting investments. But in 1974 it was argued that many supplier countries would invest only in assets immediately convertible into cash, not in assets constituting a claim on the real goods and services that would have to eventually be transferred to make a real, as opposed to debased, financial payment for oil or other resources. Further, it was asserted that supplier countries would invest surplus funds only in a limited number of developed countries of which only two, Switzerland and Germany, happened to be in Continental Europe. Rarely stated but often implied, was a refusal by Continental European governments and enterprises to accept significant investments from Islamic countries (which were sometimes former colonies to boot) in equity securities that did constitute long-term claims on the Continent's real assets: technology and know-how.

Perhaps, however, the main reason why solutions arrived at by national or new European conclaves seemed unlikely to succeed lies in the absence of rules of the economic game mutually acceptable both to Continental nations and the new protagonists to the South and South-East. There is a certain historical irony in the fact that the European Continent has become as dependent on a few North African and Middle Eastern countries for its survival as was the Roman Empire before Mediterranean trade routes were cut by the Islamic invasions.[94] Furthermore, this dependence seemed likely to increase markedly as supplier-countries invested their new-found funds to refine and process their raw materials at home, and to transport the resulting products to European markets. The Roman Empire provided some rules of trans-Mediterranean economic intercourse. Without a new set of trans-Mediterranean rules, the European oil and raw materials crises looked like preludes to European refinery, tanker, petro-chemicals and other crises.

While press commentary repeated that 'the problem was financial,' its more fundamental political aspects occasionally surfaced.[95] There were suggestions to allow important supplier countries greater voting power in the International Monetary Fund (IMF), or to supplement the IMF with a new, joint OPEC–OECD investment bank.[96] There were also proposals that the ecumenical council grouping the American and European parts of the West (the 'Group of 12') should go beyond mutual assistance and organize a crusade to force raw-materials prices down, or to reduce supplier-country power to disrupt importing economies by withholding materials.[97] But the limited scope for serious aid from Anglo-American allies, the wholly different degree of Continental dependence on foreign supplies, and the short-term nature of the financial palliatives usually discussed, left unanswered the longer term question about the Continent's fate. How, in fact, were hundreds of years of alternatively predatory, hostile, or colonial relations between Europe and less developed raw-materials suppliers to be forgotten and a visibly equitable

---

[94] Pirenne, 1939.
[95] Lewis, 1974.
[96] De Bondt, 1974; Zombanakis, 1974.
[97] Kleiman, 1974: p 2; *International Herald Tribune*, October 24, 1974: p 2.

trading system to be devised? Was there any alternative to a system of 'cartels for us, the market for you' which OPEC felt it was merely turning back on the West?

To some extent, the Continental countries and their large enterprises may be able to obtain needed raw materials by following a course usually associated with small resource-poor countries: flexible, non-predatory dealings with a diversified group of trading partners. Perhaps this strategy was uppermost in the minds of the German officials who toured Latin America to explore materials-for-technology trades in the aftermath of the oil crisis.[98] But the risk was that the time was past for such easy, purely economic solutions. Not only was there disaccord over the rules of trade, but there was also a risk that Continental countries and firms could see their fate chosen by others. The resource problems of the United States and the United Kingdom appeared short-term in nature, but the fact that these countries had any resource problem at all came as such a shock, that domestic pressures for action could be well-nigh irresistible. Continental countries have to reckon with the fact that American or British threats, promises or actions could provoke supplier-country reactions which would rebound on the West as a whole.

Continental countries thus face unique constraints, but history has also provided them with some unique opportunities: the Continent has had a good deal of experience with outsider countries which wished to obtain their place in the sun, and it knows the price of failure to devise ways of easing outsider countries into the international system. It should also know the price of allowing other nations, even allies, to unilaterally determine the solutions. The Eastern Roman Empire paid that price many times up to the fall of Constantinople in 1453. Riven by discord among territorial subunits, unable and unwilling to agree with Western allies – on whose ships it was dependent for raw materials, it tried and failed to observe the crusades as a passive bystander. Closed to non-Christian influences, associated in spite of itself with the actions of the more self-sufficient West by the Turks, it became an object, not a subject of history.[99] In the twentieth century France and Belgium twice paid similar prices at the hands of a different outsider, Germany, although, to be sure, that outsider laid claim to being an insider not on the basis of raw materials but of industrial prowess. Was the price not perhaps a bit higher because of the enthusiasm of allied nations for dismembering Austria-Hungary? Would Continental governments and enterprises remember such lessons? The vetoing in 1972 by Germany's partly state-owned Veba of the National Iranian Oil Company's attempt to enter a marketing joint-venture in Germany suggested that the Continent might not remember.[100] So did the flat statement made by a French diplomat, in the Spring of 1974, to the author that 'there would never be a *Compagnie Franco-Arabe des Pétroles*'. In a world where the distribution of natural resources has made political entities such as Continental nations or Western Europe increasingly irrelevant, what alternatives were there to broader, trans-Mediterranean political integration?

[98] Carr, 1974: p 4.
[99] Bryer, 1972; Gill, 1972.
[100] Kokxhoorn, 1974: p 193.

Chapter IV

Patterns in the Spread of Multinational Manufacturing

Unlike the causes underlying the spread of European firms into foreign manufacturing, the forces behind the development of US multinational enterprise are reasonably well understood. American firms innovated new, labor-saving, highly income-elastic products; they specialized in 'product pioneering'.[1] As innovators, they had proprietary knowledge of the production of these goods which were clearly differentiated by their novelty.[2] Rising *per capita* incomes in Europe and elsewhere first pulled such new American products into these nations as imports. When income distributions in Europe shifted toward the US pattern, as they did in post-World War II Britain, Sweden and Holland, the pull was probably all the harder.[3] The American Challenge thus met the European attraction, most often in the form of foreign customers' requests.[4]

For American firms, the transition from exporting to foreign manufacturing often came as non-American markets for new products became large enough and certain enough to warrant someone investing in additional plant capacity. Foreign production seemed in order when scale economies in US production were about to be exhausted, when foreign production could be undertaken for an average cost less than US marginal cost plus transport and tariffs, and when customer needs and production techniques were standardized enough to enable such costs to be calculated. All these events inevitably occurred as new American products went from birth to maturity over their life cycles.[5] These events were hastened by the fact that wage rates were almost invariably lower outside the United States. In such circumstances, even profit-maximizing firms with world-wide product monopolies had reason to put up foreign plants.

Conceptually, the decision of an American firm to expand abroad was like that of a domestic manufacturer considering expansion in a less developed region of his home market. Nevertheless, the evidence suggests that managers of few US firms reasoned so comfortably: threat, not opportunity, was the most frequent trigger of foreign manufacturing investment. Even in the early days of their international export expansion, most US firms were threatened by competition. Sometimes the threat came from local entrepreneurs, as they awakened to new production possibilities.[6] Local competitors were situated in countries with lower-labor costs, and, when product novelty wore off to the point where costs mattered, they began to think of imitation. Nevertheless, this source of threat has perhaps been overemphasized by observers of American international investment. As one delves more and more deeply into the history of US foreign production, it seems a different process was at work: that of US firms responding to potential or actual moves of American oligopolistic competitors abroad.[7]

---

[1] Vernon, 1971: Chapter III; Vernon, 1966.

[2] Caves, 1971.

[3] Fortune, 1972. See Chapter II for a discussion of international contrasts in patterns of income distribution.

[4] Robinson, 1961: p 37.

[5] Vernon, 1966; Hirsch, 1967.

[6] Vernon, 1971: Chapter III.

[7] Knickerbocker, 1973.

The companies in the best position to seize foreign-market opportunity from US firms were their US compatriots, at least in industries where there were few European-based companies with major US operations. Other American firms were those most exposed to the market stimuli that called forth the innovators' distinctive products. They were therefore the firms that could most rapidly introduce alternative versions of those products. The result of this imitative behavior was a series of American duels involving a repetitive sequence of attempted pre-emption followed by investment matching around the globe. The statistical evidence for such a pattern of multinational oligopolistic threat and reaction is most complete for the post-World War II era, but company histories show that this process antedated World War II. General Electric and Westinghouse checked and counter-checked one another in England and Russia in the 1890's and early 1900's.[8] Ford's moves into England and Germany also appear to have antedated significant threat from local firms;[9] pre-emption of foreign moves by Detroit rivals may have been uppermost in his mind. One thing is fairly certain: host government policies played a minor role in many foreign manufacturing decisions by American industrial enterprises.

When European or other governments imposed protective tariffs, they hastened the moment at which an American oligopolistic exporter might wish to pre-empt, or avoid pre-emption of an expanding foreign market through local production. Nevertheless, the weight of empirical evidence on American foreign investment suggests that the role of trade barriers in triggering US foreign manufacturing was a secondary one at best.[10] Foreign market growth attracted not only American goods, but also American production. References to tariffs were particularly sparse in discussions of US investment in Europe after World War II; they were more frequent in discussions of US company activity in Canada and the less developed countries.[11]

The relative lack of emphasis on barriers to trade as a trigger of US foreign manufacturing is consistent with the view of American trade and investment embodied in the international product cycle model of US multinational company growth.[12] This lack of emphasis on trade barriers is also consistent with the phenomenon of continuous growth in the dollar value of US manufacturing investment in Europe during periods of rising European incomes and labor costs, and the stagnation and decline of the dollar value of US foreign investment during the early 1930's, particularly in countries where growth was low or nil.[13] Neither the dollar figures, nor data on decisions to enter manufacturing subsidiaries in Europe taken by US parent firms show sharp discontinuous jumps at times of trade-barrier increases.[14] US manufacturing investment in Europe also grew at an increasing rate after the

---

[8] Wilkins, 1974; Jones and Marriott, 1970.
[9] Wilkins and Hill, 1964; Fridenson, 1972.
[10] Horst, 1974, provides the most complete survey of the literature bearing on this point.
[11] Horst, 1974 and sources cited therein: Vernon, 1971: Chapter III; Robinson, 1961; Horst, 1970.
[12] Vernon, 1966.
[13] Wilkins, 1974.
[14] See Table 4.4, *infra*.

Kennedy Round tariff cuts in the 1960's.[15] And company histories show a number of US firms putting up manufacturing in Europe well before governments raised tariff or other trade barriers. Ford, for example, began assembling in the United Kingdom in 1911, well before the British government imposed tariffs on autos in 1915.[16] Such gross indicators, of course, cannot show exactly to what extent government trade policy affected the spread of US multinational manufacturing, but they suggest that the erection of barriers to international commerce was of limited importance in the story of US international manufacturing. There is good reason to think that it was quite otherwise in the history of Continental European multinational enterprise.

Continental Patterns

Industries

The story of the spread of Continental European enterprises into foreign manufacturing is distinctive partly because the products and product varieties exported by Continental companies prior to undertaking foreign production differed from those produced by American enterprises. Continental firms, as Chapter II showed, rarely pioneered in the production of labor-saving, middle-income goods: their innovative leads were in synthetics, working-class, and luxury products. Even when Continental and American firms produced similar products, Continental firms often did so with different, material-saving processes.

Some of the distinctive features of the foreign manufacturing spread of Continental enterprises emerge from the comparisons presented in Table 4.1. There one observes the 1971 industry distribution of foreign manufacturing subsidiaries owned by enterprises headquartered in various parent nations. A number of clear contrasts emerge from Table 4.1, even though the very broad industry categories used to classify subsidiaries' activities obscure differences in product varieties. (And product-oriented industry classifications, by definition, do not distinguish among processes.)

American firms, one notes, often manufactured abroad in the processed food industry. So did firms based in Britain, a country which once had had the highest *per capita* income in the world.[17] The processed-food industry is made up of products that serve customer needs for convenience and the saving of preparation time. German, French, Italian, Belgian and Swedish activity in this sector was negligible. And the involvement of the Dutch predecessors of Unilever and Swiss-based Nestlé was *sui generis*. The Dutch part of Unilever began its international activities on the basis of innovations in margarine, a substitute for butter.[18] The principal precursor of Nestlé, the Anglo-Swiss Condensed Milk Company, was founded by two Americans, the brothers Page, who brought the American product innovation, condensed milk, to Europe outside the usual multinational enterprise channels.[19]

---

[15] US Survey of Current Business, various issues.
[16] Wilkins and Hill, 1964: pp 46–47.
[17] See Chapter II.
[18] Wilson, 1954: Volume II.
[19] Heer, 1967: p 32.

Table 4.1   Percent of Foreign Manufacturing Subsidiaries of US, British, Japanese and Continental European Multinational Enterprises Active in Various Industries, as of January 1, 1971 (US as of January 1, 1968)

Industry Group	National Base of Parent Enterprises:									
	US	UK	Japan	Germany	France	Italy	Bel & Lux	Holland	Sweden	Switzerland
Food and tobacco	14%	25%	5%	—%	—%	—%	2%	—%**	—%	21%
Textiles and apparel	3	4	28	—	2	5	—	3	13	—
Wood, paper and furniture	5	6	3	2	—	—	7	—	14	—
Chemicals and drugs	29	21	8	46	24	20	25	32	—	40
Petroleum refining	6	3***	—	—	10	12	6	10***	—	—
Rubber and tires	3	2	3	2	4	10	—	2	—	—
Primary metals	3	8	9	7	11	3	15	2	6	4
Fabricated metals	5	4	8	8	5	8	12	3	—	7
Non-electrical machinery	10	4	6	4	2	3	4	3	26	11
Electrical†	10	11	17	18	10	21	9	34	25	12
Transport	6	5	8	6	9	17	—	—	8	—
Instruments	2	—	—	3	—	—	2	3	—	2
Other	6	5	4	2	21	2	17	8	6	—
Total Percent*	**100%**	**100%**	**100%**	**100%**	**100%**	**100%**	**100%**	**100%**	**100%**	**100%**
Total Number	**3756**	**2160**	**438**	**666**	**376**	**101**	**253**	**410**	**157**	**371**

Notes: *Column totals may not add to 100 due to rounding.
        **Unilever is counted in the UK column, reallocation to 'company-parent' Holland would increase this number significantly.
        ***Royal Dutch-Shell is counted as Dutch in this tabulation.
        —Indicates 1 % or less.
        †Includes office equipment and computers.

Source: Comparative Multinational Enterprise Project.

One-tenth of the foreign subsidiaries of American enterprises were manu-facturing non-electrical machinery. This industry is made up of goods such as farm machinery and materials-handling equipment which are generally labor saving. German, French, Italian, Belgian and Dutch foreign activity was negligible in this industry. Swedish and Swiss enterprises did, however, have important proportions of their foreign manufacturing in non-electrical machinery (as one might have expected from the nature of the innovations stimulated by the unusual characteristics of these firms' home markets).[20]

Large Continental enterprises did display a bias toward undertaking foreign manufacturing in the electrical sector, however. Table 4.1 shows that large enterprises in all the Continental countries (except Belgium) had proportions of their foreign manufacturing subsidiaries in electrical products equalling or exceeding those of American enterprises. The greatest propensity to manu-facture electrical products abroad was displayed by enterprises originating in the countries with the oldest traditions of combating Anglo-Saxon control of oil supplies with hydro- or coal-powered electric alternatives (Germany and Italy), or in countries with the poorest domestic fuel endowments (Sweden and Holland). Only Japanese enterprises showed a similar propensity to undertake foreign manufacturing in electrical products, and Japan too was poorly endowed with fuel resources.

Enterprises based in all Continental countries had considerable proportions of their foreign manufacturing activity in the chemical industry. In 1971, German and Swiss companies had nearly half of their foreign manufacturing subsidiaries in chemicals; American companies had less than one-third of theirs in this industry. The Continental concentration in chemicals was a consistent reflection of the home-market conditioning of Continental, and especially of German and Swiss enterprises toward synthetics, as described in Chapter 2. It also was a reflection of the early German and Swiss lead in pharmaceuticals, as one finds from breaking down the aggregate data pre-sented in Table 4.1.[21] Ten percent of German subsidiaries, and 20% of Swiss subsidiaries were producing pharmaceutical preparations in 1971. These are percentage concentrations approached only by American subsidiaries, of which nine percent were producing drugs. One other segment of the chemi-cals industry also strongly reflects the effects of home-market conditioning on subsequent foreign manufacturing. Soaps and cosmetics, a middle-income, convenience-oriented product group were almost unrepresented in the foreign manufacturing activity of Continental firms, yet four percent of American, and seven percent of British foreign subsidiaries manufactured such products.

Continental enterprises thus displayed a special predilection to undertake foreign manufacturing in electrical and chemical products in the 1970's. This bias had, in fact, been even stronger during the earlier history of Continental European multinational activity. The foreign manufacturing operations of Europe's automobile, petroleum, and tire companies were largely a post-World War II phenomenon. Between the mid-1800's and 1955,

---

[20] See Chapter II.
[21] On the early Swiss and German dominance of the pharmaceutical industry, see Chapter II *supra*, and Reekie, 1973.

Table 4.2 Geographical Distribution of Foreign Manufacturing Subsidiaries of Large American, British, European and Japanese Firms: Percentage in Main Areas of the World
(US data as of January 1, 1968; all other data as of January 1, 1971)

National base of parent enterprises	Geographical Region of Subsidiary's Country							Total number 100%
	US & Canada	Developed Europe	LDC* Europe	Latin America	Asia & Oceania	Africa & Middle East		
United States	13%	35%	4%	27%	15%	7%		4246
United Kingdom	13	26	3	6	27	25		2265
Japan	5	1	2	18	65	9		479
Germany	10	42	11	18	10	10		788
France	7	38	13	17	6	19		425
Italy	6	27	18	33	5	10		129
Belgium & Luxemburg	21	53	9	5	1	11		272
The Netherlands	23	51	3	9	9	5		425
Sweden	4	65	3	14	9	4		167
Switzerland	10	57	7	14	8	4		393

Note: *Less developed Europe includes Spain, Portugal, Greece and Turkey.
Source: Comparative Multinational Enterprise Project.

almost two-thirds of all foreign manufacturing by Continental enterprise had been concentrated in chemical and electrical products. It was only after 1955 that the Continental firms began to set up significant numbers of subsidiaries in other industries.[22] In contrast, American foreign manufacturing activity proceeded on a much broader product front continuously from its inception in the nineteenth century. Non-electrical machinery and transport equipment (products with obvious labor-saving characteristics) were particularly prominent categories in the early spread of American multinational enterprise.[23]

Host Countries

The distinctive industry spread of the foreign manufacturing subsidiaries of large Continental European enterprises was accompanied by a unique geographical orientation. Table 4.2 shows that the foreign subsidiaries of Continental enterprises in 1971 were located first and foremost in other European countries. Indeed, except in the case of Italian firms, manufacturing operations of Continental enterprises were located primarily in other *developed* European countries. Continental enterprises had long located a majority of their foreign subsidiaries in Europe: prior to World War I, almost 90% of the subsidiaries of Continental enterprises were located in Europe, including the United Kingdom. In the inter-war period, this percentage remained above 70. Not until the late 1950's and early 1960's did the number of new foreign plants located outside of developed Europe exceed those within. Then, after 1965, Europe once again became the focus for approximately 60% of the foreign subsidiaries set up or acquired by Continental firms.

Not only had large Continental enterprises established a majority of their foreign subsidiaries in Europe, but they had also established many of these subsidiaries in geographically contiguous countries. Table 4.3 demonstrates that Continental enterprises had a greater propensity than their American counterparts to manufacture in their closest neighbors. Over one-third of all Continental subsidiaries were in contiguous countries, while only one-fifth of American subsidiaries were in Canada and Mexico. The contrast with the behavior of British enterprise is even more striking. Although any classification of neighbors of an island nation is a bit arbitrary, only 13% of the foreign manufacturing subsidiaries of large British enterprises were located in Ireland, France, Belgium and the Netherlands. Evidently a different geographical force was attracting British firms. As Table 4.3 shows, two-thirds of British foreign manufacturing was located in the former British colonies and dominions (not including the United States).[24]

When Continental enterprises manufactured outside of Europe, they did so in Latin America (especially if they were Italian, German, French, Swiss or Swedish), North America (especially the Dutch and Belgians), and Africa (the French). The Continental enterprises rarely went to Asia, as one sees from Table 4.2, or to the former British Empire, as shown by Table 4.3

---

[22] Comparative Multinational Enterprise Project.

[23] Wilkins, 1970.

[24] This estimate of British manufacturing in former colonies and dominions is based on numbers of subsidiaries of the 47 largest British enterprises. It happens to correspond almost exactly to the British government's estimate of the proportion in the former Empire of the value of all UK foreign direct investment. (*Board of Trade Journal*, 1970.)

Table 4.3   Percentage of Foreign Manufacturing Subsidiaries of Large American, British, European and Japanese Firms in Host Countries with Various Characteristics
(US data as of January 1, 1968; all other data as of January 1, 1971)

National base of parent enterprise	Percentage of Foreign Manufacturing Subsidiaries in:			
	Bordering countries	Latin countries	Former British Empire (not including UK or US)	In host countries where 1970 GNP *per capita* exceeded that in parent country
	(%)	(%)	(%)	(%)
US	23	36	31	0
United Kingdom	13	17	67	55
Japan	22	17	38	10
Germany	34	48	19	30
France	42	51	11	16
Italy	30	61	12	34
Belgium & Luxemburg	43	41	20	50
Netherlands	34	25	12	53
Sweden	27	32	15	2
Switzerland	38	37	16	11

Note: Bordering countries were classified as follows:
US: Canada and Mexico.
United Kingdom: Ireland, Netherlands, Belgium and France.
Japan: Taiwan.
Germany: Belgium & Luxemburg, Netherlands, Denmark, Austria, Switzerland and France.
France: Germany, Belgium & Luxemburg, Switzerland, Spain, UK and Italy. (If Algeria, Tunisia and Morocco were included, the total would be 50 %.)
Italy: France, Switzerland, Austria, Tunisia and Spain.
Belgium and Luxemburg: France, Germany, Netherlands and UK.
Netherlands: Belgium & Luxemburg, Germany and UK.
Sweden: Norway, Finland, Denmark and Germany.
Switzerland: France, Germany, Italy and Austria.

Source: Comparative Multinational Enterprise Project.

To some extent, the foreign manufacturing of Continental enterprises in and outside Europe followed lines of linguistic and cultural affinity. Table 4.3 shows that more than three-fifths of the foreign operations of Italian firms were located in countries whose languages have Latin roots. French companies had the second highest proportion of foreign subsidiaries in Latin countries (although the German companies were close behind). Among the Continental firms, Swedish enterprises had the lowest proportion of operations in Latin host countries, although it was still well above the proportions for British and Japanese firms. Nevertheless, the relationship between the location of European foreign manufacturing and cultural commonness was obscured by the overlap between cultural and geographical proximity, the proclivity of German enterprises for Latin lands (near and far), and the cosmopolitan be-havior of the Dutch and the Swedes who had proportioned their subsidiaries almost equally among Anglo-Saxon, Germanic and Latin countries.

At first glance, the role of geographical and cultural proximity in determining the spread of Continental multinational enterprise looked similar to that played by these factors in the evolution of American multinational firms.[25] Nevertheless, distance and culture had influenced, but had not dominated the multinational spread of American enterprises. The principal determinant of the American multinational spread was the *size* of the host country's market. There was a relatively close correlation between the total 1968 GNP of a host country and the percentage of all American subsidiaries one found therein in 1968.[26] There was *no* correlation between a country's 1970 total GNP and the proportion of the subsidiaries of German, Italian, Dutch or other Continental enterprises one found therein.

The absence of a correlation between a foreign market's size and its ability to attract Continental subsidiaries argued that factors other than foreign market growth were the principal stimuli to foreign manufacturing by Continental enterprise. Table 4.3 shows, moreover, that between one-third and one-half of the foreign subsidiaries of large German, Belgian, Dutch and Italian enterprises were located in countries with 1970 *per capita* incomes (and wage rates) *higher* than those prevailing in home markets. Such large proportions were not, *prima facie*, consistent with the notion of products' spreading into foreign production from higher- to lower-income countries in the fashion of the international product cycle. But why did Continental enterprises undertake so much foreign manufacturing in nearby countries, or in directions opposite, or bearing no relationship to those typical of American and British firms?

From Trade to Manufacture

The fact that intense trade in manufactures should arise among European countries seems no particular puzzle – at least if one accepts Staffan Burenstam Linder's theory that home-market demand, and the subsequent appearance of similar demand in other countries, are the true causes of exports of manufactured goods.[27] Since income and relative factor-cost levels on the Continent often came to have much in common, innovation in manufacture in one Continental market was almost sure to find other markets in Europe as they took on similar characteristics.

Why did intra-European trade so frequently give way to intra-European foreign manufacturing, however? The explanation seems to lie in the fact that it was the policies of national governments which produced much of the convergence of market characteristics in Europe, especially in regard to the supply of raw materials. Government-imposed trade and exchange controls were a major reason for the relatively high cost of raw materials. These widespread controls helped create similar demands for substitute products

---

[25] Vaupel, 1971; Vernon, 1971.
[26] The correlation coefficient was 0·63 and significant at the 5% level of probability. The hypothesis tested was: $X_{ij} = A + BY_j$ where X_{ij} = the percentage of manufacturing subsidiaries of companies based in country i located in country j, and Y_j = the total GNP of host country j. The correlation coefficient was only significant (at the 5% level of probability) in the American subsidiary case. R^2 equalled 0·40 when i was the United States and was nil otherwise.
[27] Linder, 1961.

and material-saving processes in different European countries. And, since controls rarely distinguished between natural and synthetic products, or products made by different processes, they obliged Continental firms wishing to exploit material-saving advantages to jump trade barriers and produce locally. In contrast, similarity between American companies' domestic and foreign markets was correlated to increases in total and *per capita* incomes of the foreign markets. Although American firms often produced in foreign lands (especially in Europe) for reasons having little to do with barriers to trade, Continental European foreign investments in manufacturing were almost always responses to trade barriers, both before and after World War II.

Foreign Manufacturing Before 1945

When foreign governments imposed trade barriers, certain Continental companies had particularly powerful reasons for switching from exporting to foreign manufacturing. These were the enterprises that had developed new processes for existing products, or new synthetics. Among them were the firms selling goods such as synthetic nitrate fertilizers, like BASF of Germany; or soda-ash, like Solvay of Belgium; or basic dyestuffs, like Hoechst; or margarine, like the Dutch predecessors of Unilever. Such products faced highly price-elastic demand. Although they could be differentiated from the natural products with which they competed, their substitutability with natural products was undoubtedly high. When trade barriers went up for a product such as dyestuffs they went up for all imports of such goods – synthetic or not. Thus exporters were threatened by competition both from protected local producers of natural products and from domestic or foreign firms that produced with other processes. To survive such competition, the firms that had been exporting set up manufacturing subsidiaries in the countries to which they had previously only sold their products. They could then exploit their distinctive processes behind protective barriers. In the late 1800's, for example, Belgium's Solvay faced local competition in France, Germany and other foreign countries from manufacturers using the Le Blanc process for soda-ash. BASF faced competition for its Haber-Bosch nitrogen-fixation process (which it developed in 1914) from alternatives like the Caro-Frank and Eyde-Norsk-Hydro processes developed in Germany and Norway respectively.[28] Both Solvay and BASF were stimulated to move rapidly into foreign manufacturing by the need to counter such competition.

Foreign manufacturing was stimulated not only by trade barriers and competitive pressures, but also by government incentives for the production of material substitutes and the use of material-saving processes. The Italian government, in particular, solicited Swiss and German hydro-electric and aluminum know-how during its inter-war quest for independence from imported fuels and copper.[29] Much foreign manufacturing thus was a consequence of the rise of an economic environment dominated by a governmentally instigated or tolerated arrangement, not market forces.

---

[28] Haber, 1971: pp 86 and 88; Siemens, 1957: p 217. (The Caro-Frank process was electrolytic and threatened to bring electrical firms into the fertilizer business.)
[29] Wallace, 1937: pp 91 and 92.

Governmental Trade Barriers

The relationship between host-government trade policy and foreign manu-facturing activities of Continental European companies began well before World War I. The relative freedom of trade achieved in Europe in the 1860's began to disappear with the raising of enormous tariff barriers in Czarist Russia during the late 1870's: the average level of Russian tariffs on manu-factures was over 100%. The Russian barriers, along with a rate of industrial development higher than that of any country other than the United States between 1880 and 1913, stimulated much local manufacturing by foreign firms, European and American.[30]

The 1870's also saw a continual increase in protectionism in the United States, culminating in the highly restrictive McKinley tariff of 1890. Between 1879 and 1892, Germany, France and Italy adopted protectionist tariffs. By 1913, average French, German and Italian *ad valorem* import duties on manufactures were above ten percent, as can be seen from Table 4.4.[31] American duties, on the average, were far higher. Incongruously, however, vigorous lobbying by textile interests meant that European dyestuffs entered the US at a nominal rate; US firms had produced some dyestuffs 'until a change in the tariff had knocked the bottom out of this business in 1883.'[32]

Table 4.4 Tariff Levels on Manufactured Goods in Europe and the US, 1904, 1913, 1927, 1935, 1950 and 1955

| Country | Percent of Value of Product | | | | | |
	1904*	1913	1927	1935	1950	1955
Germany	25%	10%	19%	18%	27%	16%
France	34	16	25	29	27	18
Italy	27	15	28	42	26	17
Belgium (Benelux for 1950 and 1955)		9	11	13	12	10
Switzerland		9	17	22		
Great Britain		nil	15	25	23	
Russia	131					
US	73	40	39	43	13	

Notes: *Duties levied on principal British manufactured products only.
Series may not be consistent from year to year due to differences in estimating methods.

Sources: **For Great Britain until 1935:** Friedlaender and Oser, 1953: pp 434 and 438. Figures for Great Britain in 1927 and 1935 are approximate percentages. British tariffs in 1927 applied only to a few products including dyes, autos, jewelry and watches.
For 1904: Clapham, 1951: p 322.
For Germany, France, Italy, Belgium and Switzerland in 1913, 1927 and 1935: Liep-mann, 1938.
For European levels in 1950: Woytinsky and Woytinsky, 1955: p 285.
For 1955, for Germany, France, Italy and Benelux: Bertrand, 1958.
For the United States in 1913, 1927, 1935 and 1950: United States Bureau of the Census, 1949: United States, various issues. These US data refer to actual customs collections as percentage of dutiable imports. *Ad valorum* tariff rates were clearly much higher.

[30] McKay, 1970: Chapter 2 and p 300; Bairoch, 1972: Vol 3, pp 211–245; Henderson, 1963: pp xi and 108; Wilkins, 1970: pp 101 and 212; Sutton, 1968.
[31] Woytinsky and Woytinsky, 1955: pp 247 *et seq.*
[32] Haber, 1971: pp 29 and 180. See also Chapter VII.

During World War I, almost all industrial countries set up manufacturing facilities, under pressure of war-time insecurity and demand, to supply explosives, fertilizers, dyes, vehicles and electrical communication equipment. Immediately after the war, fears of gluts in these industries and a certain amount of vengefulness toward Germany caused an enormous spurt of protectionism: average Italian and French duties came to exceed 25%. Britain, in 1920, prohibited all imports of dyestuffs – an act clearly aimed at German industry. The 1921 Safeguarding of Industries Act brought British duties on a number of products of interest to Continental manufacturers nearly level to those on the Continent.[33] In 1922, the United States enacted a tariff law with the highest duties the country had ever had; this time dyestuffs were included.[34]

With the 1929 depression came a strengthening of protectionist policies: The United States enacted the infamous Hawley–Smooth tariff in 1930; the United Kingdom completed its move away from free trade and set up the Imperial Preference wall around its Empire in 1932.[35] By 1935, European tariffs had increased yet again by roughly the same magnitude as their post-World War I jump. They were not to be lowered until post-World War II reconstruction had begun to show its results in the 1950's. Indeed, until the formation of the EEC in 1958, tariff levels in Europe were greater than they had been on the eve of World War I.

Tariff barriers, however, were only the most visible part of a whole network of trade restrictions. Exchange controls, quantitative quotas, outright import prohibitions, patent-working regulations and international private restrictive agreements also played a reinforcing role in affecting foreign manufacturing.[36] Indeed, some measures, like the laws regulating the working of patents, were specifically and often successfully aimed at enticing a number of Continental firms to produce locally.[37]

Trade Barriers and Foreign Investments

Tables 4.5 and 4.6 illustrate the importance of trade barriers in triggering foreign production of European material-saving innovations prior to World War II. Originally, foreign markets for German and Swiss exports of synthetic dyestuffs appear to have been created by a number of factors. These included the scarcity of indigenous sources of natural substances in importing countries, occasional user preference for the more constant quality of synthetics, and the inability of domestic firms to respond to market opportunity. This inability was due, in part, to patent laws and educational practices that prevented the rise of certain national chemical industries.[38] Prior to World War I, France, Britain, the United States and Italy had almost no locally-owned chemical dyestuffs producers.[39]

---

[33] Haber, 1971: Chapter 8, pp 218 *et seq*; Siemens, 1957: Vol II, p 27.
[34] Haber, 1971: pp 238 and 239.
[35] Woytinsky and Woytinsky, 1955: pp 258–261.
[36] Friedlaender and Oser, 1953: Chapter 26 *et seq*.
[37] Michel, 1936: p 15.
[38] Haber, 1958: Chapter 8.
[39] Haber, 1971: pp 29, 145 and 157.

Table 4.5 Circumstances Related to Establishment of Foreign Manufacturing Facilities by Large Continental European Firms: Selected Cases, Prior to World War I

Parent firm	Date	Product	Circumstances related to establishment
Subsidiary Establishments in France:			
Hoechst	1881	Synthetic dyes	
Bayer	1883	Synthetic dyes	Increased duties in the 1880's led German companies to manufacture.
Agfa	ca 1895	Synthetic dyes	
Geigy	ca 1895	Synthetic dyes	The Franco-Swiss tariff war 1892–1895 led Geigy to build a factory near Rouen.
Siemens	1879	Electrical lighting equipment	French patent working laws compelled local manufacture.
Subsidiary Establishments in the United Kingdom:			
Ciba	1909	Aniline oil, trinitrotoluene and intermediaries	The 1907 Patent Act compelled local manufacture.
Mannesmann	1899	Seamless steel tubes	Manufacturing was undertaken in order 'to be able to export to the British Empire'; apparently there were non-tariff barriers facing German direct exports.
Subsidiary Establishments in Germany:			
Unilever (Van Den Bergh & Jurgens' predecessors)	1888	Margarine	The initial decisions to invest were speeded up by the Bismarck Tariff of 1887 which protected domestic butter substitutes such as margarine.
Brown, Boveri	1898	Steam turbines	Demand by municipal authorities in Frankfurt-am-Main for local supply of electric generating equipment led to company's first foreign subsidiary in Germany.
Subsidiary Establishments in Russia:			
Hoechst	1878	Aniline dyes	Extremely high tariffs on finished dyestuffs stimulated manufacture.
BASF	1878	Aniline dyes	
Agfa	1888	Aniline dyes	
Ciba	1899	Aniline dyes	
Cockerill	1885	Steel plate, ships	Export sales dropped from 5 million to 300 thousand Belgian Francs between 1877 and 1885 after imposition of tariffs. Local competitors in a price-ring were extremely hostile to Cockerill's manufacturing venture. It was eventually founded as a joint Russian-Belgian venture.
Siemens	1880	Cables, telegraph apparatus	High tariffs on electro-technical goods, especially cables made supply from Germany impossible; assurances of government contracts had been given by court circles.
Subsidiary Establishments in Norway:			
Nestlé (Anglo-Swiss Condensed Milk)	1895	Condensed milk	Trade barriers were less important than was the desire to lower production costs.

Table 4.5—continued

Parent firm	Date	Product	Circumstances related to establishment
Subsidiary Establishments in Italy:			
Mannesmann	1906	Seamless tubes	Extremely high duties on tubes in Italy made it impossible for exporters to compete with domestic producers.
Subsidiary Establishments in Belgium:			
Unilever (Van Den Bergh & Jurgens)	1906	Margarine	High tariffs to protect Belgian producers led to local manufacture.
Subsidiary Establishments in Austria:			
Brown, Boveri	1910	Locomotives	High tariffs, combined with a preference for indigenous products by the Austrian state railways, led to the setting up of production.
Subsidiary Establishments in The United States:			
Nestlé (Anglo-Swiss Condensed Milk)	1900	Baby food	Consumer demand for exported product rapidly become large and tariff barriers were high.

Sources: **For Hoechst, Bayer, Agfa, Ciba and Geigy, 1881–1899:** Haber, 1958: pp 114 and 142; Masnata, 1924: p 76; **For Ciba, 1907:** Haber, 1958: p 149; **For Mannesmann,** 1899: Mannesmann, 1965: pp 81 and 84; **For Unilever predecessors from Holland:** Wilson, 1970: Vol II, pp 45, 49, 133 and 265; **For Brown, Boveri of Switzerland 1898:** Brown, Boveri, 1966: pp 244 and 227; **For Cockerill of Belgium:** McKay, 1970: pp 300 and 301; **For Siemens of Germany:** Siemens, 1957: Vol I, pp 104 and 106; **For Péchiney, and Alusuisse, 1927:** Wallace, 1937.

N.B.: The above mentioned sources include those for the following table, 4.6.

Before 1914, German and Swiss dyestuffs exports gave way to subsidiaries only when trade restrictions or patent-working regulations threatened to eliminate synthetics from the market entirely. Little threat of local chemical dye competition seemed in the offing.[40] World War I awoke Britain, the United States and Italy to the dangers of being even partially dependent on others for supplies of dyestuffs and other chemicals. During and after the war, each of these countries' governments stimulated local chemical production by import licensing, tariffs or outright subsidies to local firms. Once local companies could produce the products in question, Swiss producers faced the threat of competition from local firms and, in certain cases, the outright closure of markets. If the Swiss wished to maintain their markets it was necessary to set up local manufacturing, a step they promptly took.[41]

Foreign subsidiaries were often established in high-income, high-wage countries because of tariff walls or other protective trade barriers. Table 4.7 shows that prior to World War I more than half of Continental European

[40] Haber, 1971: pp 29, 145 and 157.
[41] Haber, 1973: Vol XI, No 1: Haber, 1971: pp 238 and 239; interviews with company managers.

Table 4.6 Circumstances Related to Establishment of Foreign Manufacturing Facilities by Large Continental European Firms: Selected Cases During the Inter-War Period

Parent firm	Date	Product	Circumstances related to establishment
Subsidiary Establishments in France:			
Jurgens (predecessor of Unilever)	1920	Margarine	The Germans after their retreat in 1918 had left France short of food and livestock. Demand for a butter substitute was high.
Subsidiary Establishments in Italy:			
Geigy	1926	Blending factory for dyes	Tariffs and licenses blocking imports led to local manufacture.
Geigy	1926	Synthetic dyes	
Ciba	1926	Synthetic dyes	
Sandoz	1926	Synthetic dyes	
Subsidiary Establishments in Spain:			
Subsidiary jointly owned by Péchiney, Alusuisse, and Aluminum Co Canada	1927	Aluminum	The Spanish government encouraged the creation of this company. Tariffs were raised to about 30%, *ad valorem* from about 3%.
Subsidiary Establishments in Czechoslovakia:			
Siemens	1930	Telephone equipment and cables	Local production was instigated by the Czech government in the interests of national economic development.
Subsidiary Establishments in Brazil:			
Geigy	1938	Dyes	Import restrictions led to local production.
Subsidiary Establishments in The United States:			
Ciba Geigy	1920	Synthetic dyestuffs	Prohibition of imports, followed by 55–60% tariffs assessed on the selling price of comparable American goods (the American Selling Price evaluation) led to local production.
I G Farben	1924	Dyestuffs	

Sources: Listed on previous page, 88 together with sources for Table 4.5.

firms' foreign subsidiaries were established in countries where *per capita* income levels equalled or exceeded those prevailing in the parent-company nations. Although the proportion of subsidiary implantations in high-income countries by firms based in low-income countries was lower in the inter-war era, such moves were still far from negligible. As nearly as one can judge, synthetics or novel processes for price-elastic goods were involved in roughly two-thirds of these early moves to establish subsidiaries in foreign countries with income and wage levels exceeding or equalling those prevailing at home. The German and Swiss chemical enterprises which had led in the development of synthetics accounted for a majority of such counter-product-cycle moves, as Table 4.7 shows.

Table 4.7   Direction of Foreign Manufacturing Investment by Large Continental European Firms: 1870–1939

Country of parent	Number of Foreign Manufacturing Subsidiaries Established:	
	In countries with incomes lower than parent	In countries with incomes equal or higher than parent
Prior to World War I:		
Switzerland	8	14
Germany	16	21
France	3	2
Netherlands	3	2
Belgium	4	4
Sweden	1	4
Total	**35**	**47**
During the Inter-War Period:		
Switzerland	8	5
Germany	15	9
Italy	3	2
France	—	2
Netherlands	23	4
Belgium & Luxemburg	4	5
Sweden	12	4
Total	**65**	**31**

Sources: Comparative Multinational Enterprise Project. *Per capita* income estimates obtained from Clark, 1951: pp 46, 47, 63, 80, 84, 85, 87, 89, 100, 108 and 109.

Continental Enterprise and New Products

Trade barriers were the primary force, but not the only force, pulling Continental enterprises to manufacture in high-cost locations. A few Continental innovations did find a market which warranted foreign production in high-income nations, as we shall see in more detail in Chapter VII. These innovations were sometimes new luxury products developed for Europe's wealthy, aristocratic élites. Daimler and Benz, inventors of the automobile, had followed commercial introduction of their hand-crafted luxury cars in Germany with foreign production in Britain in 1893 and in the United States a few years later. Labor in Britain may have been more expensive than in Germany at the time, but demand for Daimler cars was clearly not so price elastic as to make labor cost an important factor in the decision on production location. The United Kingdom and the United States were the highest-income markets before World War I, as well they had to be to attract Daimler and Benz: the American Mercedes sold for $7,500 when Ford's model T was selling for $500.[42]

New products developed on the Continent for moderate or low-income customers were also sometimes drawn into higher-income nations by the

---

[42] Wells, 1974: p 231; Daimler Benz, 1961.

sheer size of market demand. As Table 4.5 indicates, Henri Nestlé exported his baby food (a mother's milk substitute) from Switzerland to the United States until 1900, when customer demand (as well as tariff barriers) grew to such a size as to stimulate an investment decision.[43]

When Continental enterprises carried new products into foreign production, however, they usually did so to lower-income, lower labor-cost markets, as Table 4.5 shows. Between one-third and one-half of these subsidiary implantations in lower income countries concerned neither synthetics nor material-saving processes, but rather new products aimed at low-income consumer groups or at governments taking their first steps toward building modern military and industrial infrastructures. Europe's working classes had long provided mass markets for new products aimed at low-income consumers. Some European governments (especially that of Germany) had also guaranteed markets for new products aimed at military communication, transport and medical needs. These products were subsequently desired by other countries which followed the leading Continental countries toward industrialization. The new products called for in these low-income markets were sometimes pulled into foreign manufacture by market growth, local competition and lower foreign costs. In 1895, as one observes from Table 4.5, the Anglo-Swiss Company set up a subsidiary for the production of condensed milk in Norway where manufacturing costs were low. In the 1880's, the German firm of Siemens set up a dial telegraph equipment and cable factory in Russia to supply that government's basic military communication needs. Similarly, in 1930 Siemens invested in foreign manufacture of its telephone equipment and cables in Czechoslovakia. The Czech government instigated the move in the interests of its own national economic development. The opening of two plants for truck production in Russia, one before, and one during World War I by the French firm, Renault, provided another illustration of the taking of new products to less developed nations.[44]

Prior to World War II, however, very few of these investments in manufacturing in lower-income nations occurred in what are today thought of as the less developed countries. Table 4.8 shows that about three percent of the foreign manufacturing subsidiaries of Continental enterprises were regularly located in LDC's prior to World War I, and about 15% were so located during the inter-war period. All but a handful of these pre-1945 manufacturing subsidiaries in the LDC's were in Latin America. When Continental enterprises ventured to lower-income nations before World War II, they were much more inclined to do so in Eastern and less developed Europe; there they had about one-fifth of their early foreign operations.

Many of the new products being carried into foreign production by European companies turn out to have had various links with the more developed, American and British high-income markets of the time. Condensed milk and the telephone were both American innovations; the dial telegraph was a British invention.[45] In some cases, as in those of condensed milk and the dial telegraph, Continental firms innovated alternative versions of American or

---

[43] Heer, 1966: pp 79 and 118.
[44] Fridenson, 1972: p 66.
[45] Siemens, 1957: Vol I, p 14.

Table 4.8   Percentage of Foreign Manufacturing Subsidiaries Established by Large Continental Enterprises: Flow by Areas, 1900–1970

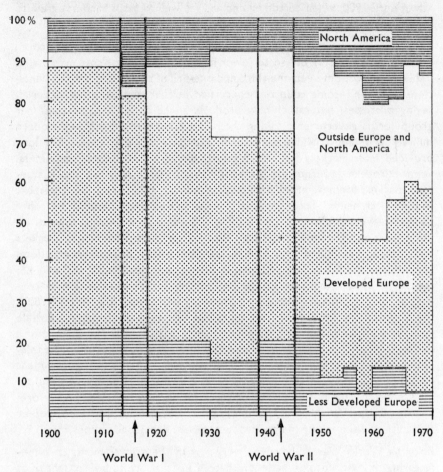

Notes: Countries included in Developed Europe:
United Kingdom, Germany, France, Belgium-Luxemburg, Holland, Switzerland, Sweden, Italy, Denmark, Norway, Austria, Ireland, Finland.
Countries included in Less Developed Europe:
Russia, Spain, Greece, Yugoslavia, Poland, Czechoslovakia, Hungary, Turkey, Portugal.

Source: Comparative Multinational Enterprise Project.

British products, versions presumably better adapted to Continental income and labor-cost conditions. In other cases Continental European firms put new products into foreign production, because of private agreements with American and British producers.[46] During the inter-war period, licensing and cross-licensing agreements were negotiated, reserving to certain Continental companies the whole or part of Europe for particular new products.[47] The *quid pro quo* for Continental producers was that they would not export such

---

[46] See, for example, the Siemens-Strowger relationship concerning automatic telephone exchanges. (Siemens, 1957: Vol I, p 262.) See also the Siemens-Westinghouse accord which lasted from 1922 to the Second World War. (Siemens, 1957: Vol II, p 215.)
[47] Stocking and Watkins, 1946.

products to Anglo-Saxon markets.[48] German and Dutch companies were often selected by the Americans and British to play a role in these divisions of world markets because of their technical ability to imitate (and later compete with) American or British products, and their potential advantages in exporting, due to their location in countries with lower wages than those in the United States or United Kingdom.

Restriction of competition was only one motive behind international agreements on market divisions. Licensing accords were used by US firms when they were wary of entering unknown markets with new products. These accords were sometimes complemented by equity participation in Continental companies, or in Continental firms' domestic subsidiaries.[49] Joint venture companies might then put the American product into production in other European markets. AEG, in which US General Electric owned (and still owns) a minority share, often acted in this manner. Accords that divided up world markets were all the more tempting when US and Continental European companies occasionally introduced new products nearly simultaneously, as in the case of the tungsten filament lamp and the vacuum tube.[50]

Whatever their genesis, agreements between American and European firms concerning new products often limited the Europeans to Continental markets. The pattern of location of manufacturing within Europe that followed then emerged from a dialectic between government protective policies and competitors' threats to set up manufacturing plants behind such barriers. Siemens began to produce telephone equipment in Czechoslovakia in 1930 not from any sense of great market opportunity or exhaustion of scale economies in Germany, but apparently out of fear that ITT might pre-empt the market by being the first to jump newly imposed trade barriers.[51]

Government measures were, therefore, important stimulants to foreign manufacturing by Continental enterprises. These measures explain some of the striking irregularities observable from Table 4.9 in the timing of entry into foreign manufacturing by Continental European firms. A major spurt in the establishment or acquisition of foreign manufacturing operations by Continental enterprises clearly coincided with the great increases in trade barriers which occurred in the World War I period and its aftermath. German, Belgian, Luxemburg, Dutch, Swedish and Swiss firms all established or acquired more foreign manufacturing subsidiaries between 1914 and 1929 than they had prior to the First World War, or were to do in any period of similar length up to the late 1950's.[52]

---

[48] Hexner, 1946: eg p 445 where the American-German agreement of 1938 concerning electro-appliances is cited.
[49] Franko, 1971(B).
[50] Siemens, 1957: Vol I, pp 290 et seq, and Vol II, pp 14 and 15.
[51] Siemens, 1957: Vol II, p 106.
[52] It is probable, although not certain that this statement also holds for French enterprises. After the data gathering for the Comparative Multinational Enterprise Project had been completed, new sources became available concerning French investments in Eastern European manufacturing between the World Wars. These sources indicate that large French companies acquired several Czechoslovak firms between 1919 and 1929 which in turn owned enough foreign subsidiaries to double the number underlying the 1914–1929 percentage reported in Table 4.9. (See Teichova, 1974: Chapters 3 and 4.)

Table 4.9   Percentage of Foreign Manufacturing Subsidiaries Established in Various Periods by Large American, British and Continental European Companies (US data as of January 1, 1968; all other data as of January 1, 1971)

| Country of parent | Period | | | | | | Total number of subsidiaries established (=100%) |
	Before 1914	1914–1929	1930–1945	1946–1955	1956–1964	1965–1970	
United States	3%	8%	11%	14%	46%	18%	9,127
United Kingdom	2	6	5	10	30	47	2,530
Germany	6	9	3	8	21	53	1,024
France	2	3	4	7	18	67	457
Italy	2	4	5	18	34	37	123
Bel & Lux	8	15	4	8	12	53	311
Netherlands*	3	11	4	6	21	55	455
Sweden	3	19	10	11	16	41	209
Switzerland	12	13	9	9	19	38	458

Notes: *Excludes Unilever.
Total percentages may not add to 100 due to rounding.

Source: Comparative Multinational Enterprise Project.

Negotiable Environments and International Combine Behavior

The term 'multinational' enterprise was coined at the end of the 1950's. Before then, a multinational production system, linked together simply through common ownership of plants by a single parent, was referred to as an 'international combine'.[53] This terminology may well have been related to the behavior of Continental European firms during the inter-war period, when governmentally imposed and privately negotiated divisions of international markets prevailed.

In international combines, foreign manufacturing subsidiaries often acted separately from one another, at least in matters concerning finished products. Trade barriers meant that price levels could differ markedly among subsidiary countries. Many subsidiaries produced identical product lines, often at scales too low to achieve minimum costs. Little evidence can be found of any international division of labor or specialization within multinational firms. Philips, the Dutch electrical concern, notes, for example, that the numerous foreign factories it set up during the inter-war period:

'. . . were at that time established in the various countries for the respective home markets only under the pressure of economic conditions and measures of trade policy. Of necessity, large sums had to be invested in relatively small, often not very profitable production units.'[54]

Van den Bergh's and Jurgens, Unilever's Dutch predecessors, behaved in a similar manner.[55] When factories that were set up under government pressure did export, it was only to particular spheres of political influence. Such

---

[53] Mason, 1946; Edwards, 1963: p 163 et seq; Plummer, 1934.
[54] Philips, 1972: p 6.
[55] Wilson, 1954: Vol II.

was the case with the pre-World War II Siemens factory in Czechoslovakia.[56] This plant exported to the small Eastern European countries whose trade was gradually becoming conditioned by a network of bilateral accords dominated by Germany.

During the inter-war era of negotiable, non-competitive environments, there occurred a distinct change in patterns of establishment and acquisition of foreign manufacturing.[57] Prior to World War I, the decisions of Continental firms to enter into foreign manufacturing had been conditioned by markets that were neither wholly competitive nor wholly suppressed. That the synthetic dyestuffs firms, Ciba, Geigy, BASF, Bayer and Hoechst, all decided to set up manufacturing plants in Russia and France during the same period of the 1880's, suggests that these companies wanted to match rivals' international moves in order to maintain a certain share of the whole European market for their product. And, prior to their merger into Unilever, Jurgens and Van den Bergh engaged in a good deal of subsidiary matching in Continental markets for margarine.[58]

As economic space contracted, however, and as disbelievers in market forces dominated post-World War European governments, another pattern of foreign entry behavior set in. Not only did governments discourage international competition by setting up trade barriers, but they tolerated the suppression of domestic competition. Oligopolistic matching in foreign markets then often gave way to entry *en famille* in manufacturing subsidiaries jointly owned by international rivals. *En famille* or 'foreign-foreign' joint ventures were not very widespread, since even during their hey day (1930–1938) they probably only accounted for about ten percent of the foreign manufacturing operations begun by Continental companies.[59] Nevertheless, this percentage of subsidiaries begun as joint ventures among international rivals has never been equalled.[60]

Joint foreign entry was particularly favored for dyestuff activities of the major Swiss companies during the period of their 1918–1951 Interest Association.[61] Similarly, the German Osram Company, a joint venture for the production of electric lamps formed in 1919 by Siemens, AEG and the smaller Auer interests, came to manufacture in numerous countries after the First World War. Competition between Siemens and AEG was thus reduced by a means that provided automatic matching and equilibration of market shares.[62]

Occasionally, the fact that the degree of competition in both domestic and

---

[56] Siemens, 1957: Vol 2, p 59.
[57] The term 'the negotiable environment' was first used by Van der Haas (1967) to describe the peculiar character of competitive conditions in most European countries prior to the establishment of the EEC in 1958. It was meant to describe economies which had neither a competitive market system of the American variety nor a centralized, command system of the communist variety.
[58] Wilson, 1954: Vol II, p 45.
[59] Comparative Multinational Enterprise Data Bank; Vaupel and Curhan, 1973: Table 11.17.1, p 309.
[60] Vaupel and Curhan, 1974: p 310.
[61] Bürgin, 1958: pp 246 *et seq* and 296.
[62] Siemens, 1957: Vol II, pp 31 and 32; Stocking and Watkins, 1946: pp 323 and 324.

foreign markets was negotiable, enabled former international competitors to combine in mergers. The most notable example was the combination of BASF, Hoechst and Bayer into I G Farben between 1925 and 1945. When only a few international competitors existed, they could parcel out manufacturing in protected markets, domestic and foreign. International cartel agreements stipulated which of the competitors would invest in which foreign country. This was the case, for example, in certain of the accords between I G Farben and the members of the Swiss Interest Association.[63] Accords such as these partially accounted for the fact that the number of foreign subsidiaries established by Continental parents decreased from 249 during the period 1920–1924 to 112 during the period 1930–1938. Since tariff barriers continued to increase, and the world economy began to recover after 1934, one probably would not have expected such a sharp drop. US parents' foreign start-ups and acquisitions increased from 299 in the earlier period to 315 in the latter.[64]

When inter-related innovative advantages were held by a few firms that were all based in one country, the merger of the domestic firms into a local mono-poly was sometimes only a first step toward the building of an international system consisting of a series of national manufacturing monopolies. Ivar Kreuger launched the Swedish Match combine in this fashion in the 1920's.[65] Kreuger first merged the various Swedish match firms, which had been export-ing on the basis of innovations in safety matches dating back to 1840.[66] Sensing that extraordinary profits were to be made if nations would grant local monopolies behind trade barriers in return for local production, Kreuger persuaded many governments which had been financially strained by World War I to offer such a monopoly in return for hard-currency loans and invest-ments. Where local match factories already existed, he offered to buy them out. When their owners resisted, he brought his technological and financial trump cards into play and forced them into submission by cutting prices. By 1930, Swedish Match was manufacturing in 11 countries. The strength of Kreuger's trumps is perhaps even better attested to by the success of Swedish Match in forcing American-owned Diamond Match out of many foreign markets. Diamond had owned numerous foreign production subsidiaries prior to Kreuger's onslaught.[67]

Kreuger did not live to see the fruits of his scheme, however. The growth of his combine had been financed with borrowed money, largely raised in the United States. World depression prevented the expected monopoly profits from materializing. Kreuger falsified his accounts or forgot to keep them in good order, or both. The result was the business equivalent of a Greek tragedy. He committed suicide in 1932 and left his bankers to sort out the pieces. Still, Kreuger's actions do not seem different in kind, but only in degree, from those undertaken by many firms in the age in which he lived; only the dénouement itself was different.

While international companies were substituting agreement for rivalry in

---

[63] Bürgin, 1958: p 255.
[64] Vaupel and Curhan, 1974: Table 1.17.2, p 79 and Table 1.17.4, p 95.
[65] Shaplen, 1960.
[66] Friedlaender and Oser, 1953: p 417.
[67] Wilkins, 1974.

foreign markets, both they and large national firms were trying to reap the benefits of protected markets at home. National cartels and mergers were formed by both domestic and international firms in each European country. Privately and publicly sponsored international cartels were negotiated to insulate home markets more thoroughly than was possible through tariffs alone.[68]

The emergence of such cartels and mergers had a special effect on foreign investment across borders within Europe by enterprises based in small countries. Firms in the large countries were not under the same compulsion to export as those in the small ones, particularly in those countries containing large plants that had been designed for the export markets existing prior to World War I. As trade barriers went up, firms exporting from these small countries had more than the usual reasons to make foreign manufacturing investments. They had an incentive to establish subsidiaries which could function as fifth-columns in large foreign markets where local producers could keep out imports. Threat of exclusion from markets could be met with counter-threat only if the exporter had a credible means to increase capacity, cut prices, or influence customer demand inside the national markets of the larger countries.[69] ARBED, the Luxemburg steel company, had almost been 'born' multinational, since the Treaty of Versailles traced new national frontiers around (and even across) its various plants. Yet it continued to acquire other foreign manufacturing subsidiaries in steel and steel-using sectors in the early 1920's. Only then, after subsidiaries had been established in larger nations, did the company become among the first to call for the international steel cartel of 1926.[70] Such considerations played an important role in the sudden post-World War I spurt of foreign manufacturing by firms whose parents were based in the smaller European countries.

The Decline of Market Forces within Nations

The transformation of Continental European multinational enterprise into a network of international combines during the inter-war period occurred in response to both the Balkanization of international markets and the reduction of competitive pressures within nation states. Cartelization and combination were also rendered attractive by some other, more national, political and economic conditions.

One of these conditions was the lack of effective antitrust or anti-cartel legislation in European countries prior to the mid-1950's. Indeed, national governments often supported the suppression of market forces through national and international cartels. In the 1930's, legislation promoting cartelization came into being in Belgium, the Netherlands, Italy and Germany.[71] Business conduct was aligned with the political philosophies of '*Gleichschaltung*' or Corporate State co-ordination prevailing in Germany and

---

[68] Plummer, 1934; Stocking and Watkins, 1946; Hexner, 1943.
[69] The establishment of fifth-column subsidiaries is a first-cousin to the exchange of threat behavior discussed by Caves (1971), Vernon (1974; p 278), and Graham (1975). See also Chapters VI and VII *infra*.
[70] Hexner, 1943: pp 70 and 71.
[71] League of Nations, 1947: pp 10 and 11.

Italy.[72] Even the non-Fascist governments of Europe promoted cartelization, for they felt that competition implied not only entry of foreign goods but also increased dependence on unpalatable neighbors.[73]

A second condition that helped make domestic as well as international environments negotiable was the fact that European competitors had many more tempting opportunities to co-ordinate actions and strategies than did their American counterparts. Short geographical distances, and the existence of stable, inter-married social élites helped to produce opportunities for arrangements between competitors unimaginable in America.[74] In Europe, competitors of the same nationality were usually personal friends. It was exceptions to this rule which were remarked upon. Discussing the foundation of a single French aluminum sales company in 1910, the *Syndicat français de l'aluminium*, one protagonist wrote:

> 'By getting together the two leaders of the industry, Adrien Badin and Jules Dreyfus – who, very strangely, did not know each other – I helped them come to an arrangement. It was done in a most friendly fashion, over lunch at the Café de la Paix.'[75]

Multinational Manufacturing after World War II

Table 4.9 shows that the great majority of Continental European firms' foreign manufacturing activities came into being after 1955. This proliferation of international operations occurred during a time when the walls of the negotiable environment were crumbling.

In the late 1940's and early 1950's, US antitrust initiatives inhibited American firms from further participation in international cartels.[76] Creation of private spheres of influence became harder, and European firms faced the threat of new American competition in home and third markets.

The EEC was created in 1958, and the difficult road toward the abolition of intra-EEC industrial tariffs was begun. Tariff barriers around the EEC were then lowered by international negotiations. Non-tariff barriers became less severe than they had been in the pre-1959 days of currency inconvertibility and quotas, although they were still far from negligible in the 1970's.[77]

The Continent's post-war move to political liberalism was gradually accompanied by increasing acceptance of the notion of competition within markets. By the mid-1950's, all major European countries (except Italy) had legislation against price-fixing and cartel abuses. In 1956, the United Kingdom became the first country outside of North America to adopt legislation to control or block mergers of cross-shareholding alliances. Price-fixing, abuse of dominant position and other restrictive practices, became legally prohibited or limited by Articles 85 and 86 of the Treaty of Rome for the EEC member countries in

---

[72] Siemens, 1957: Vol II, pp 229–236, especially p 234; Bosch, 1961: Chapter 6, pp 72 *et seq.*
[73] Private discussions with Swiss industrialists. See Teichova, 1974: p 57 on Czech tolerance for cartelization during the 1930's.
[74] Vernon, 1972.
[75] Pitival, 1946: pp 83 and 84.
[76] Bewster, 1958.
[77] Baldwin, 1970. See also Chapter VI.

1958. Still, the first action against restrictive practices taken by the EEC Commission dates from 1964, and the first fine for anti-competitive practices in the Community was meted out in 1969. Germany was the only Continental country with a consistent record of enforcing anti-cartel laws, but only in 1973 did Germany become the first Continental country to adopt merger-control legislation.[78]

The post-war reductions in government and private barriers to trade after World War II enabled Continental firms with little or no early history of foreign sales to test foreign markets through exports, and, if they had the requisite innovative advantages, embark on the road to multinationality. Less centrally directed and less cartelized domestic markets also allowed the rebirth of competitive rivalry – although not exactly of perfect competition – among large firms. Meanwhile, existing multinationals were obliged to think of protecting established market positions.

The influence of both home and host governments on the decisions of large European enterprise remained, nevertheless, very much in evidence. Sometimes European national governments strained to help 'their' firms acquire technological advantages. And, while governments of importing countries viewed international trade with an attitude of 'none is best' before World War II, many had shifted to 'not too much, please' by the 1970's.

The Rebirth of Rivalry

One event in particular promoted the decline in the negotiability of the market environment and the subsequent proliferation of foreign operations by Continental firms. That event was the deconcentration of I G Farben by the Allied Control Commission during the post-war occupation of Germany. The author of the one-hundred year jubilee book of *Farbwerke Hoechst* notes that:

> 'The American surgeons in the Control Commission carried out the cutting up of Farben's body with great thoroughness. The factories in the American zone were cut off from their traditional relationships with their cousins elsewhere in Germany, and each had to invent their own management organization from the ground up. Above all, each piece had its own finance, purchase, and sales department .... It goes without saying that there was no more unified foreign department.[79]

Hoechst and Bayer reappeared as independent entities in December 1951. BASF followed in January 1952.

One of the first items on the agendas of these re-born firms was re-entry into their once-important Latin American markets. During World War II, confiscations cut ownership ties with some 27 pre-existing I G Farben sales subsidiaries and even with a half-dozen manufacturing operations, but technological relations with former corporate relatives were less easily severed. Bayer bought back previously confiscated plants and sales subsidiaries from local firms which had purchased them to regain its pharmaceutical trademarks. Hoechst decided to go it alone and set up its own net-

---

[78] Brun and Franko, 1974.
[79] Baümler, 1963: p 4.

work for sales and later production.[80] BASF left Farben without pharmaceutical operations. It too made its way back into foreign markets, but in heavy chemicals.

The I G successors were joined by other German companies with similar aims to recapture Latin American markets. Siemens, AEG, Daimler-Benz and Bosch, for example, quickly began rebuilding their sales networks.[81] However, Latin American governments were conscious of their need for economic development and were not content to merely import basic pharmaceuticals, chemicals and electrical products. The era of import substitution and government stimulation of development had begun.[82] New tariffs – helped by reborn company rivalries – triggered new investments. As Table 4.9 shows, the foreign manufacturing activity of German firms took a leap upward in the mid-1950's and did not stop growing thereafter.

The effects of the deconcentration of German industry were also felt by European firms located outside of Germany. With the dispersal of the market power of I G Farben, the Interest Association (I G) of the Swiss chemical and pharmaceutical manufacturers came to be viewed as a bothersome constraint by some of its members. The Swiss I G had entered market division accords with I G Farben and had set up profit-pooling and joint-venture arrangements among its own members. But after deconcentration any fruits of voluntary restraint by the Swiss firms might have merely fallen to one of its competitors, including the newly independent German companies. Agreement among only a few of the relevant firms in the industry would not insure stability. The Swiss I G was dissolved in 1951.[83] As the foreign manufacturing subsidiaries of Swiss companies had not been generally confiscated during the war, the new intra-Swiss rivalry did not lead to a dramatic increase in foreign subsidiary formation. Yet it was one factor behind the post-1955 increase in Swiss foreign production discernible from Table 4.9.

The Rise of Italian Multinationals, 1945–1958

Deconcentration in Germany was not the only force that impelled a new wave of interest in foreign markets by European enterprises after World War II. The fall of fascism and its autarkic aims in Italy unleashed an internationalist reaction by large Italian firms.[84] Between 1946 and 1955, a surge occurred in the foreign manufacturing activities of Italian firms, shown in Table 4.5. Fiat's cars, Olivetti's office machinery and Snia Viscosa's synthetic fibers had been seen to some extent in international markets before the war. Now these companies were to use production skills developed in an autarkic economy to undertake production in a number of foreign nations.

Fiat, for example, was already aware in the 1930's of the market possibilities inherent in a mass-produced, working-class small car that would not use much fuel. Fiat was also conscious of the possibilities for such a product in

---

[80] Winnacker, 1972: pp 340 et seq.
[81] Bosch, 1961.
[82] See Chapter V.
[83] Sandoz, 1961: p 127.
[84] Mack Smith, 1969: especially Chapter 58.

France, where it already possessed car-producing facilities.[85] In 1936, 'the world's smallest mass production car was born – the 500. The public immediately nicknamed it "*Topolino*", or Mickey Mouse'.[86] A mass product such as this, plus mass production experience gained by Fiat in wartime, quickly led to exports to lower-income markets. Fiat was encouraged to assemble and then produce in countries like France, Spain, Yugoslavia and Argentina whose governments' policies after World War II instituted higher tariffs and import-substituting development programs.[87] Foreign production became mandatory for Fiat to keep former export markets when other Continental European companies threatened to enter the international arena with small cars. Government-owned VW, Renault (newly nationalized in 1945), and Citroën all began setting up foreign subsidiaries to avoid having their foreign markets pre-empted.* At least one attempt was apparently made during the early 1960's to bring this rivalry to a halt. It is reported that Fiat proposed a market division and price-fixing arrangement to Volkswagen in 1964.[88] VW, the newcomer, apparently declined the proposal; rivalry continued.

Fiat's experience suggests that a type of international product cycle affected the foreign spread of products (or, more exactly, product varieties) innovated for low-income European markets. Olivetti's post-war history showed a similar process at work. Its war-tested typewriters and calculators rapidly became the most popular models in government offices in Latin America.[89] Italian exports were then superseded by foreign production, as host countries pursued import-substitution policies and American, and then Japanese competitors threatened Olivetti's markets.

Continental Europe, led by Italy, began to produce for low-income markets products which moved from higher to lower income countries. As Table 4.1 showed, the foreign manufacturing activity of Italian parents was, of all the large Continental companies, the least centered on Europe. The Italian auto and office-machinery companies did not concentrate their foreign investments in developed, European countries; unlike most Continental enterprises, the distinctive thrust of Italian enterprise was to less developed Europe and the developing countries.

Some foreign manufacturing by Italian enterprises did take place in developed European countries after World War II, however, partly because of uncertainty over the degree to which barriers to international trade really would disappear. Olivetti, for example, established a subsidiary in the United Kingdom in 1947 as a means of entering both the British and the British

---

*VW, however, was consistently less adventurous in undertaking foreign production or assembly than either privately-owned Fiat, or wholly government-owned Renault. The possible reasons for this divergence in behavior are numerous. Full government ownership during the 1950's, as well as personal inclinations of VW's then general manager may have led to its more 'national' approach. Management succession difficulties may then have perpetuated this bias during the 1960's and early 1970's – in spite of some outstanding successful Latin American ventures. (See: Manchester Business School, 1973.)

[85] Fridenson, 1972.
[86] Fiat, 1970: p 266.
[87] Agnelli, 1973.
[88] Sidjanski and Maynaud, 1967: p 106.
[89] Harvard Business School, 1969: p 978.

Commonwealth markets, but neither of these markets had been closed for 12 years prior to 1966 and there seemed to be little likelihood of their closing again in the near future. By 1967, the original *raison d'être* for the plants' existence had been lost. This fact coupled with Britain's uncertain relationship with the European Common Market, was cause for considerable debate among Olivetti's top management regarding the future of the Glasgow plant.[90]

New Entrants and New Entrepreneurs: The Case of French Enterprises

The immediate post-war spread of French multinational manufacturing was not, as in the case of the Italian spread, stimulated only by a spirit of private entrepreneurship. Before World War II, the French state appeared to be a willing, even active partner in the prevailing preference for stability over growth.[91] In contrast, after 1945, its role was frequently that of '*L'État Entrepreneur*.'[92] Managers appointed by the French state decided that newly nationalized Renault would introduce France's version of the *Topolino*, the 4 CV.[93]

In its successive plans, the French state also placed increasing emphasis on exports. Soon after the war, and on into the 1970's, the French government exhorted business to export and to make the country as industrialized as Germany. Sometimes more than generalized exhortations were made: individual firms were contacted and told to export specific products to specific countries.[94] Competitive inroads into home and export markets by foreign, and especially by American firms, were viewed in France with an alarm quite beyond that shown elsewhere in Europe, particularly during the de Gaulle period. The anxiety produced in some French enterprises was reflected by a statement in a French company publication which referred to the multinational enterprise as 'the armored weapon of modern economic warfare'.[95] Perhaps paradoxically, however, successful efforts of French firms to fight off the multinational enterprises of other nations led in turn to their own multinationalization.[96]

Although the French government planners promoted the exports of long-established national industries such as steel, they placed their main emphasis on more sophisticated products. Substantial government subsidies were channelled through the state-dominated banking network to support R&D programs and technological education.[97] Some state-supported efforts were resounding failures: much has been made of France's inability to develop oligopolistic advantages in civilian aircraft, computers, nuclear-power plants, and semiconductors.[98] Much also has been made of spectacular cases of export-market failures such as Renault's abortive attempt in the 1960's to challenge

[90] Harvard Business School, 1969: p 978.
[91] Kindleberg, 1964.
[92] Naville, et al, 1971.
[93] Private communication from Patrick Fridenson.
[94] Interviews with company managers.
[95] Compagnie Générale d'Electricité, 1973: p 84.
[96] Michalet and Delapierre, 1974: pp 121–125.
[97] Gilpin, 1968.
[98] *L'Express*, 1972: pp 22–25; *Der Spiegel*, 1974: p 101.

Volkswagen in the US market. Yet, French manufacturers learned from their failures, and the groundwork was laid for multinational expansion. By 1960, France was regaining her long-forgotten, early twentieth-century role as one of the world's leading auto exporters.[99] Auto exports led along well-trodden paths to foreign assembly and production, especially in the LDC's, as rising foreign incomes and protectionist development policies pulled in companies' investments. Technological advances in radial tires and in electricity-saving aluminum production underlay the internationalization of French production in those goods.[100] As a result of such technological advantages, France took her place among the countries whose firms possessed many foreign manufacturing subsidiaries.

New Foreign Destinations

After World War II, operations in the less developed countries loomed large among the foreign manufacturing activities of Continental enterprises. Indeed, Table 4.8 shows that the increased involvement of Continental firms in Latin America, Africa and Asia represented the greatest single change in the geographical orientation of their activities after 1945. German, French and Italian firms were particularly prominent among those setting up factories in the LDC's.[101] However, the story of Continental manufacturing in the LDC's, which will be taken up in detail in Chapter V, was only part of the post-war spread of Continental multinational enterprise.

In the 1950's and 1960's, nearly one-third of the foreign manufacturing subsidiaries of Continental firms were in countries where *per capita* incomes equalled or exceeded those in home countries, as Table 4.10 shows. This was the same proportion of subsidiary implantations in high-income countries that had occurred during the inter-war period. Somewhat more than 30% of these new subsidiaries in high-income, high-cost markets were in North America, but the bulk continued to be established in nearby, developed, European countries.

Did the continuing orientation of European enterprises to foreign manufacturing within Europe imply that as tariff barriers went down, non-tariff barriers were going up? Certain fragments of information suggested that such was the case. Wherever barriers seemed to exist, Continental firms had set up or acquired subsidiaries in Europe. Pharmaceutical legislation, for example, became progressively more protectionist after the war.[102] Many new foreign manufacturing operations were then entered in that industry, but for old reasons. In 1972, the EEC Commission pointed out that there was almost no international trade in Europe in the telecommunications and heavy electrical sectors.[103] One found Continental companies in these industries undertaking numerous foreign manufacturing operations in Europe. Sometimes national subsidies added the carrot of government grants to the stick of trade barriers. Government subsidization underlay most of the mushrooming of automobile

---

[99] McKern, 1972.
[100] *Entreprise*, 1973; Sheahan, 1963.
[101] See also Table 4.2.
[102] Discussions with company executives; Witter/Technomics.
[103] *Journal de Genève*, 1972.

Table 4.10   Direction of Foreign Manufacturing Investment by Large Continental European Firms after World War II

	Number of Foreign Manufacturing Subsidiaries Established:			
	In countries with lower incomes than parents		In countries with equal or higher incomes than parent	
Country of parent	Number	%	Number	%
	1950–1959			
Switzerland	44	81	10	19
Germany	120	75	39	25
Italy	19	61	12	39
France	33	77	10	23
Netherlands	37	48	40	52
Belgium and Luxemburg	23	66	12	34
Sweden	17	77	5	23
Total	**293**	**70**	**128**	**30**
	1960–1970			
Switzerland	227	88	30	12
Germany	444	68	208	32
Italy	58	67	28	33
France	300	89	38	11
Netherlands	263	51	256	49
Belgium and Luxemburg	81	36	94	54
Sweden	100	98	30	12
Total	**1,473**	**69**	**656**	**31**

Source: Comparative Multinational Enterprise Data Project.

assembly plants in Belgium during the first two post-war decades.[104] A number of French, German and Swedish auto firms were conspicuous owners of such Belgian plants.

What underlay the increased involvement of Continental enterprises in North America, and particularly in the United States? Were Continental enterprises manufacturing in the US markets to find out how the American multinationals operated? Highly publicized US investments, such as that of Olivetti in 1959, had suggested that some European firms were undertaking manufacturing in the United States to learn from the distinctive stimuli of the world's largest market.[105] But there was also evidence that American trade barriers, real or threatened, were forcing Continental European firms to try to substitute US production (with unique processes) for European exports.[106]

The evidence presented in the next three chapters argues that the influence of trade barriers has been just as present in the multinational spread of Continental enterprise after World War II as it was before. The visible hand of the state was more subtle after the war than before, but it was still present. It was perhaps the degree to which national policies influenced Continental behavior that most distinguished the story of Continental multinational enterprise from the story of the American multinationals.

[104] Maillet, 1972: p II.21.
[105] Vernon, 1971: p 111.
[106] See Chapter VII.

Chapter V

Continental European Multinational
Enterprise and the Less Developed
World

Continental European companies began long ago to be interested in the world's less developed regions. Prior to World War I a few enterprises sought raw-material sources in those then largely colonial areas; most looked upon the less developed countries of Latin America, Africa, Asia, and Western Europe as market outlets. Export sales to these regions were common before 1914, but manufacturing operations there were almost non-existent.[1] The Indonesian refineries of Royal Dutch and the Mexican smelting operations of Metallgesellschaft were exceptions to the rule.[2]

During the inter-war period, a few Continental enterprises ventured into foreign manufacturing in less developed areas, as one observes from Table 5.1.

Table 5.1 Number of Manufacturing Subsidiaries Formed and Acquired in Developed and Less Developed Regions in Various Periods by the 85 Largest Continental European Enterprises

| Period | Region of Subsidiary Location: | | | | | |
	Developed Europe & N America	Eastern Europe	Less developed Europe*	Latin America	Asia & Africa	Total number
Prior to 1914	122	27	10	2	6	167
1914–1919	36	5	6	3	1	51
1920–1929	162	27	22	15	23	249
1930–1938	69	8	10	16	9	112
1939–1945	25	2	8	4	5	44
1946–1952	62	—	14	30	23	129
1953–1955	60	—	16	23	18	117
1956–1958	69	—	9	27	26	131
1959–1961	128	—	14	30	60	232
1962–1964	120	—	34	30	45	229
1965–1967	346	—	39	76	71	532
1968–1970	659	4**	86	130	151	1,030

Notes: *Greece, Portugal, Spain, Turkey, Israel.
        **Joint-venture subsidiaries in Yugoslavia.

Source: Comparative Multinational Enterprise Project.

In the early 1920's the Luxemburg steel firm, ARBED, acquired affiliates in Brazil and Argentina in order to retain markets threatened by the inter-war climate of protectionism and cartelization.[3] Siemens acquired a telephone-equipment firm in Argentina in the twenties as an aid to keeping its share of the local market in the face of incursions by the newly organized American firm, ITT. 'Later on, the ITT were given an interest in the concern for the sake of ensuring friendly relations with its subsidiary, the River Plate Telephone Company in Buenos Aires.'[4] I G Farben formed and acquired a few Latin American pharmaceutical operations. Nestlé acquired a condensed milk

---

[1] Manchester, 1969.
[2] Metallgesellschaft, 1931; Royal Dutch Shell, 1950: Chapters I and VI.
[3] ARBED, *Annual Reports*, various years, especially 1922.
[4] Siemens, 1957, Vol II: p 60.

company in Brazil.[5] One French firm, a predecessor to today's Rhône-Poulenc, developed a perfume thrower in the late 1800's that

> '. . . met no success whatever in Europe, but, in contrast was greeted with great enthusiasm in Brazil. It quickly became an indispensable accessory to the Carnival celebration.'[6]

Brazil was the only real market for such a product, and a subsidiary, the Companhia Quimica Rhodia Brasileira, began local production in 1921. Not only was the perfume itself put into production, but it was also accompanied by the manufacturing of basic chemicals necessary to its preparation. Thus was formed, almost by accident, the nucleus of what is now Brazil's largest chemical enterprise. It was to expand in response to local market growth, to tariff and currency barriers to imports, and to the need to replace imported intermediates while Brazil was cut off from France by World War II blockades.[7]

Many of the manufacturing subsidiaries established or acquired by Continental enterprises in low-income countries prior to 1945 were located in Eastern Europe. Continental enterprises had numerous factories in Russia under the Czars and during Lenin's New Economic Policy.[8] Between the wars, Continental investments in raw-material ventures in the East were parallelled by moves made to set up or acquire manufacturing behind the trade barriers raised by Poland and the Austrian successor states.[9] For a time the importance of these ventures in the East overshadowed that of Continental manufacturing activity in Latin America, Africa, Asia and even less developed Europe, as Table 5.1 shows. But the era of Eastern investments began to end when French enterprises were obliged to sell their Czech subsidiaries to German interests in the aftermath of the Munich accord in 1938.[10] Expropriations and state monopolization of trade by communist governments after World War II then obliged Continental enterprises to turn to the West.

The story of European manufacturing in the less developed countries thus belongs essentially to the post-1945 era. In the 1920's and 1930's, contacts between the Third World and Continental firms were primarily maintained by the latter's salesmen.[11] In contrast, during the 13 years separating World War II and the founding of the EEC in 1958, the largest Continental enterprises established almost the same number of manufacturing subsidiaries in LDC's as they did in developed countries. This shift in geographical orientation is shown in Table 5.1.

The volume of manufacturing undertaken by Continental enterprises in the LDC's was modest compared to that of American enterprises, even after 1945.

---

[5] Iffland and Stettler, 1973.

[6] Rhône-Poulenc, 'Histoire de nos sociétés,' No 3: p 4.

[7] Rhône-Poulenc, *Groupe Rhodia Brésil: Historique*, 1969: p 16.

[8] McKay, 1970; Sutton, 1968. McKay and Sutton also show that these enterprises first met in Russia many of the management problems they were later to encounter in Western LDC's.

[9] Teichova, 1974; see Chapter III *supra* on the raw-material ventures of Continental enterprises.

[10] Teichova, 1974.

[11] Hinden, 1921. Twenty percent or more of the imports of Brazil, Chile, Guatemala, and El Salvador in 1935 came from Germany, see Dietrich, 1939: p 136.

Table 5.2 Percentage Distribution of Foreign Manufacturing Subsidiaries of Large American, British, Japanese, and Continental Enterprises Located in Various Less Developed Regions, January 1, 1971 (US data as of January 1, 1968)

National base of parent enterprise	Region of Subsidiary Location:						Total:	
	Latin America	British Africa* & Mid-East	French & other Africa	Less developed Asia	Less developed Europe	Developed** countries	%	Number
United States	27%	6%	1%	6%	6%	54%	100	4,246
United Kingdom	6	27	2	10	4	51	100	2,269
Japan	18	9	2	63	2	6	100	483
France	18	6	15	4	13	44	100	429
Germany	18	10	1	8	11	51	100	792
Italy	34	10	6	6	18	26	100	133
Bel & Lux	5	7	5	2	9	72	100	276
Netherlands	9	5	3	8	3	72	100	429
Sweden	15	4	1	6	3	71	100	171
Switzerland	14	5	—	6	7	68	100	397

Notes: *Includes South Africa.
**Countries with 1970 per capita GNP exceeding US $1,200.

Source: Comparative Multinational Enterprise Project.

Table 5.2 shows that American multinationals had located more than one-quarter of their 4,246 manufacturing subsidiaries in less developed regions by 1968, while Continental enterprises had less than one-fifth of their subsidiaries in the Third World in 1971. Nevertheless, the rate of increase in the number of manufacturing operations of Continental enterprises in the LDC's came to be equal to that of the number of American subsidiaries in the mid-1960's. Between 1962 and 1967, US multinationals were regularly setting up or aquiring about 140 subsidiaries per year in less developed countries; Continental firms established LDC operations at a rate of 40 per year between 1962 and 1964, 70 per year between 1965 and 1967, and 140 per year between 1968 and the end of 1970.[12]

Interest in the developing world, however, varied greatly among enterprises based in different European countries. Large companies based in Italy had 56% of their foreign manufacturing outposts in Latin America, Africa and Asia in 1971, whereas Belgian firms had but 19%. Indeed, enterprises based in the smaller European countries have undertaken the least manufacturing in the LDC's, as Table 5.2 shows. In 1971, companies from Belgium, Luxemburg, the Netherlands, Sweden, and Switzerland had less than one-quarter of their foreign manufacturing in less developed countries (defined as those with 1970 GNP's *per capita* of under US $1,200). In contrast, large German firms had over 40%, French about half, and Italian enterprises more than 60% of their foreign production subsidiaries in nations with *per capita* GNP's under US $1,200. One notes that Japanese firms had over 90% of their foreign manufacturing in less developed areas. US multinationals had slightly over 40% of their manufacturing subsidiaries in LDC's at the beginning of 1968.[13]

The variations in Continental involvement in the emerging nations according to the countries from which parent enterprises came could not be easily accounted for by parent company characteristics. Neither the size nor the previous foreign manufacturing experience of the Continental enterprises was related to their propensity to establish manufacturing operations in the Third World.[14] On the other hand, most US-owned operations in the LDC's had been undertaken by the largest American firms, and by those with the greatest foreign manufacturing spread.[15]

A Colonial Heritage?

It would be tempting to infer that the pattern of involvement of Continental enterprises in the less developed world was the result of Europe's colonial past. Assertions to this effect have been made frequently.[16] The United Nations Report on Multinational Corporations in World Development

---

[12] This increasing European activity in the LDC's has been emphasized – and perhaps over-emphasized – by a number of authors in recent years. See, for example, Evans, 1972.

[13] Comparative Multinational Enterprise Project.

[14] Insignificant results were obtained from Chi-square tests applied to cross tabulations of numbers of firms classified by the percentage of their subsidiaries in LDC's versus measures of size, and the numbers of countries in which they manufactured. These tests were not quite comparable to those performed on American multinational data by Vaupel (1971), but there is no reason to suspect that his more complex manipulations would give different results.

[15] Vaupel, 1971.

[16] Mennis and Sauvant, 1973; Bornschier, 1973.

stated, for example, that multinational enterprises based in Continental countries which were formerly colonial powers had many more ownership 'links' with subsidiaries in LDC's than did firms from lands without a colonial past.[17] Unfortunately, the data on which such statements are based count not only links between parent firms and manufacturing subsidiaries, but also those concerning sales, service, and extractive operations. A look at just the foreign manufacturing operations of the large Continental companies suggests a rather different conclusion.

In the 1970's, the Latin American countries constituted the most important sites for manufacturing in the LDC's by Continental companies, as Table 5.2 shows.[18] With the exception of the Belgian firms, Continental enterprises showed a penchant for manufacturing in Latin America similar to that of American and Japanese companies, and considerably greater than that of British enterprises. Even French enterprises had a larger proportion of their LDC foreign manufacturing subsidiaries in Latin America than they did in the former French colonies.

France was, of course, the Continental European country most thoroughly conditioned by a heritage of colonial expansion, and trade relationships started in colonial times were often followed by the establishment of foreign manufacturing. Still, almost none of the large French firms set up manufacturing in the French Empire prior to the mid-1950's: trade, not investment, was the norm in colonial relationships. In 1955, one year before her independence, Tunisia received 75% of her imports from France;[19] in 1956, 49% of Morocco's imports came from the mother country; and in 1959, 78% of Algeria's foreign purchases also came from France.[20]

The first major move by French enterprises into manufacturing in the colonies came as part of the effort to ward off the threat of Algerian independence between 1959 and 1961. Although no tariffs were placed on imports into Algeria, the French government offered massive subsidies to firms willing to undertake local production.[21] Subsidies were also available to non-French firms willing to manufacture in Algeria, but few had had prior business relationships with French Africa. Therefore, of the 13 subsidiaries set up in French Africa between 1959 and 1961 by large Continental enterprises, 12 were established by French parents.

During the three years following Algerian independence in 1962, French establishment of manufacturing subsidiaries in French Africa dropped to nearly nothing. Afterwards, the rate of establishment rose markedly, but many of the new subsidiaries were not set up by French companies. In 1971 French parent enterprises owned about half of the 127 manufacturing ventures

[17] UN 1973: pp 8 and 9.
[18] This conclusion has been supported by several other surveys of investments in LDC's by firms based in Continental countries. On Swedish firms, see Swedenborg, 1973: p 58. On Swiss Latin American activity, see Nobel, 1973: p 123. For German companies, see Jacobi, 1972: p 39.
[19] Nehrt, 1970: p 41.
[20] Nehrt, 1970: pp 244 and 129.
[21] Nehrt, 1970: p 126.

located in French Africa by all the large Continental, British, American, and Japanese enterprises in the Comparative Multinational Enterprise Project.[22] The increase in manufacturing activity by non-French enterprises in French Africa during the 1960's took place at a time when newly independent governments were deliberately attempting to diversify their trade and investment relationships away from France.[23] A few French enterprises may have become disenchanted with the former French colonies after five of their manufacturing subsidiaries were expropriated in Algeria (although not elsewhere) between 1962 and 1968.[24] But French enterprises were also moved to trade, and then manufacture in less developed areas with which they had no colonial ties. Only 15% of their manufacturing subsidiaries in 1971 were in former colonies.[25]

The contrast between the behavior of the large French and British enterprises is striking. The 47 largest British firms had two-thirds of their foreign manufacturing subsidiaries in former colonies or dominions.[26] Two-thirds of those colonial or commonwealth ventures in turn (or some 40% of total British foreign manufacturing) were located in less developed ex-colonies of British Africa, the Middle East, and Asia.[27]

Parent firms based in other Continental countries which had once owned colonies had but a negligible fraction of their foreign manufacturing operations in former foreign possessions. Less than one percent of the foreign manufacturing subsidiaries of large Belgian firms were located in the Congo as of 1971; fewer than four percent were located in Black Africa as a whole. Less than one percent of large Dutch firms' foreign manufacturing activity in 1971 took place in Indonesia.[28] Indeed, as many subsidiaries of British as of Belgian enterprises were to be found in the former Belgian Congo, and Dutch activity in Indonesia was dwarfed by Japanese enterprises by a margin exceeding ten to one.

Part of the explanation for the limited involvement of Dutch and Belgian enterprises in manufacturing in former colonies in the 1970's lies in the relatively loose trading relations Dutch and Belgian overseas territories had had with mother countries. For example, even before Indonesia became independent during World War II, its trade with Holland had been modest. Between the World Wars, less than 20% of Indonesia's imports had come from Holland.[29] Such ties were of a different order than those which regularly led French colonies to obtain more than half their imports from France, or British colonies and dominions to obtain between one-third and one-half of their imports from Britain.[30]

The limited foreign manufacturing activity of Dutch and Belgian enterprises

---

[22] Comparative Multinational Enterprise Project.
[23] Nehrt, 1970: p 137; Brandell, 1974.
[24] Comparative Multinational Enterprise Project. On post-independence nationalizations in Algeria, see also, Nehrt, 1970: pp 188–192.
[25] Comparative Multinational Enterprise Project.
[26] See Chapter IV.
[27] Comparative Multinational Enterprise Project; see also, Stopford, 1974.
[28] Comparative Multinational Enterprise Project.
[29] Van der Wal, in Bromley and Kossman, 1968: p 202; Baudet, in Bromley and Kossman, 1968: p 210.
[30] Fontaine, 1926: p 86; Nehrt, 1970; Lewis, 1949: p 83.

in former colonies was not a consequence of confiscation and nationalization. Newly independent countries had rarely expropriated manufacturing operations. None of the half-dozen manufacturing subsidiaries in former Belgian Africa of large Belgian firms suffered such a fate up to 1971, and, of the 30 subsidiaries established by Continental enterprises in Indonesia, two had been sold, two confiscated, and 26 carried on regardless of changes in regimes.[31]

French, Belgian and Dutch colonial attachments thus had only a minor influence on the pattern of Continental firms' foreign manufacturing activity in the LDC's. It would nevertheless be wrong to infer that colonial expansion had had *no* impact on the spread of Continental firms in the less developed world. British colonial expansion strongly conditioned Continental choices. Not until 1959 did one find the slightest trace of manufacturing activity by large Continental enterprise in the British Middle East or in British Africa – except for 14 post-war subsidiaries established in South Africa. With the exception of a handful of subsidiaries in Australia and India (owned by partly-British Shell and the British affiliates of Swedish Match and Switzerland's Ciba), there were no Continental manufacturing operations in British Asia or Oceania until the late 1950's either. Meanwhile, between 1930 and 1958 the 47 largest British enterprises had established or acquired more than 200 manufacturing operations in these parts of the Empire.

British colonial trade and tariff preferences had obliged Continental firms to compete in the more open market of the Third World, notably those of Latin America, and less developed Europe.[32] Continental opportunities for trade with the Empire had been limited by the workings of the Colonial Office, many of whose purchasing agents had been seconded to colonial service by British enterprises. More formal barriers to Continental trade with the Empire were added when the Imperial Preference system of tariffs came into being in 1932. The development of the Sterling Area completed the protection of Empire markets from Continental exports between the 1930's and the 1950's. Colonial and Dominion members of the Sterling Area deposited their non-Sterling earnings with the Bank of England, and the Bank of England then re-allocated such non-Sterling currencies according to its own lights. Unsurprisingly, imports into the Sterling Area from the Continent were discouraged whenever remotely similar goods were available from member countries.[33] The upshot of these protective measures was that close to half of the imports of the Empire countries regularly came from Great Britain alone prior to the Second World War, and the bulk of the remainder came from Empire cousins.[34] Canada was the exception to the rule: there one saw occasional Continental trade precede Continental manufacturing investment, but Canada was the only important Empire country which was not a member of the Sterling Area.

Only where trade could first occur did Continental investment follow. In the more open LDC markets, however, Continental sales were important only when Continental goods and technologies met LDC economic and political

[31] Comparative Multinational Enterprise Project.
[32] Stopford, 1974; Bornschier, 1973: pp 28 and 29.
[33] Fitch and Oppenheimer, 1966: pp 42–47; Balogh, 1966: Chapter 2; Robertson, 1954: p. 39.
[34] Lewis, 1949: p 83.

demands at least as well as goods and technologies of American and Japanese competitors. Continental sales to the LDC's, and the investments that followed them, were therefore concentrated in particular product lines in which Continental firms had developed strong oligopolistic advantages.

European Products in the Less Developed Countries

The Continental goods which competed best in the open LDC markets were the products or product varieties originally innovated in Europe for low-income customer groups. Pharmaceuticals, small automobiles and trucks, and basic electric lighting apparatus had all first met substantial demand in low-income mass markets on the Continent. It is only in these product groups (along with the relatively unimportant one of rubber footwear and belting) that Continental enterprises had a majority of their foreign manufacturing subsidiaries in individual industries located in less developed countries in 1971. In all other industries, Continental enterprises had located a majority of their foreign production outposts in developed countries, that is, in countries with 1970 Gross National Products *per capita* exceeding US $1,200.[35] Over one-third of all the 766 manufacturing subsidiaries of Continental enterprises in less developed countries were producing pharmaceuticals, motor vehicles, electric lighting and wiring equipment, and non-tire rubber goods.

The association of Continental activity in the LDC's with a few specific product groups is in marked contrast to the pattern of activity of American, British, and Japanese enterprises. The latter have been deeply involved in production in the LDC's on a much broader product front. The extreme case is that of large Japanese enterprises. A majority of Japanese foreign manufacturing took place in LDC's in all industries in which Japanese enterprises were active abroad. More than 90% of all the foreign manufacturing subsidiaries of the 67 largest Japanese firms were located in the less developed world.

American multinational companies had a majority of their foreign operations in LDC's in ten industries. The foreign manufacturing activity of US enterprise was oriented primarily toward LDC's in grain-mill products, bakery products, tobacco, paper, pharmaceuticals, agricultural chemicals, tires, other rubber products, metal cans, and farm machinery. Continental European and American firms had a similar predilection for manufacturing in the Third World only in pharmaceuticals and non-tire rubber products. Due to their privileged position in former Empire markets, British firms had a majority of their foreign manufacturing subsidiaries located in the LDC's in no less than 47 out of 54 industry groups.

The story of foreign manufacturing by Continental European enterprise in less developed regions has thus been linked to a few oligopoly advantages in distinctive products and product varieties, rather than to special relationships with colonial or semi-colonial preferential markets. The presence of German immigrants in Brazil perhaps facilitated Volkswagen's entry into that market, but it was the Beetle's appeal to Brazil's emerging mass market which made

---

[35] Enterprises in the Comparative Multinational Enterprise Project Survey had foreign manufacturing activities in 54 different 3-digit US Standard Industrial Classification industries.

it the largest selling auto in the country.[36] Similarly, more than Latin cultural links led to Fiat's 25% market share in Argentina.[37]

The role of advantages in products and product varieties in the spread of Continental manufacturing to the LDC's considerably outweighed the role played by product advantages in enabling foreign manufacturing to be undertaken in developed nations. Distinctive processes or synthetics had often enabled Continental firms to jump trade barriers in developed countries, especially in the chemical industry. The same Continental firms often produced both chemicals and pharmaceuticals, for example. Yet, while Hoechst, Bayer, Ciba-Geigy, Sandoz, and Rhône-Poulenc all produced chemicals and pharmaceuticals, the LDC manufacturing operations of each were more numerous (and usually considerably so) in pharmaceutical-product specialities than in synthetics or chemical material-substitutes.[38]

A number of older European processes which used a relatively large amount of labor found their way to the developing countries.[39] Nevertheless, few European firms systematically followed the Japanese penchant for undertaking production in LDC's on the basis of oligopoly advantages based on long experience in labor-intensive technologies.[40] Had oligopoly advantages in labor-intensive production processes been of much import in the manufacturing operations undertaken by Continental companies in the LDC's, Continental firms would have located a disproportionate number of their producing subsidiaries in countries even less developed on the average than those in which American multinationals were prominent. Continental wage rates had long been lower, and Continental processes more labor intensive, than American. A Japanese concentration was apparent in the least developed countries (those with less than US $200 *per capita* GNP in 1970). Yet, in only three industry categories – refined petroleum products, engines and turbines, and construction machinery – did the percentage of all European foreign manufacturing subsidiaries in the *least* developed countries exceed the percentage of all American multinationals' manufacturing operations in these least developed lands. Moreover, American companies had a greater absolute number of manufacturing subsidiaries in the least developed countries in both petroleum products and construction machinery.

Both the limited absolute amount of manufacturing activity in LDC's by Continental enterprises, and the skewed industry distribution of that activity appear in large measure to have resulted from the orientation of so much European innovative activity toward material-saving processes and synthetics. Two post-War reconstructions and British Imperial policies undoubtedly retarded Continental activity in the Third World. But even without these influences, many Continental skills were not particularly relevant to LDC economies. Uniquely European material-saving processes were unlikely to convey particular oligopolistic advantages in countries where natural resources

[36] Baker, 1971.
[37] Fox, 1972.
[38] Comparative Multinational Enterprise Project. See also, Iffland and Stettler (1973: pp 37–43) for evidence concerning Swiss enterprises' activity in Brazil.
[39] Von Bertrab, 1968: pp 35, 59 et seq.
[40] See, Tsurumi (1973: pp 83 and 84) on Japanese enterprise behavior; See, Awni-Al-Awi (1969: p 220) for evidence on German enterprises.

were abundant, or where political and military ambitions were yet too modest to nurture hopes of autarky. Old American production processes developed when US labor costs had once been lower might well have been more warranted. Whatever the cause, only one out of the 85 largest Continental firms was found to have an explicit strategy of attempting to exploit its more labor-intensive skills through manufacture in the least developed countries 'before the Americans'.

Establishment and Acquisition of LDC Manufacturing

Trade barriers were the main triggers of Continental European foreign manufacturing. The coercive power of states bent on industrial development pushed and pulled European companies to replace imports with local production, much as it had pushed and pulled American enterprises to manufacture in the LDC's.[41] Given the price-elastic nature of products such as small autos, basic electric lighting apparatus, mechanical typewriters and calculators and the like, trade barriers may well have been a more important stimulus for Continental manufacturing in developing countries than for American-owned production. Fragments of evidence suggest that this was so, much as trade barriers seemed more critical to the establishment of foreign production by Continental firms in the developed world.[42] But the Continental Europeans, too, were following an international product cycle to the LDC's, and trade barriers and protected markets may have been less important than projections of market growth to their decisions to manufacture in LDC's. Philips of Holland in 1974 described LDC tariffs and development policies as 'speeding-up' the change from selling to manufacturing; in the 1930's, Philips' operations in foreign, developed countries were described as having resulted 'only' from market protection.[43] The difference, one suspects, was more than a matter of rhetorical flourish.

Obstacles to trade nonetheless played a paramount role in provoking Continental firms to manufacture in the LDC's, particularly since World War II. Italy's Olivetti started up plants in Colombia, Mexico, and Brazil in the late 1950's to assemble and produce typewriters and calculators, initially in order to continue selling behind high tariff barriers in closed markets.[44] Swiss pharmaceutical firms responded to similar pressures in Brazil, and gradually moved from export to production operations after that country's wartime surplus of foreign exchange was exhausted in 1947. In response to ever tighter Brazilian exchange control and import restrictions, and explicit industrialization policies, plants were started up by Hoffmann La Roche, Ciba-Geigy, and Sandoz in the late 1940's and early 1950's. All followed the progression typical of foreign pharmaceutical operations, beginning with packaging and then progressing to more complicated, higher value-added stages of production.[45] Increasing barriers to imports of transformers also triggered Brown-Boveri's 1952 acquisition of a majority position in a small Brazilian company

---

[41] On American multinational enterprise in the LDC's, see, Vernon, 1971: Chapter III.
[42] Reuber, *et al*, 1973: pp 126–128. Reuber unfortunately aggregates British and Continental firms in reporting his results.
[43] Philips, 1974: p 6; Philips, 1972.
[44] Harvard Business School, 1969: pp 967 and 980.
[45] Iffland and Stettler, 1973: pp 30–43.

which had been producing small electric motors before Brown-Boveri's involvement led it to manufacture transformers. This partial acquisition was a prelude to the start-up of a larger plant in 1957.[46] Sulzer's manufacturing subsidiary in Brazil started producing compressors and refrigeration equipment in 1960, but the plans to set it up had commenced in 1954, and were directly stimulated by rapidly increasing trade and exchange controls.[47] Surveys of German and French company behavior, not only in Latin America, but elsewhere in the less developed world have also concluded that host-government measures constituted the major stimulus to LDC production during the post-war era.[48] Well into the 1970's the prevailing Continental view of LDC operations was that once expressed by the former Chairman of Volkswagen, Heinz Nordhoff, who remarked in 1964 that his company 'was not inclined to increase overseas output without being forced to do so.'[49]

Exceptional matches between LDC markets and European innovations had occurred which had nothing to do with government policies. Brazil's largest chemical enterprise had started with the attraction of Rhône-Poulenc to Brazil by the needs of carnival revellers for perfume throwers. Nestlé, too, acquired a Brazilian firm and began producing its condensed milk and mother's milk supplement in the 1920's, nearly three decades before Brazil erected significant barriers to imports.[50] But perhaps it is more than coincidence that these exceptions occurred before the LDC's began concerted efforts to industrialize.

When state pressure did trigger manufacturing decisions, it usually did so best when the carrot of protected markets was supplemented by the stick of competitive threats. For example, a survey made of 115 decisions taken to manufacture in the LDC's by 61 German parent enterprises concluded that 95% of the 115 subsidiary operations examined would probably have been undertaken by competitors in similar form.[51]

Many of the threats which provoked LDC manufacturing decisions by Continental European enterprises undoubtedly came from other foreign firms. Often these foreign competitors were other Continental firms carrying forth distinctively European low-income products. There was little mystery concerning the identity of Fiat's principal rival in Latin America, for example. In 1969, *Business Latin America* described Fiat's strategy for expansion in Argentina as aiming 'to so saturate the market that it will be henceforth impossible for Volkswagen to enter'.[52] On other occasions, the main rivals were American. Siemens and ITT alternately fought and co-operated in South American cable and telephone equipment markets.[53] And the advertising of L M Ericsson, the Swedish telephone manufacturer, rather obviously hinted

[46] Iffland and Stettler, 1973: pp 51–52. Brown-Boveri, 1966: p 233. Trade barriers also triggered start-ups of Brown-Boveri plants in Mexico and Peru (Brown-Boveri, 1966: p 236).
[47] Iffland and Stettler, 1973: pp 53–55.
[48] Jacobi, 1972: pp 52–65; Michalet and Delapierre, 1973: pp 101–102.
[49] *Die Welt*, No 104, May 5, 1964. For a similar French view, see Michalet and Delapierre, 1973: p 86.
[50] Iffland and Stettler, 1973: pp 20, 21 and 55.
[51] Jacobi, 1972: pp 55 and 56.
[52] *Business Latin America*, 1969: p 420.
[53] Siemens, 1957, Vol 2: p 60.

that Ericsson's main competitor was Siemen's old nemesis, the same ITT.[54] Whether it was Continental or American rivals who got the bandwagon rolling into LDC markets, however, Continental firms were as prone as American multinationals to jump on to it.

As in the developed world, rivalry did not always lead to the establishment of subsidiaries by all Continental competitors in each market. Sometimes, Continental enterprises seemed to reach more or less stable understandings with other Continental firms as to which enterprise would produce in which LDC market. On other occasions, Continental firms were able to equilibrate market shares by undertaking joint ventures in LDC's with other Continental rivals. There were no antitrust barriers to hinder Hoechst and Péchiney-St-Gobain (itself a joint venture of two large French companies!) from each taking a 20% interest in a three-way joint venture with local partners in a Mexican polyvinyl chloride plastics plant, or to hinder Volkswagen and Daimler Benz from having joint assembly subsidiaries in Indonesia and Spain.[55] Continental enterprises were much more prone to enter *en famille* joint ventures with foreign rivals than were American enterprises, in both less developed and developed countries, as Table 5.3 shows. But *en famille* joint

Table 5.3 Principal Partners in Foreign Manufacturing Joint Ventures of Large Enterprises Based in Various Parent Countries, January 1, 1971 (US data as of January 1, 1968)

National base of parent enterprise	Principal Partners: Local private	Local state	Foreign private	Widely dispersed	Total %	Total numbers of joint venture subsidiaries where partners known
In All Countries:						
United States	58%	1%	14%	26%	100%	930
United Kingdom	56	8	27	9	100	498
Japan	62	9	28	1	100	362
France	37	20	37	6	100	81
Germany	70	8	19	3	100	187
Italy	50	27	20	3	100	30
Bel & Lux	42	3	39	15	100	33
Netherlands	58	7	22	13	100	91
Sweden	51	20	20	9	100	35
Switzerland	72	4	21	4	100	53
In Less Developed Countries*:						
France	23	35	38	5	100	40
Germany	64	13	17	6	100	98
Italy	50	32	18	5	100	22
Bel & Lux	17	8	50	25	100	12
Netherlands	76	8	11	5	100	37
Sweden	45	30	15	10	100	20
Switzerland	71	6	18	6	100	17

Note: *1970 *per capita* GNP under US $1,200.
Source: Comparative Multinational Enterprise Project.

[54] *Vision*, 1972: p 126.
[55] *Business Latin America*, 1970: p 22; Holthus, 1974: p 95.

ventures were not noticeably more frequent in the LDC operations of Continental companies than they were in subsidiaries in developed nations. And *en famille* joint ventures constituted only a small fraction (10 to 20%) of all Continental subsidiaries in the LDC's.

Although the legal ability of Continental enterprises to reduce competitive uncertainty by sharing markets exceeded that of the American multinationals, there was little evidence that Continental enterprises were often able to significantly to reduce rivalry among international firms within LDC's in the absence of local government support for co-operation and cartels. The great majority of the partly owned manufacturing subsidiaries of Continental firms in the LDC's were joint ventures with local, not foreign partners as Table 5.3 shows. In Latin America, at least, when one Continental enterprise embarked on foreign manufacturing in a given country, other Continental firms were not far behind. Both Renault and Volkswagen, for example, agreed to make a low-price 'people's car' in Venezuela, even although the decision was followed by much grumbling about elusive profits.[56] When one firm embarked on auto or truck assembly in Argentina, all, or nearly all the rest followed – not that the proliferation of small, high-cost plants in one market pleased local governments more than might have anti-competitive market sharing.[57] Indeed, when Continental behavior in responding to competitive threat differed somewhat from that of the American, the result was often pleasing to local governments. Having allowed oligopolistic imitation by vehicle producers to lead to numerous tiny assembly plants during the 1960's, Peru then decided that its national interests would be better served by a rationalized industry in which a (hopefully) lower-cost monopoly would replace the high-cost plants which had resulted from oligopoly rivalry. Perhaps it was an accident, but a Swedish, not an American, firm was chosen to have the monopoly on truck assembly in that country.[58]

When Continental enterprises responded to protected markets and competitive threat by deciding to manufacture in less developed countries, they typically set up new production facilities rather than acquiring all or part of the shares of local enterprises. This propensity of Continental firms to start up a majority of their LDC manufacturing operations from the ground up contrasted with their behavior in developed countries: in the latter (as Table 5.4 shows), Continental firms had acquired a majority of their subsidiaries, either directly or through the acquisition of enterprises which in turn had foreign subsidiaries.

The predilection of Continental enterprises for starting up, rather than acquiring LDC operations might seem only natural, given the existence of fewer companies which might be acquired in less industrialized regions. It takes on added significance, however, in the light of the fear often expressed in the Third World, and especially in Latin America, that foreign firms were

---

[56] *Business Latin America*, 'Renault and VW Find Profits Elusive in Venezuelan Economy Car Program', November 30, 1972: p 379.

[57] Agnelli, 1973.

[58] *Business Latin America*, 'Volvo Wins Exclusive Truck Assembly Right in Peru', December 17, 1970: p 406.

pursuing strategies of aggressive acquisition of local companies in order to suppress potential local competitors.[59]

In Latin America, however, the LDC region where the denationalization of local industry through foreign acquisition was most dreaded, only a limited number of acquisitions by Continental enterprises had taken place. Perhaps Continental firms found that protected markets gave profits which were sufficiently high to make the aggressive suppression of potential local competitors superfluous. Perhaps the oligopolistic advantages of Continental firms (in, say, small motor vehicles) were so strong as to preclude the possibility of local competitors. Or perhaps Continental habits of negotiating market shares in countries lacking antitrust traditions made it unnecessary for them to indulge in implacably aggressive behavior.

Table 5.4 Percentage of Foreign Manufacturing Subsidiaries Formed or Acquired by Large American and Continental European Enterprises (US data from 1900 through January 1, 1968, all other through January 1, 1971)

| National base of parent enterprise | Method of Establishment: | | | | |
	Newly formed	Acquired directly	Through acquisition of another parent, or reorganization	Total %	Total number established
Subsidiaries in All Areas of the World:					
United States	49 %	— % 51 %	— %	100 %	4,512
France	51	21	28	100	297
Germany	40	26	34	100	937
Italy	72	21	7	100	102
Bel & Lux	40	32	28	100	255
Netherlands	40	24	36	100	413
Sweden	39	46	15	100	195
Switzerland	39	37	24	100	411
Subsidiaries in Latin America:					
United States	57 %	— % 43 %	— %	100	1,178
France	51	11	38	100	53
Germany	61	25	14	100	126
Italy	82	18	0	100	39
Bel & Lux	20	80	0	100	10
Netherlands	74	6	20	100	34
Sweden	57	35	8	100	23
Switzerland	67	17	16	100	36

Source: Comparative Multinational Enterprise Project.

The data presented in Table 5.4 contrast the propensities of Continental and American companies to acquire and form subsidiaries in Latin America with their acquisition propensities worldwide. These data, one notes, refer to behavior antedating the formal restrictions on acquisitions which Latin American nations, such as the members of the Andean Common Market,

[59] Vaitsos, 1973; Hymer, 1970.

Mexico, and Argentina, have enacted since the beginning of 1971.[60] The data shown in Table 5.4 are limited by insufficient information concerning subsidiaries which entered multinational systems through the acquisition by parent firms of other parent firms, or through legal reorganizations: such indirectly acquired subsidiaries may or may not have been started up when manufacturing was first commenced. In the light of host-country concerns, what matters is the comparison between start-ups and direct acquisitions. The unfortunate mixing of direct and indirect acquisitions in the available data concerning American multinational enterprises allows only guesswork about American behavior. We know, however, that Continental enterprises established 321 Latin American subsidiaries, of which 200 were formed and 69 were acquired directly. Whether or not the 200:69, or nearly four-to-one ratio of formation to acquisition held for the indirectly acquired subsidiaries is not known. But the magnitude of this ratio, combined with the fact that only a handful of Continental enterprises obtained more than half of their Latin American (or other LDC) subsidiaries by acquisition, suggests little predatory, denationalizing behavior on their part. Moreover, over half of the acquisitions of Continental firms in Latin America were partial acquisitions of joint venture positions in local enterprises (although nearly half of the local partners were subsequently bought out by the European parent). Many of the partially acquired firms had been distributors of products of Continental enterprises which had been imported prior to the commencement of local production; others had invited the European partner to invest capital and know-how to better compete with other, often American, multinational enterprises.[61] Full 100% acquisitions were few and far between.

Patterns of Subsidiary Ownership

While the initial stimuli to Continental and American decisions to manufacture in the LDC's may have had much in common, patterns of subsequent operating behavior have often diverged. The greater Continental use of *en famille* joint ventures with competitors was one area of divergent practice; the greater Continental use of joint ventures with local partners was another.

It has often been asserted that multinational enterprises have a marked preference for 100% ownership of their foreign manufacturing subsidiaries. *American* multinationals clearly had a preference for 100% ownership of subsidiaries, even although the extent of that preference was often exaggerated.[62] About three-fifths of American firms' foreign manufacturing subsidiaries were wholly owned in 1968, both in developed and less developed countries. This American preference can be seen from Table 5.5. British firms, as one also sees from Table 5.5, had a similar preference for 100% ownership of foreign manufacturing operations.

In the case of Continental enterprises, however, 100% ownership has been more the exception than the rule, especially in the LDC's. Table 5.5 shows the

[60] Andean Common Market, 1970.
[61] *Business Latin America*, 'Agfa-Gevaert Links with Argentine Firm to Gain Larger Market, Lend Know-How', 1972, p 128.
[62] Franko, 1974 (A): Stopford and Wells, 1972.

Table 5.5 Percentage of Foreign Manufacturing Subsidiaries of Large Enterprises Based in Various Parent Countries which were Wholly Owned or Joint Ventures, January 1, 1971 (US data as of January 1, 1968)

National base of parent enterprise	Ownership Position:				
	Wholly owned subsidiaries*	Majority-owned joint ventures**	Minority & 50–50 joint ventures***	Total %	Total number of subsidiaries known
In All Countries:					
United States	63 %	15 %	22 %	100 %	3,720
United Kingdom	61	19	20	100	2,236
Japan	9	9	82	100	445
France	24	29	47	100	333
Germany	42	28	30	100	753
Italy	42	24	35	100	106
Bel & Lux	37	34	29	100	184
Netherlands	61	18	20	100	401
Sweden	64	17	19	100	155
Switzerland	59	29	19	100	292
In Less Developed Countries†:					
United States	57 %	19 %	24 %	100 %	1,583
France	11	37	52	100	157
Germany	44	31	25	100	323
Italy	33	25	45	100	67
Bel & Lux	21	51	28	100	39
Netherlands	33	28	39	100	82
Sweden	39	32	29	100	44
Switzerland	54	33	26	100	84

Notes: *Owned 95 % or more by a foreign parent.
      **Owned more than 50 %, but less than 95 % by a foreign parent.
     ***Owned more than 5 % but less than 50·01 % by a foreign parent.
      †1970 *per capita* GNP under US $1,200.

Source: Comparative Multinational Enterprise Project.

Continental penchant for joint ventures in less developed countries. Enterprises based in Switzerland were the only group of Continental firms to have a preference comparable to that of American firms for wholly owned operations in less developed countries. Moreover, between 80% and 90% of the joint ventures of Continental firms in the LDC's were with local private or state partners – despite the propensity of French and Belgian firms to undertake joint ventures with foreign partners, as shown by Table 5.3.

The Continental practice of including partners in LDC operations was one of long standing. Even before World War II, 60% or more of the Continental manufacturing subisidiaries in less developed countries were jointly owned. Moreover, there was no particular trend toward increased use of joint ventures by Continental enterprises such as that observable in the case of American multinationals during the post-war era.[63]

---

[63] Stopford and Wells, 1972: p 144.

After the set-up or acquisition of joint ventures, Continental firms did some-times buy out their joint-venture partners. The phenomenon of joint-venture instability which occurred during the multinational spread of American enterprise existed for Continental multinationals, too.[64] Partners had been bought out by Continental firms in 25 (or about 8%) of the subsidiaries in LDC's known to have been joint ventures. Continental firms had also increased their ownership shares from minority to majority positions in about the same number of joint ventures. Most of these ownership changes took place in subsidiaries in which initial Continental positions had been acquired. But few of these changes were associated with the wholesale simultaneous buy-outs of numerous foreign joint venture partners sometimes undertaken by American enterprises. Furthermore, not only were increases in ownership in joint ven-tures by Continental firms apparently less frequent than by American enter-prises, but a number of Continental joint ventures had undergone a kind of ownership change almost unknown in American multinational enterprise history: a decrease in shareholdings from majority to minority occurred in 21 subsidiaries.

The relative Continental preference for joint-venture operations can be traced to many causes. Indeed, it can be traced to so many that it would be artificial to say that one or another predominated.

Continental enterprises, at least those outside the chemical and pharma-ceutical industry, were smaller than American firms in similar industries. Thus they had proportionately less access to capital and human resources, and therefore more use than American companies for such contributions from joint-venture partners. Continental enterprises were also latecomers to LDC production, relative to American firms. Thus, attempts to match American global or regional positions quickly might also have led Continental firms to accept joint-venture positions. Still, being relatively small and relatively late could have only partly accounted for Continental choices of joint ventures. In motor vehicles and parts, the choice of joint ventures followed the national preferences of enterprises based in different parent nations. As Table 5.6 shows, the large, highly multinational American firms had a greater preference for wholly owned operations than did the smaller, less widely spread German, French, and Italian companies. But the even smaller Swedish firms, which had the fewest foreign manufacturing subsidiaries, had the greatest propensity of all to have 100%-owned operations in the LDC's! Size and scope of inter-national production experience were less persuasive in explaining ownership preferences in LDC's in pharmaceuticals and office machinery. As Table 5.6 indicates, American pharmaceuticals enterprises had a greater preference for 100% ownership than did Swiss and German firms, even though the Swiss and German firms producing drugs tended to be larger than their American counterparts. And the relatively small European office-machinery companies had the same overwhelming preference for 100% ownership in LDC's and elsewhere as did American enterprises.

The fact that Continental firms tended to have more diversified product lines than US enterprises helped to account for the greater Continental preference

---

[64] On joint-venture instability in American multinational enterprise systems, see, Franko, 1971 (B).

Table 5.6 Percentage of Foreign Subsidiaries of Large Enterprises Based in Various Parent Countries Manufacturing Pharmaceuticals and Motor Vehicles and Located in Less Developed Countries which were Wholly Owned or Joint Ventures on January 1, 1971

National base of parent enterprise	Ownership Position:				
	Wholly owned subsidiaries*	Majority-owned joint ventures**	Minority & 50–50 joint ventures***	Total %	Total number of subsidiaries known
Pharmaceuticals Subsidiaries:					
United States	72 %	26 %	2 %	100 %	162
France	0	50	50	100	4
Germany	41	41	18	100	32
Switzerland	57	40	3	100	30
Motor Vehicles and Parts Subsidiaries:					
United States	43 %	30 %	27 %	100 %	96
France	16	20	64	100	25
Germany	33	19	57	100	21
Italy	36	18	55	100	11
Sweden	75	—	25	100	4

NB Only joint ventures known to have been with local partners are included in these tabulations.

Notes: *Owned 95 % or more by a foreign parent.
**Owned more than 50 %, but less than 95 % by a foreign parent.
***Owned more than 5 % but less than 50·01 % by a foreign parent.

Sources: Data for subsidiaries of French, German, Swiss, Italian, and Swedish enterprises: Comparative Multinational Enterprise Project.
Data for subsidiaries of American enterprises from Curhan, 1969: pp 461 and 489.

for joint ventures. Few Continental firms had the commitment to one product line characteristic of quite a number of American enterprises, as was seen in Chapter I. Rather, most Continental firms had a commitment to a core of technology which they exploited across numerous products. Since one product line was rarely criticial to the survival of Continental enterprises, as it often was to American firms, the looser control – and lesser commitment – of joint ventures was adequate. Thus, like diversified American firms, diversified Continental companies had few allergies to joint ventures.[65]

Still another characteristic of Continental enterprises which facilitated their acceptance of joint-venture partners was the rarity of Continental operations in consumer products like processed foods, cosmetics, and soaps – products which all lent themselves to advertising and marketing-intensive sales strategies. The fear of conflicts of interest with joint-venture partners over marketing budgets and programs had often been a major force leading American firms specializing in consumer goods to avoid joint ventures.[66]

---

[65] On the relationship of strategies of product diversification to the use of joint ventures, see, Franko, 1971: especially Chapter III; Stopford and Wells, 1972.
[66] Franko, 1971: Chapter II; Stopford and Wells, 1972.

While many factors leading Continental firms to utilize joint ventures resembled the forces pushing many an American company to do likewise, some were undoubtedly the result of Continental conditioning at home. Behavior at home (of a sort unthinkable for American enterprises subject to US antitrust laws) was often reflected in behavior abroad. The French proclivity for international joint venturing was long preceded by a quite remarkable tendency of French firms to undertake joint ventures at home. A description of the French chemical industry written in 1969 remarked, for example, that 'all major companies were in joint ventures to the point where the concept of the firm as a managerial entity had lost much of its meaning'.[67] Belgian and German enterprise interconnections at home were sometimes almost as labyrinthine.[68] The pronounced acceptance of host-government agencies as partners by French, Italian, and Swedish enterprises also seemed traceable to the habits of co-operating with home-country governments developed over the years by firms of these nationalities.[69] The extent to which local governments participated in joint ventures of Continental companies based in France, Italy and Sweden is visible from Table 5.3. Forty-five of 55 joint ventures between Continental firms and state entities were located in the LDC's.

Curiously enough, while Continental experience at home conditioned Continental ownership choices abroad, there was little evidence that such choices were much affected by host-country policies favoring or disfavoring 100% ownership of subsidiaries. Had host countries introduced explicit joint-venture policies primarily for their effect on American enterprises? American managers had been conditioned by a home environment in which any action was permitted which was not strictly forbidden by an impersonal law affecting all enterprises. Were American enterprises therefore unresponsive to administrative suggestion and suasion emanating from host-country governments? And did host-country governments then find themselves forced to adopt American-style legal regulations? Or had Continental subsidiaries been too few in number for host governments to concern themselves with Continental ownership practices? Whatever the cause, Table 5.7 shows that although there was some American response to pro-joint-venture policies by Mexico, Spain and the French African countries, those policies did not seem to alter German or Swiss ownership preferences. Moreover, French companies stubbornly seemed to prefer joint ventures even in countries such as Brazil and Argentina where they had a choice of 100% ownership.

Thus, while host-countries stimulated Continental decisions to undertake local production, the past experience, strategies, and home-market conditioning of the firms themselves largely determined Continental ownership choices. The European experience and strategies of Continental enterprises also strongly influenced another dimension of Continental operating behavior in the LDC's: except in a very few cases, production was oriented to local, not export markets.

---

[67] Scott and MacArthur, 1969: p 204.
[68] Storms, 1972; Der Spiegel, January 31, 1972: p 42.
[69] Scott and MacArthur, 1969; Vernon, 1971: Chapter 6; Prodi, 1974; Hedlund and Otterbeck, 1974; Huntsford, 1971.

Table 5.7 Proportion of Wholly Owned* Foreign Manufacturing Subsidiaries of Enterprises Based in Various Parent Nations in Selected Less Developed Countries, January 1, 1971 (US data January 1, 1968)

Country of Subsidiary Location:

National base of parent enterprise	Mexico % Wholly owned	Mexico Total number of subs	Argentina % Wholly owned	Argentina Total number of subs	Brazil % Wholly owned	Brazil Total number of subs	Spain % Wholly owned	Spain Total number of subs	French Africa % Wholly owned	French Africa Total number of subs
United States	55%	249	69%	121	75%	151	32%	116	50%	22
France	0	5	13	15	17	18	0	35	13	45
Germany	42	26	46	28	57	44	86	15	na	5
Switzerland	60	5	88	8	44	9	46	13	0	0

Note: *Owned 95% or more by a foreign parent.
Source: Comparative Multinational Enterprise Project.

Exports by Subsidiaries

How few Continental manufacturing subsidiaries in the LDC's were exporting more than half of their production is shown by Table 5.8. Roughly 97% of the subsidiaries of Continental enterprises in LDC's were mainly producing for local markets.

Table 5.8 Foreign Manufacturing Subsidiaries of Enterprises Based in Continental Countries, Britain, and Japan, Classified by Principal Market, January 1, 1971

National base of parent enterprise	Subsidiary's Principal Market:				
	Local market	Export Markets:			Total known
		Developed-country subs	Subs in LDC's	Total	
United Kingdom	1,844	94	24	118	1,962
Japan	343	0	92	92	435
Germany	621	21	3	24	645
France	133	9	11	20	153
Italy	63	0	2	2	65
Bel & Lux	123	9	0	9	132
Netherlands	310	6	10	16	326
Sweden	108	6	0	6	114
Switzerland	211	15	3	18	229
Total, Continental European parents	1,569	66	29	95	1,664

Source: Comparative Multinational Enterprise Project.

The orientation of subsidiary output to local markets facilitated the Continental use of joint ventures with local partners. Had Continental firms tried to use their LDC joint ventures as platforms for significant exports, they would have risked the same conflicts with partners experienced by American enterprises in export-oriented joint ventures. Conflicts could have arisen over production schedules dictated by export, not home markets; over the transfer prices applied to products shipped to other Continental subsidiaries abroad; or over the markets to which exports might be directed.[70] Fearing such conflicts, Continental firms either owned 100% of their few LDC subsidiaries oriented to export markets, or had partners in such export-oriented subsidiaries which (with two local exceptions) were other foreign enterprises.[71]

---

[70] On the relationship of subsidiary ownership and exports in American multinational enterprise systems, see: Stopford and Wells, 1972: pp 165 and 166; Vernon, 1972: pp 421–430.

[71] Ownership shares and partners' identities were known for 18 of the 29 export-oriented subsidiaries in LDC's owned by Continental enterprises. Eight of these subsidiaries were wholly owned, eight were *en famille* joint ventures with foreign, international firms; only two were joint ventures with local partners. Continental firms thus avoided joint ventures with local partners in export operations – as did American (and apparently Japanese) enterprises. For comparative data, see: Reuber, 1973: p 84.

It was puzzling, however, that in 1971 there were so few Continental subsidiaries in LDC's – wholly owned or otherwise – whose mission was primarily
to export on to third countries or back to home markets. There had already
been much discussion in the European press of the need for European companies to cease importing foreign workers and instead, 'to put the plants
where the labor is'.[72] One might have expected European enterprises to have
been in the forefront of moves to site export-oriented plants in LDC's with
low labor costs. One might have particularly expected such behavior from
enterprises based in Switzerland, Sweden and Germany, countries with
voracious appetites for foreign workers, and where social irritations resulting
from labor imports were increasingly serious. Some of the foreign laborers
had migrated from Southern Italy, a less developed part of developed Europe;
but many foreign workers in Northern Europe had emigrated from LDC's
such as Spain, Turkey, Greece and Portugal, and France was host to large
numbers of workers from former French Africa. Few export-oriented plants
were sited in these labor-surplus countries, however. Continental firms were
inhibited from undertaking much international sourcing by behavioral
reflexes conditioned in more autarkic times, and by management structures
adequate for tariff factories, but not for global strategies.[73]

Large Continental industrial firms hardly participated in the vigorous move of
American and Japanese firms into 'offshore' production which occurred during
the last half of the 1960's and the early 1970's.[74] Large Continental enterprises
undertook production in less developed regions primarily to secure shares of
local markets, not to minimize labor costs.[75] Smaller Continental firms, not
large enough to be found among the largest 85, may have participated in
the move toward offshore production. A number of relatively small Swedish
textile firms, for example, established manufacturing subsidiaries in less
developed Europe and Africa during the 1960's, most of whose output was
exported, largely to Sweden.[76] Export subsidiaries of small German and French
clothing, textile and tableware companies were to be found in countries such
as Tunisia and Portugal.[77] But Table 5.8 shows that in the LDC's at least, large
Continental firms had only one-third the number of export subsidiaries of
Japanese enterprises. Moreover, large enterprises based in Sweden, Switzerland, and Germany were among the least (not the most) likely to have 'off-
shore-production' subsidiaries. Large French enterprises had established nine
export subsidiaries in former French Africa: six of these, however, had been
established in the late 1950's or early 1960's before the respective host
countries had become independent. Only two of large Continental enterprises'
export-oriented subsidiaries were located in the less developed European
countries from which Europe was drawing its foreign labor supply as of 1971.
Only three Continental export-oriented subsidiaries were located in the
South-East Asian countries so favored by Japanese and American firms as
offshore production sites.

---

[72] *Vision*, 1971.
[73] See also, Chapter VIII on the organizational structures of Continental European enterprise.
[74] On American offshore production see, Adam, 1971; Adam, 1972.
[75] For additional evidence see, Awni-Al-Ani, 1969: p 220; Jacobi, 1972: p 160; Michalet and
Delapierre, 1973.
[76] Swedenborg, 1973: pp 66, 68 and 152.
[77] Author's personal observations.

Developed Europe, of course, has its own less developed regions, notably in Italy. One might have expected Continental European firms to establish or acquire a significant number of export-oriented operations in Italy, perhaps as a prelude to offshore production elsewhere. No such phenomenon took place, however: of the 77 subsidiaries of Continental firms in Italy, for which data is available, only five exported more than 50% of their sales volume.

Data for large American-based companies comparable to those presented in Table 5.8 are unfortunately not available. Nevertheless, various studies have shown that the export orientation of American subsidiaries in the LDC's had become considerable by the late 1960's.[78] And certain studies indicate that in a number of industries, the use of export-oriented subsidiaries by American companies was greater than that of European firms by some very large order of magnitude. A 1971 survey of offshore production for export by South-East Asian, Mexican and Caribbean subsidiaries of international firms in the electronic components industry, found over 30 subsidiaries of American firms and only three, much smaller, manufacturing subsidiaries of European companies in these areas.[79] The survey noted that 'every established US semi-conductor firm appears to be engaged in some offshore assembly without exception'. While the majority of the American-owned factories were exporting more than 50% of their production, not one of the three European factories existing in the South-East Asian area was export oriented. Although large Continental European enterprises had some 44 foreign subsidiaries producing electronic components, only one of those subsidiaries exported more than 50% of its production – and that one was in a developed European country. In addition, it was owned by a company for which electrical products were something of a sideline.

Although few of the subsidiaries of Continental enterprises in the LDC's were export oriented, some Continental subsidiaries did, of course, do some exporting. There were also fragmentary indications in the early 1970's that the proportion of LDC subsidiaries' output for export was increasing. A census of all 107 Swedish firms with foreign manufacturing operations reported that 2% of their Latin American and Asian subsidiaries' output was exported in 1970, but individual subsidiaries were sometimes exporting much more than such low averages might suggest.[80] Germany's Siemens had a subsidiary in Greece which was exporting 40% of its telephone, relay and switch production in 1970. Siemens had also begun to build a plant in Mexico which was to produce telex apparatus for the whole of the Latin American region.[81] The foreign subsidiaries of Bosch, the German auto-electric and appliance company, exported over 10% of their production, and by mid-1973, Bosch was opening up a 100%-owned plant in Malaysia whose principal purpose was the exporting of cameras and film projectors to Asian markets.[82] Volkswagen was using

---

[78] Vernon, 1971: pp 102–104 and sources cited therein; Helleiner, 1972: p 30.
[79] Chang, 1971: pp 17–20; Adam, 1971: p 353. The parents of the three European-owned subsidiaries in Chang's sample were also among the 85 largest Continental European industrial enterprises.
[80] Swedenborg, 1973: p 66.
[81] Jacobi, 1972: p 159.
[82] Holthus, 1974: pp 73 and 74.

Mexico as a base for worldwide exports of its 'safari' wagon. Under Brazilian-government urging, VW also agreed to increase the exports of its Brazilian operations from $13 million in 1971 to $400 million in 1980.[83] French companies such as state-owned Renault were reported to be making increasing use of LDC sourcing in their operations, although it was difficult to come by estimates of the quantities of goods involved.[84] Agfa-Gevaert, the Belgian-German photo-products firm, was reported to be planning its first low-wage sourcing venture in Portugal in December 1973.[85] Cross-border integration and worldwide sourcing were reported to be increasing within subsidiary networks in LDC's such as those owned by Philips of Holland and Olivetti of Italy.[86]

This swelling list of examples, nevertheless, did not dissipate the impression that most of the international firms of Continental Europe had hesitated to take advantage of the export opportunities offered by LDC's. And the reluctance of Continental enterprises to use LDC subsidiaries as significant bases for exports was already causing a few political and commercial difficulties for Continental firms as the 1970's progressed.

Emerging Pressures and Trends

Two of the major pressures on international firms manufacturing in less developed countries in the mid-1970's were the simultaneously increasing demands by local governments for local ownership participation and for exports. These pressures were, moreover, strongest in Latin America, the less developed area of greatest importance to Continental European enterprise. The Andean Common Market's Decision 24, which established a rigorous policy for the treatment of foreign investment in Colombia, Bolivia, Ecuador, Chile, Peru and Venezuela was the most explicit legal instrument for achieving such host-country aims.[87] The Andean Code was accepted by the member countries of the Andean Market in July 1971. Among its many provisions were requirements for the cession of majority ownership to local partners over a number of years and prohibitions on contracts restricting subsidiaries from export markets. The Andean measures were a precedent for legislation embodying similar principles in Mexico and Argentina.[88] Companies reported that even in Brazil, a country often thought of as being more 'liberal' toward foreign firms, pressures for exports and local ownership had increased markedly.[89] It is said that part of this pressure resulted from the desire of the Brazilian military government not to appear too pro-foreign compared to its small, Spanish-speaking Andean neighbors.

Outside Latin America, such forces were perhaps less manifest, but they nevertheless existed. The Andean regulations have often been spoken of as a

---

[83] Holthus, 1974: pp 97 and 98.
[84] Discussions with company officials.
[85] *Business International*, December 21, 1973: pp 404 and 405.
[86] Philips, 1974: p 11; *Business Week*, 1973: p 64; *Business Latin America*, March 23, 1972: p 89.
[87] *Junta del Acuerdo de Cartagena*, Decision No 24, 1972.
[88] Discussions with Andean Common Market and Argentinian government representatives.
[89] On changing Brazilian views of foreign investment, see: *Politika*, 'Multinacionais', Rio de Janeiro, April 14, 1974.

precedent for the emerging countries of Africa and Asia, and they clearly influenced the recommendations of the United Nations Group of Eminent Persons to Study the Role of Multinational Corporations in World Development.[90] India has required local ownership in most subsidiary operations since the mid-1950's, as has Algeria more recently.[91]

Continental European enterprises, or at least those based in France, Italy and Germany, appear to have had little trouble adapting to the pressures for local ownership coming from less developed countries. There was a possibility that the tolerance for joint ventures exhibited by some of these companies was only the temporary variety often displayed by American firms new to foreign production.[92] Nonetheless, European firms' experience in home markets that had often been negotiable seemed to make them willing to exchange any inconveniences arising from sharing ownership with local partners against the privilege of a local market monopoly. One example of acceptance of partial ownership in return for a protected market was that of the Italian company Fiat's entry into Morocco in the early 1960's. There, Fiat agreed to provide cash and technical know-how for a joint venture between the Moroccan state, Fiat and Simca (the French subsidiary of Chrysler), in the belief, if not on the specific understanding, that they would be granted a monopoly of that country's auto market.[93]

Similarly, in Central America, Nestlé traded off its ownership position for market protection in a powdered-milk venture. The Nestlé group had decided to begin operations in the Central American Common Market and approached the nations within that organization in order to obtain support. Because Nestlé desired to build facilities large enough to service the entire region, and was doubtful of the venture's success in the absence of protection, it sought and obtained an agreement from the members of the Common Market to severely restrict imports. Nestlé in turn agreed to a 26% share participation (and 40% board representation) in the venture.[94] A German enterprise, Mannesmann, negotiated a similar arrangement in Turkey. In 1954, the Turkish state economic-development bank opened negotiations with Mannesmann for the construction of a plant in Turkey to build steel tubing. The company agreed to a joint-venture format in order to satisfy the Turkish government's desire for a domestic source of supply. In exchange, the government banned all steel-tubing imports.[95]

European companies do appear to have been more adept at negotiating joint-venture *cum* protected-market arrangements than American firms. Some American enterprises may have acquired such negotiating skills: an American company *was* indirectly included in the Moroccan-Fiat-Simca venture. Yet, the distinctively Continental acceptance of local partners, and the even more distinctively French, Italian and Swedish acceptance of partnerships with local states suggests that some such special ability existed.

---

[90] United Nations, 1974.
[91] India made her local ownership law more stringent in 1973. See *Business Asia*, 1973: p 295. The ownership and export behavior of Sweden's SKF is also cited in this article.
[92] Franko, 1971.
[93] *Business Europe*, November 9, 1966: p 358.
[94] Friedmann and Béguin, 1971: p 131.
[95] Friedmann and Béguin, 1971: pp 201–208.

The behavior of Continental firms concerning exports from LDC's up to 1971 was somewhat less in tune with the changing aspirations of local governments, however. Urged and pressured by governments, Continental enterprises had set up many import-substituting plants in the LDC's in the 1960's. But by the 1970's developing countries, especially those in Latin America, had become disillusioned with import substitution. Government officials were beginning to be increasingly critical of European subsidiaries, because European-owned ventures were conspicuously absent from lists compiled of manufacturing firms exporting from Latin America.[96] There was a chance that Continental European companies' reluctance to export from emerging nations would augment the LDC's fear of falling victim to private restrictions on international trade, even when public restrictions were absent or unimportant. Whether or not such fears were justified, they were a source of tension in relations between some host countries and some Continental firms – even 'though these tensions seemed still to be relatively mild'.

The most pressing reason for Continental enterprises to use more of their LDC subsidiaries as bases for exports was commercial, not political, in nature, however. In the increasingly open, interdependent world economy, there were commercial penalties attached to failure to take advantage of the cost-minimization opportunities offered by offshore production in the LDC's. In the case of one product produced by several Continental enterprises, integrated circuits, those penalties were to be laid bare in a singularly dramatic way.

The integrated circuit was invented in 1957 by the British firm Plessey.[97] Texas Instruments developed a prototype in the United States in 1958. These circuits were etched on silicon chips smaller than a fingernail. Such circuits saved space, for each chip was the equivalent of five to eight transistors. The production process developed to produce them saved labor, for it eliminated the need to wire transistors together. As has so often happened, an American company brought the product to market. In 1960, Fairchild developed the planar process, said to be analagous to Henry Ford I's moving assembly line in autos, which made possible the mass production of integrated circuits. Price cuts followed apace. At first the market grew very rapidly in the United States. In 1964, US shipments equalled $100 million: in 1966, they reached $490 million. Fairchild and Texas Instruments started exporting to Europe in 1964. By 1965 Texas Instruments and the large Dutch company, Philips, were producing integrated circuits in Europe. By 1968, it was estimated that the European market was growing by 50% per year, double the US rate. In 1969 there were 15 producers of integrated circuits in Europe. Three of these were American and 12 were European. Several of the European firms produced under US license. Major expansion plans were announced by the European companies.

---

[96] See, Casas, 1973: p 21 *et seq*; Campos, 1974: p 171. Wipplinger, 1971.

[97] This discussion of the history of integrated circuits has been adapted from Franko, 1973, especially pages 65 and 66. It owes much to discussions between the author and Mr Murray Duffin, Manager, Strategic Planning, Europe, of Motorola, Inc. Sources on the recent evolution of the industry include: Tilton, 1971; Chang, 1974; *Fortune*, September 1971: p 47; and, *The Economist*, July 17, 1971.

About that time, however, conflicting claims had virtually eliminated patent protection in integrated circuits. Standardization of specifications by computer-industry customers was increasing, and integrated circuit technology was rapidly being diffused among many firms. Fairchild decided to attempt to minimize costs immediately rather than be forced to do so later. Thus, in 1966, only six years after the integrated circuit was born as a commercial product, Fairchild and others started putting the standardized, labor-intensive stage of the integrated-circuit production process into Hong Kong, Taiwan and Mexico.

In 1971, a number of events happened simultaneously. US defense spending went down, creating excess capacity in the US market. A technological innovation also occurred in the US that decreased material wastage and allowed the same number of people, using the same plant, to increase production by about 40% with the same material input. These events were happening while the American companies had considerable production capacity in the lowest-cost sites.

Prices suddenly dropped by approximately 75%. One American company closed a two-week old German plant. English Electric closed a two-year old £4 million plant. Among the Continental firms affected by the crisis were Philips, Olivetti and SESCOSEM, a relative of France's Thomson-Brandt. Philips lost millions of dollars both at home and in its British operations. Olivetti sold its various components' operations (located in Italy, France, the United Kingdom, Germany and Sweden) at distress prices to IRI, the Italian state holding company. The French semi-conductor company, SESCOSEM required a roughly 100 million Franc transfusion from the French government. American companies, with their global networks and global horizons, survived.

The story of integrated circuits has thus far had an unhappy ending for European companies. It has been perhaps even more disheartening to European politicians who wanted integrated circuits to become a spearhead of European advanced technology.[98]

How quickly might large Continental enterprises adopt the global outlook which the 1970's appeared to demand? The answer to this question was closely linked to the willingness and ability of these firms to adjust their behavior outside the LDC's to allow for a greater international division of labor. The degree to which Continental enterprises could or would facilitate an international division of labor close to home in Europe thus took on a special importance. Their role in the integration process in the European Common Market was not only relevant to the success or failure of the EEC, but also relevant as a portent of the progress – or failure – of a broader integration. But what had been the behavior of Continental enterprises in developed Europe where, as we have seen, they established many more foreign manufacturing operations than they had ever done in the less developed world?

---

[98] For one such expression of hope, see: Layton, 1969: pp 195–204.

Chapter VI

Foreign Manufacturing in Europe
Since the EEC and EFTA

Throughout the 1960's much of Europe's attention was riveted on the American Challenge. One body of opinion had it that the EEC was little more than a playground of American multinational companies.[1] The EEC Commission itself published a report on *Industrial Policy in the Community* which concluded that:

> 'The only international linkages that are expanding relatively rapidly are those between Community firms and firms in third countries, generally the United States. Most often they consist in a more powerful firm in a third country acquiring or taking over control.'[2]

It is undeniable that American firms massively expanded their activities in Europe in the 1960's and early 1970's. The book value of direct foreign investment in the EEC by American firms grew from $2·1 billion in 1959 to $11·8 billion at the end of 1970. In 1972 it reached almost $16·8 billion.[3] Direct investment in manufacturing industry by American firms in EEC Europe (a statistic which included investment in sales companies, but which excluded investment in petroleum refining) grew from $1·1 billion to $9·7 billion between 1959 and 1972.[4]

The EEC Commission drew its dramatic conclusion concerning the role of American enterprise in the Community from a survey of publicly announced start-ups and acquisitions in the Six between 1961 and 1969 involving foreign parent companies. Acquisitions or start-ups in the EEC by parents based outside the Community appeared to substantially exceed foreign acquisitions or start-ups in the EEC undertaken by companies based in the EEC countries during that period.[5] The data gathered for the EEC mixed a few apples and oranges by including establishment and acquisition of sales as well as manufacturing operations. Nevertheless, it showed that new start-ups of wholly owned subsidiaries in the EEC by American and other third-country firms exceeded intra-EEC foreign subsidiary establishment by a factor of 1·5 to 1. Third country operations exceeded intra-EEC operations in the acquisition or establishment of joint ventures involving foreign firms in the EEC countries by a factor of about three to one. Take-overs in the EEC by non-Community companies were said to exceed international take-overs within the Six by EEC-based firms by a similar three-to-one margin.[6] The Commission later updated its survey for 1970 and 1971, and, while noting an increase in intra-EEC operations, maintained that 'its general conclusions were essentially the same'.[7]

Continental Manufacturing in the EEC

Important as American activity was in the EEC, however, the obsession with the American Challenge obscured the fact that international linkages with firms in the EEC were very far from being an exclusivity of American

---

[1] Rosenstein-Rodan, 1968: p 35; Servan-Schreiber, 1967: p 10.
[2] EEC, 1970: p 27.
[3] US Department of Commerce, *Survey of Current Business*, various issues.
[4] US Department of Commerce, *Survey of Current Business*, various issues.
[5] EEC, 1970: pp 89–95.
[6] EEC, 1970: p 92.
[7] EEC, 1972: p 167; EEC, 1973.

enterprise. The large Continental European enterprises based in the original six member countries of the EEC were establishing and acquiring foreign subsidiary links elsewhere in the Community at a rate very much like that of their large American counterparts. Between January 1, 1958 and January 1, 1968, the 187 US companies covered in the Comparative Multinational Enterprise Project established or acquired 1,434 sales and manufacturing subsidiaries in the EEC of the Six.[8] Between January 1, 1959 and January 1, 1971 (a slightly longer period) the 69 largest Belgian, Luxemburg, French, German, Italian and Dutch companies entered 1,436 foreign sales and manufacturing subsidiaries in the EEC. The links with the EEC established by the 16 largest Swiss and Swedish enterprises brought to 1,738 the total of subsidiaries of all sorts which the 85 largest Continental companies entered between 1959 and the beginning of 1971.

If one considers only foreign manufacturing activity, one also finds virtual parity between the activities of large American and European enterprises in the EEC. By the beginning of 1971, the 69 largest firms based in the Six had nearly 600 foreign manufacturing subsidiaries located in EEC countries, as one sees from Table 6.1. Comparable data for the 187 largest US multinationals ends three years earlier, with the beginning of 1968. At that time the American multinationals owned wholly or partly 758 manufacturing subsidiaries in the EEC, as Table 6.1 shows. Despite the time lag, the difference in orders of magnitude was very much smaller than one would imagine from reading popular accounts of foreign investment in Europe. Moreover, that difference was due entirely to the greater propensity of American firms to undertake foreign manufacturing in Germany and Italy, compared to EEC-based firms. In France and the Benelux countries the numbers of foreign production activities of large American and EEC enterprises were close to being equal.

During the latter half of the 1960's, the importance of foreign manufacturing within the EEC for firms based in the Community increased rapidly. One sees from Table 6.2 that large parent companies based in EEC countries entered a larger proportion of their foreign operations between 1966 and 1971 in the EEC than they had in almost any other period. The rise in the proportion of manufacturing operations entered elsewhere in the Community was especially striking in the case of French companies. Large French firms had fewer than 15% of their foreign manufacturing subsidiaries in EEC countries between 1955 and 1965, and 35% thereafter. The reorientation of investment was nearly as striking, however, in the case of German, Italian, and Belgian enterprise. Indeed, Table 6.2 shows that out of all the 908 foreign manufacturing subsidiaries set up or acquired between 1966 and the end of 1970 by large enterprises based in France, Germany, Italy, or Benelux, fully 434, or 48%, were in the EEC.

In the light of all the pages that have been written on the subject it is perhaps worth noting that only a handful of these intra-EEC manufacturing linkages could be remotely termed 'transnational mergers'.[9]

---

[8] Vaupel and Curhan, 1969: p 122.
[9] On transnational mergers in Europe, see: Goldberg, 1971; Feld, 1970; Whitehead, 1971; Mazzolini, 1975.

Table 6.1 Foreign Manufacturing Subsidiaries in the EEC Owned by the 85 Largest Continental and by 187 American Multinational Enterprises (January 1, 1971, US data as of January 1, 1968)

	Parent Company From:					Total EEC parents	Switzerland	Sweden	Total Continental parents	American parents
Host country	Germany	France	Italy	Bel & Lux	Nether-lands*					
Germany	—	42	3	25	42	112	57	15	184	214
France	128	—	11	49	33	221	44	16	281	205
Italy	36	34	—	15	13	98	24	6	128	174
Bel & Lux	24	36	2	10	16	88	10	6	104	85
Netherlands	24	14	4	18	—	60	15	9	84	80
Total in EEC	**212**	**126**	**20**	**117**	**104**	**579**	**150**	**52**	**781**	**758**

Note: *Includes data for Royal Dutch-Shell, but not for Unilever.

Source: Comparative Multinational Enterprise Project.

Table 6.2 Entries into Foreign Manufacturing Subsidiaries in the Original Six EEC Countries, in Non-EEC Europe and in the Rest of the World by EEC-Based Parent Firms, Various Time Periods

Country of parent		Pre 1913	1914– 1945	1946– 1958	1959– 1965	1966– 1970
Belgium and	EEC	10	23	14	17	71
Luxemburg	Other Europe	13	25	9	12	26
	Rest of World	1	8	14	15	63
France	EEC	4	11	7	12	102
	Other Europe	2	13	14	23	49
	Rest of World	2	9	32	67	138
West Germany	EEC	16	26	26	51	165
	Other Europe	39	89	49	56	127
	Rest of World	8	42	92	121	216
Italy	EEC	0	6	3	7	11
	Other Europe	3	5	5	14	13
	Rest of World	0	3	27	30	20
Netherlands	EEC	9	48	18	32	85
	Other Europe	13	42	18	38	96
	Rest of World	19	71	41	123	471
Total parents	EEC	39	114	68	119	434
based in EEC	Other Europe	70	174	95	143	311
	Rest of World	30	133	229	356	908

Note: Figures for the Netherlands and Totals are not strictly comparable with Tables 6.1 and 6.2, since Unilever subsidiaries are included in this Table, but not elsewhere.

Source: Comparative Multinational Enterprise Project.

The EEC countries were also an important location for foreign manufacturing by large Swiss and Swedish enterprises. There were 202 subsidiaries of Swiss and Swedish firms in the EEC. The country distribution of these operations can be observed from Table 6.1. The large Swiss and Swedish firms had 131 manufacturing ventures in EFTA countries, as is shown in Table 6.3. In 1971, subsidiaries of Swiss enterprises in the EEC outnumbered subsidiaries in EFTA by a margin of two to one. Much of this orientation to the Six was accounted for by operations established long ago. Still, new Swiss entries into EEC manufacturing were 50% greater than those into EFTA between 1959 and 1970. Nearly 40% of *all* foreign production operations formed or acquired by Swiss firms after 1958 were located in the Six. Swedish company activities were more oriented to EFTA countries in 1971: they had 58 subsidiaries in EFTA as opposed to 52 in the EEC.

Continental Manufacturing in EFTA

Whereas the EEC countries loomed large in the foreign manufacturing activity of firms based on the Continent, interest in EFTA bases was more muted. One sees from Table 6.3 that large enterprises based in the EEC had important numbers of foreign production operations in the United Kingdom. One joint Dutch-British company, Royal Dutch-Shell, owned nearly half of those

Table 6.3 Foreign Manufacturing Subsidiaries in EFTA Owned by the 85 Largest Companies Based in Continental Europe (January 1, 1971)

Host country	Parent Company From:					Total EEC parents	Switzerland	Sweden	Total Continental parents
	Germany	France	Italy	Bel & Lux	Netherlands				
UK	35	20	9	8	78	150	43	22	215
Denmark	4	1	1	1	6	13	2	5	20
Norway	3	1	0	0	1	5	9	14	28
Sweden	20	4	0	0	6	30	1	—	31
Finland	3	0	0	2	—	6	1	11	18
Switzerland	22	6	1	1	8	38	—	3	41
Austria	34	5	2	3	9	53	13	1	67
Portugal	14	10	2	6	1	33	4	2	39
Total	**135**	**47**	**15**	**21**	**110**	**328**	**73**	**58**	**459**

Source: Comparative Multinational Enterprise Project.

'foreign' operations, however. Except for the German-owned subsidiaries in Austria, Switzerland and Sweden, the operations of EEC-based firms elsewhere in EFTA were almost negligible. One observes that Swiss firms were not much more active in manufacturing in EFTA than were companies based in the EEC. In contrast, Swedish firms had 58 producing subsidiaries in EFTA – of which 30 were in other Nordic countries – compared to only 52 in the EEC.

As in the case of the EEC, the difference between the foreign production activity of American and Continental European firms in EFTA was small. The number of foreign manufacturing operations in EFTA of the 85 large Continental firms in 1971 came close to equalling the number of subsidiaries of the 187 US multinationals three years earlier. Continental firms had 459 foreign manufacturing subsidiaries in EFTA at the beginning of 1971: US companies had 494 at the beginning of 1968. US companies, however, had no less that 356 (or 72%) of their EFTA-based production operations in the UK alone; Continental firms had only 215 (or 47%) in the UK in 1971.

Causes and Cross-currents of Investments

This kaleidoscope of investment patterns by European firms provides little support for some of the tidier generalizations that could be advanced to explain enterprise behavior in post-war Europe. For example, little support emerges from Tables 6.1 through 6.3 for the proposition that EEC-based firms were mainly investing in EFTA to jump EFTA tariff barriers, or that EFTA firms were primarily preoccupied with jumping the EEC common tariff. In individual cases, to be sure, managers of Continental firms have affirmed that the division of Europe into regional blocs has played a role in foreign manufacturing decisions. Officers of the Swedish company Volvo state that they probably would not have established an assembly plant in Belgium in 1963 had it not been for the 22% common tariff wall then being erected around the EEC for automobiles.[10] Observers of Swiss company behavior argue that some of the post-1958 surge in Swiss company activity in the Common Market had such straightforward tariff-hopping motives.[11] And a tendency of producers in the aluminum industry to attempt to divide their production between EFTA plants (largely based in Norway) and EEC plants protected by the 9% outer tariff has been noted by writers and industry executives.[12] Nonetheless, Tables 6.1 and 6.3 demonstrate that over 70% of all foreign manufacturing subsidiaries established by Continental firms in Europe were set up or acquired within trading blocs. EEC – EFTA crossover investment was the exception, not the rule.

There is a little evidence for the existence of a relationship between location decisions and linguistic and geographical affinities. These affinities were particularly noticeable in the case of the relatively few EEC – EFTA crossover decisions. The Swiss showed an affinity for German locations; the Germans were attracted to Switzerland, Austria, and Sweden; and the Dutch went to Great Britain as we see from Tables 6.1 and 6.3. When investments were

---

[10] *Business Europe*, 1963: p 4.
[11] Schwamm, 1971.
[12] Evans, 1974: p 234.

influenced by the cost of tariffs, companies behaved as if they were also trying to minimize other costs, such as those of language and communication. The fact remains, however, that EEC – EFTA crossovers were of marginal importance compared to decisions to set up or acquire foreign manufacturing *within* supposed free-trading areas. The data on the exchange of foreign manufacturing within the EEC and EFTA areas displayed no clear-cut predominance of moves to cultural brethren, save in the case of a certain concentration of Swedish manufacturing in Nordic countries noticed from Table 6.3.

Common Market Expectations versus Company Behavior

Perhaps the greatest puzzle is the fact that there is such a large number of foreign manufacturing subsidiaries within EEC and EFTA which were set up or acquired by firms themselves located within these trading areas. It seems doubly odd that the establishment and acquisition of such foreign manufacturing ventures by parents located in these regional groupings should also be growing at a rate greater than that of their foreign production in most other areas of the world. This proliferation of foreign manufacturing within free-trade regions at first glance seems in outright contradiction to what many economists would have anticipated.

It has often been argued that European economic integration would lead to a greater international division of labor within Europe and to the realization of economies of scale previously unobtainable because of Europe's fragmentation into small national markets.[13] Industrial production in an integrated Europe was expected to become concentrated in large, specialized plants in industries in which scale economies were possible. Small national units, viable in a Europe cut up by trade barriers, would be closed; such closures would be especially numerous in the case of sub-optimal tariff factories set up by multinational enterprise during the days of negotiable environments. The plethora of European plants found by Bain to have capacities of around half those of their American counterparts in the 1950's were to give way to larger, specialized units.[14] In sum, it was increases in international trade – rather than in intra-regional investment – that were contemplated.

The *prima-facie* discord between anticipation and realization appeared greatest within the original six countries of the EEC. At the beginning of 1971, our 85 Continental parents had 781 foreign manufacturing subsidiaries, or an average of nine foreign subsidiaries per parent, in the Community. The number of foreign manufacturing subsidiaries per parent in the eight nations of EFTA was closer to five. When one eliminated the great concentration of EFTA subsidiaries in the UK, this measure of the density of foreign manufacturing by Continental enterprise in EFTA dropped to less than three.

---

[13] The 'Spaak Report', as cited in Frank, 1961: pp 94 and 95; Swann, 1972: p 38. Most discussions of the relationship between European integration and scale economies appear to have taken into account only the production scale economies obtainable in individual plants. Consideration of the scale economies in R&D, marketing, purchasing, administration and finance available to multi-plant enterprises might have conceivably altered expectations concerning industrial location in Europe. For discussions of various types of scale economies see Scherer, 1974; Pratten, 1971; Vernon, 1970.
[14] Bain, 1966: pp 34–42 and appendices.

The following examination of these puzzles concentrates on events in the EEC. It was in the EEC that the Continental firms made the bulk of their foreign manufacturing commitments in Europe. And it was there that the seeming dissonance between integration theory and company practice was largest.[15]

Subsidiary Closures and Liquidations

Had integration proceeded in the EEC as foreseen, one would have anticipated the sale, closure or liquidation of plants in the industries where scale economies were greatest. But in fact, there were very few sales or liquidations of foreign manufacturing interests in the Community – whatever the industry – by large Continental enterprises between 1958 and 1971. Only 35 subsidiaries in the EEC (5% of the total existing in 1971) were terminated during this period. These terminated ventures were to be found in a randomly scattered selection of industries, except for seven sales in a miscellaneous group of chemical products accounted for by the actions of only one parent company. These seven terminated ventures in chemicals still were a small fraction (less than 10%) of the foreign chemicals operations in the EEC remaining in 1971.

The Comparative Multinational Enterprise Project data on foreign manufacturing subsidiaries relates, to be sure, to legally incorporated entities; these do not precisely correspond to individual plants. Executives, especially in the electrical machinery industry, occasionally pointed out that products have often been phased in and out of factories in Europe without inducing a change in the legal structure of operations. Nonetheless, reallocation of production did not seem to be a major preoccupation for most Continental firms prior to 1971; only later were there indications that data on subsidiaries as such might understate plant closures and product reallocations.[16] Liquidations and sales would have continued to involve legal units as a matter of course, and not many of these were publicly announced in the EEC during the early 1970's.[17]

Proliferation of Subsidiaries in the EEC

It was indeed in some of the industries in which the minimum economic scale of production is said to be the greatest, that Continental European enterprises were establishing the largest number of manufacturing subsidiaries in the EEC.

Table 6.4 presents several measures of the density of the foreign manufacturing operations in the EEC of Continental enterprises. These measures are given for 37 industry groups. The industries are presented in decreasing order of the percentage of foreign manufacturing subsidiaries found in the EEC. Thus, the metal-can industry is listed first, since 67% of all production

---

[15] Hufbauer and Chilas, 1974, have argued that the dissonance between integration theory and European practice is also noticeable from intra-European trade patterns. They point out that although traditional trade theory stresses the international division of labor, 'the postwar experience (in Europe) has been an experience with "balanced trade" at the industry level'. They argue that the origin of balanced trade was to be found largely in non-tariff barriers – the same barriers that, as seen below, seem to have so influenced intra-European subsidiary establishment.

[16] *Business Week*, 1973; Lorenz, 1973: p 21.

[17] Funk and Scott International Index, various issues.

Table 6.4   Density of Foreign Manufacturing Subsidiaries Located in the EEC and Owned by Continental Parents, Various Measures by Industry, January 1, 1971

Industry: *Seventeen High-density Industries*	% of all world-wide subsidiaries in EEC	% of subsidiaries in Europe in EEC	Number of EEC subsidiaries per Continental parent	Number of subsidiaries in EEC	Number of parents
Metal cans	67 %	100 %	4·0	4	1
Glass	57	64	6·7	27	4
Paints	57	69	4·5	27	7
Engines & turbines	55	86	4·0	12	3
Iron & steel	43	74	3·1	40	13
Non-ferrous smelting	42	73	2·7	11	4
Food (all categories)	41	55	11·0	22	2
Soaps & cosmetics	40	60	1·2	6	5
Plastics & synthetics	39	58	2·3	37	16
Special industrial machinery	39	47	2·6	18	7
General industrial machinery	39	70	19·0	19	1
Rubber (ex tires)	38	56	3·0	9	3
Transport (ex motor vehicles)	36	57	1·3	4	3
Tires	35	43	2·0	6	3
Stone, clay, concrete	34	67	6·7	20	3
Precision goods	33	57	1·5	16	11
Industrial chemicals	31	60	3·7	49	13
Twenty Low-density Industries					
Non-ferrous metal products	30 %	46 %	1·7	10	6
Paper	28	42	1·3	8	6
Printed matter	27	50	1·8	7	4
Electrical transmission	27	46	2·7	16	6
Electronic components	26	47	2·6	18	7
Petroleum refining	26	68	3·4	17	5
Wood products	26	54	3·5	7	2
Fabricated wire products	24	63	2·5	5	2
Radios, TVs & appliances	22	41	2·2	11	5
Furniture	20	25	1·0	1	1
Pharmaceuticals	20	46	3·7	37	10
Office machines	19	36	2·0	4	2
Structural metal products	19	42	1·7	5	3
Autos, trucks & parts	17	47	1·3	16	12
Electric lighting	17	32	2·0	12	6
Agricultural chemicals	16	45	1·0	9	9
Communication equipment	8	18	0·6	5	3
Apparel	0	0	0·0	0	2
Construction machinery	0	0	0·0	0	
Farm machinery	0	0	0·0	0	1

Source: Comparative Multinational Enterprise Project.

subsidiaries of Continental firms were located in the Six at the beginning of 1971. Apparel, construction machinery, and farm machinery are listed last, since all the foreign manufacturing subsidiaries owned by large Continental enterprises in these product groups were located outside of the Common Market. The first column provides a measure of the orientation of foreign manufacturing to the Community in each industry in terms of the percentage of worldwide manufacturing operations located in the EEC. The second column relates the percentage of all European subsidiaries located in the Community. The third column shows the average number of EEC manufacturing subsidiaries wholly or partly owned by each parent firm active in an industry. These three measures of the EEC-orientation of foreign manufacturing of Continental firms are supplemented in column four with the absolute number of foreign ventures-per-industry in the EEC, and in column five with the number of parent firms to which subsidiaries are linked.

Although Table 6.4 presents a large array of figures, matters quickly become simplified when one observes that there is a high degree of concordance among the three alternative measures of foreign manufacturing density in the EEC. Of the 17 industries in which more than 30% of all foreign manufacturing was concentrated in the EEC, all but two (tires and special industrial machinery) also had more than 50% of their European operations in the EEC. Among the 17 high-EEC-density industries, one also finds 12 of the 16 sectors in which the average number of EEC subsidiaries-*per*-parent exceeded 2·5. Nearly two-thirds of the absolute number of EEC subsidiaries for which industry information is available (or 333 out of 521) were found in these 17 most EEC-oriented branches.

Whatever density measure is chosen, one sees from Table 6.4 that large Continental enterprises have forged a striking proportion of their foreign manufacturing links within the EEC in industries such as cans, glass, power turbines, iron and steel, non-ferrous smelting, processed foods, industrial chemicals, and paints. A bit further down the list one finds industries such as petroleum refining and pharmaceuticals in which the number of EEC-subsidiaries *per* parent is high, even though the percentage of manufacturing operations found in the EEC is below 30%. It is only toward the bottom of Table 6.4 that we find the two oft-cited success stories of the Common Market: appliances, and motor vehicles.[18] We also find several categories of electrical products and non-electrical machinery.

The most comprehensive studies available on scale economies in manufacturing industry unfortunately do not provide us with rankings for all industries listed in Table 6.4, or with rankings for precisely the same industry or product categories as those for which we have foreign investment data. Nonetheless, it is evident that there are enormous economies of large-scale manufacture in iron and steel, non-ferrous smelting, and the fabrication of turbines for electric power generation. Those in petroleum refining and industrial chemicals, while perhaps lower, are still considerable.[19] Although scale economies of

---

[18] Maillet, 1972: Part II.
[19] Pratten, 1971. Pratten's estimates refer only to the minimum optimum scale of production in individual factories (plant scale economies).

production in motor vehicles and appliances are hardly negligible, they are of a lower order than those available in the other industries mentioned.

Some of the highest EEC concentrations of foreign manufacturing subsidiaries of large Continental firms were thus to be found in the very industries where scale economies were highest – in the industries where it was trade links, not foreign manufacturing links that were expected.

A number of the industries with the highest EEC-density of foreign manufacturing by Continental companies have also been those where intra-Community trade was expanding most slowly. Data on trade expansion in the EEC do not allow exactly comparable statistical relationships to be established for the 37 industry groups presented in Table 6.4. Statistics published by the OECD and GATT, however, show that intra-EEC trade in all manufactures expanded by a factor of 3·2 between 1963 and 1971. Trade in iron and steel and non-ferrous metals (smelting and products) expanded 2·4 and 2·8 times respectively. Meanwhile, intra-EEC trade in chemicals was expanding by a factor greater than four.[20] Trade in motor vehicles was expanding by 3·7 times, or almost as much, and trade in engineering products (including appliances, machinery, etc) by a factor of 2·97.[21]

These seemingly negative relationships between the growth of foreign manufacturing in the EEC and industry trade and scale economies, suggest that during the decade of the 1960's something rather different from the sort of economic integration imagined in the 1950's was going on in many sectors of European industry. In a few sectors like motor vehicles and electrical appliances, growth in trade accompanied a relative lack of establishment or acquisition of intra-EEC foreign manufacturing subsidiaries.[22] In some others, it appeared highly probable that proliferation of foreign manufacturing subsidiary links by European firms in Europe was a consequence of national government or private efforts to limit integration. The elimination of tariff barriers did not eliminate tariff factories. Rather, it frequently acted as a great stimulus to government innovation in non-tariff barriers (NTB's) and subsidies that resulted in a great number of NTB factories.

Responses in Different Industries

Confronted by the dual threats of NTB's and foreign competition, business responded in a number of ways, all of which meant an increase in intra-EEC foreign manufacturing links. One response was neo-traditional NTB jumping. Another was putting subsidiaries behind competitors' home lines. A third was that of defensively acquiring potential competitors at home or across national boundaries. Many of these competitors also had foreign operations, so acquisition often meant acquisition of many intra-EEC links. This interplay of thrust and riposte by government and business is illustrated by a more detailed look at a number of the industries listed toward the top of Table 6.4

---

[20] This classification unfortunately groups into 'chemicals' all the following sectors listed in Table 6.4: paints, soaps and cosmetics, plastics and synthetics, industrial chemicals, pharmaceuticals, and agricultural chemicals, as well as 'other' chemical products such as inks not covered in Table 6.4 because of a lack of detailed product data.

[21] GATT, various issues.

[22] Maillet, 1972: Part II.

Iron and Steel

The iron and steel industry has an image of being made up exclusively of national firms. Nonetheless, one observes from Table 6.4 that the absolute number of manufacturing subsidiaries located in the EEC by Continental firms in this industry is larger than that in any other, excepting only industrial chemicals. The percentage of all subsidiaries in the industry in the EEC is high, as is the number of EEC manufacturing operations *per* parent. All 13 parents accounting for the 40 foreign operations within the EEC were, incidentally, themselves headquartered in the Community.

This singular foreign manufacturing behavior – in a supposedly 'national' industry – is almost certainly linked to the particularities of the evolution of the European Coal and Steel Community (ECSC). According to one recent study of the steel industry in Europe, the ECSC, far from leading the Six countries of the European Community into free trade, became a means of maintaining an uneasy truce among industry and government protagonists.[23] The cease-fire lines of this truce did not always correspond to national borders – as they had during the 1920's and 1930's. The ECSC treaty had had that much effect. Nor was supranational competition of the sort hoped for by some of the founders of the ECSC entirely absent. Still, fears and threats of closure of national markets were still around, whatever the ECSC treaty said.

In such an atmosphere, it seemed only prudent for firms based in the small countries of the Six to keep their 'fifth-column' subsidiaries established long ago behind competitors' lines.[24] It was also prudent to add to them over time, for profit margin squeezes resulting from rising labor costs, revaluations and the like in the EEC countries with big markets led to a recrudescence of defensive protectionist sentiments. Fully half of the EEC subsidiaries of EEC companies were those set up or acquired by Benelux firms in France and Germany. Many of these subsidiaries were insurance policies against market closure.

The iron and steel industry in Europe was, of course, going through something of an economic revolution during the 1950's and 1960's. The producers with sea-coast locations had substantial transport-cost advantages over those without. The inland, high-cost producers merged and concentrated along national lines – with the help of national governments, and made the threat of market closure yet more menacing.[25] Sea-coast producers in small countries faced a choice between producing at lowest cost and hoping that markets would remain accessible, or running inland foreign plants for little or no return both as a 'fifth column' deterrent and as a gesture of social responsibility to uneconomic regions. They often chose the latter course.

The economic revolution in European steelmaking did lead to the creation of a few foreign subsidiaries, for reasons of the sort one might expect in a single market. ARBED, a Luxemburg firm, did take part in the SIDMAR joint project on the Belgian coast.[26] Thyssen, Germany's and Europe's largest steel producer is eventually to have a share in the Fos-sur-Mer venture on the

---

[23] Hayward, 1974.
[24] See Chapter IV.
[25] Hayward, 1974.
[26] *Société Générale de Belgique*, 1972: pp 216–218; *European Intelligence*, July 6, 1972: p 13.

Mediterranean near Marseilles.[27] Still, it was the rare foreign venture that was formed as part of an effort at restructuring Europe's steel industry on an international basis.

In fact, it was the rare steel venture that was formed in the EEC. Less than a quarter of the foreign manufacturing subsidiaries located in the EEC at the start of 1971 had been built from the ground up; more than three-quarters had been acquired; and almost half had been acquired as a result of acquisitions of other parent-firms during the process of agglomeration of the industry into one consisting of a few large national groups. The proportion of subsidiaries that were acquired (as opposed to formed) in the iron and steel industry in the EEC was equalled or exceeded only in paper products, pharmaceuticals, paints, dairy products, bearings and communications equipment. Contrary to what some static theories suggest, however, it is arguable that these foreign acquisitions promoted, rather than restrained competition in the European iron and steel industry. The number of independent firms in the industry was reduced by such international acquisitions. But the main decline in independent firms was occurring because of national concentration moves. Indeed, the fifth column subsidiaries seemed among the few remaining elements keeping some semblance of competitive instability in the market.

When one added up all the known facets of the behavior in the European iron and steel industry in the post-war era, the picture that emerged was one of individual enterprises attempting to defend themselves against a real or imagined threat that the history of the negotiable environment might repeat itself. The foreign investment pattern that emerged in the EEC conformed to one predictable in a common market in only a limited way. The industry climate was one dominated by national mergers and acquisitions, basing-point pricing, and even explicit market-sharing agreements (the German participant in Fos-sur-Mer was being required by the French government to sell its share of output outside of the French market).

Moreover, little change seemed in the offing as the 1970's reached their midpoint. Only one transnational Dutch-German merger (compared to 40 foreign subsidiary relationships) had emerged by the early 1970's, but it had been instigated by a company based in Holland, a small country, for the traditional small-country-reason of maintaining access to a foreign market.

Non-Ferrous Metals

The smelting of non-ferrous metals is another industry in which there is a relatively high density of foreign manufacturing in the EEC. The reasons for this focus of foreign manufacturing on the Community had much in common with those behind the cross-border moves in iron and steel. Public intervention in the Common Market by national authorities was nonetheless more noticeable. Industry executives claimed that progress toward free trade had been made during the first decade and one-half of the EEC, although no statistics of any kind seemed to be available to show degrees of market interpenetration by firms headquartered in different nations. Yet, the steps toward free trade – whatever they might have been – were often offset by autarkic and protective reflexes.

---

[27] *Financial Times*, February 7, 1973; *American Metal Market*, February 16, 1973.

Protective moves were rampant in the most important non-ferrous metal industry in Europe, aluminum. Behavior in that product seemed to set the pace for copper and zinc. The super-protection of the EEC as a whole by the 'gentleman's agreement' between the leading European and Canadian companies and the USSR, is well known.[28] The resistance of Péchiney and of its national government, France, to the reduction of the 9% EEC outer tariff in aluminum during the Kennedy Round has also been much noted.[29] But while France supported EEC protection in order to boost Péchiney's sales elsewhere in Europe at the expense of outside suppliers, the response of some countries in the Community to such trade diversion was to stimulate national production. National production was often supplied by a foreign subsidiary of a European firm.

People active in the industry noted that West German state and federal governments had created 'special conditions' to foster an aluminum smelting industry 'that never should have been built.'[30] Government electric power subsidies and grants facilitated local smelter constructions, in spite of Germany's relatively liberal post-war market philosophy. Some of the new smelters were foreign subsidiaries of Continental firms.

Sometimes, of course, government subsidies or NTB inducements constituted only one of several motivations for intra-EEC investment. Péchiney put up a smelter in Holland in the late 1960's partly out of a desire to take out an insurance policy against high and rising French power costs. The new smelter was part of a complex linked to a plant that produced nuclear energy. The Dutch government helped, nevertheless, with 'a special lump-sum subsidy (of 60 million guilders) that offset power costs'.[31]

Developments in the early 1970's suggested that, if anything, the intervention of national governments in the EEC aluminum market was likely to increase. In 1972, Italy announced the setting up of an 'aluminum plan' that industry observers noted was likely to-cause 'the situation . . . to evolve in the direction of autarky'. Italy's balance of payments problems constituted the immediate rationale for this plan, although it was also seen as one move among many to develop Italy's South. The national champion, Montedison, a firm with foreign subsidiaries of its own in other products, was given state aid to concentrate and expand the industry. But room was left for partly owned affiliates of other Continental producers.[32] In such a climate, old tariff factory subsidiaries in the different European countries had not disappeared.[33]

Indeed, when the author asked aluminum industry executives whether state-stimulated, foreign manufacturing operations in the EEC countries were likely to one day cease to be so prevalent, their answer was a disquieting one. They were able to imagine a day when there would be few, if any, multinational ownership links between parents and subsidiaries located in certain Common Market countries, but not because free trade had actually come into being.

---

[28] Mikdashi, 1974: p 185.
[29] Mikdashi, 1974: p 191; Curzon and Curzon, 1973.
[30] Interviews with industry executives.
[31] Business Europe, 1969: p 123.
[32] *Revue de l'Aluminium*, September 1972: p 673.
[33] Mikdashi, 1974: p 182.

Rather, there was a fear of the day when one or another government might simultaneously pursue policies of both autarky *and* exclusion of foreign subsidiaries.

Engines and Turbines for Power Generation

While subsidies and cash grants inhibited trade in primary non-ferrous metals, purchasing policies of national electricity boards came close to eliminating it altogether in power generation equipment.[34] The very marked orientation of foreign manufacturing to the EEC in engines and turbines observable from Table 6.4 is one result of this near-prohibition of intra-EEC commerce.

The EEC Commission itself has pointed out that very little international trade within the Common Market occurs in power-generation products.[35] When trade in such products has occurred in Europe it has been but a prelude to government insistence on local production.[36] The reaction of firms based in the large countries of Europe that produce power turbines has essentially been to stay in their own protected markets, and export to (and occasionally produce in) the Third World. The reaction of the firms based in smaller Continental countries has been to set up no less than 11 foreign manufacturing operations in the Six EEC countries.

Foods

Foods constitute another industry – or set of industries – shown by Table 6.4 to have a high density of manufacturing subsidiaries in the EEC. Indeed, the number of EEC-subsidiaries *per* parent firm in this industry is one of the two highest to be found listed in that table.

Part of the explanation for Continental firms' exploitation of oligopolistic advantages in the food industry in the EEC countries by manufacturing rather than by exporting doubtless has to do with the high transport costs associated with many processed food products. Even if trade were fully free within the Common Market, one would expect to find numerous production *loci* for the bulky, perishable products such as those of the dairy industry. Within a national market like France, one finds firms with multiple production locations for similar products, some of which may be legally incorporated as subsidiaries. Shipping costs offset economies of large-scale production beyond a certain point.[37] Language and taste differences among different Common Market countries – and within those countries – would also lead one to expect a high frequency of foreign production operations, even in the absence of trade restrictions.

It is clear, however, that transport costs and differences in tastes are far from the whole explanation of the large number of foreign manufacturing subsidiaries found within the EEC. Widely diverging health and labelling regulations continue to act as NTB's for many food products.[38] Thus, despite

---

[34] Surrey and Chesshire, 1972.
[35] *Journal de Genève*, November 1, 1972.
[36] Surrey and Chesshire, 1972.
[37] Ghertman and Siegmund, 1973: Case 'A'.
[38] Ghertman and Siegmund, 1973: Case 'B'; Communautés Européens, 1974: p 139.

some attempts by Continental firms to 'rationalize' production on a Common Market basis, one found but one instance of a sale or liquidation of a foreign subsidiary in the EEC in the food sector, and no subsidiaries exporting more than half their production at the beginning of the 1970's.

Chemicals, Synthetics and Plastics

Although the chemicals, synthetics and plastics industries appear further down in the listing of Table 6.4, many of the private and public motivations for intra-EEC investment were similar to those prominent in the sectors with the highest proportion of foreign subsidiaries in the Community. Once again, the hand of national governments – and of the political forces acting on governments – was occasionally visible.

Governments had a hand in preventing the closure of foreign chemical operations put up in the EEC to jump the tariff barriers that existed prior to July 1968. The most famous example of state intervention was that which followed AKZO's announcement, in early 1972, of its desire to eliminate four of the 37 EEC foreign manufacturing subsidiaries in synthetics noted in Table 6.4, as well as two of its factories in Holland which also produced synthetic fibers.[39] AKZO management maintained that it would be possible both to reduce costs considerably and to maintain output by concentrating the production of certain varieties of synthetic fibers for the EEC market in two or three rather than eight separate units. Labor unions objected to AKZO's brusquely announced decision, however, and various national governments pressured the company to rescind or postpone action.[40]

Government subsidies, too, occasionally played a role in stimulating subsidiary proliferation and maintenance in the EEC. Nevertheless, subsidies apparently affected location decisions less in industrial chemicals and synthetics than they did in other industries.

Some cost-minimizing industrial relocation of the sort one would expect in a single market has occurred in industrial chemicals and synthetics production in the EEC. Common Market behavior apparently underlay the siting of a number of the dozen or so foreign chemical subsidiaries in the Benelux. A number of these subsidiaries were formed to take advantage of access to inexpensive, sea-borne raw materials.[41] Two were exporting more than half their production. Some managers noted that such investment decisions often were made in response to competitors' plans and threats.

Indeed, foreign location decisions in industrial chemicals and synthetics in Europe seem to have been influenced rather frequently by private attempts to negotiate market access and market share. Location decisions were also influenced by the continual spontaneous breakdown of those accords, and by the breaking up of them by EEC or German antitrust authorities. The German Cartel Office has gone so far as to suspect that the foreign manufacturing links among Continental European firms and their subsidiaries in polyurethane fibers, plastics and raw materials constituted an arrangement akin to the

---

[39] Northrup and Rowan, 1974: Part II, p 49; Tudyka, 1973: p 308.
[40] Northrup and Rowan, 1974: Part II, p 50; Tudyka, 1973.
[41] Interviews with company executives.

exchange of hostages in warfare, the aim of which was to deter any member of the 'ring' from cutting prices. This charge was reported in the German press in an article which also included a diagram of the cross-border owner-ship interconnection of some large European firms.[42] The presumed purpose of such interconnections was to deter any one member of the ring from hurting its 'own' joint venture across EEC borders.

Sometimes, foreign investment in industrial chemicals by Continental firms in the EEC seems to have been undertaken as a response to competition, rather than as a preventative of it. Some moves by Continental firms were stimulated by American company decisions to locate in the EEC that threatened to uncover sites reputed to have lower costs than those prevailing in headquarters countries. What occurred next then suggested a recapitu-lation in miniature within the EEC of the product-cycle, oligopoly-reaction sequence of investment matching so often observed among American multi-national firms. Europeans were involved in a way suggested by Bayer's account of one of its investments in France:

'Bayer came to know of the intentions on the part of US enterprises to set up isocyanate plants in France. [As] . . . it was also necessary for Bayer to expand their own isocyanate production, it appeared opportune to anticipate these plans and to establish a manufacturing firm in France . . . . In July 1959 an agreement was concluded with two important French companies (Société Progil and Société d'Electrochimie, d'Electro-métallurgie et des Aciéries Electriques d'Ugine) regarding the foundation of the firm of Progil-Bayer-Ugine (PBU) in which Bayer participated to the extent of 50% and two French partners were to hold 25% each. . . . the manufacturing units were set up in Pont-de-Claix near Grenoble in the immediate vicinity of the Progil. All . . . products are being manu-factured in accordance with Bayer processes for which PBU were granted corresponding licences.'[43]

In the early 1960's, when this investment was made, tariff barriers around the French market were still in existence: thus there was all the more reason for Bayer to protect its French market position by an investment in that country.

As the 1970's unfolded, a number of signs began to indicate that competitive behavior along the lines one might expect in a common market was beginning to occur. At the start of 1971, one found five foreign subsidiaries of German chemical giants located in the EEC exporting more than half of their pro-duction.[44] AKZO was prevented from rationalizing in Europe by abruptly closing down tariff factory subsidiaries in 1972, but the enterprise nonetheless intended to gradually implement the plan it could not effect all at once. Rhône-Poulenc sold its 50% share in its former Italian tariff-factory fiber operation, expanded capacity at home in France, and apparently kept access to the Italian market.[45] The planning director of one Continental chemical

---

[42] *Der Spiegel*, March 5, 1973: pp 95 and 96.
[43] Bayer, 1963: p 62.
[44] Comparative Multinational Enterprise Project.
[45] *Oil Paint and Drug Reporter*, December 20, 1971: p 1; *European Chemical News*, December 31, 1971.

Table 6.5   Antitrust Decisions of the EEC Commission, Industry Distribution, 1964–1972

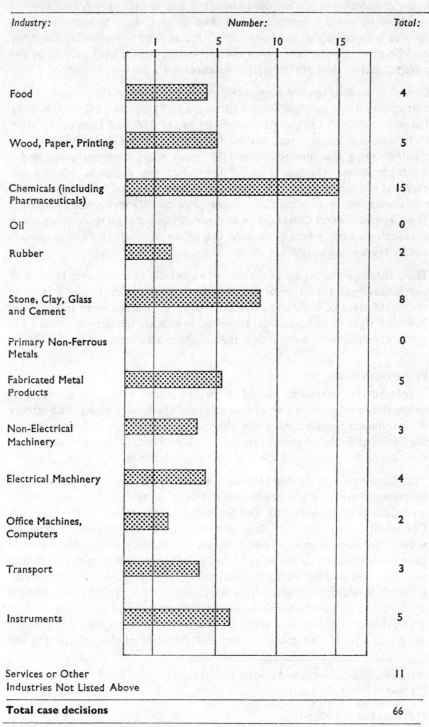

Industry:	Number:	Total:
Food		4
Wood, Paper, Printing		5
Chemicals (including Pharmaceuticals)		15
Oil		0
Rubber		2
Stone, Clay, Glass and Cement		8
Primary Non-Ferrous Metals		0
Fabricated Metal Products		5
Non-Electrical Machinery		3
Electrical Machinery		4
Office Machines, Computers		2
Transport		3
Instruments		5
Services or Other Industries Not Listed Above		11
Total case decisions		66

Source: Derived from *EEC, First and Second Reports on Competition Policy*, EEC, Belgium and Luxemburg, April 1972 and 1973.

multinational remarked in 1974 that an international view of the world was rapidly gaining ground in his firm 'even if the dream of many managers in our heavy chemicals production departments is still to build plants that are not so big as to upset competitors, and then protect them by market-sharing accords with colleagues in the industry'. Italian firms were finding that they could capture a major portion of the German synthetic fiber market by exporting, rather than entering joint ventures with German firms.[46]

Part of this move toward more competitive behavior in chemicals and synthetics may have resulted from antitrust activity of the EEC Commission. Between 1964 and 1968, antitrust activity in the EEC had been negligible.[47] Only nine decisions in total, and no fines, were handed down by the Commission during that period. Since 1968, many more decisions came, and a disproportionate number of them concerned the chemical, plastic, and chemical fibers sectors, as one sees from Table 6.5. Indeed, the largest of the two fines meted out by the Commission prior to 1972 concerned dyestuffs.[48] The German Federal Cartel Office also added some stimuli to competition in chemicals by early morning raids on the offices of synthetic fiber producers and by the levying of stiff fines.[49]

Thus, although the legacy of the era of negotiable environments seemed to weigh heavily on the behavior of the multinationals of Continental Europe in chemicals, signs of movement toward a common market were in evidence. Few such signs were noticeable, however, in another industry in which most of the chemical firms were active, that of pharmaceuticals.

Pharmaceuticals

Thanks to the worldwide spread of foreign manufacturing by Continental enterprise in drugs, only a small percentage of the foreign production activity of Continental firms active in the pharmaceutical industry is located within the EEC. But Table 6.4 shows that the number of EEC subsidiaries-per-parent company in drugs is among the highest of all industries.

That Continental firms should have a marked penchant for establishing or acquiring pharmaceutical production facilities in several EEC countries is perhaps only to be expected. The Seventh General Report of the European Communities remarks that: 'It is in the sector of pharmaceutical products where there has been the least progress in obtaining a free circulation of products within the Community.'[50] In few other sectors does one find location decisions so affected by national safety, packaging, and licencing regulations.[51] In addition to these NTB's one finds the markets of the Six separated by the fact that government-owned hospitals or insurance agencies – which give preference to national suppliers – account for a majority of European drug purchases.[52] The continued national character of medical training and

---

46 Industrievereinigung ChemieFaser, 1974: pp 18 and 19.
47 Brun and Franko, 1974.
48 Brun and Franko, 1974.
49 Business Europe, 1972: p 115.
50 Communautés Européens, 1974: p 132.
51 Baldwin, 1970: Technomic Research Associates, 1973.
52 DAFSA, 1974: p 60.

licensing has also been said to contribute to separating pharmaceutical markets in Europe. One result of the continued existence of barriers to trade in drugs in the EEC has been the creation of conditions favoring greatly differing prices for similar products among national markets. Another has been the continuation of classical stimuli to foreign production.

Restrictions on trade imposed by French public policies have perhaps had the greatest effect on foreign location decisions in the EEC. Nine of the ten Continental parent firms that have any foreign pharmaceutical production in the EEC have plants in France. A few have several subsidiaries in that country. Indeed, in 1971, almost half of the pharmaceutical manufacturing subsidiaries of Continental parents found in the EEC were French. One obvious stimulus to foreign production in France arises from the fact that the forms of dosage traditionally used in French medical practice – notably the use of suppository rather than capsule forms – often require special packaging. The influence of such traditions on location decisions, however, appears to have been minor compared to that of the French system of requiring visas for all new varieties and brands of pharmaceuticals. This visa system, it is said, virtually precludes access to the French market to drugs not undergoing some stage of fabrication in France itself.

In Italy, not only NTB's, but also that country's refusal to grant patent protection to drugs have combined to provoke Swiss, German, French, and Dutch producers of pharmaceuticals to undertake some production in that market. Local production did not fully prevent local or other international firms in that market from helping themselves to products and processes. Nonetheless, production in Italy did provide an observation post on competitors' activities and, if it was undertaken immediately after new products were developed at headquarters, gave some hope of confronting Italian imitators with a well entrenched position.

Restrictions on trade in pharmaceuticals by EEC countries tended mainly to affect finished products, or, in the jargon of the industry, compounds. Trade was often still possible in the basic ingredients for drugs, the so-called active substances. Thus, although it was not visible on the surface, a certain amount of cost minimization through the exploitation of economies of large-scale production was said to be occurring. Yet, insofar as large scale production, and hence exporting were happening, it was clear that only headquarters operations were involved: only one of the many drug subsidiaries in the EEC was exporting more than half of its output.

The fact that national legislative and administrative barriers to trade tended to affect only the final stages of production may have underlain the extraordinarily high frequency of acquisitions in pharmaceuticals in the EEC. Only one out of every five EEC subsidiaries had been started up by its parent, compared to an average ratio of start-ups to acquisitions of two to five in all industries. The practice of blocking trade in final products while allowing it in intermediates may have made intra-EEC acquisitions particularly attractive. Acquisitions did not visibly upset the structure of national industries, and therefore seemed unlikely to provoke retaliatory pressures from entrenched producers for more complete closure of national markets at the basic production stages. Acquisitions nevertheless provided the 'fifth-columns' necessary for the maintenance of some export activity by multinational parents.

Petroleum Refining

Petroleum refining is another industry found fairly far down on Table 6.4, but for which one finds a high ratio of EEC-subsidiaries per-parent. Once again, the hand of the state seems responsible for much of this subsidiary proliferation. The interplay between government and enterprise activity in the search for crude petroleum by large Continental enterprise was described in Chapter III. This interplay continued in the production stages that followed finding oil and getting it out of the ground.

France has had a system of quotas for crude oil since 1928.[53] This system, still in effect, allocates imports of crude to petroleum companies on the basis of their existing or planned refining capacity in France. By augmenting the pull of the French market, the quota system has attracted a third of the foreign refinery subsidiaries of the Continental companies within the EEC. Although this legislation has been noted for favoring the development of French-owned oil companies, one of its original aims was to promote the development of refining in France by whatever companies could be induced to enter the country.

In Italy, foreign firms were encouraged to undertake refining by subsidization rather than by a system of controls. Such subsidies pulled much investment in refining capacity to Italy that might not otherwise have gone to Italy at all. Most of this subsidized refinery capacity was built by American and British enterprise, but a few of the new, post-war refineries were built by European firms headquartered outside of Italy. Still, the location of refineries in Italy was not only the result of subsidies. The threat of a 'French solution' to the organization of petroleum refining and distribution had not been implemented in Italy between the mid-1940's and the mid-1970's. Nonetheless, close state regulation of the industry had often been discussed, and the threat of trade barriers hung like a sword of Damocles over non-Italian firms that might have wished to simply export refined products to Italy.

German policies, or perhaps more accurately the regional development policies of the German *Länder* or states, had much the same effect on company behavior as did those of Italy. Eight of the 17 Continental-owned foreign refining subsidiaries in the EEC are located in Germany. These operations appear to have been largely triggered by subsidies, like those offered by rural Bavaria as part of its program to attract industry.[54] The economics of refining allowed for some inland refineries, but it is virtually certain that in the absence of subsidies more seacoast locations would have been chosen.

Curiously, the increasing visibility of these foreign-owned NTB refineries apparently was partly responsible for provoking the German government into an even more nationalistic policy during the mid-1960's. Many of these foreign-owned refineries were American, but not all. And when a rush began among American, local and other European firms to acquire positions in the German market before import controls could threaten, it was a French firm that found its bid for acquisition blocked. *Compagnie Française des Pétroles* had wished to buy 40% of Gelsenberg for what appear to have been classical,

---

[53] Rondot, 1962: p 35; Adelman, 1972: p 234.
[54] Vice, 1971: p 135; Bossenecker, 1972: pp 34–51.

'fifth-column' reasons. The German government refused, and Gelsenberg became the seed from which Germany's own national champion in petroleum began to grow in the 1970's.[55]

Industries with Little Foreign Manufacturing in the EEC

It is only in the industries with relatively low densities of foreign manufacturing by Continental firms in the EEC that one finds the success stories of European economic integration: automobiles and appliances.

The story of the internationalization of trade in the EEC in autos and parts has been told a number of times.[56] In 1958, countries such as Italy had imposed tariffs of up to 45% on automobiles produced in other EEC countries. The progressive elimination of these high protective tariffs was accompanied by the considerable, even spectacular increases in interpenetration among EEC markets shown in Table 6.6.

Table 6.6 Percentage of Automobile Market in EEC Countries Supplied by Imports from Other EEC Countries, 1958 and 1970

Market	1958	1970
France	1%	16%
Germany	7	25
Italy	2	28
Belgium	14	49

Source: 'Driving For Cars', *Economist*, October 7, 1972, page 95.

The fourfold increase in motor-vehicle trade within the EEC and the manifold increases in interpenetration among Community markets was accompanied by minimal foreign production of European companies within the EEC:

'... the general pattern under the freer trade arrangements of the 1960's and 1970's was for European firms to supply European countries from home; by 1973, for example, Fiat was closing its German assembly plant.'[57]

Fiat's *de facto* disengagement from its ownership participation in Citroën in 1973 suggested that yet more reliance on home production to meet Community markets was in the offing.[58]

Already in 1971 the motor-vehicle industry ranked low in all three of the measures used in Table 6.4 to determine the density of foreign production by large Continental European companies in the EEC. Moreover, nearly half of the Continentally owned, EEC foreign manufacturing operations in motor vehicles was owned by producers of parts, not by auto assemblers. The major

---

[55] Vice, 1971: pp 136 and 137.
[56] Wells, 1974: *The Economist*, October 7, 1972: p 95; Maillet, 1972.
[57] Wells, 1974: p 247.
[58] *Business Week*, June 30, 1973: p 20.

automobile firms had very few foreign operations within the EEC, in 1971, apart from four assembly plants that had been put up in the 1950's in Belgium in response to both tariffs and considerable government subsidies.[59]

The few subsidiaries producing motor vehicles and parts that were located in the EEC also exhibited a propensity to export that was quite dramatically greater than that exhibited by manufacturing subsidiaries in other industries. In most industries in 1971 the number of EEC subsidiaries exporting more than 50% of their production was zero, or not much above zero, but in vehicles and parts, over one half, or five out of the nine manufacturing subsidiaries of Continental firms in EEC countries for which data was available, exported more than 50% of their output. In no other industry were EEC subsidiaries so intensively used as platforms for trade.

The automobile producers of Continental Europe thus gave numerous signs of acting as if they indeed were located in one, large, supranational European market. This market behavior was consistent with the establishment of only a relatively few foreign operations in the EEC. Supranational behavior in this industry did not require much multinational plant location.

Household electrical appliances constitute another product group where most signs have pointed to very considerable economic integration in Europe. Maillet points out that intra-Community trade in refrigerators, washing-machines, small household appliances, radios, and TV's increased by roughly six times between 1960 and 1970.[60] Moreover, in these product sectors, one notices moves to close down or re-allocate operations among Community countries resembling those which occurred in autos.

'While Germany and France produced the same number of refrigerators in 1970 as they did in 1958, production was stopped altogether in Belgium and the Netherlands, and Italian output increased ten times.'[61]

The moderate density in the EEC of foreign production subsidiaries of Continental firms shown in Table 6.4 is consistent with the growth in trade in appliances. Less than one-quarter of the foreign subsidiaries of the five large Continental firms that produced appliances in 1971 were located in the Common Market. And these five firms averaged little more than two foreign production subsidiaries in the EEC in the appliance sector. Of the seven EEC-based subsidiaries for which data was available, one was exporting more than half its production.

A few of the Common Market subsidiaries of Continental enterprises in appliances had begun their productive operations as independent companies. These companies, particularly the ones based in Italy, were among the relatively small firms that had aggressively revolutionized the European appliance markets in the late 1950's and early 1960's. They produced relatively simple, standardized models for export and caused considerable discomfiture to many of the large Continental enterprises who had dominated their home markets when tariffs had been high. The largest Continental firms in the industry thus appear to have been responding initially to the threat of smaller

[59] Maillet, 1972: p II.27.
[60] Maillet, 1972: p II.42.
[61] Maillet, 1972: p II.59.

firms when they began selling and re-allocating production on a Community-wide basis. Their initial response appears to have been that of forming anew, rather than acquiring, foreign manufacturing subsidiaries in lower-cost EEC countries. Nearly two-thirds of the EEC subsidiaries of the Continental enterprises in appliances were new start-ups, a percentage of new formations equalled in only one other industry, structural metal products.

By the late 1960's, thanks to more saturated EEC markets, high Italian costs, and increased competition, a number of the independent firms were beginning to experience financial difficulties. A few of the biggest Continental electrical firms then acquired shares in some of the initial challengers.

The precise meaning of these acquisitions was still obscure in 1975: some of the events following these acquisitions suggested that common market behavior in the industry was being reinforced; others raised the possibility that these acquisitions had been undertaken to block further changes in production locations to least-cost sites. On the one hand, Philips, the Dutch multinational, transferred the head office of its major domestic appliance division to Italy 'where the main production was already concentrated' after its acquisition of Ignis and IRE.[62] On the other, the German Cartel Office prevented AEG from increasing its 20% holding in the Italian Zanussi to a majority share out of fear that AEG would then have had 'control over much of the cheap Italian imports that were holding down prices in the German markets'.[63] Nonetheless, despite – or because of – such moves by the large Continental multinationals, behavior in household appliances seemed consistent with the existence of a common market.

While there were still gaps between theory and practice in the Common Market with respect to appliances, radios and TV's, the policies and ambitions of nation states contributed at least as much to these gaps as did moves by private companies. Manifold differences in national standards for radios and TV's culminated in the incompatibility between France's SECAM and the PAL system developed by Germany's AEG in color television.[64] Companies could compensate for such NTB's to a limited extent by exploiting scale economies through plant specialization one stage earlier in the production process, whence the relatively high proportion of the intra-EEC 'export subsidiaries' in components. Two of the seven component subsidiaries for which data were available were exporting more than half of their production, a propensity exceeded in the EEC only by subsidiaries in the motor vehicle industry. Location of production 'as if' there were a complete economic community was, however, still to occur.

Questions and Conclusions

The conclusion that emerges from this survey of the foreign production choices of the largest Continental firms within the EEC is a relatively somber one for advocates and well-wishers of European integration. As far as can be judged, the sort of behavior expected from the large Continentally based

---

[62] Philips, Annual Report, 1973.
[63] *The Economist*, March 16, 1974: p 96.
[64] *Entreprise*, 13 September, 1974: p 52.

multinational enterprises in a common market has been more the exception than the rule. Perhaps this judgement should not be pushed too far, for there is much that is not known about industrial behavior in the EEC. Data concerning market interpenetration among the Six is available for only a few product and industry categories, or for one or two countries. The situation is the same with respect to plant size and scale economies. Only one serious study of the relationship – or lack thereof – between the establishment of the EEC and company behavior has been undertaken by the EEC Commission.[65] It discusses the two obvious success stories of integration, autos and appliances. It then discusses some of the problems of Europe's 'non-industries': the high technology sectors almost exclusively in the hands of American firms. Until some of the other industries which constitute the vast bulk of Europe's industrial production are subjected to similar analyses, uninformed views of large European enterprise may well prevail.

To a great extent, Continental European enterprises have been locating foreign subsidiaries in the EEC in a manner one would anticipate with respect to any moderately protectionist group of foreign countries. In the industries we have examined, governments appear to have shifted their attitude toward international, and even intra-community trade from the pre-World War II view of 'none is best' to only as far as 'not too much please'.

Although government non-tarriff barriers, purchasing preferences, subsidies and the like loomed largest in affecting the location decisions of large Continental enterprises in the Community, it was not always clear to what political forces governments were responding. In some cases, like that of AKZO's abortive decision to close plants in several Community countries, it was clear that national union pressures blocked or delayed moves toward common market behavior.[66] In others, government fears of losing face through balance of payments difficulties, or desires to 'keep up with the Joneses' led to the subsidizing of economically questionable plants. But on other occasions, it seemed that some enterprises with high sunk costs in uneconomic NTB or subsidy-factories may themselves have been pressing for public measures to protect against ungentlemanly, disturbing intra-community competition.

Where common-market behavior did occur, it seemed that there was more at work than just an elimination of trade barriers within the EEC: the catalyst of industry outsiders was necessary to provoke large Continental-based enterprises to behave as if there were an EEC.

American companies active in Europe played this catalytic role in automobiles. They may also have played it in some of the electrical machinery sectors we have not discussed in depth, but which have low EEC-subsidiary densities. The effects of the behavior of American-owned companies on European firms, and particularly on Continentally based firms probably should not be exaggerated. Table 6.7 presents estimates for 1964 of the market penetration of subsidiaries of US companies in Europe in nine industry categories both including and excluding the UK. American penetration rates ranging from 1·2%

[65] Maillet, 1972.
[66] Northrup and Rowan, 1974: Part I; for commentary on similar pressures in Italy, see Prodi, 1974.

Table 6.7 Estimates of Sales of US-Controlled Foreign Manufacturing Subsidiaries in Relation to Sales of all Manufacturing Establishments in Europe, 1964

Industry	Sales of US-controlled manufacturing subsidiaries (billions of dollars)		Total sales of manufacturing establishments (billions of dollars)		Subsidiaries' sales as % of all sales (percent)	
	UK and Europe	Europe minus UK	UK and Europe	Europe minus UK	UK and Europe	Europe minus UK
	$	$	$	$	%	%
Food products	1·4	0·5	46·2	37·2	3·1	1·3
Paper and allied products	0·1	0·1	11·0	8·9	1·2	1·0
Chemicals	2·2	0·7	36·3	28·2	6·2	2·5
Rubber products	0·5	0·2	4·2	3·2	12·7	6·0
Primary and fabricated metals	1·0	0·1	43·7	36.6	2.4	0·3
Machinery, except electrical	2·9	1·3	29·7	19·8	9·7	6·6
Electrical machinery	1·7	0·7	18·6	10·6	9·1	6·6
Transport equipment	4·7	2·6	36·6	35·1	12·8	7·3
Other products	1·8	1·0	65·4	34·3	2·8	3·0

Sources: Data grouping the UK and Europe: *Survey of Current Business*, November 1965, page 19; and Hufbauer, G C, and Adler, F M, *Overseas Manufacturing Investment and the Balance of Payments*, US Treasury Department, Washington, DC, 1968, pages 37–8. Data for Europe minus the UK was derived by subtracting adjusted estimates of total sales and US subsidiaries' sales for the UK in 1966 from the global estimates. Figures for total and US subsidiary sales in the UK are found in the US Tariff Commission Report, *Implications of Multinational Firms for World Trade and Investment*, US Senate, Finance Committee, US GPO, Washington, February, 1973, pages 695 and 733–47. Operations in the petroleum sector are excluded from the definition of manufacturing in all of these sources.

to 13% in Europe including the UK, and from 0·3% to 7·3% on the continent do not seem staggering. Still, for particular products, the market share held by US-owned firms is greater. Moreover, it is evident from Table 6.7 that American penetration on the Continent has been high in industries for which Continental firms have displayed common-market behavior in the EEC, as in transport equipment and electrical machinery, and very low in sectors such as primary and fabricated metals.

The exact impact of the 'American challenge' on European companies cannot presently be quantified for any but the very gross industry categories shown in Table 6.7. Nonetheless, European business and government élites have often accused American companies of engaging in unruly and ungentlemanly competitive behavior in order to break into markets.[67] Conditioned by their relatively competitive US home market, they have frequently been said to have disturbed European national market order. American auto companies in particular have often been said to display particularly aggressive behavior

---

[67] Vernon, 1971; Behrman, 1970: Chapter V.

in the EEC. Hearsay indicates that American firms in Europe have frequently assimilated local patterns of industry behavior when they have achieved a 'reasonable' market share. Yet, even when American firms have behaved in non-threatening ways, they have often been suspected of using the gentleman's agreements to lull competitors into a false feeling of security.

In household appliances, the competitive catalysts were relatively small Italian outsiders. Large Italian firms were said to have played this role in synthetic fibers in 1971 and 1972, thus supplementing any effect EEC antitrust action may have had in pushing the European chemicals industry to behave more supranationally.

Notwithstanding the fact that it is one thing to explain the past behavior of large Continental enterprises in the EEC and another to assess future trends, insofar as the past is prologue, certain events seem more likely to occur than others. Few signs of change are in evidence in the industries in which Continental enterprises have established a high proportion of their foreign manufacturing subsidiaries in the EEC. And, as noted in the discussion of the case of the smelting of non-ferrous metals, the change toward fewer intra-EEC subsidiaries that seems in the offing might well be a change provoked by ultra-nationalist policies of eliminating not only foreign suppliers but also foreign ownership.

In some industries, notably in chemicals, efforts to move toward a common market seem under way, although some might see them as both slow and belated. And in these sectors, as well as in those where a common market more or less exists, EEC antitrust efforts and the unsettling influence of American outsiders may help to preserve these fragments of European integration.

Perhaps the main forces working for competitive, common market behavior on the part of the large multinational enterprises of Continental Europe, however, are those that some of these firms have adopted as their own. A number of these enterprises have come to have important operations in North America, and that experience seems to have influenced their comportment at home. Others have reorganized their internal management structures along lines that now conflict with, rather than complement those that trace national, protected borders. These changes in the stimuli operating on and within large Continental enterprise are described in the following chapters.

Chapter VII
The Venturers to The United States

For as long as statistics have been kept, the direct foreign investment in manufacturing in Europe by American multinational enterprises has considerably exceeded the lesser investment in the United States by European firms. For some observers, this asymmetry, presented in Table 7.1, meant that foreign operations in America were an anomaly.[1] This view was reinforced by non-American managers' complaints about the difficulties of US operations,[2] and by heroic tales of European entrepreneurs' leaps into the American unknown.[3] Indeed, some observers speculated that the decisions of foreign firms to invest in manufacturing in the United States might fit no rational model; it was argued that these investments could be understood only by appealing to a 'great man' theory of international enterprise.[4]

The experience of Continental enterprises suggests, however, that rational causes underlay most of their involvement in the United States. Innovations, not great entrepreneurial leaps, underlay trade, and then investment in the United States. Exceptionally, the desire to learn from the stimuli of the high-wage, high-income US market provided the motivation for some spectacular adventures (and misadventures) into American manufacturing. But when Continental firms went to the US without strong innovative advantages,

Table 7.1   Direct Investment in the United States by Companies based in Continental European Countries, Various Years (US $million)

In the United States, from Continental countries	1937	1962	1970	1972	1973
Bel & Lux	71	158	338	309	603
France	57	183	286	321	473
Germany	55	152	680	807	768
Italy	na	100	100	107	85
Netherlands	179	1,082	2,151	2,357	2,550
Sweden	30	179	208	256	291
Switzerland	74	836	1,545	1,567	1,825
Total Continental investments in the United States	**436**	**2,690**	**5,308**	**5,724**	**6,595**
In home countries of Continental European enterprises by American companies	785	5,383	16,520	21,206	23,581

Note: These data include direct investment in sales, financial extractive and service enterprises, as well as that in manufacturing. Data is not available on the value of foreign manufacturing investment in the United States broken down by country of origin.

Sources: For 1962 through 1973, US Department of Commerce, *Survey of Current Business*, various issues, and, *Annual October Survey of Foreign Direct Investment in the United States.*
For 1937, US Department of Commerce, *Foreign Long Term Investments in the United States, 1937–1939*, Washington, GPO, 1940.

[1] Vernon, 1971.
[2] Franko, 1971(A): Chapter I, especially p 10; Michalet and Delapierre, 1973: pp 138 and 139.
[3] Faith, 1971: pp 2 and 3.
[4] Stopford, 1972: pp 14–16.

the competitiveness and unfamiliarity of the American market led to a very high rate of mortality.

The Growth of Continental Manufacturing in the US

A large number of the Continental ventures existing in the United States in 1971 were of very recent origin. Table 7.2 shows that in 1960, 12 large Continental firms owned US manufacturing operations, a number already reached in 1913. These 12 Continental parents owned 25 US manufacturing subsidiaries. A decade later, there were 25 parents and 68 US subsidiary offspring. Some German firms whose US subsidiaries had been confiscated during both world wars, had re-entered, and the Swiss and Dutch companies whose American production experience often dated back to the 1920's, had added new activities. By the beginning of 1971, 46 of the 85 largest Continental firms were involved in manufacturing in the United States, and these 46 firms (42 of which were multinational in the sense of manufacturing in at least seven nations) had spawned no less than 230 US manufacturing subsidiaries. The large German and French companies had increased the number of their US operations with particular rapidity. The 230 US manufacturing subsidiaries nonetheless represented less than nine percent of the total number of foreign manufacturing operations of Continental firms around the world in 1971.

Table 7.2 Manufacturing Subsidiaries in the United States Owned by Continental Enterprises (Selected Years)

Country of parent system	1913	1930	1938	1950	1960	1971
	Number of Parent Systems Manufacturing in the US:					
Germany	6	2	2	0	5	16
France	1	1	0	0	3	9
Bel & Lux	1	1	1	1	2	4
Italy	1	0	0	1	3	4
Netherlands*	2	3	4	4	4	6
Sweden	0	1	1	2	3	2
Switzerland	2	4	4	5	6	6
Total	**12**	**12**	**12**	**12**	**25**	**46**
	Number of Manufacturing Subsidiaries in Operation:					
Germany	7	12	13	0	10	48
France	1	1	0	0	4	20
Bel & Lux	1	1	1	1	3	12
Italy	1	0	0	1	4	6
Netherlands*	2	8	8	9	24	95
Sweden	0	1	1	2	5	3
Switzerland	2	15	9	9	15	29
Total	**14**	**38**	**32**	**25**	**68**	**230**

Note: *Includes the operations of Anglo-Dutch Unilever.
Source: Comparative Multinational Enterprise Project.

Early Continental Activity in the US

Although Continental manufacturing in America grew most rapidly during the 1960's, some of the forces behind its establishment, and some of the parent companies involved, emerged at a very early date. Before the First World War, Siemens had founded the Siemens and Halske Electric Company of North America.[5] Italy's Fiat was assembling in the US[6]. Bayer had established a plant to produce dyestuffs in 1882 and Solvay a soda company in 1881.[7] Metallgesellschaft owned a metals-refining company that later grew into American Metal Climax.[8] Bosch was producing automobile ignition systems.[9] Geigy of Switzerland began producing dyes in the US in 1903.[10] And one of Nestlé's predecessors had been manufacturing condensed milk in America, although it was obliged to sell out its US subsidiary to Borden in 1902.[11]

Several of the Continental European innovations which gave rise to the exports that preceded these early investments were of the labor-saving variety that occasionally first appeared on the Continent. Labor-saving innovations, like the magneto for auto ignitions developed by Bosch of Germany, met a brisk import demand in the US where stupendous tariff barriers encouraged a move into local production in 1906.[12]

European luxury products were also pulled to the high-income United States market before World War I. Some very wealthy Americans provided a limited but profitable market for Mercedes' $7,000 autos. By the turn of the century Mercedes was producing its luxury cars, introduced in the German market 13 years earlier, in a US joint venture with Steinway of piano fame.[13]

Resource-rich America had a limited, but rapidly growing demand for synthetic dyestuffs during the end of the nineteenth century. Almost all of the pre-World War I demand thereof was supplied by German and Swiss exports, since tariffs were kept low by pressure from US textile-industry users. Yet the small Bayer and Geigy plants were kept in operation. Prices could be kept high enough to permit their high-cost production, for US patent laws protected products, not processes, and thus stopped development of alternative paths to the same products by potential American competitors. American synthetic dyestuffs production was negligible at the time, however, and did not assume any importance until the German supply was cut off by the entry of the United States into the war.[14]

Most of these Continental operations in the US were small, yet their number seems to have been equal to the number of American enterprises active on the

---

[5] Siemens, 1957: Vol I, p 309.
[6] Wells, 1974.
[7] Haber, 1958: p 145; Bolle, 1963: p 139.
[8] Metallgesellschaft, 1931.
[9] Bosch, 1961: p 34.
[10] Bürgin, 1900: p 296.
[11] Heer, 1966: p 78.
[12] Bosch, 1961: p 34.
[13] Wells, 1974; Schildberger, Undated: pp 4 and 14.
[14] Haber, 1971: pp 179, 180, 184 and 185. The capability of American firms to produce dyestuffs may also have been low. The suddenness with which American firms embarked upon dyestuffs production during World War I argues, however, that lack of chemical engineering skill was not a serious constraint.

Continent before the First World War. Had Péchiney succeeded in implementing its war-aborted plans to build an aluminum smelter in North Carolina, the Continentals in America might have outnumbered the American companies expanding in Europe.[15] Indeed, one wonders how much transatlantic investment asymmetry would have arisen had not wars, and the confiscations that accompanied wars, intervened. The first six German entrants into US manufacturing were confiscated during World War I. Two of their parents re-entered in the 1920's, brought back their former subsidiaries, and were re-confiscated during World War II. Four of the first six were again among the 16 large German firms that rapidly expanded their manufacturing operations in America after the US government permitted re-entry in the 1950's. A fifth announced major US investment plants in 1973.

Industries with US Activity

Chemical and electrical products, the sectors in which Continental enterprises had their oldest and strongest innovative advantages, have accounted for the bulk of Continental companies' US operations ever since the 1880's. This was the case even during the inter-war period, when there were cartel agreements in force which were supposed to prevent foreign investments in those industries. Swiss and Dutch firms, partly taking advantage of the post-World War I restrictions on German investment brought innovations in dyestuffs, pharmaceuticals, synthetic fibers, and medical electronics into US production in the 1920's.[16] Notwithstanding anguished protestations from American chemical company executives, Bayer re-entered the US in 1924. In 1925 Bayer merged with Hoechst and BASF to form I G Farben, and Farben's US manufacturing subsidiaries came to account for 28% of the US synthetic dyestuffs market by 1940.[17] Holland's AKU started plants for rayon production in the United States in 1928 and 1929, much to the irritation of America's Du Pont and the British-owned American Viscose Corporation. Du Pont and AVC officers had promoted international market-sharing agreements to supplement the protection of the US market afforded by tariffs. Despite the agreements, firms such as Italy's Snia Viscosa kept exporting (dumping?) to the United States. AKU seemed to restrain its exports, but then attacked the US market by local production.[18] Bosch re-purchased its auto-electric subsidiary in 1930.[19]

After World War II, the US subsidiaries of Continental firms continued to be oriented towards chemicals and electrical equipment. In 1971, 56% of the Continentals' US manufacturing subsidiaries were producing chemical and electrical products, as can be seen from Table 7.3.

Although numerous manufacturing subsidiaries had been established around the world by Continental enterprises in motor vehicles, tires and rubber, and

---

[15] On Péchiney's 1913 American project, see: Pitaval, 1946: pp 97–98; Péchiney, 1970. Germany's Metallgesellschaft also had a capital participation in this American venture.
[16] Haber, 1971; Coleman, 1969: p 191.
[17] Stocking and Watkins, 1946: p 472. The US subsidiaries of Swiss enterprises accounted for at least another 12% of the market before World War II, see, Hexner, 1946: p 311.
[18] Coleman, 1969: pp 297 and 298. The AKU plants in the US were owned by its Dutch Enka, and German Glanztoff subsidiaries.
[19] Bosch, 1961: p 124.

Table 7.3 Industry Distribution of Manufacturing Subsidiaries of Continental Firms in the US, Compared with Subsidiaries of US Companies in Continental Europe

	Manufacturing Subsidiaries of:			
	Continental Enterprises in the US		American Enterprises in Home Countries of Continental Firms	
Industry group	1971		1968	
	Number	%	Number	%
Food	12*	5%	91	10%
Textiles and apparel	0	0	22	2
Wood, paper, printing	11	5	38	4
Chemicals	58	24	180	20
Drugs	21	9	49	5
Petroleum refining	6	3	56	6
Rubber and tires	0	0	20	2
Primary metals	7	3	20	2
Fabricated metals	22	10	63	7
Non-electrical machinery	13	6	91	10
Electrical machinery	48	21	104	11
Transport	3	1	59	7
Instruments	12	5	56	6
Other and unknown	15	7	56	6
Totals**	**228**	**100%**	**905**	**100%**

Notes: *Excludes Unilever.
**Percentage totals may not add to 100 due to rounding.
Source: Comparative Multinational Enterprise Project.

petroleum refining, few of these operations were located in the United States. Until Sweden's Volvo announced its intention to build an American plant in 1973, no European firm had produced autos in the US since Mercedes' and Fiat's pre-World War I ventures.[20] Until Michelin of France announced its plans for a radial tire plant in 1973, no Continental firm had owned US tire-fabricating facilities since Michelin itself had made an aborted pre-World War I entry into US production.[21] Shell came to have enormous interests in American petroleum refining since it entered the US oil market in retaliation for Standard Oil's attacks in South-East Asia in 1913, but the refining activity of other Continental oil firms in the US was of marginal importance.[22]

Exchange of Threat or Innovative Advantage?

The skewed industry distribution of Continental manufacturing operations in the United States suggests that the appeals to Newton's Third Law of Motion occasionally used to explain foreign investment in the US do not explain a great deal: American actions in Europe only infrequently led to equal and opposite reactions by European firms in the United States. The

[20] For an excellent discussion of Volvo's move, see: McLain, 1974: pp 153–164.
[21] *Entreprise*, 1973.
[22] On Shell's entry into the US see: Vernon, 1971: p 110; Graham, 1974.

Continental reaction was not equal, nor, except in the chemical and electrical industries, was it particularly opposite, as Table 7.3 shows.[23] In 1971, the number of US manufacturing ventures owned by the 46 largest Continental enterprises active in the US totalled only 25% of the number of operations owned by the 187 largest US multinationals in 1968 in the Continentals' home countries. And US ventures in Europe were frequently numerous in industries such as transport and rubber and tires in which Continental activity in the United States was nil.

Some of the considerable increase in Continental investment in US manufacturing during the 1960's was indeed related to European responses to American company invasions of Continental territory. Subsidiaries could be – and sometimes were – used as pawns in games played among international rivals who alternately challenged and defended established world-market positions.

Exchanges of threats across the Atlantic were particularly characteristic of industries such as basic industrial chemicals and synthetic fibers.[24] European and American companies had come to have roughly equal technological capabilities in these product lines well before World War II. Individual firms each had distinctive advantages in products and processes in chemicals and chemical fibers, but basic technological know-how was widely diffused among a group of large enterprises based in several countries. Continental firms also had financial resources equal to American companies; despite small home markets, the Continentals were of a size roughly equivalent to that of the Americans. Chemicals and fibers were industries which some observers termed mature, as opposed to technological, oligopolies: oligopolistic industry structures seemed more the result of barriers to entry such as capital requirements, company reputation, size, and scale, rather than scientific mystery. Companies were therefore often torn between the desire to exploit quickly advantages that might soon be imitated by other oligopolists, and the desire to retain some semblance of price and share-of-market stability in sectors of great capital intensity.

Before World War II, it was possible for European and American chemical and chemical-fiber firms to seek stability through explicit market-division agreements. These accords were often complemented by cross-licensing agreements which allowed for some immediate and predictable return in foreign markets from innovation. Nonetheless, agreements and accords broke down even before World War II, and I G Farben aggressively undertook dyestuffs operations in the US when trade barriers blocked exports. Alternatively, accords between leading firms served as umbrellas for moves by lesser members of the international oligopoly. Du Pont (and Britain's Courtaulds) may have accepted AKU's establishment of a subsidiary in the US fibers market in the 1920's without counter-attacking in Continental Europe, for fear of arousing the ire of the already menacing Farben.

---

[23] Spearman's rank correlation coefficient for all industries shown in Table 7.3 is 0·62 ('significant' at the 1% level). Excluding chemicals and electrical machinery, however, this coefficient is (an insignificant) 0·33. 'Other and Unknown' were excluded from both calculations.

[24] For further discussion of the role of exchange of threat in oligopoly behavior, see Hymer and Rowthorn, 1970; Caves, 1970: p 16; Vernon, 1971: p 110; Graham, 1974.

After World War II, American antitrust proceedings and the breakup of Farben greatly inhibited the use of explicit agreements to achieve industry stability. American chemical companies increasingly set up or acquired their own subsidiaries in Europe as European economies recovered from the war, grew and provided markets for American innovations. Cross-licensing agreements in which American and European firms assigned each other exclusive rights in specific territories also became rare after World War II. Even exchanges of joint-venture hostages between American and European rivals' home markets were few in number.

Exchanges of joint-venture hostages across the Atlantic did occur: at least two Continental chemical firms had established parallel US and home-country joint ventures with the same American firms in the same product.[25] But joint-venture exchanges (or at least their American halves) risked attack by the US antitrust authorities. America's Monsanto had been required to sell out its share in a US joint venture to its German partner, Bayer, after US courts decided that each firm could have entered the polyurethane-foam market independently.[26] Joint-venture interconnections among rivals, of the sort Continental chemical companies had within Europe, did not develop in America.[27] And, although American firms sometimes provided European rivals with hostages as guarantees of good behavior (in the form of joint ventures in European home countries), both American exports and American subsidiaries in Europe were often seen as threats to Continental profits and market shares.[28]

American firms were in a position to appear particularly threatening to Continental companies when the Americans could hope to recover the full costs of administration and R&D in their US home market. The American enterprises then could choose to export (or dump) at marginal cost. Dumping through trade could, of course, be attacked by the custom authorities in importing countries. But if American firms had producing subsidiaries in Europe, they could cut prices on subsidiary production, recover full costs at home, and effectively dump in the absence of trade. A Continental firm exposed to such a threat in its home market might find the threat particularly menacing, for where else could it hope to recover its full costs?

One Continental response to the menace by American subsidiaries to cut prices was to signal back to American firms that unfriendly behavior would be answered by price cutting in America. Exchange of threat was one means of groping toward industry stability in a world where cartels, agreements, and joint-venture exchanges were frowned upon.

When Continental firms could parry American assaults by the counter threat of exporting to the United States, they did so. Continental chemical firms

---

[25] In some discussions of international oligopoly behavior the terms exchange of hostages and exchange of threat are used interchangeably. The author's preference is to reserve the term exchange of hostages for mutual joint-venture exchanges in which rivals can directly influence the behavior of pieces of each others' empires. This is a different state of affairs than that prevailing when each rival has a fifth-column threat behind the other's lines.

[26] On the Bayer/Monsanto venture, see: Ellis, 1970: pp 66 and 67.

[27] On joint venture interconnections in Europe, see Chapter VI.

[28] Wilkins, 1974: p 381, suggests that many American joint ventures in Europe served such a hostage role.

countered many an American incursion into Europe in bulk plastics – goods that fit the 'mature oligopoly' category just as well as dyestuffs and fibers did – through export sales, not investment.[29]

Often, however, the export response risked being rendered ineffective by American tariff or non-tariff barriers to trade. In synthetic fibers, threats were exchanged through investment. German firms first tried to retaliate for American incursions into some of their synthetic-fibers markets by exporting other varieties of synthetic fibers to the United States. But, as the former president of Hoechst remarked in his memoirs, effective retaliation required undertaking fiber production in America.[30] During the 1960's there was a growing risk that American producers of synthetic fibers would obtain increased protection from tariffs and quotas.[31] Had protection materialized, the only effective deterrent to American price cutting abroad would have been the ability to threaten American producers in their home markets.

By 1971, something of a state of relative transatlantic balance seemed to have been reached between US investment in chemicals and synthetic fibers in Holland and Germany, on the one hand, and Dutch and German investment in the US on the other. The number of subsidiaries of Dutch chemical firms in the US in 1971 was equal to that of US firms in Holland in 1968; the number of German subsidiaries in the US seemed to be between one-half to two-thirds those established in the other direction. The balance seemed yet more even in terms of sales: the sales of majority and 100%-owned subsidiaries of American chemical firms in Germany (including exports) were $963 million in 1970;[32] the sales of Bayer, BASF, and Hoechst subsidiaries in the US were estimated to exceed that amount. These figures, of course, include sales in product lines other than basic chemicals and fibers: companies do not report detailed statistics by product. They are, however, suggestive of the state of play of the game.

Exchange of threat influenced some Continental implantations in the United States, but even in chemicals other motivations were also present. Continental chemical companies usually led from technological strength when they decided to produce in the United States, whether or not they were concerned with American behavior in Europe. Moreover, because Continental enterprises were strongest in material-saving processes and synthetics, their US implantations continued to be associated with trade barriers, as they had been during the 1920's and 1930's. Bayer and BASF's re-entry into US dyestuffs production after World War II gave them subsidiaries behind the lines of some American multinationals which were menacing German positions in Europe. But Bayer and BASF chose to produce specialty dyestuffs which were not yet being manufactured in the United States. The German firms also had the process and cost advantages of long production experience: the United States had become the largest single market for synthetic dyestuffs and fibers after World War II, but German (and Dutch) *per capita* consumption in most

---

[29] *Financial Times*, 1971.
[30] Winnacker, 1971: p 370.
[31] *Financial Times*, 1970: p 16.
[32] Figures for American companies from United States Tariff Commission, 1973: p 736.

synthetics still far exceeded that in the US in 1970.[33] In addition, the German firms faced tariffs on organic chemical products (including dyestuffs) which were assessed on the basis of the American Selling Price valuation system. Import duties were levied on the basis of prices prevailing in the protected US market for 'similar' products, not on import prices. The ASP valuation system had originally been imposed to protect American firms against the innovations and cost advantages (especially in R&D) that German and Swiss enterprises already possessed in 1922.[34] Continental chemical companies had jumped the ASP barrier at that time; in the 1960's the successors of I G Farben repeated history, for the cost and trade barrier conditions confronting them bore a remarkable similarity to those prevailing 40 years earlier. German costs were below American costs during the 1960's, and the German interest in exporting, not investing, was demonstrated by the vigorous lobbying of the American chemical companies in favor of the ASP.

In specialty chemicals, pharmaceuticals and electrical equipment, Continental investment in the US followed the classical sequence of distinctive innovation, export, and then manufacture. We can document the rationale for about two dozen of the post-1960 Continental subsidiary establishments in these sectors in the US; all but a handful of these were traceable to European innovations. Geigy's DDT, an insecticide, was exported to, then produced in the United States in the 1950's and early 1960's, as were the herbicides and agricultural chemicals subsequently innovated by that firm.[35] Montecatini-Edison's polypropylene;[36] Sandoz's psycho-pharmaceuticals; BASF's magnetic recording tapes (an I G Farben innovation of the 1930's)[37] and Philips' convenience recording cassettes[38] had all been sold, then produced in the United States. Some of the decisions to produce these products in the US were influenced by tariff and non-tariff barriers to trade; none seem to have been provoked by American actions in Europe.

Dutch and Swiss enterprises were particularly prominent in Continental moves to carry new products and processes in electrical goods, fine chemicals and drugs to the United States in the 1960's. This was perhaps to be expected of enterprises like Philips, AKZO and Hoffmann-La Roche, all of which spent more than seven percent of their yearly sales' revenue on R&D.[39] These enterprises' American ventures constituted more than responses to US invasions of European home markets. It is difficult to satisfactorily define the home markets of firms based in small countries like Switzerland and Holland. Yet it is noteworthy that the dozen Swiss chemical and drug-production subsidiaries in the US have no US-owned counterparts in Switzerland (except for a few small R&D laboratories), and that Dutch-owned electrical products

---

[33] *Chemical Engineering News*, 1973: p 53.
[34] Haber, 1971: p 240. The American Selling Price valuation principle was written into the Fordney-Macomber Tariff Act. For a detailed description of the American Selling Price import valuation system, see, Baldwin, 1970: pp 134–136.
[35] Discussions with company executives.
[36] Discussions with company executives.
[37] BASF, 1965: p 54.
[38] *Barrons*, October 13, 1969.
[39] The (statistically significant) relationships between the propensity of European enterprises to establish US subsidiaries and their R&D intensity (as measured by R&D as a percentage of sales) has been emphasized by Franko, 1971(A) and, McClain, 1974.

subsidiaries in the US outnumbered American electrical subsidiaries in Holland by 32 to three. One US subsidiary of a Swiss pharmaceutical company, Hoffmann-La Roche, was itself the single largest producer in the United States of ethical drugs sold by doctors' prescriptions.[40]

Even in aluminum, an industry which in many ways fits the image of a mature oligopoly *par excellence*, Continental enterprises ventured into manufacturing in the United States only when they were simultaneously confronted by the threat of trade barriers and were convinced that they had a technological advantage. Péchiney and Alusuisse each set up two smelting subsidiaries in the United States during the 1960's. The establishment of these ventures may in part have constituted moves in a series of exchanges of threats with American producers.[41] However, it is arguable that the Europeans were the first to threaten American positions. Throughout the 1960's, the United States was a large net importer of aluminum metal. Most US imports came from Canada, but particularly in the early 1960's, significant amounts came from Péchiney's French smelters or from smelters in Norway (which were owned by Continental, Norwegian, and Canadian firms).[42] American firms responded both by vigorous lobbying for US protection and by marginal-cost pricing of exports to Continental countries (especially to Germany, a country without its 'own' major entrant in the industry). Péchiney 'sought a means to stabilize its sales in the United States'.[43] First it acquired a fabricating company (Alusuisse had fabricated in the US since 1948); shortly thereafter Péchiney was invited by an American firm (which had a market position in competitive non-ferrous metals) to undertake a joint smelting venture to be based on Péchiney's energy-saving technology. The venture enabled Péchiney to hedge against the imposition of US trade barriers and to capitalize on fuel-saving process innovations. In this energy-intensive industry, Péchiney's electricity-saving technology more than enabled the firm to overcome the disadvantages of applying relatively labor-intensive European production methods in the US context of high labor cost. As a result of limited hydro-electric sources and American protection of high-cost domestic oil sources, Péchiney's US competitors were experiencing higher energy costs relative to their labor costs. It seemed the turn of the United States to provide a fertile ground for the application of a European innovation, especially when trade was inhibited.[44]

To what extent was there an exchange of threat? Some American aluminum firms did eventually establish smelters in Norway and Britain, but American facilities in the Continental markets were limited to Germany until the 1970's.[45] Still, American smelting capacity in Europe, including capacity in

---

[40] This statement cannot be fully verified since Hoffmann-La Roche publishes no statistics concerning its operations. Industry sources often estimated Roche's 1970 US sales as being around $500 million. America's Merck had consolidated worldwide sales of $748 million in 1970, of which about two-thirds came from ethical drugs. (Willatt, 1971; Fortune, 1971.)

[41] Vernon, 1971: p 110; Forbes, 1964: p 41.

[42] OECD, 1962: p 61.

[43] Péchiney, 1970: p 1.

[44] During the early 1960's US aluminum imports from France had exceeded 30,000 tons per year; by 1972 they had dropped to less than half that amount. OECD, 1962: p 61; OECD, 1972: p 54.

[45] OECD, 1973: pp 27 and 28. Vaupel and Curhan, 1969: p 210.

the UK and in Norway, consistently lagged behind European capacity in the United States. Furthermore, on a worldwide basis, American firms appeared to be losing market share relative to European companies.[46]

The tire and rubber industry is another sector which superficially fit the mature oligopoly category, and Michelin's decision to manufacture in the US in the early 1970's was occasionally interpreted as a response to American activity in Europe.[47] Other factors were also at work, however. First, there was the pull of US market demand on Michelin's innovation:

'In 1972, Michelin sold 35% of all radial tires sold in the US, and its sales volume approached 250 million dollars. The tires came from Spain . . . .'[48]

Previously, when American raw-material costs favored the shorter-lived, belted tire, there was little demand for radial tires in the United States:

'Michelin invented (the radial) . . . before the second world war . . . France was the first country to adopt the radial before being imitated by other European countries, then the United States.'[49]

In spite of the rapidly growing demand for radials in the United States, Michelin almost desperately sought to *avoid* producing in the high-labor cost American market; it saw no special advantage or insurance effect from having the same cost structure as American firms. The company's first North American production site was in Canada. That investment was prompted by fears of US protectionist moves against Spanish production and represented an attempt simultaneously to get a low labor-cost production site, a subsidized plant in a depressed Canadian region, and duty-free access to the US market via the US–Canadian free-trade agreement on autos and parts. American competitors protested that Canada's subsidization of Michelin's New Brunswick facilities gave Michelin an unfair advantage; the US government responded to these complaints by putting a six percent surtax on Michelin's imports from its Canadian plant.[50] Only after US demand had created a market, and US government policy had prevented that market from being profitably supplied from abroad, did Michelin become convinced of the practicability of investing in South Carolina in 1973.

Market Convergence

Industry patterns and company examples thus argue that the desire to capitalize on innovative advantage was involved in the majority of the forays of Continental firms into US manufacturing. But why should the American market have shown an interest in Continental innovations in the first place?

Occasionally, European firms did innovate labor-saving or high-income products. Sometimes US demand was large enough to encourage the establishment of Continentally owned production facilities in America. A sizable US demand for a European product could occasion diseconomies in supply or

---

[46] Kuhn, Loeb, & Co, 1968.
[47] Tsurumi, 1974: p 14.
[48] *Entreprise*, April 27, 1973: p 101.
[49] *Entreprise*, February 9, 1973.
[50] *Entreprise*, April 27, 1973.

transport which would favor an American production location. The marketing of new European products (like the marketing of new American products) also often required that production take place close to customers. Customer needs were often ill-specified at early stages of product life cycles, and product modifications were often desired; these could not always wait to fit European production or shipping schedules. But if European products were new in the US, demand for them was typically insensitive to price, and higher US labor costs could be passed on to customers.[51]

Mercedes, Bosch, and Nestlé, all carried labor-saving or high-income innovations to America before 1914. Their precedent was followed a number of times after World War II. Geigy's herbicides, for example, found their largest market in the US, for American labor-saving farm machinery could not be used on crops ridden with weeds, and US labor was too expensive for the weed-removing job to be done by hand. Geigy responded to this demand with US production; other European firms were to respond in a like manner to US demands in electrical equipment, psycho-pharmaceuticals, and medical and scientific instruments.

Some US demand for Continental innovations arose in the 1960's and early 1970's because the cost of certain raw materials was rising relative to labor costs in the United States. This change in relative factor costs in America provided a stimulus to the application of European material-saving innovations and synthetics in the US – much as increases in labor costs relative to material costs in Europe provided a demand for American labor-saving products and processes on the Continent. For example, US import quotas during the 1960's raised the price of oil and petrochemical feedstocks above those current in Europe. Once imports of organic chemicals were inhibited by the ASP barrier, occasions arose for Continental firms to employ European processes in America for the utilization of waste petroleum refinery gases which had been developed at a time when European feedstock costs had been highest.

Relatively high US oil prices were also partly responsible for the opportunity given to Péchiney to apply successfully its European, energy-saving technology in the US: protected, high-cost oil meant higher electricity costs for American firms.

The convergence of American and Continental relative factor prices gathered steam during the early 1970's when the sudden escalation of oil and raw-materials prices, combined with doom-preaching of the *Limits to Growth* variety, gave impetus to a search to conserve materials in the United States.[52] One result of the shift in the price of petroleum relative to labor in America was that a German firm with long experience in a fuel-short country was prompted to announce its third entry into US manufacturing. In 1973, Bosch announced plans to start up US production of gasoline-saving, fuel-injection

---

[51] On the marketing requirements of new products, see: Vernon, 1966; Hirsch, 1967.
[52] See, Meadows, *et al*, 1972. On July 5, 1974, it was reported that the US Defense Department was opposing the free purchase of gold by US citizens on the grounds that the 'precarious US raw-materials position' might require use of US gold reserves for imports during some future war. See, *Journal de Genève*, July 5, 1974.

equipment – a product line whose innovation in Germany commenced in the inter-war period.[53]

In all probability, a gradual shift in the cost of raw materials relative to that of labor in the US commenced around the turn of the century. It was then that the US ran out of unlimited supplies of land.[54] The implication for European products of this shift toward more expensive raw materials can be seen in the cases of two synthetics innovated on the Continent: rayon-staple fiber and margarine.

Table 7.4 World Staple-Fiber Production (In Thousands of Pounds)

Year	United States	Japan	Great Britain	Germany	Italy	Total
1930	350	0	850	4,350	700	6,250
1935	4,600	13,625	9,320	37,900	67,675	120,820
1939	53,000	309,500	60,000	440,000	191,000	1,053,500

Source: Encyclopaedia Britannica, 1951: p 709E.

Table 7.4 shows how the German and Italian market demand for rayon staple – a product that substituted for both wool and cotton – led US demand during the 1930's. The German and Dutch firms that were to achieve an important position in synthetic chemical-fibers production in the United States had first supplied a very large fraction of the demand in the Continental markets in which the first demand for synthetics had appeared. These firms reinforced their advantages in innovation with production experience gained not only in home-country plants, but also in Dutch-owned tariff factories in Germany and Italy, and in German plants in Italy.[55]

Table 7.5 illustrates the increase in margarine demand relative to that of butter in the United States. Before World War I, when the manufacturing subsidiaries of Unilever's Dutch predecessors were proliferating in Europe, an abundance of dairy products in the US minimized the US demand for margarine. After World War II, the price of dairy fats rose relative to the price of vegetable fats. This shift in relative prices had occurred on the Continent nearly one half-century earlier. Few US companies had much experience in margarine. But the Dutch part of Unilever had first introduced margarine as a butter substitute in 1871.[56] In 1948, Unilever acquired a failing US margarine company in time to meet the boom in US margarine demand shown in Table 7.4.[57]

Until the early 1970's, however, there were few European synthetic or material-saving innovations which seemed to meet a demand so large, so price inelastic or so unpredictable, (or which had a production scale so small), as to prompt US manufacturing without protection. The evidence presented

[53] Bosch, 1961: pp 60, 124 and 126.
[54] Habbakuk, 1962.
[55] Fauquet, 1960: Chapter 2, Annexe 7.
[56] Wilson, 1954: p 29.
[57] Wilson, 1968: p 230.

Table 7.5 Consumption of Butter and Margarine in the United States, 1930–1973

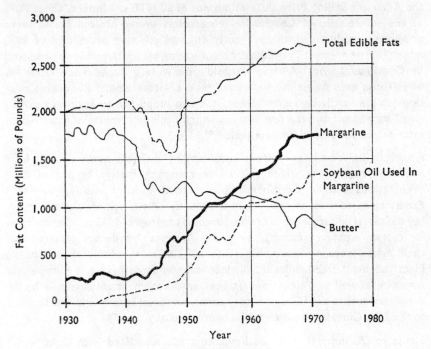

Source: Dovring, in *Scientific American*, February 1974: p 18.

in Chapter III showed that the raw-materials problem of the United States was of a wholly different order from that of Western Europe. And, while shifting relative prices in America may have created niches for European materials-saving processes and products, the reluctant US entry of Michelin and others spoke again of the role of the policies of a host-country government in stimulating multinational production activity by Continental enterprise.

US Trade Barriers

The role of American trade barriers in stimulating non-American manufacturing investment in the US has received some notice.[58] But it has surely been underemphasized – at least in the Continental case. Much of the rapid increase in the number of US subsidiaries of Continental enterprises during the 1960's was a by-product of efforts by high-cost American producers of price-elastic products to get the US government to stop American imports of goods produced by European firms with more favorable cost structures.

The sectors in which Continental firms' exports were most likely to hit US government limits to trade also happened to be those in which they had their most notable histories of innovation. Effective rates of US tariff protection in chemicals, drugs, electric lighting, fabricated-metal products, and scientific

---

[58] Daniels, 1971; McClain, 1974.

instruments in 1964 were all estimated to equal or exceed 20%. These estimates took into account the incidence of some non-tariff barriers (such as the American Selling Price system) but not of all NTB's.[59] Indeed, about 70% of the subsidiaries of Continental enterprises in the United States were producing products which apparently enjoyed effective protection of 20% *ad valorum* or greater. The industry classification by which products produced by Continental firms' American subsidiaries were grouped were crude, as were those used to estimate effective rates of protection.[60] But such a relationship can hardly be a coincidence; it is also supported by European executives' statements and the few surveys which provide glimpses of Continental motivations for American production.[61]

American limits on imports from Continental firms were numerous. US food and drug regulations which refused to recognize foreign testing of drug preparations obliged Continental pharmaceutical firms wishing to reach American customers, to produce in the US. Buy-American regulations applying to federal and state government purchases augmented US tariff protection for certain customer markets by giving American producers preference if their prices were no more than 15 to 25% more expensive than imports. Electrical firms faced differential electrical standards between Europe and America, as well as Defense department encouragement to physically locate supply sources in the US on military contracts (because 'Holland was so close to the Iron Curtain that it could be overrun at any time.')

Limits to US imports, like the limits to trade associated with Continental implantations across borders in Europe after World War II, restricted trade. But they did not stop it altogether, as governmental and cartel barriers had done in the 1930's. It is perhaps for this reason that these limits were associated with increasing, rather than decreasing Continental involvement in US manufacturing. After World War II, moderate, rather than prohibitive tariffs enabled European enterprises to test US market demand; by marginal-cost pricing if necessary. During the 1950's, the innovative prowess of American firms was such that European imports were not terribly threatening. As Europe recovered from World War II, however, Continental firms were increasingly able to imitate or vary American products. And as new American products matured, standardized, and faced increasingly price-elastic demand in the US, European imitators could export to US customers and sell on the basis of price. European firms could undercut American companies (domestic or multinational) in the US if they had absolute advantages in labor costs, or if they had developed cost-cutting process innovations. Faced with foreign competition, American firms in import-competing industries sought, and sometimes obtained, protective succor from the US government.

Continental firms which had only absolute labor-cost advantages, like those in textiles, could be shut out of the US market by anti-dumping proceedings, 'voluntary' agreements, tariff increases, and NTB's. But firms with distinctive products or processes could jump those barriers.

---

[59] Baldwin, 1970: pp 163 and 164.
[60] US manufacturing subsidiaries were grouped by 3-digit US Standard Industrial Classification categories. These were not necessarily comparable to the groupings used by Baldwin.
[61] Franko, 1971(A): p 11; Daniels, 1971; Michalet and Delapierre, 1973.

Although the link between American trade barriers and Continental investment decisions was most visible at the moment of subsidiary establishment, it
surfaced again whenever public debates over American trade policy took
place. There exists no systematic survey of the attitude of managers of
European companies or their US subsidiaries toward US trade policy. Nonetheless, something is known about positions taken by executives in the most
important Continental chemical companies with US ventures. Some of the
most vigorous defenders of the American Selling Price valuation of organic
chemicals were to be found among managers of American subsidiaries of
European dyestuffs firms.[62] These managers greatly feared seeing production
re-allocated back to non-American sites, an event which might have occurred
had the promises to eliminate the ASP system made by the US executive in
the Kennedy Round negotiations actually been implemented by the US
Congress. Moreover by the mid-1970's, managers of the Continental parents
had lost interest in persuading the United States to remove the ASP valuation
system. Since their companies had by then jumped the US barrier, they
informed their governments that European diplomatic pressure on America
over ASP was 'no longer necessary'.[63] When proposals to increase tariffs
on synthetic fibers were being considered by the US Congress in 1970 and
1971, top managers of one of the oldest and largest Continental-owned
US fibers producers sent out letters to American shareholders (who owned
a minority of the subsidiaries' stock) urging them to support protectionist
legislation, because the US venture was being threatened by non-American
products – many of which were coming from corporate relatives in Continental Europe!

The most common single cause for the existence of European manufacturing
in the US after World War II was thus the same as that which led Continental
investment to spread throughout Europe and the less developed countries:
companies had jumped trade barriers to exploit innovative advantages born
in Continental markets.

Learning and Failure

In the light of the importance of trade barriers and technology in Continental
implantation in America, entries motivated by a desire to learn provided
interesting, but atypical counterpoint to the main themes. Moreover, it was
the rare Continental 'gamble of leaping to a global logistical structure that
would match US controlled enterprise' that was fully successful.'[64]

A number of Continental enterprises did use US subsidiaries as a means of
diversifying into technologies and products which they had not previously
produced in Europe. By 1971, nine firms had subsidiaries which had acquired
or started US operations in products or processes not previously produced
by parent companies or subsidiaries elsewhere in the world. This phenomenon
of diversification in a foreign market preceding diversification at home was

[62] Faith mentions the views of the American managers of Ciba-Geigy, US (Faith, 1971: p 74).
Other examples have been mentioned to the author in discussions with executives.
[63] Dale, 1972.
[64] Quote from Vernon, 1971: p 111.

practically unknown in the foreign-manufacturing history of American enterprises.[65]

The Continental enterprises which were most successful in tapping American skills and in responding to peculiarly American market needs were not taking gambles or leaps into the unknown, however. They diversified in the US years after they first commenced manufacturing in the United States with products and processes that had originated in Europe. Shell, after it had already refined petroleum in the US for more than 20 years, chose to make its first entry into petrochemicals in America in the 1930's.

'... the reason was simple: the supply of excellent scientists available in California. Even by today's standard it was a bold move to allow a foreign subsidiary to lead an important, research-based piece of diversification; then it was a virtually unprecedented piece of 'multinationalism' ... all the development work on Shell's extremely profitable weed killers was done in the US.'[66]

After 30 years of experience in the United States, the American Enka subsidiary of Holland's AKU (later AKZO) diversified from synthetic fibers to plastic-covered wire and cable and electrical insulating material in the 1960's. It did so by acquiring American companies.[67]

An initial leap into establishment or acquisition of US operations out of a desire to learn-by-doing, rather than out of an ability to exploit an oligopoly advantage, was a more dangerous affair. Olivetti's 1963 purchase of Underwood furnished the most widely known post-war case of a Continental investment in US manufacturing undertaken largely for the sake of learning. The risks of such a strategy were made amply evident, however, by the fact that the venture very nearly failed. And, to make its US operation viable, Olivetti invested nearly 100 million dollars – an amount once called 'the highest tuition fee in history'.[68] Olivetti found, as did many other Continental firms, that most of what was learned in the US was unplanned and involuntary – and involved a substantial chance of failure.

Continental firms that established US manufacturing operations without a clear competitive advantage based on technological innovation often ended up making unceremonious exits from the United States. Twenty-nine of the Continental subsidiaries established in the United States between 1900 and 1971 were sold or liquidated by their European parents.[69] Indeed, nearly 40% of all 78 subsidiaries ever sold or liquidated by Continental enterprises around the world were located in America. This was a wholly disproportionate number of sales and liquidations: Continental firms had established only a tenth of their manufacturing subsidiaries in the United States.

These exits from US operations were often disagreeable affairs. One of the predecessors of Nestlé, the Anglo-Swiss Consolidated Milk Company, had

[65] See Table 1.2 in Chapter 1 for comparative data on foreign and domestic product diversification by Continental and American enterprises.
[66] Faith, 1971: p 53.
[67] AKU, 1964: p 21; American Enka, 1965: p 8.
[68] Vernon, 1971: p 111.
[69] Comparative Multinational Enterprise Project.

achieved a success in European operations based in imitation and improve-
ment of condensed milk, a product innovated by Borden in the United States.
But technological equivalence was not sufficient for Anglo-Swiss to have
profitable US manufacturing operations in the competitive American environment.

> 'The Dixon factory was hardly completed (in 1890) when five com-
> petitors launched similar products on the market.'[70]

That operation hung on to existence until it was sold to Borden in 1902. The
American manufacturing subsidiaries of the Swiss Brown-Boveri electrical
company established between the world wars met a similar fate.[71] During the
1960's it was the turn of France's St-Gobain to experience failure in the
United States. Thinking that its 300 years of experience in polished plate-
glass would be a sufficient guarantee of viability in US manufacturing, St-
Gobain responded to a threat of American import restrictions in 1958 by
deciding to build a factory in Kingsport, Tennessee, completed in 1962.[72]
The company did not reckon with the possibility that the float-glass process,
innovated at about the same time by Britain's Pilkington, might be made
operational by Pilkington's US licensees. At the opening ceremonies of the
Kingsport plant, the president of America's Pittsburgh Plate Glass (PPG)
Company was heard to remark that the St-Gobain venture was 'the most
modern obsolete plant in the world'.[73] PPG had its Pilkington-licensed float
plant in operation in 1963, and was followed by nine other US firms in rapid
succession.

> 'The result of SG's miscalculation of US competitive behavior (among
> other things) followed with all the inevitability of a Greek tragedy.
> American Saint-Gobain (ASG), the US subsidiary, chalked up losses
> almost every year. In 1969 its losses topped $one million, and in the first
> quarter of 1970 they reached $658,000.
>
> SG finally sold its 57% participation in ASG, which had carved about
> 6% of the US plate glass market, to Nelson Loud & Associates for $one
> million (and later repayment of company debts to SG of some $2·35
> million), after having spent more than $19 million on the subsidiary over
> 12 years.'[74]

The failure of one tenth of Continental ventures into US manufacturing –
and the teething troubles of a good many more – amply demonstrated that
manufacturing in America was fraught with special difficulties for enterprises
conditioned in a non-American market setting.

Adaptation to the US Environment

Many of the difficulties faced by Continental firms in America could be traced
to the long-standing differences in attitudes toward competition on the part

[70] Heer, 1966: p 74.
[71] Brown-Boveri, 1966: p 213.
[72] On American tariff increases on sheet glass – and the ambivalence of American St-Gobain
toward them subsequent to its plant's coming on stream – see: Curzon and Curzon, 1973.
[73] Smith, 1965: p 150.
[74] Franko, 1971(A): p 10.

of American and Continental governments.[75] Compared to the environment in which the large enterprises of Continental Europe grew to maturity, that of America was 'non-negotiable'. As Nestlé, St-Gobain and many others discovered, there were bound to be American competitors. American trade barriers could inhibit competition from imports, but they could not confer protection from US enterprises. The United States had antitrust traditions going back to the 1880's, while market-sharing agreements had been frowned on in Europe only since the Treaty of Rome and went unpunished until 1969 when the EEC levied its first fine. US law forbade acquisitions of shares in competitive companies if significant proportions of an industry or product group were involved, while in Europe French firms, say, could buy into Belgian companies – or trade joint-venture bargaining counters with them – in order to deter market invasion.

When US competitors struck, European enterprises were often handicapped in their response both by reflexes conditioned to seek negotiated arrangements and by the frequent inapplicability of European production and distribution techniques to American relative-factor costs. Continental firms often had difficulty in coming up with *encores* once the initial margin of Continental monopolistic technological advantage had worn off. When St-Gobain's American subsidiary found its European processes an insufficient match for the Pilkington float-glass method perfected by US competitors, it was suddenly confronted by the problem of high US labor costs. When the US subsidiary of one European chemical enterprise misjudged the ability of American firms to innovate around its material-substituting product, it too found itself saddled with a labor-intensive plant which no longer had competitive costs. As Table 7.6 indicates, the home-country experience of Continental firms conditioned them to use more labor per unit of sales than

Table 7.6 Sales per Person in Large American and Continental European Enterprises Classified by Selected Main Industries of Company $'000, 1970

Main industry	Fortune '500' American companies	81 Continental firms on Fortune '200' list	Continental sales per employee as a percentage of American
	($'000)	($'000)	(%)
Food	44·4	28·6	64%
Rubber	27·5	17·6	64
Chemicals & drugs	37·2	27·3	73
Petroleum	113·4	73·5	65
Glass	29·1	20·1	69
Iron & steel	34·1	28·9	85
Non-ferrous metals	37·7	34·7	92
Non-electrical machinery	28·1	23·0	82
Electrical machinery	25·7	19·3	75
Office machinery	28·2	13·0	46
Motor vehicles & parts	41·3	24·7	60

Source: Calculated from information provided in *Fortune.*

[75] See also Chapter IV.

their US counterparts. Only in the non-ferrous metals sector did the 1970 sales volume per person in Continental firms reach more than 85% of the US company level.

The difficulties of adaptation to American labor costs, once the menace of competition appeared, were compounded for Continental firms operating in the US by a host of other competitive disadvantages. Unlike British and Canadian firms operating in the United States, Continental firms had to cope with more or less severe linguistic, ethical, culinary, religious and personal differences in behavior. They also had to cope with the US style of business-government relationships. Unlike the cordial, close relationship prevailing in most Continental countries, that between government and business in the United States was arms'-length, impersonal, and even hostile.[76] These cultural changes, plus the crude economic fact that average US income levels were much higher than those on the Continent, led to customer and employee behavior quite unlike that to which most Continental firms were habituated. When competition threatened, Continental firms had only two choices: learn and adapt, or withdraw and admit failure.[77]

The nature of the adaptation to the US *milieu* by European firms displayed a multiplicity of forms.[78] Perhaps the most far-reaching adaptation occasioned by the impact of American competition on US subsidiaries was the nearly universal undertaking of research and development in the United States. In 1971, nearly all the American subsidiaries of Continental European firms were undertaking some R&D activity; the few exceptions were either very recent ventures or were in some stage of financial difficulty. A number of withdrawals from US manufacturing by Continental parents – including St-Gobain – were directly linked to parental reluctance to allow US subsidiaries to do R&D.

It was unusual for a Continental European firm to allow any foreign subsidiary to do its own R&D.[79] And none seemed to have planned to do R&D in the United States when US manufacturing was first established. US R&D activity was usually initiated under the pressure of competitive challenge, which eventually provided the focus for the kind of learning that helped some

---

[76] For a comparison of the radically different American and French styles of business-government relations, see, Vernon, 1971: Chapter 6. For illustrations of European problems in adjusting to these differences, see, Faith, 1971; Franko, 1971(A).

[77] The interrelationship between the competitiveness of product markets and the likelihood of company adaptation of production processes to factor price levels has been emphasized for multinational-company behavior in less developed countries by Wells, 1973(A).

[78] Ward, 1973; Leontiades, 1973.

[79] Currently available data tell one little about the propensity of European firms to undertake R&D activities outside of their home-country markets. No systematic data seems available on American practice either. The general rule in both American and European practice seems to have been to keep R&D at home. Illustrative examples for US practice are found in Duerr, 1970.

Holthus, *et al*, 1974, cite Bayer as undertaking research on veterinary products in Argentina in addition to US R&D, and Hoechst as undertaking R&D in eight countries outside of Germany. *Business International*, 1972: p 287, notes that the practice of doing foreign R&D seems to be growing while describing the 'offshore' efforts of SKF and other Swedish firms. *Business International*, 1972: p 115, describes the Indian R&D laboratory of Hoechst, as well as the foreign R&D operations of numerous American firms. Much light remains to be cast upon this question.

Continental enterprises to 'evolve from a parochial national orientation to an Olympian view of their threats and opportunities'.[80] A detailed examination of the 23 Continental enterprises with the largest US manufacturing operations indicated that all but five of these companies had received 'feedback' from American operations that had had some visible impact on parent product lines or marketing practices.[81] Still, the desire to get such feedback had consciously motivated the establishment of US R&D activities in only a handful of cases.

Adaptation and Ownership

Competition in America not only obliged Continental firms to allow their US subsidiaries to undertake R&D, but also pushed Continental enterprises to own 100% of their US operations. In 1971, a much greater proportion of Continental companies' American manufacturing subsidiaries were wholly owned than the proportion typical for Continental subsidiaries elsewhere in the world. Two-thirds of the Continentals' US subsidiaries were wholly owned, compared to 46% of all Continental foreign manufacturing operations. Moreover, moves by Continentals to buy out their joint-venture partners following entry into the US were common: at least a dozen of the 126 wholly owned ventures operating in the US in 1971 had started out as joint ventures with American corporate partners.[82]

The Continental preference of 100%-ownership of operations in the United States largely stemmed from the need to respond quickly to competitors' moves.[83] Under the competitive conditions prevailing in the US, joint-venture partners could not separate marketing and technical functions: marketing decisions frequently involved R&D activities and vice-versa. Partners could not keep out of each other's way by any simple division of labor within the venture. And the speed of competitive play made meetings and discussions aimed at harmonizing partners' interests an expensive luxury.

The problems of using joint ventures in the US market were well illustrated by the experience of one US subsidiary which found itself cut off from new application developments in its line of specialty plastics until it developed its own marketing competence, under its own ownership umbrella. While the subsidiary was a joint venture, its sales network was managed by the US partner. Only after buying out the partner's sales network could the firm reintegrate the marketing and R&D functions in the US and go from rather dismal failure to quite considerable success over the subsequent five years.[84]

---

[80] Vernon, 1971: p 109.

[81] Research done in connection with Franko, 1971(A): pp 28 and 33, and reported therein together with findings for British firms.

[82] Franko, 1971(A). Although the data is fragmentary, moves by European parents to take over 100%-ownership of US operations initially entered as joint ventures appears to have been common during the inter-war period. On I G Farben's progressive takeover of the US General Aniline and Film Company, see Stocking and Watkins, 1946: p 472.

[83] For a more detailed discussion of the link between speed of response in the US market and 100%-ownership, along with some specific case histories of moves from joint ventures to wholly-owned forms, see, Franko, 1971(A): Chapter V, p 48; Franko, 1972; Wells, 1973(B).

[84] Franko, 1971(A): p 48.

Nationality of US Subsidiary Managers

Continental success in US operations was critically dependent on *what* was done in America. It was not dependent on whether an American or a European managed the US subsidiary, however. There was no consensus among managers in Continental enterprises that adjustment to the US market required American presidents for American operations. And no correlation could be found between success in US operations and management nationality. Local managers were used in US manufacturing subsidiaries only slightly more often than in Europe or in the Third World, according to information provided by 20 Continental companies active in America.[85]

Toward a Global Outlook?

Adapting to the US market environment was a first step on the road toward a global perception of threat and opportunity by Continental enterprises. As the American market environment moulded and shaped the research and development efforts of their US subsidiaries, some Continental enterprises found themselves able to introduce innovations in a market other than their own. Such enterprises were multinational in a different sense than firms which simply owned factories in several countries. Enterprises with R&D on both sides of the Atlantic henceforth had the capability to have their strategies conditioned by more than one 'home' market. In addition to taking European innovations into foreign production, they could, and sometimes did, take new, labor-saving, high-income products developed in the United States into production abroad.

Becoming a global enterprise and allowing a US subsidiary to respond to its immediate market were different things, however. Continental headquarters often resisted the influence of American operations on parent-company strategies. Several Continental parents seemed to view too much innovation by their American subsidiaries as a worrisome phenomenon. Within Continental multinational systems, the locus of innovation seemed to have much to do with the locus of personal power.[86] Managers of American subsidiaries that had responded too well to US conditions had been known to make what amounted to take-over bids for parent enterprises. They had sometimes also attempted to secede from Continental parents when parents were no longer visibly necessary to the success of US ventures. The experience of one Swiss enterprise was well-remembered in Europe. Just prior to World War II the American managers of the firm's US subsidiary had become convinced of the superfluity of Swiss ownership and tried to wrest legal control of the US operation by having Switzerland declared as enemy territory at the outbreak of the war. Their attempt was unsuccessful.[87] But other American efforts to impose American strategies (by secession or take-over) have been known to occur. Mindful of such power considerations, Continental enterprises seemed often to prefer the risk of missed global opportunity, or that of American

---

[85] See Table 8.4 in Chapter VIII for further details.
[86] British parent-US subsidiary relationships also were often strained as a result of 'too much' innovation in the US operation. See, Franko, 1971(A); Skinner, 1973.
[87] Fehr, 1971: pp 46 and 47.

managerial dissatisfaction, to the risk of Americanization. In the 21 Continental firms with American subsidiaries with 1970 sales exceeding $50 million, only two had internally acknowledged the importance of US operations to the extent of having American managers on their executive boards. And even they had taken the step with a certain reluctance.

Three Continental enterprises had attempted an indirect solution to the problem of 'too much innovation' by US subsidiaries. US ventures which developed new products or processes had themselves been allowed to become multinational enterprises as foreign demand arose for their goods or methods. These companies had an arm's-length, holding-company relationship with the parent, although product lines sometimes overlapped. The direct impact of American products, processes, and people on the European parent was thus minimized.

The Swiss and Dutch enterprises operating in the United States were the firms most capable of responding to stimuli from multiple markets. They had the oldest US subsidiaries, as Table 7.2 showed. They also had the largest US subsidiaries: Swiss and Dutch enterprises accounted for two-thirds of all Continental direct investment in the United States, as can be seen from Table 7.1, and the largest Swiss and Dutch firms seemed to account for almost all of it in 1972.[88] The combined sales of the US subsidiaries of Shell, AKZO and Philips exceeded five billion dollars (although four billion of that amount was accounted for by Shell alone, and the totals included sales of imported goods). The combined sales of the US subsidiaries of Switzerland's Ciba-Geigy, Hoffmann-La Roche, Sandoz and Nestlé exceeded two billion dollars in 1972.

The sheer length of time during which these enterprises have manufactured in the United States appears largely responsible for both the size of their US subsidiaries and the responsiveness of those subsidiaries to US market conditions. Had German companies avoided confiscation during World War I, they might have been the leaders in responding to both home and American markets, for a number of Swiss and Dutch investment implantations in the US during the 1920's seemed largely to fill the void left by the German pioneers. To be sure, Shell got its start in the US in a pre-World War I series of exchanges of threats with Standard Oil. Nestlé began enduring US operations with an 'American' sort of product: *farine lactée*, a mother's-milk supplement. The others, however, began American manufacturing with chemical synthetics and electrical products which had been spawned in European (and often German) environments.

During the 1950's and 1960's, there remained a strong flow to the United States of innovations based on stimuli felt closer to the headquarters of these Swiss and Dutch firms. Ciba's expansion of epoxy-resin and plastics operations in the US in the 1960's seemed traceable to discoveries in Switzerland in the 1940's.[89] Geigy's building of agricultural-chemicals facilities in Louisiana in 1968 and 1969 were a consequence of earlier innovations in Switzerland.[90]

---

[88] This estimate assumes a ratio of two dollars of sales for every one dollar invested.
[89] *European Chemical News*, May 31, 1968: p 8.
[90] *Journal of Commerce*, January 15, 1968: p 7.

However, increasingly, American subsidiaries of Swiss and Dutch firms were innovating products for the US market which were being put into foreign production within Continental European multinational systems. One of the most striking examples of this evolution was provided by Hoffmann-La Roche, the Swiss firm which was the world's largest pharmaceutical producer. Roche entered the United States in the 1920's. By World War II, its American subsidiary had developed an independent R&D capability. After the war, the subsidiary developed into the largest ethical drug manufacturer in the United States. The subsidiary's early growth was based on Swiss innovations in synthetic vitamins and drugs, but the US subsidiary developed the most famous products the enterprise was to carry forth to world markets: the psychopharmaceuticals Librium and Valium. These products were then put into production in other markets.

The American subsidiary of Nestlé, the Swiss-based foods firm, also demonstrated a similar product-development capability when it beat the American company, General Foods, to US nationwide-market distribution of freeze-dried coffee in 1969. This product, too, was later produced outside the US by other Nestlé subsidiaries.

Other Swiss and Dutch multinational enterprises were engaged in a similar international product transfer, although it was sometimes made less spectacular by virtue of the entry of American product developments into the European enterprise system by acquisition, rather than internal development.

Perhaps the Swiss and Dutch firms which were successful in both innovating for more than one market, and then obtaining the fruits of those innovations on world markets, were helped by the small size of their home markets. Having little or no home market at home, they sought one abroad; logically enough, they picked the largest possible foster home. Small home markets, however, did not prevent Swedish and Belgian firms from having relatively few subsidiaries in the US. And, toward the end of the 1960's, a few German firms were beginning to act like the Swiss and the Dutch: they too were beginning to parlay US manufacturing operations initially made possible by European innovations into a second incubator of products with multinational futures.

The Continental European enterprises which both were most successful in the United States and most successful in getting innovations from the United States, appeared to have a common denominator which was not so much nationality as it was organizational structure. Structures which facilitated the transfer of information across borders. With rare exceptions, the enterprises which succeeded in the United States were the leaders in the European movement to adopt organizational structures appropriate to multinational systems with unified strategies.

Chapter VIII

The Organization of Multinational Manufacturing

Throughout the growth and spread of their multinational operations, Continental European enterprises maintained highly personalized relations with their foreign manufacturing subsidiaries. The nineteenth century practice of appointing relatives of company owners as heads of foreign subsidiaries gradually gave way to less familial ties.[1] Nevertheless, at the beginning of the 1970's, the most important bonds between center and periphery in European multinational systems were still the personal relationships between presidents of parent companies and presidents of foreign ventures.

The personal nature of parent-foreign subsidiary relationships in Continental enterprise has come to be known as the mother-daughter form of organization. Its structure can be illustrated in chart form as in Figure 8.1. The mother-daughter reporting relationships ran from parent president to foreign subsidiary presidents and was almost always accompanied by a domestic

Figure 8.1 Basic Features of the Mother-Daughter Organizational Structure

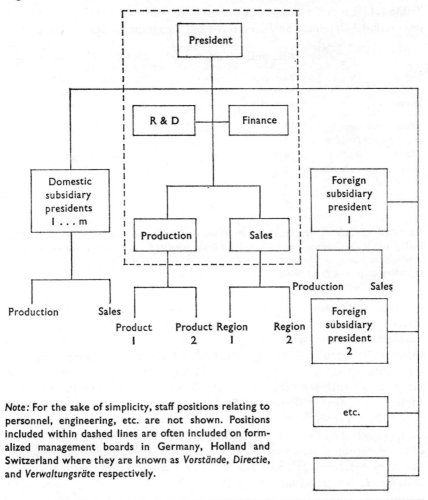

Note: For the sake of simplicity, staff positions relating to personnel, engineering, etc. are not shown. Positions included within dashed lines are often included on formalized management boards in Germany, Holland and Switzerland where they are known as *Vorstände*, *Directie*, and *Verwaltungsräte* respectively.

---

[1] For examples of family ties holding together early Continental multinational systems, see Siemens, 1957; Kocka, 1969; Degussa, 1973: p 39. For early examples of less familial, but still highly personalized management links, see McKay, 1970.

organization in which functional heads for production, sales, research and finance reported to (or served on the same managing board as) the parent president. Domestic operations outside the parents' main industry were often handled by subsidiaries whose presidents also reported to the parent head.

The mother-daughter relationship was the most common international organizational form used by Continental multinational enterprises at the start of 1971. It was used alike by firms with many and with few foreign manufacturing operations. Table 8.1 shows that 25 of the 70 enterprises for which organizational histories could be developed used the mother-daughter form. Twenty-one of the firms organized along mother-daughter lines had manufacturing operations in more than seven countries; one company maintained mother-daughter relationships while manufacturing in 17 nations.

In the past, the mother-daughter organization had been even more common. In 1961, only nine enterprises were using alternative structures.

Table 8.1   Large Continental European Enterprises Classified by International Organizational Structures and Geographical Spread, 1971

	Enterprises Manufacturing in:			
Structure	Less than seven countries	Seven to ten countries	More than ten countries	Total number of firms
Mother-daughter	5	9	12	26
International Division	1	5	5	11
World-wide product	4	6	14	24
Area and world-functional	0	0	3	3
Mixed and matrix	0	0	6	6
Total	10	20	40	70

Note: Data concerning organizational structure was not obtainable for all 85 Continental enterprises in the Comparative Multinational Enterprise study. Some enterprises which were classified as having world-wide product or area structures had one or two subsidiaries reporting to parent firms along mother-daughter lines.

American multinational enterprises had followed a very different organizational evolution. President-to-president relationships similar to the mother-daughter sort were often used by American firms during the early stages of their foreign manufacturing experience.[2] But American enterprises with such a structure rarely managed networks of manufacturing operations spanning many countries. More than 60% of the American enterprises in the Comparative Multinational Enterprise Project abandoned president-to-president, personalized reporting structures in favor of another organizational form before they had established their fifth foreign manufacturing subsidiary.[3] None of the American multinationals had even maintained president-to-president reporting relationships beyond ten foreign manufacturing subsidiaries, and none had such relationships in 1967.[4]

---

[2] Stopford and Wells, 1972; Franko, 1971(B).
[3] Stopford and Wells, 1972: p 21.
[4] Personal communication from Professor John M Stopford.

American terms do not, however, quite correspond to the behavior which typically occurred in European company systems. The mother-daughter relationship was less a formal organizational structure based on written rules, procedures, and reporting relationships than it was a structural surrogate based on career, social, friendship and family ties.

Managing the Mother-Daughter Relationships

The nature of the mother-daughter, parent-subsidiary relationship in the Continental multinationals can be glimpsed in a number of ways.[5] One way is to contrast the management practices in firms maintaining this relationship with those in firms which abandoned it. Tables 8.2, 8.3 and 8.4 present managers' perceptions of the role played by written job descriptions and rules, standardized reporting periods and formats, and the use of expatriate home-country managers in relationships between headquarters and foreign manufacturing subsidiaries. These tables are based on questionnaire and interview responses provided by 35 Continental enterprises.

Despite the great international spread of the seven mother-daughter firms that responded to the questionnaire (six of the seven were manufacturing in more than nine foreign countries), none ascribed a major role to written rules and procedures in the control of international operations. In contrast, 12 of the 28 firms with alternative structures, as seen from Table 8.2, indicated that written rules and procedures played a major role in managing foreign operations. Whereas mother-daughter firms used little standardization of reporting periods and document formats, most of the firms with other structures had a high degree of standardization, as can be seen from Table 8.3. The mother-daughter firms employed a higher proportion of home-country expatriates as presidents of foreign manufacturing subsidiaries than did firms with alternative structures. Table 8.4 shows that this contrast held true whether the comparisons were for foreign operations in North America, Europe, or the less developed countries.

Table 8.2 Continental Multinational Enterprises, Classified by International Organizational Structure and Role Played by Written Job Description and Rules in Controlling Foreign Manufacturing, 1972

Structure	A minor role	A major role	Total number of firms
Mother-daughter	7	0	7
Other	16	12	28
Total	**23**	**12**	**35**

Notes: All enterprises manufactured in more than seven countries. See appendix A for questions and method of classification.

[5] For a detailed examination of the mother-daughter relationships between large Continental (and British) enterprises and their subsidiaries in one country, the United States, see Franko, 1971(A): Chapter III and Franko, 1971(C): p 35. For impressionistic comments on the nature of the mother-daughter relationship, see Business International, 1967: p 32.

Table 8.3 Continental Multinational Enterprises Classified by
International Organizational Structures and Standardization of Reporting
Periods and Documents of Foreign Manufacturing Subsidiaries, 1972

Structure	Degree of Standardization:		Total number of firms
	Low	High	
Mother-daughter	6	1	7
Other	4	22	26
Total	**10**	**23**	**33**

Notes: All enterprises manufactured in more than seven countries. See appendix A for
questions asked and method of classification.

Although the data presented in Tables 8.2, 8.3 and 8.4 relate to only about half
of the Continental European multinational enterprises maintaining the
mother-daughter structure in 1973 (the year in which the questionnaire was
circulated), there is little doubt that the patterns shown by these data applied
just as well to firms not providing information. Our questionnaire was
complemented by press descriptions of mother-daughter relationships in
non-responding enterprises which read, for example, like: 'all the 74 subsidiary companies report to (the president), who attempts to see each company head twice a year. These are largely informal visits.' The president of
this enterprise went on to remark, 'I meet the managing director and his
production people. We talk about his problems and whether the parent
company can do anything to solve them.' The contrast could not be more
complete between the management practices of the Continental European
multinationals using the mother-daughter form and the archetypal American
multinational with job descriptions, 'bibles' of rules, and frequent use of local
nationals as foreign subsidiary presidents.[6]

Control and Constraint

Although managers in firms with mother-daughter structures often spoke
about the great independence of foreign subsidiary presidents, the kind of
autonomy granted was rarely of the sort exercised by subsidiary presidents in
American multinationals during the so-called autonomous subsidiary phase of
their earliest foreign operations. Few of the traditionally organized Continental multinationals considered their foreign, tariff or non-tariff-barrier
factories as portfolio gambles, made to insure against a feared, but incalculable
penalty for not investing.[7] When European managers described their mother-
daughter organizations, they invoked analogies of control systems used in
Roman or feudal times.[8] Like Roman proconsuls sent out to govern the colonies after being educated as good Romans, subsidiary managers in many
Continental firms were given foreign responsibilities only after years spent
absorbing the values and practices of the parent company. The absorption

[6] On the process of control of American multinational firms see: Vernon, 1971. On nationality
staffing patterns in the US multinationals see: Franko, 1973; Van Den Bulke, 1971.
[7] Stopford and Wells, 1972: p 20.
[8] For a written reference of this sort, see Cvetkov, 1972.

Table 8.4 Continental Multinational Enterprises, Classified by International Organizational Structure and Percentage of Home Country Nationals as Presidents of Manufacturing Subsidiaries in Various Regions, 1972

	Region of Subsidiaries and Percentage of Home-Country Expatriate Subsidiary Presidents:									Total companies responding
	North America:			Europe:			Less Developed World:			
Structure	0–33%	34–67%	68–100%	0–33%	34–67%	68–100%	0–33%	34–67%	68–100%	
Mother-daughter	2	0	5	0	3	5	2	1	6	9
Other	8	1	4	11	8	4	6	8	7	23
Total	10	1	9	11	11	9	8	9	13	32

Note: See appendix A for questions asked and method of classification.

process was facilitated by the fact that many of the foreign managers were of the home-country nationality, as Table 8.4 indicates. Indeed, they often came from families long-established in headquarters' cities. Written rules and reports were unnecessary in most circumstances, for headquarters managers could usually predict how their foreign presidents would act: it was said that managers in one enterprise 'simply would not do things not in the group interest'. Consequently, foreign subsidiary presidents were often allowed great autonomy – but within precise, yet unwritten constraints. Five mother-daughter organizations examined in depth were able to achieve nearly total worldwide standardization of policies relating to product mix and diversification, product quality, brand names, product design and formulae, external versus internal financing and personnel promotion and reward systems. This occurred without anything resembling a system for reporting and control.

As long as constraints were respected and dividend checks appeared when anticipated, the center rarely interfered with – or even asked for much information from – foreign subsidiaries. When information was transferred, it often travelled on lines established by friendship and acquaintance, and in a manner showing little concern for the principle of unity of command (or 'one man, one boss').[9]

Rationale of the Mother-Daughter Structure

The possible reasons for the lengthy use of the mother-daughter organization by Continental enterprises are numerous. Some managers suggested, for example, that enterprises with the bulk of their foreign subsidiaries in Europe could maintain the mother-daughter relationship simply because of the relatively short geographical distances involved. There was, however, no observable relationship between Continental firms' propensities to concentrate foreign manufacturing in Europe as of 1971 and the likelihood of their having mother-daughter structures.

Alternatively, managers suggested that multinational companies with narrow product lines could maintain the mother-daughter structure longer than highly diversified enterprises. A *priori*, they felt it was easiest to maintain simple, personalized relationships among component parts of a relatively simple (one- or few-product) multinational enterprise. It is difficult to imagine a president transferring much information among 74 manufacturing subsidiaries during twice-yearly visits in all but the most specialized firm. In practice, however, fewer than half of the Continental European multinational enterprises employing the mother-daughter structure in 1971 had narrow product lines in their foreign production operations, as one sees from Table 8.5.

But how were Continental enterprises able to maintain mother-daughter structures in the face of considerable geographical spread and product diversity (while American firms adopted alternative structures)? It may have been partly because European managers (unlike American managers) usually spent their working lives in one firm.[10] If managers' loyalty to company

---

[9] See also Lombard, 1969: p 38; Schollhammer, 1971: p 354.
[10] Franko, 1973; Stopford, 1972: p 87; Schollhammer, 1971: p 355.

Table 8.5 Continental Multinational Enterprises, Classified by Structure and by Foreign Product Diversity, 1971

Structure	Total number of firms with production in seven or more countries	Number of firms classified by foreign product diversity*		
		None	Low	High
Mother-daughter	21	3	6	12
International Division	10	3	5	2
World-wide product	20	1	6	13
Area and world-functional	3	1	2	—
Mixed and matrix	6	—	2	4
Total	**60**	**8**	**21**	**31**

Note: *See appendix B for method of calculation of foreign diversity.

objectives is a function of time spent in the firm, then there is some margin of substitutability of personalized for impersonal means of achieving organizational cohesiveness.[11] Nonetheless the evidence argues that this margin was too narrow to allow mother-daughter structures to be maintained under all pressures: despite the nearly life-long tenure of their managers, firms such as Switzerland's Nestlé and Ciba-Geigy, and Germany's Siemens, Bayer and BASF had shifted to alternative structures by 1971.

It is conceivable that many Continental mother-daughter enterprises were able to obtain some cohesion throughout their multinational systems by avoiding joint ventures with foreign partners. Table 8.6 points out that mother-daughter enterprises were particularly prone to have wholly owned foreign manufacturing subsidiaries.

Perhaps the most powerful forces behind the long predominance of mother-daughter relationships were the barriers to trade (public and private) which kept national markets separate from one another, and thus limited the need for cross-border communication in most Continental European multinational systems. The greatest contrast between the mother-daughter structure and the alternative structures sketched in Figures 2 and 3, lies in the fact that *none* of the managers in the mother-daughter organization has strictly supranational responsibilities, whereas there is an explicit recognition of cross-border responsibility, co-ordination and communication in all the alternatives to the mother-daughter relationship. In organizations in which decision-making power is held by the head of an international, a world-wide product or an area division, chiefs of national subsidiary units can no longer lay claim to a status in their fiefdoms nearly equal to that of the mother-company president; national desires and interests must go through an international filter before they can obtain the attention of the parent president. The mother-daughter structure was a logical organizational counterpart to the economic behavior of international combines of subsidiaries held together by common ownership, but not by a supranational strategy, as described in Chapter IV.

[11] Galbraith, 1969: p 12.

Figure 8.2   Basic Features of Organizational Alternatives to the Mother-Daughter Structure

I   *The international division structure*

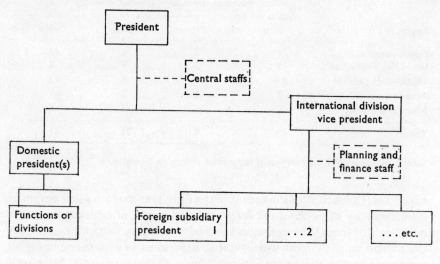

2   *The world-wide product structure*

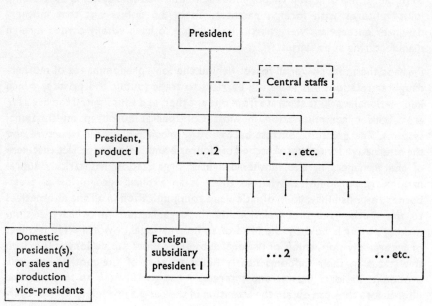

3 *The area structure*

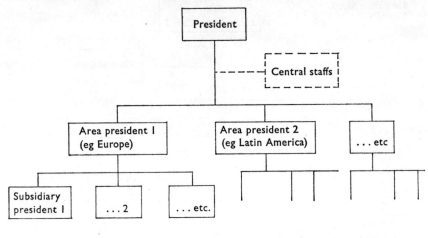

4 *The world-functional structure*

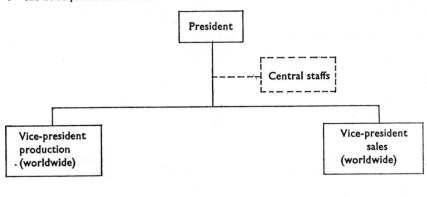

5 *A mixed structure*

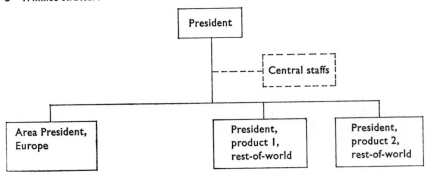

Figure 8.3   Matrix Structures for International Operations

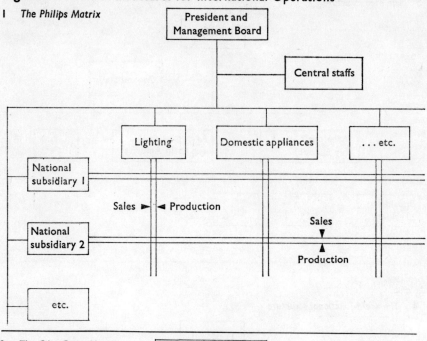

1   *The Philips Matrix*

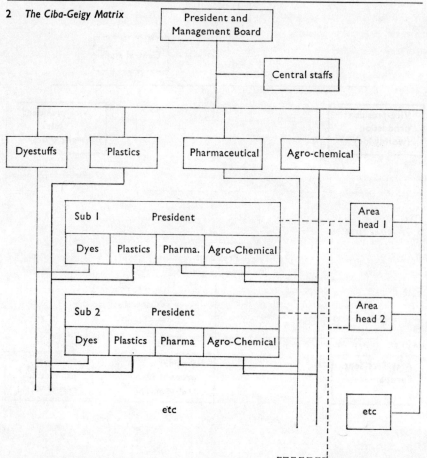

2   *The Ciba-Geigy Matrix*

Table 8.6 Continental Multinational Enterprises, Classified by
Organizational Structure and Percentage of Wholly Owned
Foreign Manufacturing Subsidiaries, 1971

Structure	Percentage of Subsidiaries wholly owned:			Total number of firms
	0–32 %	33–49 %	50 % or more	
Mother-daughter	6	6	9	21
International Division	4	2	4	10
World-wide product	8	6	6	20
Area and world-functional	0	2	1	3
Mixed and matrix	0	4	2	6
Total	**18**	**20**	**22**	**60**

Note: All enterprises manufactured in seven or more countries.

Organizational behavior was but the reflection of the tariff, non-tariff and cartel barriers to trade which kept national markets economically separated from one another.

Before World War II, in the thick of the negotiable environment, only one Continental enterprise managed relations with foreign subsidiaries through a supranational structure, even though 14 enterprises manufactured in more than seven countries by 1938. By 1968, the year when tariffs reached zero within the EEC, 12 enterprises had moved to structures with supranational centers of responsibility; by 1971 the number was 39.

In a world of separate markets, the Continental firms ignored the American paradigm of international structure following a company strategy of inter-national product diversification or geographical dispersion.[12] I G Farben, for example, produced in 13 countries and in eight industries (even counting chemicals and drugs as one industry) on the eve of World War II, yet the mother-daughter structure sufficed.

The separation of markets by trade barriers eliminated most possibilities of production specialization and trade inter-dependence among the foreign subsidiaries of Continental European multinational enterprises. This in itself minimized the need for cross-border communication about delivery times, payment terms, product specifications and quality. Since there were few transfers of goods, there was little need for discussion about transfer prices, much less about the distortions these could cause on subsidiary or parent income statements when transfer prices were set without taking due account of their repercussions on profitability throughout the multinational entity.

Separation of markets was a necessary condition of the use of the mother-daughter structure on a large scale. The sufficient condition was provided by the nature of the material-substituting or process innovations being carried into foreign productions by many Continental enterprises.

Firms engaged in the pioneering of new products, like most American multi-national enterprises, needed considerable cross-border communication within

---

[12] Stopford and Wells, 1972; Franko, 1971(B).

the organization as they spread new products around the globe in product-cycle fashion, even in the absence of an interdependent flow of goods within the multinational system. Customer demand for new products, unlike that for synthetics or old products produced with new processes, tends to be price inelastic.[13] Before deciding to purchase new products, customers require information that is not supplied in a price quotation; they ask questions about the function of the product, its reliability, where can it be used, and where can it be serviced. For sales in foreign, second markets to grow, marketing information such as this must be transferred from the market of innovation to subsequent markets. As the American multinationals learned, organizational structures assigning supranational responsibility are important means of transferring marketing information from first to second markets.

The tendency of Continental European firms to spread international production of goods with relatively high price elasticities implied that little regular transfer of marketing information was necessary. When a trade barrier was to be jumped, there occurred a unique, discrete need for technical communication. The technical knowledge necessary to starting new plants or introducing new processes and synthetics could be circulated among production departments on a non-formalized basis.

To the extent that Continental enterprises could reach a negotiated *modus vivendi* with local or international competitors the need for subsequent international transfer of technical information was reduced. When steady-states of nationally compartmentalized markets could be reached, the personalized hierarchy of the mother-daughter relationship did not need replacement by structures designed for a more efficient supranational transfer of information. Indeed, an efficient transfer of information represented a positive danger in such circumstances: it facilitated local competitive initiatives, which in turn could result in the undoing of the laborious negotiations necessary to the formation of most cartels!

Organizational Change

Enterprises with US Operations

The Continental enterprises with the largest and most successful operations in the United States led the movement away from the mother-daughter structures. The competitive nature of the American market virtually ensured that the leisurely pace of personal, unsystematized mother-daughter communications would lead to frustration on both sides of the Atlantic.[14] Table 8.7 indicates that nine of the ten Continental multinationals that abandoned the mother-daughter relationship before 1968 manufactured in the US; eight of those nine had American subsidiaries with more than $50 million in sales in 1970.

A direct connection between US operations and changes in system-wide organizational structures was often perceived by the managers of the enterprises, although not always in economic terms. Philips of Holland, and the Ciba

[13] Vernon, 1966; Hirsch, 1967.
[14] See also Franko, 1971(A): Chapter III; Franko, 1971(C).

Table 8.7 Continental European Multinational Enterprises, Classified by Importance of US Manufacturing Operations in 1970 and Abandonment of Mother-daughter Structure

	Abandoned mother-daughter structure:		Not abandoned	Number of firms
	Before 1968	Between 1968 and 1971		
Companies with US manufacturing sales exceeding $50m (1970)	8	7	6	21
Companies with US manufacturing sales less than $50m (1970)	1	10	9	20
Companies having no US manufacturing (1970)	1	12	6	19
Total	**10**	**29**	**21**	**60**

Note: Any company with fewer than 20% of foreign subsidiaries reporting on mother-daughter lines was counted as having abandoned that relationship.

predecessors of Ciba-Geigy of Switzerland, traced the breakup of their mother-daughter relationships shortly after World War II to the influence of managers returning to headquarters operations from wartime exile in America.[15] The move by American firms to organize their domestic operations by product divisions, begun in 1921 by Du Pont and General Motors, was building toward the wave of reorganizations that engulfed the majority of large American firms during the 1950's.[16] Philips and Ciba managers brought back to Europe the product-division concept, with its emphasis on assigning profit responsibility for operating decisions to managers of self-contained business units. They adapted it to Swiss and Dutch proclivities for group management by substituting collegial responsibility for American-style individual responsibility. Ciba did this by forming division boards; Philips assigned joint divisional responsibility to co-equal technical and commercial managers. Philips further adapted the divisional concept into the matrix structure shown in Figure 3 by confronting the two co-equal technical and commercial managers of product divisions with yet other co-equal technical, commercial and financial managers responsible for all products within individual nations. But Philips and Ciba then applied the notion of product responsibility not only to their domestic markets as the Americans were doing – perhaps since Holland and Switzerland were so small – but also to international operations.

Nestlé adopted the area organizational structure even before World War II, a move related to the importance attached even then to the transfer of

[15] Bouman, 1956.
[16] Rumelt, 1974.

marketing information within that Swiss multinational. The marketing information being transferred had to do with product pioneering undertaken in the US both by Nestlé and by its American competitors.[17]

Managers of the US subsidiary of one of the first German firms to have abandoned the mother-daughter structure mentioned the effect of the relative non-negotiability of the US market on their – and their parent's – operations. These managers indicated that they had implored the German headquarters to allow them to divisionalize in the US during the first decade in which manufacturing had taken place in that market, but that the German parent had insisted that US operations be organized along functional lines like those of the parent. The US managers, however, found the functional organization a serious handicap to a speedy response to competition, because no one was responsible for both the sales and production functions of the subsidiary's numerous products. Partly as a result of the difficulties encountered by its US subsidiary, the German parent eventually replaced its mother-daughter organizational structure. The company simultaneously moved from functional to product-line responsibility for its highly diversified domestic operations, allowed the US subsidiary to divisionalize by product, and linked domestic with US and other foreign operations by means of an international division.

The connection between important US operations and international organizational change was not universal, as Table 8.7 shows. Six of the 21 enterprises with large American manufacturing subsidiaries had not abandoned the mother-daughter form by the end of 1971. Yet, had the cutoff date for Table 8.7 been the end of 1972, the table would have shown that four of these six companies were no longer structured along mother-daughter lines.

Competition in Europe

A need for international communication resulting from product pioneering or competitive experience in America was not the only cause of reorganization of international operations by Continental European enterprise. Competition was beginning to break out in Europe in many sectors by 1968 (as seen in Chapter VI). Tariffs within the EEC disappeared. Penetration of Continental markets by American multinationals was becoming considerable in the motor vehicle, electrical, machinery, and rubber sectors.[18] Co-operative habits in the chemical industry were being attacked by Italian firms bent on taking market share away from older oligopolies and by EEC and German government antitrust actions.

The multinational enterprises of Continental Europe with their main base of activities in competitive industries, followed the venturers to the United States in adopting supranational structures.[19] Table 8.8 classifies the Continental European multinationals by their main industry and their propensity

---

[17] Heer, 1966: pp 140, 165–168.

[18] See Chapter VI, Table 6.7.

[19] An American influence was manifest even in many reorganizations of Continental companies without US subsidiaries. American consultants were often called into European firms to facilitate organizational change – usually after competition had cut into company profits. See, for example, *Capital*, March 1971: p 66; Hennemann, 1971: p 221.

Table 8.8 Continental European Multinational Enterprises Classified by Main Industry of Operations and International Organizational Structure, 1971

Industry	International structure				Total number of firms with information available
	Mother-daughter		Other		
	Number	%	Number	%	
Food	0	0%	1	100%	1
Wood and paper	0	0	2	100	2
Chemical and drug	4	24	13	76	17
Petroleum	0	0	5	100	5
Rubber	1	33	2	67	3
Glass	0	0	2	100	2
Iron and steel	5	83	1	17	6
Non-ferrous metals	3	100	0	0	3
Non-electrical machinery	2	40	3	60	5
Electrical machinery	3	30	7	70	10
Motor vehicles and parts	3	50	3	50	6
	21		**39**		**60**

Note: Main industry of operations refers to the two-digit, US Department of Commerce Standard Industrial Classification (SIC) industry which accounted for the largest proportion of enterprises' worldwide sales.

to abandon the mother-daughter structure. The enterprises whose main sectors of operations were in the more competitive categories were considerably more prone to reorganize by 1971 than were the enterprises based in the less competitive iron, steel, and non-ferrous metals industries. The exceptions to the rule, such as the three motor-vehicle and parts producers which retained the mother-daughter structure, can be explained by the fact that almost all their foreign manufacturing operations took place in highly protected (usually LDC) markets.

The role of competitive pressure in promoting the adoption of supranational structures is again suggested by the classification of Continental multinational enterprises by their headquarters country and their 1971 international organizational structures shown in Table 8.9. Table 8.9 also compares the 1971 structures of Continental multinational enterprise to the structures of British and American multinationals. The fact that small, internationally open Holland and Switzerland had the lowest proportion of firms retaining the mother-daughter structure (next to the United States) again suggests that supranational responsibility was especially necessary for those buffeted most by the winds of international competition.

The Sequence of Change

Unlike American multinationals, the Continental enterprises that adopted supranational organizational structures typically did so only after achieving a relatively large geographical spread of manufacturing operations. Moreover, when the Continental multinationals changed their organizational structures, they did so in a very different sequence than that followed by their American counterparts.

Table 8.9 International Organizational Structures of Multinational Enterprises Based in Continental Europe, the United Kingdom and the United States, 1971

Country of parent system	Mother-daughter	International division	Product	Area and world-functional	Matrix and mixed	Total known
Bel & Lux	1	—	3	—	—	4
France	3	4	5	1	—	13
Germany	9	3	6	—	2	20
Italy	3	1	1	1	—	6
Netherlands*	0	—	1	1	2	4
Switzerland	2	1	2	—	2	7
Sweden	3	1	2	—	—	6
Total Continentals	**21**	**10**	**20**	**3**	**6**	**60**
United Kingdom**	8	12	8	—	19	48
United States***	0	90	30	17	26	162
(170 multinationals, 1968)						

Notes: *Unilever is included with United Kingdom firms in this tabulation.
**Data for multinational enterprises based in the United Kingdom was supplied by Dr John Stopford of the London Business School.
***Data for the United States is from Stopford and Wells, 1972.
Some enterprises which were classified as having international division, world-wide product division, or area structures had one or two subsidiaries reporting to headquarters along mother-daughter lines.

Figure 8.4   International Organizational Evolution of Multinational Enterprise

Continental Multinational Enterprise

International Structures

| Domestic Structures | Mother-Daughter | International Division | Global Structures |

Functional

Divisional

American Multinational Enterprise

International Structures

| Domestic Structures | Autonomous Subsidiaries | International Division | Global Structures |

Functional

Divisional

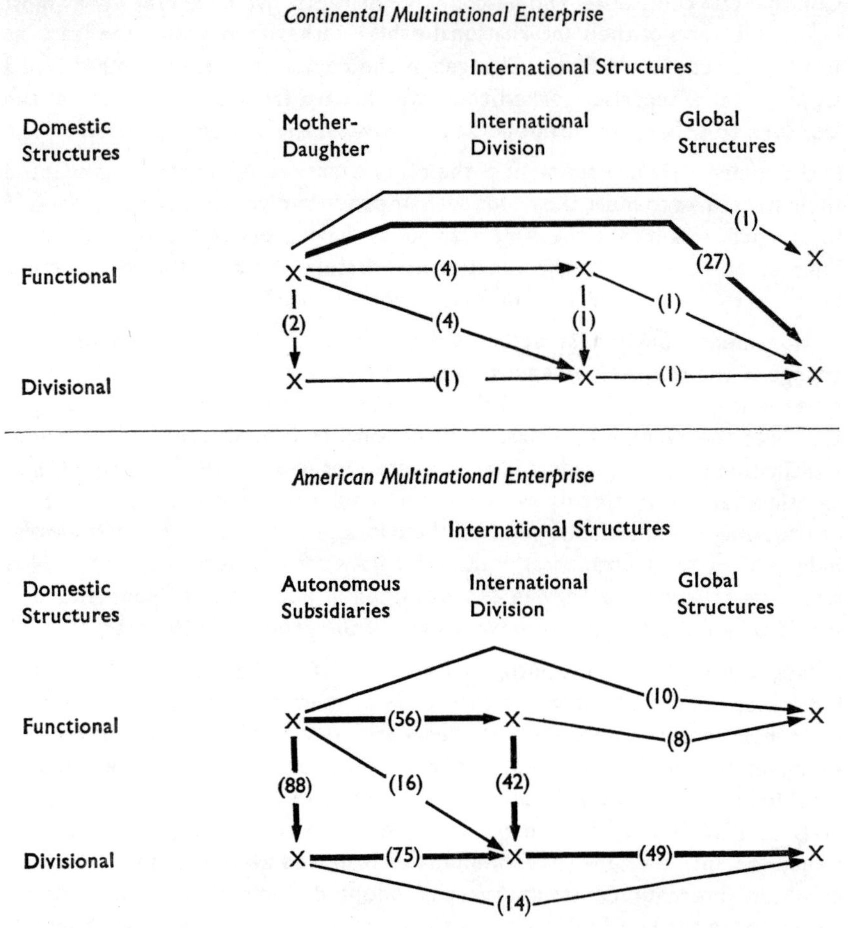

Sources: For Continental Multinational Enterprise: CEI-Harvard Comparative Multinational Enterprise Project. For US Enterprise, Stopford and Wells, 1972, p 28.

Figure 8.4 contrasts the organizational evolution of Continental European multinationals with that of American multinationals. One sees that most Continental firms simply skipped the international division phase passed through by nearly 90% of the 170 American multinationals surveyed.[20] In addition, Continental enterprises, in all but three cases, undertook both domestic and international reorganization simultaneously. Continental moves to the 'global' forms of organization (world-wide product, area, mixed or matrix structures) accompanied divisionalization by product at home. In contrast, more than three-quarters of the American enterprises classified as multinational saw fit to change their domestic structures from functional to divisional forms prior to adopting one of the so-called global structures.[21]

[20] Stopford and Wells, 1972: pp 21–28.
[21] Stopford and Wells, 1972: p 28; Fouraker and Stopford, 1968.

The disinterest of Continental enterprises in anticipating international structural change by domestic structural change can be traced to the fact that Continental companies' home-country markets were among the most negotiable parts of their international orbit – rather than among the least, as in the case of the US firms. Changes in the competitive environment facing Continental enterprise worked their way inward from the periphery of the US, then to other European operations, toward the center.

In the competitive environment of their home market, American firms adapted their structures to meet the needs of their product-diversification strategies.[22] In practice, this meant the American firms, having diversified their product lines at home, forsook the functional structure for a divisional structure before they became involved in foreign operations.[23]

In Continental Europe, structure did not follow strategy until there was a change in the competitive environment.[24] The average Continental European enterprise was actually more likely to be diversified both at home and abroad than was the average American multinational.[25] Whereas 16% of American multinationals had all their domestic operations in one industry, only 11% of Continental multinationals were similarly undiversified at home. While 35% of the American multinationals had their foreign operations in one industry, only 16% of the Continental multinationals were undiversified abroad. Had structure followed strategy in the Continental European environment, one would have expected nearly universal use of the product-division structure.[26]

In fact, at least 11 of the Continental enterprises with great product diversification at home had had more than 20% of their domestic sales outside of their main industry since long before World War II. Hoechst and Bayer, for example, produced pharmaceuticals, dye-stuffs, veterinary medicines, photographic film and other products with widely diverging customer markets as early as 1910.[27] They felt no particular need to rearrange their functional structures until the time they simultaneously moved away from their mother-daughter international structures and adopted domestic product-division structures in the late 1960's. During the inter-war period, I G Farben handled highly diverse lines of chemicals, plastics, fertilizers and pharmaceutical products with a domestic functional structure in which production was split into four regional departments – themselves very diverse – and sales were handled by one single gigantic department split into a multitude of sections. None of these departments or sections was responsible for profit centers containing both production and sales functions.[28]

Moves to Global Structures

Once Continental multinational firms began to face internationally competitive environments, Continental structures became congruent with domestic and international product-diversification strategies.

---

[22] Chandler, 1961.
[23] Chandler, 1961; Fouraker and Stopford, 1968.
[24] Franko, 1974.
[25] See Chapter I, Table I.2.
[26] Franko, 1974; Thannheiser, 1972; Pavan, 1972; Pooley-Dyas, 1972.
[27] Haber, 1971: p 121.
[28] Haber, 1971: pp 339–341.

When organizations were changed, enterprises with highly diverse foreign product lines adopted world-wide product structures. Nineteen of the 20 Continental European multinationals that moved to world-wide product structures were managing foreign operations in several industries, as shown by Table 8.5.

Area structures – or their near cousin, world-wide functional structures – were adopted by three firms by 1971, all of which had little foreign product diversity, and all of which were manufacturing in more than 14 countries. Like the American multinational enterprises that adopted the area structure, Continental multinationals with specialized product lines moved to defend themselves against the onslaughts of competition, not by abandoning the products to which they had a long commitment, but rather by building an organization permitting the exploitation of all possible economies of multinational scale. The organizational means to achieve such economies was the centralized co-ordination of operations in particular geographical areas. Centralized co-ordination sometimes culminated in the elimination of general management responsibility for individual countries and the adoption of a world-wide functional structure.[29] Such co-ordination could permit economies of scale in marketing, since successful promotion and product-differentiation methods could be rapidly diffused around the multinational system. Area co-ordination could also facilitate the use of unexploited economies in finance and production when competitive pressures made 'rationalization' necessary.

The experience of one Continental enterprise which was taking tentative steps in 1972 toward grouping its mother-daughter subsidiaries into areas, illustrates in microcosm how international competition could render traditional parent-subsidiary relationships obsolete for companies having relatively narrow product lines. The enterprise had no foreign production outside its main industry and had maintained mother-daughter relationships with its foreign subsidiaries over 60 years of multinational operations. It had long been among the leaders in an industry in which firms had traditionally maintained relatively co-operative relations in operations outside of the antitrust-conscious United States. During the 1950's, tariff barriers and more-or-less gentlemanly rivalry urged the enterprise into production in Latin America. At the time manufacturing commenced in Latin America, trade among the foreign subsidiaries in the system occurred only sporadically. Trade for the enterprise had previously meant exports from the home country – until such time as local governments forced production. Since transfers of goods among subsidiaries were rare, the prices at which transfers took place were set by individual daughter-company presidents, often without consulting or informing the mother company. After start-up, one of the Latin American daughter companies placed a small order for some intermediate component goods with one of its sister manufacturing subsidiaries; the sister, wishing to tend to its own protected national market, and not wanting to be bothered by small orders from a distant land, intentionally set a transfer price at an exceedingly high level with the aim of discouraging such bothersome orders. For more than 15 years, however, the Latin American subsidiary

---

[29] For a detailed description of management processes in area and world-functional organizations, see Franko, 1971(B): Chapter III.

refused to be discouraged. It was not aware that it was being charged a penalty price, and, as local economic growth proceded in a highly protected market, it could sell increasingly large volumes of its protected manufactures incorporating the excessively priced intermediate.

In the late 1960's, however, a relatively small American newcomer to the industry, seeing the wide gap between its costs (calculated on a basis which took into account the interdependence of the firm's world-wide operations), and prices in the Latin American country, also jumped the tariff barrier, set up production, and cut prices. The subsidiary of the European enterprise then saw its sales' growth rate start to decline, despite efforts to differentiate its product on the basis of its long experience and technical competence in the industry. It was gradually forced to meet its competitor's prices. The mother company, no longer receiving the dividends and statements of earnings to which it had been accustomed, decided that local management was not being zealous enough in cutting costs. Taking advantage of the approaching retirement of the subsidiary manager, headquarters sent another expatriate out from the center with orders to show more profit. The new president promptly began to cut local costs by embarking on a no-new-hiring policy. When locally reported profits were not restored, first managers, and then employees were let go. The Latin American country was, however, facing severe unemployment and under-employment problems. The firings were received with mass protests by workers, great unrest among remaining personnel, and more than one attempt on the life of the new subsidiary president.

Only after these disagreeable events did subsidiary managers note that the subsidiary was maintaining sales volume by taking a loss on the goods incorporating the imported component with its penalty price. The multinational system as a whole had been making a considerable profit out of the Latin American business; it showed up, however, as a particularly pleasant profit in the subsidiary that exported the intermediate goods, and as a loss on the books of the importing operation. Because of the mother-daughter organizational structure of the company, each national subsidiary was treated as a portfolio holding unconnected to the rest of the multinational system, with the result that neither headquarters, nor either of the two subsidiaries in question had a complete picture of profitability – or even the cost and price elements composing system profit.

As management recognized the fact of international interdependence of company parts, they realized that the organizational structure of the enterprise needed to reflect this interdependence. When neither governments nor firms could isolate national markets from one another and prevent competitive entry, an organization designed for supranational co-ordination became necessary.

The International Division Structure

Some companies adopted a structure in which one executive was responsible for all the foreign operations of the enterprise, once the necessity of supranational co-ordination was recognized. Such an international division structure was adopted by ten Continental multinational enterprises which had low or intermediate levels of geographical dispersion and only a moderate amount of product diversity. The geographical spread and foreign product diversity of the firms which separated domestic and foreign operations by adopting international divisions is shown in Tables 8.1 and 8.5. When competition and interdependence among subsidiaries rendered mother-daughter relationships unworkable these enterprises adopted the organizational form typical of similar American enterprises.[30]

Continental experience supported the notion that international division structures were most appropriate to enterprises with home markets which were large relative to foreign operations. Among Continental enterprises, firms based in the relatively large French and German markets had the greatest propensity to adopt international division structures as one sees from Table 8.9.

One Italian firm, and one of the three German enterprises using an international division structure excluded EEC operations from their international divisions. In dubious testimony to the continuing importance of national boundaries in Europe to Continental firms, these two enterprises were the only large enterprises of the Continent which explicitly considered the whole EEC market as their 'domestic' territory.

Mixed and Matrix Structures

Mixed or matrix structures were adopted by six Continental multinational enterprises, all of which manufactured in more than ten countries and had diverse foreign product lines. American firms faced with the problem of simultaneously managing considerable geographical dispersion and product diversity had recourse to similar international organizational structures.[31] Faced with multinational, multi-product complexity, firms of differing national origins evolved toward mixed international structures in which some responsibilities for profits were delineated by product and others by area. Other firms adopted matrix structures in which dual lines of profit responsibility existed. Four firms with highly diverse foreign product lines, and production in more than ten foreign countries, had been able to maintain mother-daughter structures through the end of 1971. By mid-1974, however, three of these four were taking steps toward mixed structures: those having elements of both product and area lines of responsibility.

Ownership and Control in Global Structures

After the mother-daughter relationships were replaced, there was concurrence between European and American enterprises' policies toward subsidiary ownership. Like their American counterparts, Continental European multinationals adopting international divisions or world-wide product divisions often conducted their international operations by means of joint ventures with local foreign enterprises.[32] Twelve enterprises both abandoned the mother-daughter structure and fully owned fewer than one-third of their foreign subsidiaries by 1971. As Table 8.6 points out, these were enterprises that had adopted international division or product division structures. The

---

[30] Stopford and Wells, 1972: p 21 *et seq*; Franko, 1971(B): Chapter III.
[31] Stopford and Wells, 1972: Chapter VI.
[32] For American comparisons, see: Franko, 1971; Stopford and Wells, 1972.

great product diversity (or limited geographical spread) of these enterprises reduced the possibilities for production rationalization and marketing coordination across borders. As in the case of American enterprises with similar characteristics, joint-venture partners could be tolerated in such circumstances.

The few Continental multinationals with area structures, or mixed, or matrix structures avoided joint ventures; all enterprises with these structures owned 100% of more than one-third of their foreign operations. Continental enterprises were more likely to have 100% ownership of foreign subsidiaries if they were defending a limited product line against competitive threat in many countries, or if they were attempting to manage a complex organization in which lines of responsibility were not straightforwardly aligned with product or area. Once competition required truly substantial cost cutting or marketing communication across national boundaries, Continental European multinationals, like American multinationals, found it difficult to maintain unified strategies in the presence of foreign ownership participation in subsidiaries.

The abandonment of mother-daughter relationships by Continental European multinational enterprises tended to go hand in hand with the adoption of more formalized rules, procedures, and reporting systems, as we have already seen. But the control systems accompanying organization in Continental multinational enterprises continued to display unique personalized characteristics. 'American' structures were not always accompanied by American management practices.

Few of the Continental enterprises which had adopted supranational structures had reached the level of formality of rules and reports ascribed to American multinationals. Table 8.2 shows that 16 of the Continental reorganizers still indicated that written job descriptions and rules played but a minor role in controlling foreign manufacturing in 1972. Furthermore, eight of 28 reorganized firms surveyed in that year attached little importance to financial measures like reported monthly or yearly return on investment, or cash flow in evaluating either managers or investments, despite their new supranational divisions. Seven companies whose foreign subsidiary managers reported to the head of an international division or world-wide product division, noted that they did not (some said did not 'yet') have consolidated income statements or balance sheets which corresponded to their supranational responsibility centers in 1972!

Continental Organizations in the Future

Although vestiges of the mother-daughter era lingered on, strong pressures were pushing Continental European multinational enterprises toward supranational structures in the early and middle 1970's. If anything, the pace of organizational change accelerated after 1971.

Competitive moves by American, Italian and, increasingly, Japanese companies led to pressures on Continental enterprises based in the chemicals and non-ferrous metals sectors, pressures which could not be immediately countered by government protection and cartelization. In 1971 and 1972, price competition broke out in the chemical fiber industry. European companies attempted to form a cartel, but the German Federal Cartel Office greeted their attempt by meting out nearly 50 million Deutschmarks in fines in 1972 to nine Continental firms.[33] In the aftermath of this treatment, two Continental chemical enterprises that had held to mother-daughter structures through 1971 began moves toward reorganizing into world-wide product divisions.

In the same years, 1971 and 1972, a slump in demand and an increasing number of entrants into the world market in non-ferrous smelting produced a time of threat to Continental enterprises in this hitherto gentlemanly sector. As a result, by 1974, moves had been taken by all the leading Continental multinationals in non-ferrous metals industries to move from mother-daughter to product division or mixed structures.

Two of the three remaining enterprises in the motor-vehicle industry which had been organized along mother-daughter lines in 1971 also had begun moving to alternative structures, even though their foreign subsidiaries were almost all located in highly protected, LDC markets. All told, of the 23 Continental multinational enterprises with mother-daughter subsidiary relationships in 1971 only 13 retained them in mid-1974.

A Move to Matrix Organizations?

Will the process of structural change in Continental European multinational enterprises eventually cause the evolutionary paths of American and Continental organizations to converge? Specifically, will the many Continental multinationals coping with extensive geographical dispersion and foreign product diversity experiment increasingly with the matrix structures of the type that have emerged in Philips, Ciba-Geigy and some American enterprises?[34]

Superficially, the conditions were in place for a wide use by Continental enterprises of organizational structures in which shared, rather than individual responsibility would be the norm. Whereas 'management in the United States has placed a high premium on the separation and specialization of managerial tasks',[35] management in Continental enterprises with functional structures at home and daughter companies abroad long placed a premium on shared responsibilities, group decision-making, and communication along lines quite unrelated to formal responsibility. Because the mother-daughter organization was based on the principle of personal hierarchy and status, not on a division of labor among managers who were specialists in particular products, cross-functional and cross-product committees and group decision-making exercises were a necessity if any communication was to take place at all. Even cross-border committees sometimes became institutionalized adjuncts of mother-daughter structures: one German multinational tenaciously retained a mother-daughter structure in 1974 (in the face of substantial internal opposition from managers who wished to form an international

---

[33] Brun and Franko, 1974: Table 1.
[34] On American company moves to matrix (therein called 'grid' organization) structures, see Stopford and Wells, 1972.
[35] Quote from Stopford and Wells, 1972: p 85.

division), by appointing increasing numbers of parent-company executives to managing boards of foreign subsidiaries. These managing boards, which included executives from both the parent and the foreign countries, had collective responsibility for foreign subsidiaries; the subsidiaries had no 'presidents' but rather, in conformity to occasional German domestic practice, a management board 'spokesman' (Vorstandssprecher).[36]

Continental enterprises that were contemplating organizational change were attracted to matrix forms not only because of traditions of group responsibility, but also because enticing examples of successful use of matrix forms were available for emulation. Until Philips' profit margins began to drop precipitously in the late 1960's, that company was 'successful' by any reasonable standard of growth and profitability. Whether it was more successful than Continental companies using other structures is difficult to judge. Variations in the accounting practices and consolidation requirements of the Continental countries preclude any meaningful quantitative comparisons of company success. Philips, as Figure 3 points out, managed its far-flung multinational operations with about as complex a grid of overlapping product, national, and functional responsibilities as it was possible to imagine. From its inception in 1968 to its mutations in 1974, the Geigy (and then the Ciba-Geigy) product-area matrix of shared responsibility illustrated in Figure 3 provided another archetype of seeming organizational modernity.

Yet, while three-dimensional drawing of criss-crossing product, geographical, and functional lines were proliferating in the Continent's board-rooms and business schools in the early 1970's, evidence was accumulating that the matrix was not a terminal structural paragon, but was rather a way station toward sleeker, specialized, supranational product management. In 1973, it was announced that Philips was beginning to try to end its recent history of 'profitless growth'.[37] The means by which growth was to become profitable again were 'more centralization' and 'seeking economies of scale by concentrating production in fewer plants' whose mission was to 'produce for the entire company and no longer for their own national markets'. Observers noted that 'obviously, the change strengthens the roles of the product groups in corporate headquarters'.[38] Although management insisted that co-responsibility of functional head, and national and product committees would be retained, some managers were clearly becoming more equal than others, particularly since Philips was discretely, but gradually putting individual managers in charge of world-wide product co-ordination where co-equal technical and sales directors had previously shared product-line responsibility. Ciba-Geigy's matrix, too, was in 1973 beginning to be described in terms which hinted that shared responsibility was giving way to world-wide product management, while heads of regional services and national 'umbrella' subsidiaries provided substantial – but not co-equal – advice and counsel.

Managers in enterprises with matrix structures were thus recognizing that much of the influence and power given to managers who identified their

[36] On collegial traditions in European enterprise see also, Parks, 1966: Stopford, 1972: p 88.
[37] Business Week, January 13, 1973.
[38] Business Week, January 13, 1973: p 67.

interests with national borders was counter-productive. Lack of world-wide product perspective – and decision-making authority – had been one of the root causes of Philips' multi-million dollar losses in integrated circuits in 1971 and 1972.[39] American and Japanese enterprises – some with narrower, simpler product lines, others with simpler organizational structures – inflicted losses on European enterprises. These losses made personalized, collegial structures obsolete.[40] Some American multinationals had been able to optimize production in the EEC, or respond to the offshore sourcing opportunities in South-East Asia while the Continental multinationals' managers met in committee. Unless borders were to be closed, and competition suppressed as in the years past, new supranational structures with single lines of responsibility were a necessity.

Structures and Behavior

In the mid-1970's, however, it was not yet evident that the new supranational organizations would ineluctably modify the managerial and competitive behavior of Continental enterprises. Only two enterprises had adopted organizational structures which explicitly treated the whole EEC as their domestic market. Moreover, there was a disconcerting possibility that there was a race going on between the fixation of the new structures and attempts to recreate a negotiable environment. Despite their moves away from mother-daughter structures, the majority of the synthetic-fiber producers attempted to obtain approval for a Europe-wide rationalization cartel from the EEC in 1972 and 1973.[41] Moves toward world-wide product management did not prevent Continental producers of consumer electrical goods from attempting to negotiate private and public agreements to resist Japanese penetration of Europe in audio-visual equipment and household appliances.[42]

Table 8.10 Continental European Multinational Enterprises Classified by International Organizational Structure and by Whether Some Subsidiaries Exported more than 50% of their Production

Structure	No subsidiaries exporting more than 50%	Some subsidiaries exporting more than 50%	Total number of firms
Mother-daughter	14	7	21
International Division	5	5	10
World-wide product	8	12	20
Area and world-functional	1	2	3
Matrix and mixed	0	6	6
Total	**28**	**32**	**60**

[39] See Chapter V for a description of the events leading to European difficulties in the electronics sector in these years.
[40] See Stopford (1972) for a more optimistic – but very highly qualified view of the utility of collegial structures for international operations.
[41] *Business Week*, March 17, 1973: p 78; *Financial Times*, June 19, 1973; *Frankfurter Allgemeine Zeitung*, March 18, 1972.
[42] *Entreprise*, February 9, 1973.

Organizational change can facilitate behavioral change; it cannot determine it. The behavior of Continental European enterprises in 1974 was still occasionally one of reflexes conditioned by a half-century of protection and negotiated market sharing. Nevertheless, there was at least one sign that some behavioral change was underway. This sign was the correlation of Continental enterprises' adoption of supranational structures with their use of their foreign manufacturing subsidiaries as platforms for international trade, as seen from Table 8.10. Seventy-six of the 89 export-oriented foreign manufacturing subsidiaries of Continental multinational enterprises (for which organizational data were available) were owned by parents with supranational organizational structures. The absolute number of export-oriented subsidiaries of Continental multinationals was not high. Yet the correlation of organizational change with subsidiaries undertaking international trade did offer promise that the multinational enterprises of Continental Europe were beginning to adopt competitive, supranational *mores*.

Chapter IX

Politics and the 'Other' Multinationals

In 1971, it was still possible for managers of large Continental European enterprises to argue publicly that conflict between multinational companies and the interests of nation-states was 'an American problem'.[1] By and large, this perception of the American essence of the multinational enterprise problem was also shared by government officials throughout the world, except perhaps in the former British Empire and in South-East Asia. In the former Empire, colonial and Dominion ties had gone, but a massive presence of British manufacturing and extractive companies had remained and grown.[2] In South-East Asia, the growing presence of Japanese enterprises was the main focus of attention and reaction.[3]

Non-governmental political élites, too, often expressed their assent to an equation of multinational and American enterprise. This assent appeared to transcend distinctions among groups favoring revolution or reform, developed or less-developed countries, or labor or managerial-class interests.[4] Explicitly or not, there were many who subscribed to the view of one spokesman for the less developed countries that ' "multinational" was a word coined by people who wanted to obscure how American the phenomenon is'.[5] Once multi-national enterprise was thus identified with American big business, it then, of course, was but a short step to link the phenomenon to a real or imagined American imperial drive to world hegemony.[6]

Insofar as the American image of multinational enterprise was a function of the sheer outpouring of American statistics and professional publications during the 1960's, it was in need of revision by the 1970's.[7] During the 1950's and early 1960's, American enterprises had, of course, accounted for the large majority of foreign manufacturing and extractive operations established or acquired by the world's large companies.[8] But it is evident that neither in those decades, nor long before, were the American multinationals alone. During the im-mediate post-World War II era the foreign activity of American, and to some extent British enterprises, was made known to the world as a result of official statistics and public disclosure requirements of stock exchanges and govern-ments. Nonetheless, Swiss, Swedish, Dutch, Belgian, Luxemburg, and even Italian enterprises also owned important foreign manufacturing and extractive operations, only they were more discreet about them. In an earlier, somewhat forgotten historical period, the foreign activity of American enterprises had even been less important than that of firms based in Continental lands. The foreign manufacturing activity of German firms alone, as nearly as one can tell, was more extensive than that of American enterprise on the eve of World War I (and, incidentally, helped spawn the works of Lenin, Hilferding and Luxemburg on imperialism).[9] During the 1920's, the rate of expansion of large

---

[1] *Vision*, 1971: p 77.
[2] Stopford, 1974; Vaupel and Curhan, 1973–1974: pp 84–87.
[3] Tsurumi, 1974: pp 23, 24 and 35.
[4] Sulzberger, 1973.
[5] Vaitsos, Constantine, statement made at a seminar at the CEI, Geneva, May 1973.
[6] Magdoff, 1969.
[7] The suspicion that the *defi américain* was largely the result of *les statistiques américaines* was expressed already in 1968 by Rolfe, Sidney (1968: p 20).
[8] As seen in Chapter I.
[9] Chapter I, *supra*; Staley, 1935: Chapter I; Lenin, 1960.

Continental firms as a group into both foreign manufacturing and extraction was nearly equal to that of American enterprise.

The statistical identification of multinational enterprise with American big business became a serious distortion, however, only after large enterprises based outside the United States began to establish and acquire foreign operations at a more rapid rate than did American firms, an event which occurred sometime in the mid-1960's. The foreign expansion of Japanese, British and Canadian enterprise played a role which was far from negligible in this upsurge of non-US multinational activity, but the major part of the postwar growth of non-US multinational enterprise was accounted for by Continental European firms. Moreover, of the five developed home countries whose enterprises had more than doubled the number of their foreign manufacturing subsidiaries during the last half of the 1960's, four were Continental European: they were France, Germany, Belgium and the Netherlands.[10] Japan was the other country (its enterprises had the second highest rate of subsidiary proliferation).

As was seen in Chapter I, by 1971, the foreign manufacturing activity of US enterprise only slightly exceeded that of non-US enterprise, however estimated, and Continental multinational activity accounted for at least half of the non-US total. Sixty-four of the 85 largest Continental industrial enterprises manufactured in more than seven countries by 1971, and all but three of the total had at least one foreign manufacturing subsidiary; thirty-four of the 85 were engaged in foreign extractive activity.

Yet, despite the long history and recent upsurge in the multinational operations of non-American enterprise, there was still a considerable element of truth to the American identification of the problems surrounding multinational company relationships with political entities. The purely quantitative indications of the multinational expansion of non-US enterprise in general, and Continental enterprise in particular, masked persistent differences in patterns of enterprise behavior between many of the Continental firms and their American counterparts. Moreover, they masked differences among the political responses of governments and national élites to Continental European and American multinational activity. Some of these differences in enterprise action and political response were especially noticeable at the time of initial establishment of manufacturing or extraction in foreign lands.

National Reactions to the Establishment of Foreign Operations by Continental Firms

From the very beginning, when the Prussian finance minister asked John Cockerill to help reduce Prussia's dependence on imports of British textile machinery in 1815, the history of the foreign manufacturing decisions of Continental industrial firms has been bound up with the trade and development policies of host-country governments. The historical evidence argues that national tariff and non-tariff barriers to trade played a considerably greater role in the spread of Continental foreign manufacturing than they did in the American multinational spread.[11]

---

[10] See Chapter IV, Table 4.9.
[11] See Chapters IV, V, VI, VII above.

In order to commence foreign manufacturing successfully, both Continental European and American enterprises needed distinctive, oligopolistic advantages over potential local competitors, for both European and American multinationals needed to overcome the special costs endemic to foreign operations. These costs included the burden on home-country managers of learning different languages, laws, and business-government and labor-relations practices. The oligopolistic advantages possessed by Continental enterprises were, however, not the same as those underpinning American multinational expansion.[12]

American enterprises pioneered new products in the United States and then carried them into foreign production: these new products typically appealed to high-income, middle-class consumer demands, or to industrial needs to employ less high-cost labor. Demand for new products, first at the time they were innovated in the US, and then again when these products were new in foreign markets, was more income-elastic than price elastic. Such new product-pioneering was associated not only with advantages in technology, as reflected in the high expenditures on research and development of the US multinationals; it was also associated with advantages in the marketing of income-elastic goods, as reflected in the US multinationals' high advertising expenditures.[13]

In contrast, Continental European enterprises tended to derive their special advantages from the innovation of processes for the production of known products, or low-income varieties of known products, or of material substitutes and synthetics. As a result of the Continent's meager resource endowment and of government policies often aimed at autarky, many Continental innovations – process or product – were of a material-saving nature. Since the products produced by Continental firms tended to be themselves well known in the market place, or to be substitutes for well known goods, their demand was sensitive to price. Consequently, although science, technology, and R&D were often associated with Continental advantages, advertising and other marketing skills associated with income-elastic products played little role in supporting the expansion of foreign manufacturing by Continental enterprise.

As a result of the kind of innovations they developed, Continental enterprises were only infrequently drawn into manufacturing in foreign lands by impersonal market forces. Continental products and processes were born in, and best adapted to countries where the cost of materials was high relative to that of labor. Due to the high price-elasticity of demand for the products produced by Continental enterprises, the incentive to manufacture outside home countries in a world of relatively increasing wage rates and incomes was weaker than that for American enterprise. Continental moves to enter foreign production were most often triggered by tariffs (which directly affected the price at which exports could be sold in foreign markets), by host-government policies to reduce dependence on foreign raw materials, or by host-government threats of non-tariff barriers to trade.[14]

---

[12] For a more detailed discussion of these points, see Chapters II and IV above.

[13] Vaupel, 1971.

[14] High price elasticity went hand-in-hand with the ability of competitors to produce similar products. When NTB's were raised, Continental firms were thus faced with the prospect of elimination from the protected market.

The foreign manufacturing decisions of American firms with monopolistic advantages in new products were less often associated with host-government policies: foreign increases in incomes and labor costs caused imports of high-income, labor-saving new products into Europe and other regions. Once markets were established, lower absolute levels of labor costs abroad often dictated foreign production by American product pioneers – tariffs or no tariffs.

The continual association of the moves into foreign manufacturing by large Continental enterprises with host-government policies almost certainly gave Continental firms a political edge over American firms in relationship with both home-country and host-interest groups.

On the Continent, it was next to impossible for home-country unions or labor ministries to accuse enterprises of putting up 'runaway' plants in foreign countries when trade barriers, not the attraction of lower-cost foreign labor, visibly 'forced' the replacement of exports by foreign manufacturing. Who could blame enterprises, when German and Swiss dyestuffs exports to the United Kingdom or the United States gave way to German and Swiss subsidiaries because of import prohibitions or protective devices like the American Selling Price?[15]

In host countries, intellectual and political élites found it relatively easy to receive Continental enterprises which were clearly responding to host-government policy measures. Continental responses to political decisions somehow seemed more obviously 'socially responsible' to host-country nation states than did American responses to local market growth. American firms often set up foreign production to meet market demands of high-income groups for 'non-essential' new products that political élites claimed were 'not really wanted or needed by the people'.[16] The process by which new, high-income American products spread into production around the world was termed the international product cycle by some economists. It was termed 'Coca-Colonization' by political élites which had little use for market forces.[17] Moreover, in countries like France or some less developed or socialist states where opinion leaders could define a non-essential good as 'anything that needed to be advertised', the heavy marketing orientation of some American multinationals made American enterprises even more suspect compared to the Continental firms and their 'essentials'.

The Underdog Advantage

Continental process innovations and synthetics often provided prospective host countries with alternatives to receiving American manufacturing multinationals, or to purchasing raw materials controlled by Anglo-American oligopolies.

Repeatedly, Continental multinational expansion was associated with host-countries' fights against nature's inequitable distribution of natural resources,

---

[15] See Chapters IV and VII.
[16] It has also been argued that the introduction and advertising of new, middle-class products distorts local consumer aspiration levels, and thence development patterns into relatively unproductive channels. See Furtado, 1974: pp 46 and 47.
[17] United States Tariff Commission, 1973: p 151.

or against an American enterprise's market dominance. Only rarely were Continental enterprises in a position to overwhelmingly dominate international markets for particular new products through early innovation of those new products. The history of Continental multinational enterprise reveals few equivalents to a Standard Oil in refined petroleum or a Ford in mass-produced automobiles before World War I, or to an IBM in computers, a Texas Instruments in semi-conductors, or an ITT in telecommunications after World War II. The names of few Continental multinationals have become household words in the manner of Kodak, Coca-Cola, Xerox and IBM. Continental firms in competitive products were latecomers, and they provided host countries with the option of receiving subsidiaries of multinational enterprises associated neither with market dominance nor with a great-power parent nation. Continental enterprises with the know-how to produce synthetics or substitutes provided options to Anglo-American controlled supplies of oil, copper, rubber and other raw materials, and Continental enterprises which produced hydro-electric power generation equipment, or aluminum or fertilizer, or dyestuffs were more often welcomed than feared.[18]

The complementarity between the multinational expansion of Continental enterprise and host-country desires for independence from American and British enterprises did not to be sure, hold true in all times and in all products. Before World War I, product pioneering in militarily important goods set the early German multinationals apart. Their advances in pharmaceuticals, explosives, X-ray equipment, and signalling and communication devices occasionally led to market shares which provoked fear and envy in nations receiving German imports and foreign investment.[19] During the inter-war period, the renewed lead of Germany's I G Farben in pharmaceuticals and insecticides placed that enterprise in the giant (or ogre) category usually reserved for American multinationals well before Farben became associated with the political machinations of the Third Reich.[20] After World War II, two of Continental Europe's multinationals also occasionally reaped harvests of resentment usually reserved for American firms: Sweden's SKF found its bid for the acquisition of Britain's Ransom and Marles (later merged into Ransom-Hoffmann-Pollard) blocked in 1968 on the grounds that the combined enterprise would have been too dominant in ball and roller bearings in the UK;[21] Switzerland's Hoffmann-La Roche found itself under attack in the early 1970's by the UK Monopolies Commission, the EEC Competition Department, and the German Federal Cartel Office for the dominant market position of its (American developed!) Librium and Valium tranquilizers.[22] One or two other Continental European multinational enterprises seemed potential candidates for castigation as monopolists, but they were exceptions

---

[18] See also Chapters IV, V and VI.

[19] See Chapter II; Siemens, 1957: Vol I; Aldcroft, 1968; Haber, 1971.

[20] Du Bois, 1953.

[21] Dunning, 1974: p 33. See Hodges, 1974: pp 112 and 113, for a detailed discussion. The fact that two other firms in the UK bearings industry – in addition to SKF's Skefco subsidiary – were owned by foreign enterprises, gave an additional incentive for the British government to block the bid. It was felt that there might soon otherwise be no British-owned company in the bearings sector.

[22] *United Kingdom, Monopolies Commission*, 1973; Bissiger, 1974: p 6.

to the rule. To nation states contemplating the receipt of foreign enterprise, Continental companies have long been the Other Multinationals.

The benefits accruing to the Other Multinationals from their underdog image were long visible in the oil industry. When Standard Oil of New Jersey was top-dog in petroleum, Royal Dutch-Shell provided the French government with an appealing alternative to Jersey's market power.[23] After Shell became identified with the Anglo-Saxon international petroleum cartel, it was the turn of the French state petroleum companies and Italy's ENI to benefit from the appeal of the challenger first at home and then abroad. Countries anxious to decrease the hold of the American and British oil companies either on raw materials concessions or on refining and marketing capacity often welcomed the Continental newcomers.

The Continental petroleum enterprises, for their part, often encouraged host-country governments to diversify the parent nationalities (and parent governments) of the large multinational firms with which they dealt. During the 1950's, ENI's leader, Mattei, actively supported African and Middle Eastern aspirations for political independence. He also supported these countries' desires to reduce the share of their commerce and investment conducted by British, American or French companies. Although Mattei's foreign policy earned him the active hostility of British and American enterprises and governments (as well as that of the French, as long as they were engaged in the Algerian war), it facilitated the multinational spread of ENI's extractive, refining, and marketing activities in Tunisia, Iran, Tanzania, Egypt, Morocco, Ghana, Zambia and Zaïre.[24] Once France had abandoned its claims to colonial empire, its oil companies too, were in a position to appear responsive to numerous host-country desires to 'get out from under' the Anglo-Saxons.[25] One suspects that Germany's new state-owned national oil champion, Veba-Gelsenberg, will be aided in some of its projected multinational expansion by a frequent congruence in goals of underdog states and underdog companies.[26]

Although the contrast between American dominance and Continental challenge has been somewhat less extreme in motor vehicles than in oil (particularly in the post-World War II era), governments have often welcomed Continental enterprise as alternatives to the Americans.[27] Thanks to their unique, low-income automobiles, Continental firms sometimes experienced the profitable (and resented) pleasures of being leaders in local manufacturing in less developed countries. Predominant market positions have occasionally led to public visibility and, as demonstrated by the assassination of Fiat's general manager in Argentina in 1971, they have occasionally been a prelude to the hostile political treatment more often meted out to American and British companies.[28] Nevertheless, the multinational spread of

---

[23] Rondot, 1962: p 100.

[24] Tiger and Franko, 1973; see also Chapter III.

[25] See Chapter III above.

[26] Veba's image as a friend of the Third World may have suffered, however, from its vetoing of Iran's desire to market directly in Germany in 1972. See Chapter III.

[27] See also Chapter V.

[28] Fiat's share of the Argentinian auto market was estimated at 25% in 1969. Fox, 1972: p 124.

American motor vehicle firms had occurred earlier, and had blanketed much more of the world with producing subsidiaries than had the spread of Continental firms.[29] Volvo was especially welcome in Peru, Renault in Colombia, and Peugeot in Chile in the 1960's and 1970's: small countries found such firms less intimidating than General Motors, Ford and Chrysler, the world's first, third and fifth largest industrial companies.[30] The welcome was even greater, since the names of the Continental enterprises carried no echo, however distant, of American diplomatic or military influence. But the mere fact of being newcomers, and of having no past history of local market dominance undoubtedly led host governments to see these enterprises as alternative sources for investment, technology and business skills.

In electrical products, Continental enterprises also provided host-countries with alternatives to American multinationals. When Belgium's public purchasing authorities decided to discriminate against the dominant American computer firms by limiting them to half of the public market, they discriminated in favor of Philips of Holland and Siemens of Germany.[31] While Belgium still did not have its 'own' computer company, it had the simultaneous satisfaction of encouraging more supply options and of reinforcing political links with the two other member countries of the EEC in which Siemens and Philips were based. Freedom of choice seemed a move away from dependence, even if total independence was unattainable. In Latin America, governments faced with the entrenched, near-monopoly position of ITT in telecommunications would doubtless have seen Ericsson of Sweden, Siemens of Germany and Philips of Holland as natural allies, even had ITT never compounded host-country fears of monopoly pricing with direct political meddling.

To a certain extent the compatibility in goals of underdog nations and underdog multinational companies would have been high regardless of the national origin of the underdog multinationals. Newer, smaller American enterprises (independents, in the parlance of the oil business) often were welcomed by host-countries as alternatives to dominant American giants. But the Other Multinationals not only brought alternative products and processes, they brought alternative home-country flags.

Allies Against 'Neo-Colonialism'?

Continental enterprises occasionally were welcomed by their hosts simply as a relief from omnipresent hordes of American, British, and even Japanese enterprises. Acting as if in imitation of the advertising slogan of America's Sherwin-Williams paint company, the American multinationals had 'covered the earth'. Moreover, as one observes from Table 9.1 the British had covered the Empire and the Japanese had covered South-East Asia by 1971. American multinationals owned a majority of the foreign manufacturing subsidiaries that had been located in most countries of the Western hemisphere by all large foreign companies. Large British enterprises owned about two-thirds of the foreign manufacturing subsidiaries located in Ireland and in former

---

[29] See also Chapter V *supra*.
[30] *Fortune*, 1974: p 185.
[31] *Business Europe*, 1970: p 178.

Table 9.1 Concentrations in Selected Host Countries of Foreign Manufacturing Subsidiaries of Large Enterprises Based in Various Parent Countries, January 1, 1971 (US Subsidiary data for-January 1, 1968)
(Percentage concentrations are indicated where subsidiaries from any one parent country equal or exceed 30% of all subsidiaries)

Host country	Total subsidiaries in host country	Parent Countries:											
		US	(%)	UK	(%)	Japan	(%)	France	(%)	Germany	(%)	Sweden	(%)
Canada	748	475	(64)	175		12		9		33		2	
Mexico	352	255	(72)	18		10		7		26		5	
Argentina	246	125	(51)	28		3		23		30		3	
Peru	78	47	(60)	4		9		—		8		2	
Chile	59	31	(53)	6		2		4		6		2	
Brazil	368	162	(44)	26		33		28		47		6	
Germany	534	214	(40)	125		—		42		—		16	
France	646	205	(32)	97		0		—		128		16	
Italy	376	174	(46)	57		—		34		36		7	
Bel & Lux	243	85	(35)	49		3		36		24		6	
UK	610	357	(59)	—		—		20		35		22	
Ireland	125	28		80	(64)	—		0		—		0	
Sweden	109	35	(32)	41	(38)	0		4		20		0	
Finland	28	6		4		0		0		3		11	(39)
Austria	108	17		23		0		5		34	(37)	—	
Greece	43	17	(40)	7		0		2		11		—	
Pakistan	58	16		24	(41)	5		—		6		—	
Zambia	44	6		36	(82)	2		0		0		0	
Kenya	52	8		38	(73)	2		0		—		0	
Nigeria	65	11		41	(63)	8		2		0		0	
Other Brit Africa	58	4		41	(71)	6		0		2		0	
Maghreb*	66	15		—		—		31	(47)	3		0	
Other Fr Africa	61	9		13		3		30	(49)	3		0	
Australia	616	209	(34)	346	(56)	16		12		6		6	
Taiwan	110	13		2		92	(84)	0		—		0	
Phillippines	78	53	(68)	2		12		—		3		—	
Indonesia	29	3		5		15	(52)	2		3		0	
Thailand	79	14		4		52	(69)	0		5		0	
India	217	65	(30)	78	(36)	27		3		20		5	

Note: *Algeria, Tunisia, Morocco.
Source: Comparative Multinational Enterprise Project.

British African countries, and the Japanese relative presence was similarly impressive in Taiwan, Thailand and Indonesia.

The Continental presence was more discreet. In no host country did enterprises from any one Continental nation own more than half of all manufacturing subsidiaries of large, foreign firms. There was a moderate concentration of French subsidiaries in former French Africa, of German subsidiaries in Austria, and of Swedish subsidiaries in Finland. But elsewhere, large enterprises based in one Continental country never accounted for more than 30% of all the foreign outposts located in a given host country.

The percentages shown in Table 9.1 are imperfect indicators of the visibility in host nations of the flags of the various home nations of multinational enterprises. But, in their imperfection, they may even understate the host-country presence of American, British and Japanese enterprises: those multinationals all spanned a much broader range of industries than did the Continentals, and the Continentals had a comparatively tiny stake in advertised consumer products.[32]

The hostility of reception being accorded to multinationals from different lands during the 1970's clearly bore some correlation to the proportions shown in Table 9.1. Canada displayed great irritation toward US firms, and British journalists complained of American colonization of the UK. Latin Americans also considered US companies as their *bêtes noires*.[33] The British were often the target in former British Africa, and the Thais and Indonesians railed against Japanese enterprise.[34] But, except for French companies in part of French Africa, Continental countries and enterprises avoided such abuse.

In the post-World War II era, perhaps one of the greatest political advantages of multinational enterprises based on the European Continent was the fact that they were not American, British or Japanese. The flags of the home countries of Continental enterprises did not connote superpower ambitions or superpower capabilities to recipient countries. Except in the case of French firms in French Africa, the home-country flags of Continental enterprises did not even have overtones of superpower memories. Receipt of a West German, Dutch or Italian enterprise did not seem to inspire any host country's governmental or intellectual élite with nervousness about the possibility that West Germany, Holland or Italy might someday apply effective military, political or economic sanctions on behalf of its enterprises. It seemed a long time since these home states had attempted military actions or even taken strong political positions on behalf of their enterprises in host countries. Host countries were not so sure about the actions of the United States, Japan Incorporated, or Great Britain. And some hosts, even in developed European countries, were quite convinced that acceptance of a Mitsubishi meant acceptance of direct pressures from the Japanese Ministry of International trade and Industry (MITI), and that acceptance of ITT and Exxon meant that the power of the US was not far behind. In the extreme case, home country weakness seemed to become a strength for the Other Multinationals:

[32] See Chapter IV above.
[33] Vaitsos, 1973; Koebner and Schmidt, 1964: especially p 299.
[34] Amsden, 1971: especially pp 51 et seq.; Nkrumah, 1965: especially pp 52 and 53; Tsurumi, 1974; Kobayashi, 1974.

managers of Swiss and Swedish enterprise could assert that their 'greatest asset' in foreign operations was the neutrality of their home countries.

The style of business-government relationships between Continental enterprises and their home-country governments may also have stood them in good stead when they ventured into foreign lands. Continental élites have rarely, if ever, proudly displayed or vigorously washed the linen of their political relationships in public. Countries which had been under military siege since time immemorial saw no virtue in advertising or publicly criticizing business-enterprise ties. Discreet arrangements were to be discreetly arrived at. Proud (or shamed) exposure of business-government links was a luxury good affordable only by nations surrounded by water which had no fear of invasion from neighbors who might take a dislike to those links.

The relationship between French firms and the French governmental élite was exceedingly close. Rare were the cases in which top managers of French firms were appointed without consultation with government ministries. Rare, also, were the cases in which the top management groups of French companies did not include former government officials.[35] Dutch business-government relationships were said to be even closer.[36] Presidents of two of Sweden's largest enterprises stated that between a third and a half of their time was spent in dealing with governmental bodies.[37] In Switzerland, political, business, and military élites were intertwined by inter-changes of management personnel as well as by family relationships.

These relationships were rarely visible in the foreign operations of Continental enterprises, however. When home-country business-government links did affect foreign operations they tended to do so in an indirect way: enterprise-government negotiations at home gave firms practice that was later useful in dealing with governments abroad. The penchant of French, Swedish and Italian firms for undertaking joint ventures with host-country governments, remarked upon in Chapter V, seems explicable only by the nature of the experience at home of these enterprises.

American enterprises were often publicly exposed when they became involved in political, ideological or military ventures of the US government; such a style was the very antithesis of Continental discretion. Whether US enterprise and government policies had mixed frequently or infrequently was beside the point: the publicity was the message, and it swamped any statistically verifiable generalization.[38] The relationship between Japanese enterprises and MITI, too, had become public legend.[39] And while the legacy of the public perception of the interconnection between British business and the Empire was perhaps fading, it had hardly disappeared.[40]

---

[35] On business-government relationships in France, see Michalet, 1974; Vernon, 1971: pp 219–223; Scott and MacArthur, 1969; Shonfield, 1969; Granick, 1962: pp 72–79.
[36] Priouret, 1970: p 359.
[37] Discussions with the author.
[38] See also Vernon, 1971; Behrman, 1970.
[39] Yoshino, 1968; Yanaga, 1971.
[40] Amsden, 1971; Nkrumah, 1965; Reid, 1971: p 17.

Being an enterprise from a Continental country was not invariably an advantage with other Continental governments. The German government blocked a bid for Gelsenberg by France's *Compagnie Française des Pétroles* in 1968, while the American company Texaco had been allowed to take over the German refiner, *Deutsche Erdöl*, in 1966.[41] Memories of Franco-German conflicts, as well as close relations between Germany and the United States may have had something to do with the preference shown for Texaco. In France, memories of German territorial ambitions made for unease over the extent of German manufacturing investment in Alsace in the 1960's.[42] The ghosts of history also caused ambivalence in Belgium and the Netherlands over German investment, and even over transnational mergers with German firms. And, unsurprisingly, the concentrations of French investment in North Africa, of German in Austria, and Swedish in Finland occasionally provided targets for accusations of French, German or Swedish imperialism.[43] But such tensions seemed minor compared to those which had been raised by the presence of American enterprises wherever they went, or by British and Japanese multinationals in their African and Asian bailiwicks.

Reactions to Operating Behavior after Entry

Once installed in foreign lands, Continental European enterprises frequently had a tension-free relationship with both host and home nation-states. Such, at least, was the case for enterprises undertaking foreign manufacturing.

While American enterprises engaged in multinational manufacturing had long exercised the production, market, profit location and financing options available to enterprises which could co-ordinate operations in many countries, most Continental multinationals only began to pay much attention to cross-border co-ordination after 1970. Observers of American multinational company behavior were quick to perceive that multinational enterprises 'can seek out the lowest-cost site for even individual components of products and cross-haul them to various assembly points. Such a high degree of specialization and exchange would have warmed the heart of Adam Smith....'[44] Whatever the reality of the optimizing image of American multinational behavior, the contrast between this image and Continental behavior was striking: the foreign manufacturing subsidiaries of Continental enterprises were rarely very specialized by product, and were rarely intensively engaged in international trade.[45]

The orientation of subsidiaries of Continental enterprises to producing for national markets was partly the result of governmentally imposed barriers

---

[41] *The Economist*, October 5, 1968: p 99; *The Economist*, January 25, 1969: p 70.
[42] See: *Documents: revue des questions allemandes*, 1969: pp 61–127, especially the article by Julliard, E, pp 74–91.
[43] In Algeria, for example, officials and politicians often equated colonialism, capitalism, and French dependence in their speeches. Algeria has deliberately tried to diversify its trade and investment partners. See Brandell, 1974. On Swedish 'imperialism in Finland', see: *To The Point International*, August 24, 1974: p 33. For an attack on 'German Monopoly Capital' in Austria, see: Hager, 1971.
[44] Krause, 1972: p 97.
[45] See Chapters V, VI, VIII above.

to trade in sectors such as metals and pharmaceuticals.[46] Yet, much of this national orientation seemed the result of organizational hierarchies and managerial reflexes which had been conditioned in uncompetitive, negotiable home-market environments. Both Continental and American multinational enterprises were active in synthetic fibers and electronic components, for example. However, the webs of supranationally intermeshed logistic systems spun by a number of the American-based enterprises in these sectors had few if any Continental counterparts before the mid-1970's.[47]

Relationships with both host and home countries were often facilitated by the minimal amount of international trade conducted by the foreign manufacturing daughters of Continental European mother companies. The limiting of international trade minimized the risk of conflicts with national governments and labor unions over profit and currency reallocations through transfer prices, the adjustment of payment terms on goods traded among subsidiaries, and the like. Minimal international trade also reduced the risk of conflicts with local workers and managers over delivery times, quality standards and control systems. With no obligation to work to the pace of a supranationally scheduled mechanism, local norms and customs could prevail in the collections of national subsidiaries which made up Continental international combines. The Continental multinationals thus avoided conflicts with national interests that were endemic to American enterprises which, like IBM and Ford, 'treated Europe or Latin America like one big plant' and gave great authority to executives with supranational regional responsibilities.[48]

On occasion, Continental enterprises paid a heavy economic price for the inefficiencies endemic to allowing subsidiaries to act as if they were national companies. Continental European parents and their subsidiaries incurred huge losses in the integrated circuit business in 1971, largely because the enterprises failed to locate production optimally on a worldwide basis.[49] Nevertheless, economic adversity could sometimes be turned to political advantage in home countries. When Continental enterprises behaving like international combines of separate national firms suffered commercial disaster at the hands of optimizing American multinationals, the Continentals were in a position to argue at home that they had been more 'socially responsible'. They had not threatened workers' jobs, or nations' trade balances and desires for technological independence by having recourse to 'runaway plants' or 'offshore sourcing'. Such an argument sometimes successfully persuaded home-country governments in Europe to grant subsidies and protection. In the aftermath of the integrated circuit debacle, the French government provided large cash subsidies to France's SESCOSEM (a domestic subsidiary of Thomas-Brandt of France), and the Italian state holding company IRI rescued Olivetti's SGS (a daughter company which itself had Italian, French, Swedish, German and British manufacturing operations). National governments also prevailed upon the EEC to severely tighten the application of rules of origin

---

[46] See Chapter VI.
[47] See Chapters V and VI.
[48] On the relationship between cross-border sourcing, supranational organizational structures and political conflicts involving American multinational enterprises, see Wells, 1971.
[49] See Chapter V for a detailed discussion.

on circuits imported into the Community.[50] Insofar as home-country governments equated social responsibility with national employment security,
(rather than, say, with a lower total cost of semiconductors to customers and
taxpayers) international combine behavior was by definition socially
responsible.

Seeds of Conflict

The seeds of conflict with national interests were nonetheless being planted
by Continental multinational enterprises, even when they behaved like loose
international combines of national companies.

A Continental multinational which behaved like an international combine of
national companies could not, for example, entirely avoid the risk of being
viewed with suspicion by national labor unions. A Continental European
multinational combine which maintained unspecialized plants producing the
same product in various countries was often accepted by host-governments
bent on import substitution and host-country businessmen fearful of con-
frontations with supranationally optimizing competitors. But the fact that a
company behaving like an international combine produced similar products
in a number of different countries made national unions uneasy. Unions
worried that such a multinational could break a strike called in one country
by shipments from other plants in the system with excess or rapidly
expandable capacity.

A Continental multinational which had daughter companies producing for
national markets also could not completely avoid the risk of conflict with
host- and home-country interests over transfer prices. Some potential for
conflict – with both home and host countries – was always latent in the widespread use of foreign financial holding companies by Continental firms. Large
European enterprises, including those with relatively few foreign production
or extractive operations, long found it useful to maintain financial holding
(or 'base') companies in countries which had low income taxes and few
restrictions on capital flows.[51] Switzerland, Luxemburg, and Holland (because
it did not tax foreign source income, even when remitted as dividends) were
the preferred locations for tax-haven base companies, although other country
locations were occasionally used.

The governments of Continental home countries had in fact traditionally
favored the use of tax-haven companies by exporting enterprises. Until 1971,
none of the Continental home countries taxed unremitted foreign income,
and none controlled exporters' transfer prices.[52] Continental enterprises
could bill exports to tax-haven companies at one price, and then on to customers (affiliated or not) at another, higher price. Small adjustments in
margins could lead to large shifts of profits into tax-haven subsidiaries.
Home-country encouragement of these shifts of profits constituted an
effective subsidy to exports.

---

[50] On IRI's purchase of a majority of SGS see *The Economist*, July 24, 1971: p 78. On rules of
origin, see *Business Europe*, April 13, 1973: p 120.
[51] For example, Stephenson, 1972: pp 135 and 136, cites ten non-Swiss Continental multinationals with base companies in Switzerland as of 1971.
[52] Hufbauer, 1974.

However, in one Continental home country, Germany, various political groups were beginning to conclude that exports no longer needed subsidization by 1971. Reducing the tax-haven privileges of German exporters (a measure which was in effect a partial revaluation of the Deutschmark) was seen as a substitute for a further revaluation of the German exchange rate. Companies were attacked in the German press for transfer-pricing profits on exports into foreign base companies. German enterprises with multinational manufacturing subsidiaries were also criticized for using tax-haven subsidiaries not only as collection points for export profits, but also as conduits for avoidance of German taxes on remittances from foreign manufacturing subsidiaries. In 1973, Germany became the first Continental home country to adopt a legal instrument for the control of the use of base companies by its enterprises. The German law (the *Aussensteuergesetz*) provided for supervision of transfer prices on exports from Germany and for the taxation of the income of tax-haven companies as if such income had been received by the parent enterprise.[53]

Host countries were often particularly suspicious of the European multinational enterprises headquartered in countries that others chose as locations for tax-haven subsidiaries. Enterprises whose headquarters were located in low-tax countries often had foreign manufacturing subsidiaries that were transferring few goods (or services) among themselves, but which were purchasing considerable quantities of intermediate goods, components or services from the parent companies. When such intermediates did not have readily visible market prices, suspicions of overpricing and underpayment of local taxes could flourish. Swiss-based companies in particular were the object of such fears.[54] Hoffmann-La Roche was thus attacked in the United Kingdom, Germany and Colombia not only because of its highly visible dominance of some segments of tranquilizer markets, but because it supplied many of its subsidiaries with intermediates from its home company.[55] The United Kingdom Monopolies Commission, for example, asserted that Hoffmann-La Roche obtained 76% of its income from its UK affiliate, Roche Products Ltd by way of an excessive transfer price on Chlordiazepoxide and Diazepan, the raw materials for Librium and Valium supplied from Switzerland. The Monopolies Commission claimed that if this amount were added to the declared profits of the UK subsidiary, the return on capital earned over the period 1966–1972 would have been over 70%.[56]

It was, of course, rather illogical for host countries to single out companies headquartered in low-tax countries for special suspicion on matters related to transfer-pricing. As long as Continental home countries did not tax foreign earnings prior to repatriation (and none did), enterprises headquartered in high-tax nations could presumably reduce host-country tax liabilities by billing

---

[53] *Business Europe*, August 31, 1971: pp 258 and 259; Business International, *Investing, Trading and Licensing Conditions: Germany*, 1974: p 14.
[54] Stonehill, 1965: pp 135ff, for example, makes a discreet reference to a *cause célèbre* in Norway which involved a Swiss firm and the Norwegian government. The dispute centered on the size of payments to be made by the Swiss firm's subsidiary to its parent for technical services.
[55] Alaya, 1970.
[56] Monopolies Commission, 1973: Chapter 6, esp p 47.

intermediates shipped to foreign subsidiaries through base companies in tax-haven countries. However, the fears of host countries were sometimes more the result of the images hosts had of home nations than the result of enterprise actions.

Sometimes the conflict between national fiscal authorities and Continental enterprises over transfer-prices took on a slightly surrealistic cast, for the foreign production subsidiary that was supposedly underpaying host-country taxes sometimes had protectionist trade barriers as its primary or only *raison d'être*. Protection as such often gave a monopoly rent to the firms which produced behind trade barriers of the kind so common in the pharmaceuticals industry.[57] Legal combat occasionally raged over whether the host nation or the foreign company was to appropriate the monopoly rent created by protection, even though that protection had been intended as an incentive to get certain stages of local production started in the first place. But few governments, however, seemed bothered by any contradiction in the fiscal authorities' trying to get back what trade or industrial policy officials had given out.

Continental enterprises seeking raw materials also found that their behavior conflicted with national interests: subsidiaries extracting minerals in one country to sell in another could rarely behave for very long in ways totally consistent with the interests of both home and host countries. Although Continental firms seeking raw materials were greeted as the Other Multinationals, they too found that theirs was an 'obsolescing bargain'.[58] The welcome accorded by Liberia to the Swedish iron-ore syndicate headed by Gränges in the late 1950's, for example, gave way to dispute and renegotiation over the terms of the LAMCO mining concession in 1973. Once successful operations were underway, initial Liberian pleasure in decreasing the relative degree of US involvement in Liberia was replaced by a desire for more income, and thus for more control over the pricing and investment policies that might affect that income. Liberia was affected by declining world prices for iron ore regardless of the nationality of the firms which mined the ore. Liberia also seemed to become increasingly sensitive to the fact that the Gränges affiliate which handled both LAMCO and Swedish iron-ore sales had a reputation as a price-cutter.[59] Liberia first pressed Gränges to make 'value-added', ore-washing and pelletizing investments in the country in 1965, in an attempt to render demand for Liberian ore less sensitive to price. Liberia then instigated a general renegotiation of the LAMCO concession in 1973. Pressures by Liberia to realize such desires could not be isolated from the operations of Gränges in Sweden or elsewhere. The LAMCO renegotiation was but one example of the hard bargaining that followed initial welcomes in most raw materials ventures.[60] Nature's scattering of markets and deposits made it impossible to treat extractive subsidiaries as isolated, national

---

[57] It is arguable that protection gives rise to incremental monopoly rents even in the case of patented products such as Librium and Valium. Few patented drugs have *no* substitutes. And the vast differences in pharmaceutical prices among countries suggest that (public or private) protection *qua* protection has an influence on the price of patented drugs. (See, *Vision*, May 1973: p 97.)

[58] Vernon, 1971: Chapter II; Wells, 1968.

[59] Mikdashi, 1971: 'Malmexport'.

[60] Tiger, 1974.

entities. Thus, much discussion, bargaining and accommodation was needed to resolve tension as interests repeatedly diverged.[61]

Changes in Enterprise Behavior

Although Continental European multinational enterprises could not completely eliminate the risk of conflict with national interests by behaving like international combines of national firms, such behavior allowed the illusion to persist that the problem of multinational enterprise was an American problem. The pattern of behavior on which that illusion was based was, however, rapidly disappearing as the 1970's reached their mid-point. Competition from American, Japanese and Italian firms had pushed many Continental enterprises to cut costs by moving toward supranational production specialization.[62] Continental firms were also increasing the authority of executives with supranational responsibilities, and reducing the authority of national managers.[63] Continental companies active in motor vehicles, electrical products and specialty chemicals had moved further in the direction of European-wide, and even worldwide scanning and resource allocation than had enterprises based in the metals and mechanical industries. But whatever the sector, moves toward international optimization were decreasing the compatibility between the objectives of Continental European multinational enterprises and the objectives of these firms' home and host nations.

Perhaps the most abrupt manifestation of the dawning of an era of contentious relationships between national élites and Continental multinationals was the announcement on April 6, 1972 by the Dutch chemical giant AKZO of its desire to close five of its tariff factories dotted around Europe and to specialize production among different plants as if a true common market existed.[64] The announcement was greeted with protests by unions in both home and host countries. The strongest objections, however, were made at home. Two of the plants AKZO wished to close were in the Netherlands, and the support given by the Dutch press to union pressures and to plant sit-ins by workers made it clear that such 'socially irresponsible' behavior on the part of a Dutch multinational was hardly consistent with national expectations. For a time the Dutch (and German) top managers of AKZO and its Dutch-German Enka-Glanztoff division were being publicly referred to as 'the Americans'. Such an abrupt announcement of the priority of economic interests over those of maintaining existing jobs in synthetic fibers would, so it seemed, not have been surprising coming from US-owned multinationals. Coming from one of the European Multinationals it was more shocking.

In France, Péchiney's increasingly frequent statements that it intended to invest less and less, and perhaps cease investing at all in its home country, created an only slightly less explosive reaction there than did AKZO's intention to disinvest in its home country.[65] During the time when Péchiney appeared to be expanding foreign aluminum smelting primarily in response

---

[61] Wells, 1968.
[62] See Chapter VIII above.
[63] See Chapter VIII.
[64] See Northrup and Rowan, 1974: Part II and sources cited therein.
[65] *L'Expansion*, 1967.

to host government proddings, trade restrictions, and investment grants, such statements could have been interpreted as mere negotiating gambits in the never-ending bargaining between electricity-using Péchiney and *Eléctricité de France*. But as Péchiney expanded abroad, and particularly as new enterprises (including some in bauxite- or electricity-rich countries) threatened to compete on a price basis in order to enter the aluminum industry, low-cost foreign production sites became ever more appealing.[66] For Péchiney managers the importance of electricity as a component element of aluminum costs meant that foreign expansion was an economic necessity. The French socialist and communist parties, however, saw Péchiney's foreign plans as a search for unjustifiable 'superprofits' sought at the expense of French workers. During the 1974 election compaign the French left proposed to nationalize Péchiney – precisely in order to resolve the conflict by blocking the company's plans to act like a global, optimizing enterprise.[67]

Yet, even while the French left was proposing to nationalize Péchiney to bring French state and enterprise goals into harmony, Renault, an enterprise nationalized 28 years earlier was receiving attention both at home and abroad on account of its obscure, but considerable multinational spread. Although Renault's annual reports said little about them, the French press reported that the firm had both a sophisticated international sourcing system and a number of holding companies in low-tax countries. As a result, some suspicion surrounded the firm's profit reports and transfer-pricing practices. Business and labor interests alike harshly criticized Renault's secrecy concerning its multinational scope, its Swiss holding companies 'through which probably transit all movements of funds concerning subsidiaries', and its publication of 'well illustrated annual reports stuffed with production and export statistics, but lacking financial meaning'.[68] Attention was called to the 'danger of a financial-base company like Renault-Finances (Switzerland) not only aiding in the financing of foreign operations, but of dipping into the Euro-dollar market to finance the development of the mother company'.[69] Responding to these criticisms an anonymous member of the company's management replied: 'People would not permit the Régie (Renault), *a multinational enterprise*, to manage its finances inefficiently.' (Emphasis added.)*

In Germany, conflicts between the proposed multinational strategy of Volkswagen's management and the interests of labor unions and local (*Land*) government officials had become even more embarrassingly public by 1974. The clash between the increasingly multinational outlook of the major firms in the European automobile industry and the interests of national élites that some observers had predicted became real in the aftermath of the 1973–1974

---

*A few days after these pages were written, a French parliamentary commission published a report containing what press reports termed 'a violent attack' accusing 100 % French-state-owned Elf-Erap and partly state-owned *Compagnie Francaise des Pétroles* of practising similar financial dissimulation. (*Journal de Genéve*, November 9–10, 1974, p 5.)

[66] Kuhn, Loeb & Co, 1968; Kuhn, Loeb & Co, 1971.
[67] For a detailed analysis of Péchiney's operations as viewed by the French left, see: Jourlin and Derrien, 1973: pp 1–56, especially pp 33 and 56.
[68] *Entreprise*, October 1973: p 138.
[69] *Renault-Finances* is one of Renault's Swiss holding companies.

petroleum crisis.[70] In September 1974, while auto sales were stagnating in Europe and some Volkswagen plants were working shortened weeks, VW management brought up its oft-postponed proposal to establish a plant in the United States for consideration by its supervisory board.[71] The board decided yet again to postpone a decision to manufacture in the United States, but less because of doubts over the economic viability of the project than because of the interests of union and local government representatives on VW's board in protecting local employment.

> 'Before the Board was an Executive Board feasibility study on the project thought by industry sources to come out in favour of a plant in Pittsburgh. On the 21-man Supervisory Board are seven union representatives led by the IG Metall Union chairman Herr Eugene Loderer, who has said a US project would endanger German workers' jobs. The two representatives of Lower Saxony – which holds 20 per cent of VW's capital – have voiced similar reservations as much of the company's export activity is centred on the Hanover and Emden plants. According to industry sources, the US plant would produce 200,000 to 250,000 vehicles a year or about half the total VW has previously exported to the US. Assuming unchanged markets elsewhere, this could lead to a domestic labour force reduction of 40,000 to 50,000 workers, although the number could be moderated by the need to carry on US-bound component production in Germany.'[72]

In the absence of clearly visible barriers to trade with the United States, a decision to produce in that country could not be politically justified to certain German national, or local interest groups at a time when existing jobs seemed threatened – even though other sectors of the German economy continued to experience shortages of labor. But there was yet another irony in Volkswagen's situation: while interests of some German political groups were blocking increased multinational activity by the firm, a number of German national governmental departments were strongly urging VW to produce more in lower-cost countries. Some of these national government agencies wanted VW to thereby help in the fight against inflation by releasing resources for alternative domestic uses. And others wished to reduce the need for foreign workers (*Gastarbeiter*) in the German economy.[73]

Faced with these conflicting pressures, the President of Volkswagen resigned on December 19, 1974.[74]

Changes in the Economic Environment

While some Continental multinationals found themselves increasingly in conflict with national interests on account of changes in their own management strategies, enterprises that wanted (or had the reputation of wanting) to maintain the international combine style of behavior found conflict inevitable on account of changes and inconsistencies in the policies of nations themselves.

---

[70] For one prediction of this conflict, see Wells, 1974.
[71] For a concise summary of the tortuous history of VW's consideration of US manufacturing, see: McLain, 1974: pp 135–153.
[72] *Financial Times*, September 3, 1974.
[73] See: *Neue Zurcher Zeitung*, September 29, 1974.
[74] Colchester, 1974.

Firms that had set up tariff-barrier and NTB factories in less developed countries pursuing policies of import substitution, found that an initial agreement between enterprise and host-government goals often gave way to tension when host countries shifted toward export-oriented development strategies. In Latin America, for example, European enterprises found their import-substituting plants welcome during the 1950's and 1960's, but, as Latin American nations slowly discovered the gains to be had from regional integration, specialization, and exports to hard-currency countries, criticism began to be directed toward European subsidiaries, for these companies were conspicuously absent from lists compiled of manufacturing companies exporting from Latin America.[75] In Africa, too, one began to see clashes between the desires of a country like Nigeria for an export-oriented petrochemicals plant, and the wishes of Royal Dutch-Shell to establish a plant only where production and sales could be essentially matched within one country.[76]

Enterprises perceived as disposed toward behavior along international combine lines could also find themselves in conflict with *home*-country governments when these governments turned from nationalist to internationalist persuasions. Tensions between some German government agencies and German-based firms (or their union board members!) were notable in this regard. Having once swallowed the pill of Deutschmark revaluation as an anti-inflationary measure, some government officials did not want the effect of revaluation to be nullified or offset by private restrictions on imports.[77] German enterprises were urged by the Central Bank to phase out domestic production of import-competing goods, and attacked by the German Federal Cartel Office for entering into restrictive agreements with European and Japanese competitors. German enterprises were also finding their foreign acquisition plans under scrutiny for possible restrictive intent. In one case, the Federal Cartel Office intervened to limit the percentage shareholding a German firm (AEG) could take in an Italian competitor (Zanussi) to a 20% stake. The Cartel Office feared that any greater influence on the part of AEG would have enabled it to shut off the flow of Zanussi refrigerators to the German market.[78]

Indeed, European multinational enterprises had shown that they could sometimes come into conflict with a large number of home- and host-country interest groups simultaneously as a result of changes or aberrations in home-government policy. When government policy objectives changed, a company president could 'wake up to find himself at the head of a multinational company' (as one put it during the 1974 United Nations Hearings on Multinational Corporations and World Development). A shift in French government policy led to such a rude awakening being visited on St-Gobain in 1968 and 1969.

---

[75] See: Casas, 1973: especially pp 21 *et seq*; Campos, 1974: p 171; Wipplinger, 1971.

[76] Stephenson, 1972: p 108.

[77] The worry that the existence of multinational enterprise might make the traditional adjustment mechanisms less sensitive has been expressed frequently. (UN, 1973: p 65.) German examples suggest that the existence of any large commitment of resources – foreign *or* domestic – is a drag on adjustment. They also suggest that managers' and shareholders' interests are only one source of inertia in the adjustment process.

[78] See Chapter VI for a more detailed discussion of the AEG-Zanussi link-up and the Federal Cartel Office's intervention in it.

For reasons which are still unclear the French government uncharacteristically tolerated a public take-over bid in 1968 by Bussois-Souchon-Neuvesel (BSN) for St-Gobain, one of the Continent's enterprises with the lengthiest history of extensive foreign manufacturing operations. Public take-over bids, common enough in Anglo-Saxon countries, had previously been almost unknown in France. Perhaps the French government was distracted as it picked up the pieces of the May 1968 riots; perhaps it wished to disturb the quiet lives to which some managers had become accustomed in the long-cartelized glass industry. In any event, the structure of the French glass industry was not amicably arranged by private negotiations among enterprises and the Finance and Planning Ministries, as was traditional in France. BSN made its bid in December 1968, and although St-Gobain's defense was successful, St-Gobain was obliged to reveal much more about its finances and operations than it had ever done before.

Previously, few Frenchmen (or citizens of countries in which St-Gobain had daughter companies) had thought of St-Gobain as a multinational. Suddenly, St-Gobain stood identified in shareholders' and unions' minds as a multi-national enterprise, with all the profit and production location options associated with US multinational enterprises. Nevertheless, the company's public relations defense against the BSN bid gave St-Gobain a reputation of having suddenly and mysteriously conjured up profits out of the nether reaches of a multinational empire. This image was quickly seized upon in the United States, Germany and Italy by labor unions, which demanded that concessions made to French workers during the May 1968 disturbances be extended on a worldwide basis. The suspicion of these unions was that the concessions in France had been made at their expense; they feared that St-Gobain was declaring artificially low profits in America, Germany and Italy in order to pay for labor peace in France. In the event, the American, German and Italian unions were able to utilize St-Gobain's new multinational image to mobilize their members' support for a three-week strike in the United States, and for protracted negotiations in Germany and Italy. Some observers termed this simultaneous union action the 'first multinational strike', others thought that unions acted at the same time only because contracts in the United States, Germany and Italy happened all to expire in early 1969. But whatever one calls those events, St-Gobain was made abruptly aware of unions' perception of the company as a multinational enterprise capable of transfer-pricing profits to or from one or another subsidiary as a bargaining weapon.[79]

The Future of Continental European Multinational Enterprise

No reduction of tensions between national interests and the multinational enterprises of Western Continental Europe seemed in the offing as of 1974. Forecasting is a hazardous activity even in the most tranquil of times, and, at first glance, the turbulence of the world economy would appear to increase those hazards markedly. Paradoxically, however, it is the very turbulence surrounding the large enterprises of Western Europe that makes

---

[79] Vice, 1971: pp 98–115; Stephenson, 1972: pp 162; Northup and Rowan, 1974: Part I.

a prognostication of future conflicts with national interests a likely bet. Both the enterprise and the political reflexes that long permitted relatively facile relationships between the Other Multinationals and national interests were conditioned in different times. Managers who hope that political conflict can continue to be resolved by treating foreign subsidiaries as members of a combine or commonwealth of national units are likely to be cruelly disappointed.[80]

The behavior typical of international combines in which mother and daughter companies were linked only by ownership and personal ties, not by a common strategy, was possible in a world in which national élites could accept the illusion of the desirability of industrial autarky for themselves, and the legitimacy of such a goal for others. Once national élites came to hold other goals, or once there was little agreement on goals within national societies, not even the international combine mode of multinational enterprise behavior could resolve the conflict between enterprises and political interests.

In the past, the multinational expansion and the operating behavior of Continental European enterprises largely consisted of responses to the wishes of élites with homogeneous values and interests which clearly constituted nation states. Continental enterprises knew such entities well, since until recent years most of the political systems of their home or neighboring countries had been considerably less pluralistic than those prevailing in the Anglo-Saxon world.[81] In such a world enterprises and states could set unambiguous and predictable agendas for one another. The post-war increase in political pluralism has meant, however, that multinational enterprise actions cause entries in the agendas of many political interest groups.[82] Continental multinational enterprises are increasingly seen as capable of satisfying or blocking fulfilment of the objectives of any number of home- and host-country interest groups.

In the near future multinational enterprises based on the European Continent, perhaps unlike those based in America, Great Britain or Japan, may face a higher degree of political tension at home than in host countries.[83]

While the cross-winds of political pluralism are likely to buffet the Continental multinationals with conflicting claims and accusations at home, the less developed countries will probably receive Continental enterprises as the Other Multinationals for some years to come. The concentrations of US, British and Japanese investments in some less developed countries will almost certainly make Continental enterprises and their managers a welcome relief from time to time, even if a Continental firm should occasionally take advantage of the welcome to do an especially sharp deal or two. Paradoxically, Continental enterprises will probably be the multinational firms most discomfited in less developed countries' operations, if host countries increasingly

---

[80] *Vision*, December 1973: p 58.
[81] Dahrendorf, 1968; Huntsford, 1971; Shonfield, 1969; Salvemeni, 1971.
[82] On the political role of multinational enterprise in 'setting the agendas' of nation states, see Nye, 1974.
[83] Dunning, 1974: p 29, forecasts greater tensions surrounding MNE's in *host* countries, especially those which are less developed. Dunning, however, appears to have American and British enterprises in mind.

require more complete public accounting disclosure. Continental enterprises' experience in European financial markets has hardly prepared them for the sort of information disclosure urged by the UN in its Report of Eminent Persons on Multinational Corporations in World Development, or for the controls on inter-affiliate transfer prices proposed in less developed countries' foreign investment laws like the Andean Common Market's Decision 24.[84] Continental European governments have rarely required the publication of detailed, consolidated company accounts. Nor have Continental governments (except for Germany after 1972) concerned themselves much with the inter-affiliate transfer prices set by European firms. American and British companies have had much more practice in the disclosure of financial information, as a result of their income-tax and stock-exchange laws and regulations. Nevertheless, while Continental firms may find it difficult to adapt to the increasingly strict regulations on financial transactions being adopted by less developed countries, they will profit from their ability to negotiate with their hosts, to accept local ownership, and to enter market-sharing agreements among themselves (thus suppressing the oligopolistic rivalry which has led to the proliferation in certain industries and countries of many small, sub-optimal plants).[85] Most of all, the European Multinationals will profit from the small-power connotations of their parent nationalities.

Their life will be more difficult, however, in a Europe made up of countries which appear unable to choose among nationalism, full European economic integration, or something else.[86]

Throughout most of their history, large Continental enterprises have demonstrated that they can accommodate themselves to a world in which nations dominate. Especially during the period between 1900 and 1939, Continental firms showed that multinationality of manufacturing operations is quite feasible in a nationalistic environment. Trade barriers and cartels insured the profitability of operations, and supranational optimization of the sort that has come to be (erroneously) identified with 'multinational enterprises' was not necessary when competition could be negotiated away.

Continental enterprises have also demonstrated that the multinational spread of manufacturing enterprise is not uniquely associated with a free-trade world. The first burst of foreign manufacturing by the large enterprises of Western Continental Europe occurred as trade barriers were going up before World War I. On the eve of World War I there were some 160 Continental subsidiaries in operation, and although data concerning these subsidiaries' size could not be systematically reconstructed, it is known that some of these subsidiaries were very large.[87] On the eve of World War II there were at least 510 foreign subsidiaries of Continental European enterprises in operation, and many of these, like AKU's American Enka, Farben's General Aniline and Film, and the many foreign operations of Swedish Match were

---

[84] UN, 1974: p 80; Vaitsos, 1973.

[85] See also Chapter V.

[86] On the current economic and political confusion of Western Europe, and especially of its Continental component, see, Simonet, 1974; Kennan, 1974. The pessimism of these articles is in sharp contrast to the better-known descriptions of Europe's economic miracle of the 1960's. See Shonfield, 1969.

[87] McKay, 1970; Sutton, 1968; Siemens, 1957.

large firms in their own right. By 1971, the number of foreign manufacturing subsidiaries of large European enterprises had (at most) quintupled over the number extant in 1938. The overall level of European industrial production had increased by roughly 4·5 times, or very nearly the same amount.[88] Some trade was necessary for European enterprises to test foreign markets, but only some trade, not free trade. Perhaps this is why, in a 1973 survey, Swedish managers stated that they believed that an increase in protectionism by the worlds' major nations would considerably reduce the rate of growth of their firms' domestic production and exports, but would only moderately retard the growth of their firms' foreign production.[89]

History thus suggests what Continental enterprises would do in a Europe which disintegrated into its ancient nation-states. Protectionist measures might reduce economic growth, and they might again stimulate innovations that substituted for imported fuels and materials. But these long familiar measures would imply only a small adjustment in behavior for Continental enterprises.

An integrated Europe would demand a greater departure from traditional behavior from Continental enterprises. A United Europe, or a North Atlantic, or a Trans-Mediterranean Union, would require enterprises to specialise and re-locate production. In the late 1960's and early 1970's most Continental firms showed that they were able to make some adjustment to a world (and to American, Italian and Japanese competitors) that pushed toward a broader international division of labor. If free trade within Europe were to become a reality, rather than an oft-compromised principle, it is likely that Continental enterprises would be obliged to continue the tentative moves they have made in the direction of supranational coordination and optimization of operations. Continental efforts to reallocate and specialize production to least-cost sites would surely be all the greater if unambiguous political decisions were taken in Europe to maintain or increase competitive market structures through antitrust legislation and enforcement.

While it seems evident what Continental enterprises would do in response to clear political choices, political pluralism and an uncertain economic environment promise everything but clarity. Continental enterprises have begun to coordinate operations and search for information on a supranational basis at a time when fears for the fragility of Europe's postwar prosperity have come to the fore. And political turmoil seems to be a plant that flourishes when prosperity is fragile. Some voices call for increased international cooperation, others advocate national protection, cartelization and sauve qui peut. But even in the face of a European recession. Continental enterprises were being pressured not ohly to expand but also to optimize their foreign production.

In 1974 and 1975 most large Continental enterprises were announcing massive foreign investment plans, not heralding the end of multinational activity.[90] This was perhaps to be expected in a period whose most salient features were

---

[88] UN, 1958; UN 1971. This comparison of numbers of subsidiaries and the level of industrial production assumes a constant size distribution of foreign manufacturing subsidiaries. The reasonableness of this assumption cannot be verified with the data presently available.
[89] Hedlund and Otterbeck, 1974: p 111.
[90] Financial Times, 1974: Carr, 1975: p 20; European Intelligence, 1974: No 159, p 19.

the post-October 1973 quadrupling In oil prices, steep rises in the prices of many raw materials, and the revaluations of most Continental European currencies. Because of the rises in oil and other materials prices, European fuel-saving processes and synthetics seemed to be meeting growing market demand in nations that had the misfortune to be poor in high-priced raw materials. Meanwhile, the drastic drop in the price of most non-Continental currencies were acting like the tariff barriers of old by encouraging foreign production rather than export. The revaluation of Continental currencies also put increased pressure on European enterprises producing goods that competed with imports to manufacture abroad for home country demand, a step which European enterprises had, as we have seen, been notably reluctant to take up to 1971.[91]

This internationally altered pattern of relative factor costs added a novel element to the forces pushing Continental enterprises to manufacture in foreign countries. Continental enterprises were no longer considering foreign manufacturing investments only in response to visible, discrete political decisions by the government of an importing country. Instead, more impersonal American and Brazilian market demands for fuel-saving autos seemed to be creating expanding market opportunities for a firm like Volkswagen. The impersonal change in the price of the dollar and the Cruzero relative to that of the Deutschmark then provided the sufficient spur to interest management in implanting or increasing foreign production. Absolute differences in labor costs might make German processes of 1970 uncompetitive in the Germany of 1975, but eminently transferable to Brazil or another less developed country.

However, multinational production expansion in response either to foreign market demand or to absolute wage-cost differentials was a matter of indifference to home-country workers, labor ministries and governments only when there was no threat of domestic unemployment at the moment foreign plans were announced. When the jobs existing in an enterprise seemed threatened, or worse, when general unemployment was feared, convincing home-country workers that enterprise and national labor interests were in harmony, was likely to be a difficult task. Moreover, if the interest of management in expanding foreign production was additionally stimulated by hints of non-tariff barriers by importing countries (or by the imposition of the most subtle NTB of all, that of rapidly changing standards and safety regulations), enterprise management might find itself up against a nearly hopeless political task at home. It was popularly assumed that the industrial world was close to having free trade, and attempts to explain the subtleties of NTB's to home-country workers were vulnerable to being labelled an attempt by management to deceive the working class. The softly swinging doors of NTB's and exchange-rate changes did not slam in the manner of the tariffs and quotas of yesteryear, which had once made it clear that it was governments, not multinational companies, that were to blame for the setting up of plants that

---

[91] See Chapter V. Enterprises protected by NTB's, or which had monopolistic control over distribution channels for imports could, of course, continue to avoid shifting production abroad (or going out of business). Enough protection of this sort, combined with fiscal systems which subsidize exports, could put continuous upward pressure on exchange rates. Is this part of what has occurred in Continental Europe during the 1970's?

extinguished trade. In 1975, who could really tell if multinational enterprises – including Continental multinational enterprises – were in fact being 'forced' to set up many of their foreign operations? The illusion of autarky had in part been replaced by an illusion of international freedom of trade, and since neither illusion was wholly true, nor universally accepted, movements by Continental enterprises consistent with either one were bound to raise tensions with partisans of the other.

The political pulling and hauling occasioned by Continental firms' international plans for expansion during a time of stag- or slump-flation, is likely to produce more home-country reactions like that of the proposed Swedish government/labor review board for outward foreign investment. According to legislation pending in Sweden, a government board will be required to approve the foreign investment plans of Swedish enterprises only if such plans have no negative effects on Swedish employment.[92] But if Europe sorts out the economic tangle into which she has been plunged by the oil price conundrum, will the potential storms gathering over Continental multinational enterprise disperse? The answer seems almost certainly to be negative, for even if economic growth resumes, industrial adjustment problems will remain and intensify.

The industrialization plans of the oil-producing countries will be export oriented, due to the small size of their home markets. The forthcoming exports may well be eventually aimed at home- or third-country markets of Continental enterprises, not only in petroleum refining and petrochemicals but also in the energy and pollution-intensive aluminum and steel industries.[93] To the extent that world market structures in these industries are competitive, the Continental enterprises active in these industries will probably participate in moves to create a new international division of labor rather than in moves to re-create a nationalistic economic environment. If new entrants based in the US, Japan, Australia or elsewhere threaten Continental export markets with lower-cost production from the Middle East, Continental firms may have little choice but to participate.[94] Steel might be an exception, for European steel enterprises have a less multinational spread than firms in other industries, and European steel firms have been among the last to adopt organizational structures appropriate to managing a supranational division of labor. Nevertheless, it was a steel firm, Krupp, which first forged ownership links with one of the new supplier powers, Iran. To the extent that Continental enterprises participate in this export-oriented development, they will involve themselves in politically sensitive problems of adjustment in Europe, even if full employment is theoretically feasible at a macro-economic level. To the extent that Continental enterprises turn their backs on their recently acquired global habits, and refuse to participate in the industrial development of supplier countries while supporting protectionism at home, they will be involved in another, although perhaps not very multinational political process.

Toward Nation-State Control?

Most of the future international investment or operating decisions of large

---

[92] *Business Week*, March 2, 1974: p 32.
[93] Dafter, 1974; *The Economist*, October 19, 1974: p 100.
[94] For a more detailed discussion of the likely response of large Western enterprises to the industrialization policies of the oil-producing countries see: Franko, 1975.

Continental enterprises are likely to have political consequences in a world where autarky is only a dream, but a dream which is nevertheless often dreamt. Thus, the day is at hand when the large enterprises of Continental Europe will no longer be perceived as the Other Multinationals. But should that day be welcomed or cursed, and by whom?

Part of the answer may depend on what national governments are planning to 'do about' multinational enterprise. The history of the foreign expansion of large Continental European enterprises can, in large measure, be interpreted as an experiment in collaboration between national élites and multinational firms. During much of their history, the Other Multinationals were following an unwritten 'code of good conduct' for relations with nation-states. The cardinal tenet of this code was the minimization of clashes with national élites in both home and host countries by minimizing international trade and aggressive competitive behavior.

In the 1970's both enterprises and governments showed signs of unhappiness with all the implications of such a code, however. This path to the accommodation of the interests of multinational enterprises and nation states had not done much for European integration, as Chapter VI indicated. Nor had pure import substitution by Continental multinationals done as much as might have been done for the development of the less developed countries. Moreover, the following of this code had sometimes led to unhappy commercial results for European enterprises facing globally optimizing American firms. Consequently, Continental firms were under pressure to allocate resources and activities on a supranational basis as never before.[95]

Many home and host national governments did not welcome autonomous, non-governmental supranational optimization – even when the supranational optimizers had no association with the American flag. Governments have announced their intention to control increasingly the behavior of multinational enterprise: developed countries propose to place more controls on outward investment, while underdeveloped countries propose to place more controls on inward multinational enterprise activities.[96] There is something novel, however, in the latest discussions of national controls. They too, reject the international-combine style of accommodation between enterprises and states; their thrust appears to be one of national control for ends which will have an impact on other nations. Host-country governments are learning that they can use multinational enterprises to favor their own development. And development has something to do with political power. Host countries are acquiring levers of power over the foreign subsidiaries in their midst to promote exports – or withhold exports – to particular countries and areas.[97]

---

[95] See Chapter VIII.
[96] Robock, 1974; UN, 1974.
[97] Many of the clauses of the Andean Common Market's Decision 24 appear aimed at acquiring an influence in foreign subsidiaries located in the Andean area (Vaitsos, 1973). An example of export promotion – involving US companies as a transmission belt for Canadian development policies – is the history of the US-Canadian auto-parts accord. (Beigie, 1970; Fouraker, 1968: pp 242–250.)
The power of host countries to use multinationals to withhold goods was suggested by the October 1973 oil embargo. Nevertheless, rearrangements of transport and supply patterns by the oil companies concerned allowed embargoed countries to obtain considerable quantities of crude, thus suggesting that such host-country power was still limited.

Home countries are also acquiring the ability to control aspects of the behavior of their own multinationals, an ability which could be used for many purposes, including the rewarding of friends with investments and access to export markets, and the withholding of such benefits from less favored hosts.[98]

In the post-World War II period, direct use of Continental multinational enterprise for political ends by home countries has so far occasioned few outcries and few difficulties of accommodation by enterprises. Perhaps this is because home-government use of large Continental enterprises as if they were state agencies, although common enough domestically, was relatively rare in foreign operations.[99] A few instances of such use of multinational enterprise did occur: Renault, for example, was ordered by the French government to put up a commercially questionable (and subsequently closed) assembly plant in French Canada in the early 1960's heyday of Générale de Gaulle's policy of '*vive le Quebec libre*', but the move was received without noticeable irritation in Canada.[100]

Host countries (and enterprise managers) may not have such sanguine reactions to efforts by home-country governments (or labor unions) to use multinational company ownership links to restrict imports of, say, automotive components into Germany to 'protect German jobs'. The fact that multinational ownership links are useful either to promote global optimization *or* the restriction or diversion of trade, has not escaped certain pressure groups in developed European countries. German union discussions of the possible political uses of multinational enterprises may be a prelude to attempts to inhibit trade in goods (or technology) by means which would work through multinational networks and bypass more publicly visible policy instruments.

Host countries have also demonstrated the uses of having subsidiaries of Continental enterprises in their nations. Immediately after independence, Algeria was able to obtain special treatment in France, because of French concern for the investments of French firms by Algerian petroleum.[101] It also appears that the considerable stake of French enterprise in Spanish manufacturing firms may have had something to do with France's comparatively favorable view of Spanish association with the EEC. Perhaps this *entente* was also facilitated by the fact that all the operations in Spain of large French firms were at least 50% locally owned – and thus potentially responsive to requests by the Spanish government to export to particular markets.[102] Host countries that wish to shift from import-substituting to export-oriented development policies can be expected to use their power over the

---

[98] Robock, 1974.

[99] Vernon, 1974.

[100] Howe, 1973: p 54. Renault and Fiat's extensive co-operation and trade agreements with state agencies in Rumania, Poland and the USSR appear also to have been motivated partly by political considerations. Firms based in Italy and France, countries with the largest communist parties in Western Europe, had special reasons for entering co-operative arrangements with their Eastern European neighbors. Such accords are more akin to trading and licencing activities than to multinational manufacturing, with its implications of permanent company involvement in host-country economies. Consequently they do not fall within the scope of the present work.

[101] Chevalier, 1973: pp 141–152.

[102] Comparative Multinational Enterprise Project.

profitability of foreign subsidiaries in their midst as a lever to get Continental enterprises to lobby with home governments for the reduction of importing countries' tariff and trade barriers. Foreign subsidiaries can (and will) be welcomed, then used as bargaining counters in inter-governmental negotiations.

If national *use* of multinational enterprise is the thrust of current public policies, then it is evident that welcomes and curses can succeed one another, or be uttered simultaneously by different groups as national interests, objectives and fears alternately clash or harmonize in the future. In such a turbulent environment, it is doubtful that multinational enterprises can devise patterns of behavior which will simultaneously satisfy the desires of, say, the German, Iranian, and Italian governments, much less the desires of German, Iranian, and Italian workers and the desires of locally-owned competitive firms. Faced with irreconcilable interests, Continental multinational enterprises are likely to accelerate their efforts to act in the image of the globally scanning American multinationals. The Continental multinationals, too, will probably seek temporary safe havens and temporary, sequential satisfaction of the goals of diverse national élites. In a world in which negotiated compromises with national élites are unstable, Continental multinational enterprises are likely to be tempted to manoeuver among the interstices of nation states. It is probable that Continental enterprises will attempt to keep the growing national thrusts for international power at bay by exercising supranational market, production location, and financial options to the fullest.

A different future might be possible if nation states could agree on rules for the international trade and investment game. But some of the necessary rules might limit national sovereignty much more than does the existence of multinational enterprises manoeuvering in interstices of nation states. Without a reduction of national sovereignty through a supranational agreement on taxation some nations will benefit more than others from tax avoidance by multinational enterprises, and tension over multinational enterprise behavior will result. Without a sovereignty-reducing accord on international rules of competition and on acceptable rates of adjustment for declining industries, tensions will surround multinational enterprises, whether they limit or accelerate exports from foreign affiliates back to home countries.

At the 1973 annual shareholders' meeting of a large Swiss enterprise with manufacturing operations in some 30 countries around the world, a shareholder stood up and asked the firm's chairman if the enterprise in question was 'a multinational enterprise'. The chairman responded that no, the firm was not a multinational enterprise, but rather was an international enterprise. The shareholder was silent for a moment, and then, somewhat impolitely by the standards of Swiss shareholders' meetings, asked the chairman why the firm was an international, not a multinational enterprise. The chairman responded; 'nobody likes multinational enterprises nowadays'.

Whatever the large enterprises of Continental Europe are called, it is probable that they, too, will become unliked. But their ability to help, or hinder nations' economic and technological development will undoubtedly continue to make them useful for many economic and political ends.

Appendix A

In order to obtain a better understanding of the processes accompanying organizational structure in Continental European enterprises, a questionnaire was mailed to the presidents of the sixty-four large continental firms with manufacturing operations in six or more countries. Usable responses were obtained from 33 of these enterprises. The tables presented in the text, the relevant questions posed to managers, and the simplified classifications (if any) used in the tables were the following:

Table Number	Question asked

8.2   *Question*

To what degree did *written* job descriptions, performance targets, and policy guidelines (for example, maximum capital expenditure allowances) play a role in controlling your company's foreign manufacturing operations in:

		1965	1972
A	No role at all:	_____	_____
B	A minor role:	_____	_____
C	Some role:	_____	_____
D	A major role:	_____	_____

Simplified classification
A, B, and C responses for 1972 are grouped in Table 8.2 under 'a minor role'; D responses only are labelled 'a major role'.

8.3   *Question*

On a scale ranging from 1 to 5, please indicate the degree to which internal, parent-company and foreign-manufacturing-subsidiary reporting periods and document formats were standardized. (1 = not standardized at all, to 5 = identical for both.):

1965	1972
1 2 3 4 5	1 2 3 4 5

Simplified classification
Responses of 1, 2, or 3 for 1972 are grouped in Table 8.3 under the heading 'low degree of standardization'; responses of 4 or 5 are grouped as 'high standardization'.

8.4   *Question*

Please indicate the approximate percentage of the presidents of your foreign manufacturing subsidiaries who were citizens of the country in which your company's *headquarters* is located:

	1965			1972		
	0–33%	34–67%	68–100%	0–33%	34–67%	68–100%
A in Europe:	___	___	___	___	___	___
B in North America:	___	___	___	___	___	___
C Outside of Europe and North America:	___	___	___	___	___	___

Appendix B

In the study of 187 American multinational enterprises undertaken by Stopford and Wells (1972) a highly diversified product line was defined by the condition that:

ns is greater than 1, where n = number of two-digit US Standard Industrial Classification (SIC) industries represented in the product line

and s = proportion of total sales generated by products outside the major industry.

Using this definition, a firm with sales divided in the percentages of 40, 30, 30, among three industries satisfied the condition of ns greater than 1, since $n = 3$ and $s = 0·60$. Such a firm was defined by the condition that ns lies between 0 and 1. Thus, a firm operating in two two-digit industries was necessarily classified in the low category even if there is an equal share of the total sales in the two industries. Firms that have all their operations entirely within a single two-digit industry were classified as having no product diversity.

In the study of American enterprise values of n for each firm were available for 1965 product lines. The sales data to calculate the relative industry importance measure, s, were collected from published sources and interviews. Separate classifications of the diversity of the product lines in the United States and abroad were made for each firm by this procedure.[1]

In the present study it was not possible to apply precisely the same methodology to estimating the domestic and foreign product diversity of the 85 largest Continental European industrial firms. Data for s was often not available, and, when it was, did not differentiate between foreign and domestic sales.

Values for n were, however, available both for the domestic operations and the foreign manufacturing subsidiaries of all 85 enterprises as of 1971. Thus, it was possible to classify Continental firms as having no foreign or domestic product diversity if they manufactured only in a single two-digit industry: a procedure identical to that used in the American study. Firms manufacturing in two to four two-digit SIC industries domestically were arbitrarily classified as having low domestic product diversity. Firms manufacturing domestically in five or more (to a maximum of 11) two-digit industries were classified as having high domestic product diversity.

Continental enterprises were classified as having high foreign product diversity when they satisfied the condition that:

np is greater than 1,

where p = the proportion of the number of foreign subsidiaries manufacturing products outside of the firms' major industry.

---

[1] For a further discussion of the methodology used in the US study see Stopford and Wells, 1972: pp 185–187.

p was assumed to be a reasonable surrogate for the unavailable variable, s, and was available for all enterprises. When np lay between 0 and 1, Continental enterprises were classified as having low foreign product diversity.

Rough classifications of these types are subject to numerous shortcomings and possible biases. They are presented only to indicate possible contrasts between the product ranges of European and American enterprises, and possible differences in the nature of pressures on management in Continental and US firms.[2]

---

[2] See also Stopford and Wells, 1972: pp 186–187.

References

ADAM, G, 'New Trends in International Business: Worldwide Sourcing and Dedomiciling', *Acta Oeconomica*, Vol 7, 1971, pp 349–367.

ADAM, G, 'Some Implications and Concomitants of Worldwide Sourcing', *Acta Oeconomica*, Vol 8, 1972, pp 309–323.

ADELMAN, M, *The World Petroleum Market*, Resources for the Future, Johns Hopkins University Press, Baltimore, 1972.

AEG, *50 Jahre AEG*, Berlin, December 1956.

AGNELLI, G, 'Statement Before the Group of Eminent Persons to Study the Impact of Multinational Corporations on Development', United Nations, Geneva, November 1973.

AHARONI, Yaïr, 'On the Definition of a Multinational Corporation', in KAPOOR, A and GRUB, Philip D (eds), *The Multinational Enterprise in Transition*, Darwin Press, Princeton, New Jersey, 1972.

AKU, *AKU-ENKA Commonwealth of Companies*, Arnhem (Holland), 1964.

ALDCROFT, Derek, *The Development of British Industry and Foreign Competition, 1875–1914*, University of Toronto, Toronto, 1968.

ALLEN, J A, *Studies in Innovation in the Steel and Chemical Industries*, Manchester University Press, Manchester, 1967.

ALUMINIUM-INDUSTRIE-AKTIEN-GESELLSCHAFT. *Geschichte der Aluminium-Industrie-Aktien-Gesellschaft Neuhausen 1888–1938*. Herausgegeben vom Direktorium der Gesellschaft, Chippis, 1942–1943. 2 vols.

ALUSUISSE, *Aluminiumindustrie AG*, Zurich, 1960.

AMERICAN ENKA CORPORATION, *This Is American Enka Corporation*, Enka (North Carolina), 1965.

AMERICAN METAL MARKET, 'To Buy 5 % of Solmer Fos Steel Plant', February 16, 1973.

AMSDEN, Alice H, *International Firms and Labor in Kenya*, Frank Cass, London, 1971.

ANDEAN COMMON MARKET, *Junta Del Acuerdo De Cartagena*, Decision No 24, Lima, Peru, July 1972, as translated in *International Legal Materials*, Vol II, p 126, 1972.

ANDERSSON, I, *A History of Sweden*, Weidenfeld and Nicolson, London, 1955.

ARBED, *Annual Reports*, various issues.

ARPAN, Jeffrey S and RICKS, David A, 'Foreign Direct Investments in the US and Some Attendant Research Problems', *Journal of International Business Studies*, Spring 1974.

ARROW, Kenneth, *The Limits of Organization*, W W Norton, New York, 1974.

ASEA, *ASEA Today*, ASEA, Vasteras, Sweden, 1972.

ASZKENAZY, Heinz, *Les grandes sociétés européennes*, Centre de Recherche et d'Information Socio-Politiques (CRISP), Bruxelles, 1971.

AVRAM, M, *The Rayon Industry*, Van Nostrand, New York, 1927.

AWNI-AL-ANI, 'German Investment in Developing Countries', *Intereconomics*, No 7, 1969, pp 219–221.

AYALA, J, 'Hasta 8,000 % de Sobre Facturacion', *El Espectador*, Bogota, Colombia, date unknown, 1970.

BAIN, J S, *International Differences in Industrial Structure*, Yale University Press, New York and London, 1966.

BAIROCH, P, 'Free Trade and European Economic Development in the 19th Century', *European Economic Review*, Vol 3, November 1972.

BAKER, Betsy, 'West German Investment in Latin America', *Bank of London and South America Review*, Vol 5, No 60, December 1971, pp 692–701.

BALDWIN, Robert E, *Nontariff Distortions of International Trade*, The Brookings Institution, Washington, DC, 1970.

BALOGH, Thomas, *The Economics of Poverty*, London, 1966.

BANDERA, V N, *Foreign Capital as an Instrument of National Economic Policy*, Nijhoff, The Hague, 1964.

BANDERA, V N and WHITE, J H, 'US Direct Investment and Domestic Markets in Europe', *Economia Internazionale 21*, August 1968.

BANK OF ENGLAND, *Quarterly Bulletin*, various issues.

BARRON'S, 'North American Philips Finds Strength in Unity', October 13, 1969.

BARRON'S, 'Pharmaceutical Headache', April 8, 1974.

BASF, *Au Royaume de la Chimie*, Econ Verlag, Düsseldorf/Vienna, 1965.

BATTELLE INSTITUTE, *Interactions of Science and Technology in the Innovative Process*, NSF, C667, Washington, DC, 1970.

BAUDET, H, 'The Dutch Retreat from Empire', in BROMLEY, J S and KOSSMANN, E H (eds), *Britain and the Netherlands in Europe and Asia*, Macmillan, London, 1968.

BÄUMLER, Ernest, *Ein Jahrhundert Chemie*, Econ Verlag, Düsseldorf, 1963.

BÄUMLER E, *Etappen des Fortschrittes*, Hoechst, AG, Dortmund, 1966.

BAYER, *Bayer-Berichte*, '100 Jahre Bayer Leverkusen', No 11, English edition, 1963.

BEER, John Joseph, *The Emergence of the German Dye Industry*, University of Illinois, Urbana, 1959.

BEHRMAN, Jack, *Some Patterns in the Rise of the Multinational Enterprise*, University of North Carolina, Chapel Hill, 1969.

BEHRMAN, Jack, *National Interests and the Multinational Enterprise*, Prentice-Hall, Englewood Cliffs, New Jersey, 1970.

BEHRMAN, Jack, *US International Business and Governments*, McGraw-Hill, New York, 1971.

BEIGIE, Carl, *The Canada-US Automotive Agreement: An Evaluation*, The Canadian–American Committee, Washington, DC and Montreal, 1970.

BEROV, L, 'Le capital financier occidental et les pays balkaniques dans les années vingt', *Etudes Balkaniques*, Sofia, 1965.

BERTRAND, R, *Comparaison du niveau des tarifs douaniers des pays du marché commun*, Cahier de l'INSEE, Serie R, No 2, February 1958.

BETTELHEIM, Charles, *Bilan de l'économie Française, 1919–1946*, Presses Universitaires de France, Paris, 1970.

BISSIGER, Jürg, 'Encore le Valium et le Librium: Roche prépare sa défense en Allemagne', *Journal de Genève*, August 13, 1974, p 6.

BOLLE, Jacques, *Solvay, l'invention, l'homme, l'entreprise industrielle, 1863–1963*, Solvay et Cie, Bruxelles, 1963.

BONJOUR, E, OFFLER, H and POTTER, G R, *A Short History of Switzerland*, Oxford University Press, London, 1952.

BORNSCHIER, V, 'Der Einfluss der Grösse von Industrie ländern auf die Multinationalisierung ihrer Wirtschaftsunternehmen', manuscript, October 1973.

BOSCH, Kornelis Bauwe, *De Nederlandse Beleggngen in de Verenigde Staten*, Elsevier, Amsterdam, 1961.

BOSCH, Robert, GmbH, *75 Jahre Bosch*, Stuttgart, 1961.

BÖSSENECKER, Hermann, *Bayern, Bosse und Bilanzen*, Verlag Kurt Desch, München, 1972, especially Chapter 3, 'Auf einer Woge von Öl'.

BOUMAN, P J, *Anton Philips of Eindhoven*, Weidenfeld and Nicolson, London, 1958.

BRANDELL, Inga, 'L'Algérie et les sociétés multinationales', United Nations, *Institut Africain de Développement Economique et de Planification*, Dakar, August 1974.

BROOKE, Michael and REMMERS, H Lee, *The Strategy of Multinational Enterprise*, Longman, London, 1970.

BROWN-BOVERI, *75 Years Brown-Boveri*, Brown-Boveri & Co Ltd, Baden, 1966.

BRUN, S and FRANKO, L G, 'Antitrust Policy In Europe: The Emergence Of Strict Enforcement?' *Journal of World Trade Law*, Vol 8, No 5, September–October 1974

BRYER, Anthony, 'The First Encounter with the West – AD 1050–1204', and GILL, Joseph S J, 'The Second Encounter with the West – AD 1204–1453', in WHITTING, Philip, *Byzantium*, Basil Blackwell, London, 1972.

BUNDESMINISTERIUM FÜR WIRTSCHAFT, *Runderlass Aussenwirtschaft*, various issues.

BÜRGIN, A, *Geigy 1758 bis 1939*, J R Geigy, SA, Basel, 1958.

BUSINESS ASIA, 'New Indianization Legislation Evokes Quick Corporate Action', September 14, 1973, page 295.

BUSINESS EUROPE, 'Volvo's Entry into Common Market', October 30, 1963.

BUSINESS EUROPE, 'North African Governments Play "Divide and Rule" with Car Makers', November 9, 1966, page 358.

BUSINESS EUROPE, 'Péchiney Wins Dutch Treat', April 18, 1969, page 123.

BUSINESS EUROPE, 'Belgium Initiates Protectionist Action', June 5, 1970, p 178.

BUSINESS EUROPE, 'German Two-Pronged Tax Assault Drafted Against Exported Profits', August 13, 1971, pp 258–260.

BUSINESS EUROPE, 'German Mergers And Markets Overhauled By Cartel Law Revision'' June 29, 1973.

BUSINESS INTERNATIONAL, *Indicators of Market Size*, various issues.

BUSINESS INTERNATIONAL, *Organizing for European Operations*, Business International Corporation, New York, 1967.

BUSINESS INTERNATIONAL, 'Wage Costs at Home Drive German Firms Abroad', December 21, 1973, pp 404 and 405.

BUSINESS LATIN AMERICA, 'Fiat Expansion in Argentina', February 6, 1969, p 42.

BUSINESS LATIN AMERICA, 'Expansion by European Firms in Mexico', January 15, 1970.

BUSINESS LATIN AMERICA, 'How Olivetti Deploys Its Subsidiaries for Profits in Latin America', March 23, 1972.

BUSINESS WEEK, 'Philips: A Multinational Copes with Profitless Growth', January 13, 1973.

BUSINESS WEEK, 'A New Glut Of Chemicals In Europe', March 17, 1973.

BUSINESS WEEK, 'Why Fiat-Citroën Called It Quits', June 30, 1973, p 20.

CAMPOS, Jaime, 'La Participacion Empresarial En El Proceso De Integracion: Las Reuniones Sectoriales De La ALALC', *Revista de la Integracion*, No 16, May 1974, BID-Intal, Buenos Aires.

CANADIAN DEPARTMENT OF INDUSTRY, Trade and Commerce, 'Direct Investment Abroad By Canada, 1964–1967', Mimeo, Ottawa, 1971.

CAPITAL, 'Management-Beratung McKinsey – Die Jesuiten der deutschen Wirtschaft', March 1971.

CARR, Jonathan, 'German Interest in Latin America', *Financial Times*, August 28, 1974, page 4.

CARR, Jonathan, 'Overseas Orders Will Maintain Steady Growth at Siemens', *Financial Times*, February 6, 1975, p 20.

CARSTEN, F K, *The Origins of Prussia*, Oxford University Press, London, 1954.

CASAS, Juan Carlos, *Las Multinacionales y El Comercio Latinoamericano*, Centro de Estudios Monetarios Latino-americanos, Mexico, 1973.

CASTRONOVO, Valerio, *Agnelli*, Unione Tipografico – Editrice Torinese, Torino, 1971.

CAVES, Richard E, 'International Corporations: The Industrial Economics of Foreign Investment', *Economica*, February 1971.

CENTRE FOR DEVELOPMENT PLANNING, Projections and Policies of the Department of Economic and Social Affairs of the United Nations Secretariat, United Nations, Undated.

CHANG, Y S, *The Transfer of Technology: Economics of Offshore Assembly, The Case of the Semiconductor Industry*, UNITAR, New York, 1971.

CHANDLER, Alfred, *Strategy and Structure*, MIT Press, Cambridge, 1961.

CHANNON, Derek, 'A Note on the European Automobile Industry', Manchester Business School, Manchester (UK), 1973.

CHANNON, D, 'Volkswagen', Case Study, Manchester Business School, 1973.

CHEMICAL ENGINEERING NEWS, Multinational Supplement, April 16, 1973, p. 53.

CHEVALIER, J-M, *Le nouvel enjeu pétrolier*, Calmann-Lévy, Paris, 1973.

CHIADO-FIORO, Elena, *Il Caso ENI*, G Giappichelli, Editore, Torino, Italy, 1973.

CHOFFEL, J, *St-Gobain, du miroir à l'atome*, Plon, Paris, 1960.

CLAPHAM, J H, *Economic Development of France and Germany, 1815–1914*, Cambridge University Press, Cambridge (UK), 1951.

CLARK, Colin, *The Conditions Of Economic Progress*, Macmillan and Co, London, 1951.

COCKERILL, A, *The Steel Industry: International Comparison of Industrial Structure and Performance*, Cambridge University Press, November 1974.

COHEN, Benjamin J, *The Question of Imperialism*, Basic Books, New York, 1973.

COLCHESTER, Nicholas, 'Volkswagen's Leiding: Success But Not Enough', *Financial Times*, December 21, 1974, p 8.

COLEMAN, D C, *Courtaulds, An Economic and Social History*, Vol II, 'Rayon', Oxford University Press, London, 1969.

COLLIER'S ENCYCLOPEDIA, 'Romania', Vol 20, 1962.

COMMUNAUTES EUROPÉENNES, *Septième rapport général sur l'activité des communautés européennes*, Bruxelles et Luxembourg, February 1974.

COMPAGNIE GÉNÉRALE D'ÉLECTRICITÉ, *L'Europe électrique*, CGE, Paris, 1973.

CURZON, Gerard and CURZON, Victoria, 'Industrial Trade Cooperation in the 1960's', IER Group, Royal Institute of International Affairs, Chatham House, 1973, pp 110–113.

CVETKOV, Pierre, 'Le contrôle de la Société Générale sur les principales enterprises belges et ses mécanismes', *La revue nouvelle*, November 1972.

DABRITZ, W, *Fünfzig Jahre Metallgesellschaft, 1881–1931*, Metallgesellschaft, Frankfurt-am-Main, 1931.

DAFSA, *The Pharmaceutical Industry in Europe*, DAFSA, Paris, 1974.

DAFTER, Ray, 'Waiting for Arab Chemicals', *The Economist*, October 19, 1974, p 100.

DAFTER, Ray, 'The Oil Producers Move on Downstream', *Financial Times*, November 4, 1974, p 16.

DAHRENDORF, Ralf, *Society and Democracy in Germany*, Weidenfeld and Nicholson, London, 1968.

DAIMLER BENZ, AG, *75 Jahre Motorisierung des Verkehrs, 1886–1961*, Daimler Benz, Stuttgart – Untertürkheim, 1961.

DALE, Reginald, 'Nine Withdraw Chemical Tariffs Offer from US,' *Financial Times*, December 20, 1972.

DANIELS, John, *Recent Foreign Direct Investment in the United States*, Praeger, New York, 1971.

DAVID, Rhys, 'Alcan and Péchiney Join in French Alumina Project', *Financial Times*, December 12, 1974.

DE BONDT, Frank, 'Contraints de relever le défi pétrolier les pays industrialisés tentent de mettre de l'ordre dans leurs économies', *Le Soir*, Brussels, September 29–30, 1974, page 10.

DE GEEST, Johan, 'La Stratégie de la Société Générale dans le secteur des non-ferreux', *La Revue Nouvelle*, November 1972.

DEGUSSA, *Aller Anfang ist schwer, Bilder zur hundertjährigen Geschichte der Degussa*, Frankfurt, 1973.

DENNIS, W H *100 Years of Metallurgy*, Duckworth, London, 1963.

DER SPIEGEL, 'Die Macht der Konzerne', January 31, 1972, p 42.

DER SPEIGEL, 'Markt Aufgeteilt', March 5, 1973.

DER SPIEGEL, 'Frankreich', No 15, 1974.

DESAI, A V, *Real Wages in Germany, 1871–1913*, Oxford, London, 1968.

DIE WELT, No 104, May 5, 1964.

DIETRICH, Ethel, *World Trade*, Henry Holt, New York, 1939.

DOCUMENTATION FRANCAISE, La 'Fusions et concentrations d'entreprises en république fédérale d'Allemagne', *Notes et Études Documentaires*, No 3688–3689, May 12, 1970.

DOCUMENTS: REVUE DES QUESTIONS ALLEMANDES, 'Dossier: investissements allemands dans l'est français', July–August 1969, pp 61–127, see especially: JUILLARD, Étienne, 'L'Alsace va-t-elle basculer dans l'orbite économique allemande?', pp 74–91.

DOTTI, H L and FONTELA, E, 'Distribution des revenus et intégration de l'Europe', *Revue du Marché Commun*, Paris, January 1970.

DOVRING, Folke, 'Soybeans', in *Scientific American*, Vol 230, February 1974 (especially page 18).

DU BOIS, Josiah E, Jr, *Generals in Grey Suits*, The Bodley Head, London, 1953.

DUERR, M, *R&D in the Multinational Company*, National Industrial Conference Board, New York, 1970.

DUNNING, John H, 'The Future of the Multinational Enterprise', *Lloyds Bank Review*, July 1974, No 113, pp 15–32.

DUESENBERRY, J, *Income, Saving and the Theory of Consumer Behavior*, Harvard University Press, Cambridge, 1949.

D'YDEWALLE, Charles, *L'Union Minière du Haut Katanga*, Plon, Paris, 1960.

ECO, U and ZORZOLI, G B, *Histoire Illustrée des Inventions*, Pont Royal, Paris, 1961.

ECONOMIST, THE, 'Microcircuits: GEC Bows Out', July 17, 1971.

ECONOMIST, THE, 'Microcircuits: Fresh Victim', July 24, 1971, p 78.

ECONOMIST, THE, 'Driving For Cars', October 7, 1972.

ECONOMIST, THE, 'Antitrust: Unmunificent Seven', November 16, 1974, pages 72 and 73.

EDWARDS, Corwin, 'Size Of Markets, Scale Of Firms And The Character Of Competition' in ROBINSON, E A G (ed), *Economic Consequences Of the Size Of Nations*, Macmillan, London, 1963.

EEC, *Industrial Policy in the Community*, EEC Commission, Brussels, 1970.

EEC, *First Report on Competition Policy*, Brussels–Luxemburg, April 1972.

EEC, *Second Report on Competition Policy*, Brussels–Luxemburg, April 1973.

EEC, *Third Report on Competition Policy*, Brussels–Luxemburg, May 1974.

EISENHANS, Hartmut (Hrsg), *Erdöl für Europa*, Hoffmann und Campe, Hamburg, 1974.

ELLIOTT, W Y (ed), *International Control in the Non-Ferrous Metals*, Macmillan, New York, 1937.

ELLIS, J J A, 'The Legal Aspects of European Direct Investment in the United States', in Rolfe, S E and Damm, W, *The Multinational Corporations in the World Economy*, Praeger, New York, 1970.

ENCYCLOPAEDIA BRITANNICA, Vol XXI, New York, 1951, p 709E.

ENCYCLOPAEDIA BRITANNICA, 'Immigration Law', Vol 11, New York, 1973.

ENCYCLOPAEDIA BRITANNICA, *Book of the Year, 1973*, New York, 1973.

ENI, *Annual Report*, 1968.

ENOS, J L, *Petroleum Progress and Profits: A History of Process Innovation*, MIT Press, Cambridge, Mass, 1962.

ENTREPRISE, 'Belgique: Les Affaires 72/73', February 9, 1973.

ENTREPRISE, 'Michelin: Le grand dessein', February 9, 1973.

ENTREPRISE, 'États Unis: des soucis pour Michelin?', April 27, 1973, p 101.

ENTREPRISE, 'Renault gagne-t-il de l'argent? Ce qui n'a jamais été dit sur la Régie'. No 945. October 19, 1973, p 138.

ENTREPRISE, 'Vers une super Elf-Erap allemande', May 24, 1974, pages 44 and 45.

ENTREPRISE, 'Les leaders des non-ferreux', May 31, 1974, pages 26 and 27.

ENTREPRISE, 'Télévision: SECAM marque un point', No 992, September 13, 1974.

EUROPEAN CHEMICAL NEWS, May 31, 1968, p 8.

EUROPEAN CHEMICAL NEWS, 'Montedison Acquires 100 % of Rhodiatoce', December 31, 1971.

EUROPEAN COMMUNITIES, *First Report on Competition Policy*, EEC, Brussels–Luxemburg, 1972.

EUROPEAN COMMUNITIES, *Second Report on Competition Policy*, EEC, Brussels–Luxemburg, 1973.

EUROPEAN COMMUNITIES, *Third Report on Competition Policy*, EEC, Brussels–Luxemburg, May 1974.

EUROPEAN INTELLIGENCE, 'SIDMAR', No 103, July 6, 1972.

EUROPEAN INTELLIGENCE, 'CIBA-Geigy Sustains States-side Expansion Drive', September 5, 1974, No 159, p 19.

EUROPEAN INTELLIGENCE, 'Reasons for Price Differences in the Community', No 113, November 23, 1972, pages 2–30.

EVANS, P B, 'National Autonomy and Economic Development: Critical Perspectives on Multinational Corporations in Poor Countries', p 326 in KEOHANE, R O and NYE, J (eds), *Transnational Relations and World Politics*, Harvard University Press, Cambridge, Mass, 1972.

EVANS, John W, *The Kennedy Round in American Trade Policy: The Twilight of the GATT*, Harvard University Press, Cambridge, 1971.

EXPANSION, L', 'La mue difficile de Péchiney', November 1967, pages 122–127.

EXPRESS, L', 'Les mauvaises affaires de la France', November 20–26, 1972.

FAITH, Nicholas, *The Infiltrators*, Hamish Hamilton, London, 1971.

FARBEN, I G, *Annual Report*, 1927.

FARBEN, I G, *I G Farbenindustrie*, AG, Frankfurt, 1933.

FAUQUET, L G, *Histoire de la rayonne et des textiles synthétiques*, Paris, 1960.

FAYERWEATHER, J, *International Marketing*, Prentice Hall, Englewood Cliffs, 1965.

FEHR, Hans, *Fragmente aus der Roche-Geschichte*, F Hoffmann-La Roche & Co, AG, Basel, 1971.

FEIS, Herbert, *Europe: The World's Banker*, Yale University Press, New York, 1930.

FELD, Werner, *Transnational Business Collaboration Among Common Market Countries*, Praeger, New York, 1970.

FIAT, SpA, *All The Fiats*, Editoriale Domus, Milan, 1970.

FIGARO, LE, 'L'Euroafrique: Double pari, l'or noir et l'Europe', March 16–17, 1974, page 3.

FINANCIAL TIMES, 'World Fibers', August 3, 1970, p 16.

FINANCIAL TIMES, 'International Plastics: Worldwide View of Investment Decisions', May 17, 1971.

FINANCIAL TIMES, 'Hoogovens-Hoesch Merger Approved', January 19, 1972, p 18.

FINANCIAL TIMES, 'Actively Negotiates For State', February 7, 1973.

FINANCIAL TIMES, 'Synthetic Fibre Safeguards', June 19, 1973.

FINANCIAL TIMES, 'Iran May Take Stake in AGIP External Operations', August 13, 1974, page 16.

FINANCIAL TIMES, 'VW Board Discusses US Production', September 3, 1974.

FINANCIAL TIMES, 'AEG Intensifies Output in Brazil', September 20, 1974, p 4.

FINANCIAL TIMES, 'Why Citroën and Fiat Are Breaking Up', June 25, 1973.

FISHLOCK, David, 'That Menthol-Fresh Feeling', *Financial Times*, October 17, 1974, p 24.

FITCH, Bob and OPPENHEIMER, Mary, *Ghana: End of an Illusion*, Monthly Review Press, New York, 1966.

FONTAINE, Arthur, *French Industry During the War*, Yale University Press, New Haven, 1926.

FORBES, 'The Game that Two Could Play', Vol 94, December 1, 1964, page 41.

FOREIGN POLICY, 'One, Two, Many OPEC's', Spring 1974.

FORTUNE, 'Electronic Warfare', September 1971, p 47.

FORTUNE, *Double 500 Directory*, Time, Inc, New York, 1971.

FORTUNE, J Neill, 'Income Distribution As A Determinant Of Imports Of Manufactured Consumer Commodities', *Canadian Journal of Economics*, Vol V, No 2, May 1972.

FOURAKER, Lawrence, 'The Automotive Products Trade Act Of 1965', in VERNON, Raymond, *Manager In The International Economy*, Prentice-Hall, Englewood Cliffs, New Jersey, 1968.

FOURAKER, Lawrence E and STOPFORD, John M, 'Organizational Structure and the Multinational Strategy', *Administrative Science Quarterly*, Vol 13, No 1, June 1968.

FOX, James, 'The Automotive Industry', in BEHRMAN, Jack, *The Role of International Companies in Latin American Integration*, Lexington Books, D C Heath, Lexington (Mass), 1972.

FRANK, Isaiah, *The European Common Market*, Praeger, New York, 1961.

FRANKEL, P H, *Mattei: Oil and Power Politics*, Praeger, New York, 1966.

FRANKFURTER ALLGEMEINE ZEITUNG, May 8, 1969, as cited in JACOBI, Ingo, *Direktinvestitoinen und Export*, HWWA-Institut, Hamburg, 1972, p 159.

FRANKFURTER ALLGEMEINE ZEITUNG, 'Bussgeld gegen Chemie-Faser Kartell?' March 18, 1972.

FRANKFURTER ALLGEMEINE ZEITUNG, 'Bosch baut in den Vereinigten Staaten', June 5, 1973.

FRANKO, Lawrence G, *European Business Strategies in the United States*, Business International, SA, Geneva, 1971 (A).

FRANKO, Lawrence G, *Joint Venture Survival in Multinational Corporations*, Praeger, New York, 1971 (B).

FRANKO, Lawrence G, 'Strategy + Structure — Frustration = Experience of European Firms in America', *European Business*, Autumn 1971 (C).

FRANKO, Lawrence G, 'The Art of Choosing an American Joint Venture Partner', in BROOKE, M Z and REMMERS, H L, *The Multinational Company in Europe: Some Key Problems*, Longman, London, 1972.

FRANKO, Lawrence G, 'Strategic Planning for Internationalization: The European Dilemma and Some Possible Solutions', *Long Range Planning*, June 1973.

FRANKO, Lawrence G, 'Who Manages Multinational Enterprise?', *Columbia Journal of World Business*, Summer 1973.

FRANKO, Lawrence G, 'Joint Ventures in Developing Countries: Mystique and Reality', *Law and Policy in International Business*, Vol 6, No 2, Spring 1974.

FRANKO, Lawrence G, 'The Move Toward the Multidivisional Structure by European Organizations', *Administrative Science Quarterly*, December 1974.

FRANKO, Lawrence G, 'Problems of Middle Eastern Entry into Western Industries', Ms, CEI Geneva, 1975.

FRANKO, Lawrence G, 'Arab Countries and Western Oil Companies: Is Co-operation Possible?' in MIKDASHI, Zuhayr (ed), *The Administration of Arab Oil Resources*, Arab Planning Institute, Kuwait, forthcoming.

FRIDENSON, P, *Histoire des usines Renault*, Seuil, Paris, 1972.

FRIEDLAENDER, H E and OSER, Jacob, *Economic History of Modern Europe*, Prentice-Hall, Inc, New York, 1953.

FRIEDMANN, Wolfgang G and BEGUIN, Jean-Pierre, *Joint International Business Ventures in Developing Countries*, Columbia University Press, New York, 1971.

FUNK AND SCOTT INTERNATIONAL INDEX, Predicasts, Inc, Cleveland, various issues.

FURTADO, Celso, *Analyse du 'modèle' brésilien*, Editions Anthropos, Paris, 1974.

GALBRAITH, Jay R, 'Organization Design: An Information Processing View', unpublished Ms, MIT, Cambridge, Mass, October 1969.

GATT, *International Trade*, GATT, Geneva, various annual issues.

GHERTMAN, M and SIEGEMUND, M, 'Danone avec fruits', Cases 'A' and 'B', *Centre d'Enseignement Supérieur des Affaires*, Jouy-en-Josas, France, 1973.

GILPIN, R, *France In The Age Of The Scientific State*, Princeton University Press, Princeton, 1968.

GLOYSTEIN, Peter, 'Multinational Enterprises and the International Division of Labor in The European Community', HWWA Institut, Hamburg, unpublished Ms, 1974.

GORDON, R L, *The Evolution of Energy Policy in Western Europe*, Praeger, New York, 1970.

GOLDBERG, Paul M, 'The Evolution of Transnational Companies in Europe', PhD Dissertation, Massachusetts Institute of Technology, 1971.

GRAHAM, Edward Montgomery, 'Oligopolistic Imitation and European Direct Investment in the United States', Unpublished DBA Thesis, Harvard Graduate School of Business Administration, Ms in preparation, 1975.

GRINDROD, M, *The Rebuilding of Italy*, Royal Institute of International Affairs, London, 1955.

GROSS, H, *Further Facts and Figures on I G Farben*, Kiel University, Kiel, 1950.

GRUBER, W, MEHTA, D and VERNON, R, 'The R&D Factor in International Investment of United States Industries', *Journal of Political Economy*, Vol 75, No 1, February 1967.

HABAKKUK, H J, *American and British Technology in the Nineteenth Century*, Cambridge University Press, London, 1962.

HABER, L F, *The Chemical Industry During the 19th Century*, Oxford University Press, London, 1958.

HABER, L F, *The Chemical Industry 1900–1930*, Oxford University Press, London, 1971.

HABER, L F, 'Government Intervention At The Frontiers Of Science: British Dyestuffs And Synthetic Organic Chemicals, 1914–1939,' *Minerva*, Vol XI, No 1, January 1973.

HAGER, Franz, 'Contribution by Franz Hager, Communist Party of Austria', in *The International Firms and the European Working Class*, Communist Party of Great Britain, London, 1971.

HANDELSKAMMER HAMBURG, *Deutsche Direktinvestitionen im Ausland*, 1969.

HARMANN, A, *The International Computer Industry*, MIT, Cambridge, 1970.

HARVARD BUSINESS SCHOOL, 'Ing C Olivetti & Co, SpA,' Case Series in LEARNED, E, CHRISTENSEN, C, ANDREWS, K, and GUTH, W, *Business Policy, Text and Cases*, 2nd edition, Irwin, Homewood, Illinois, 1969.

HARVARD BUSINESS SCHOOL, *Note on the Watch Industries in Switzerland, Japan and the United States*, 1972.

HAYWARD, J E S, 'Steel', in VERNON, R (ed), *Big Business and The State: Changing Relations in Western Europe*, Harvard University Press, Cambridge, 1974.

HECKSCHER, Eli, *An Economic History of Sweden*, Harvard University Press, Cambridge, Mass, 1954.

HEDLUND, Gunnar and OTTERBECK, Lars, *Det Multinationella Företaget, Nationalstaten Och Fackföreningarna*, P A Norstedt and Sons, Stockholm, 1974.

HEER, Jean, *Reflets du Monde, 1866–1966, Présence de Nestlé*, Château de Glérolles, Rivaz, Suisse, 1966.

HELLEINER, G K, 'Manufactured Exports from Less Developed Countries and Multinational Firms', *The Economic Journal*, March 1973.

HENDERSON, W O, *The Genesis of the Common Market*, Quadrangle, Chicago, 1963.

HENNEMANN, Friedrich, *Organisationstruktur und Produktion im Ausland*, Universität Karlsruhe (West Germany), 1971.

HEXNER, Erwin, *The International Steel Cartel*, University of North Carolina Press, Chapel Hill, 1943.

HEXNER, E, *International Cartels*, University of North Carolina, Chapel Hill, 1946.

HINDEN, H, *Deutsche und deutscher Handel in Rio de Janeiro*, Witte, Rio de Janeiro, 1921.

HIRSCH, Seev, 'An International Trade And Investment Theory Of The Firm', Unpublished Ms, University of Reading, Discussion Paper in International Investment and Business Studies, No 17, September 1974.

HIRSCH, Seev, *Location Of Industry And International Competitiveness*, Oxford University Press, London, 1967.

HODGES, Michael, *Multinational Corporations and National Governments*, Saxon House, Westmead (UK), 1974.

HOGAN, Michael J, 'Informal Entente: Public Policy and Private Management in Anglo-American Petroleum Affairs, 1918–1924', *Business History Review*, Summer 1974, pages 187–205.

HOGAN, W T, *Economic History of the Iron and Steel Industry in the US*, Heath Lexington Books, Lexington, Mass, 1971.

HOLTHUS, M, JUNGNICKEL, R, KOOPMANN, G, MATTHIES, K and SUTTER, R, *Die Multinationalen Unternehmen der Bundesrepublik*, HWWA-Institut, Hamburg, 1974.

HORST, Thomas Osborn, 'A Theoretical And Empirical Analysis Of American Exports And Direct Investments', PhD Thesis, University of Rochester, 1970.

HORST, Thomas Osborn, 'American Exports And Foreign Direct Investments', *Harvard Institute of Economic Research*, Discussion Paper No 362, May 1974.

HOWE, Richard, 'Le Canada: Banc d'essai du marché US', *Vision*, June 1973, p 54.

HUFBAUER, G C, *Synthetic Materials and the Theory of International Trade*, Duckworth, London, 1965.

HUFBAUER, G C, 'The Taxation of Export Profits', Unpublished Ms, Stockholm School of Economics, May 1974.

HUFBAUER, Gary C and CHILAS, John G, 'Specialization By Industrial Countries: Extent and Consequences', *Weltwirtschaftliches Archiv*, Institut für Weltwirtschaft, Kiel, 1974.

HUNTSFORD, Roland, *The New Totalitarians*, Allan Lane, The Penguin Press, 1971.

HYMER, Steven, *The International Operations of National Firms: A Study of Direct Investment*, MIT, unpublished Doctoral Dissertation, Cambridge, Mass, 1960.

HYMER, Steven, 'The Efficiency (Contradictions) of Multinational Corporations', *American Economic Review*, Vol 60, No 2, May 1970.

HYMER, Steven and ROWTHORN, Robert, 'Multinational Corporations and International Oligopoly: The Non-American Challenge' in KINDLEBERGER, C P, *The International Corporation*, MIT Press, Cambridge, Mass, 1970.

IFFLAND, C and STETTLER, A, *Les entreprises Suisses au Brésil*, Centre de Recherches Européennes, Lausanne, 1973.

INTERNATIONAL HERALD TRIBUNE, 'France Leads the Way', September 28–29, 1974, page 6.

INTERNATIONAL HERALD TRIBUNE, 'Oil War Not Barred by Bonn Aide', Statement of the West German Financial Minister, October 24, 1974, page 1.

INTERNATIONAL LABOR ORGANIZATION, *Year Book of Labor Statistics*, various issues.

ITT RESEARCH INSTITUTE, *Traces*, NSF, C535, Washington, DC, 1969.

JACOBI, Ingo, *Direktinvestitionen und Export*, HWWA-Institut, Hamburg, 1972.

JACQUEMIN, A and CARDON, M, 'Size Structure, Stability and Performance of the Largest British and EEC Firms', *European Economic Review*, No 4, 1973.

JAPANESE MINISTRY OF INTERNATIONAL TRADE AND INDUSTRY, *White Paper on Foreign Trade*, 1972.

JEWKEŞ, J, SAWERS, D and STILLERMAN, R, *The Sources of Invention*, Macmillan, second edition, London, 1969.

JONES, Robert and MARIOTT, Oliver, *Anatomy Of A Merger: A History of GEC, AEI And English Electric*, Jonathan Cape, London, 1970.

JOURLIN, A and DERRIEN, P, 'Le Groupe Péchiney-Ugine-Kuhlmann', *Economie et Politique*, August 1973, pp 1–56, especially pp 33 and 56.

JOURNAL DE GENEVE, 'Les marchés publics de fourniture restent trop cloisonnés dans la CEE', November 1, 1972.

JOURNAL DE GENEVE, 'Vers un cartel des exportateurs de bauxite?' February 3, 1974.

JOURNAL DE GENEVE, July 5, 1974.

OURNAL OF COMMERCE, January 15, 1968, p 7.

KEBSCHULL, Dietrich and MAYER, Otto, G, *Deutsche Investitionen in Indonesien*, (in German with English summary) HWWA-Institut, Hamburg, 1974.

KENNAN, George, 'Europe's Problems, Europe's Choices', *Foreign Policy*, No 14, Spring 1974.

KINDLEBERGER, C P, *Economic Growth in France and Britain, 1851–1950*, Harvard University Press, Cambridge, Mass, 1964.

KLEINMAN, Robert, '12 Oil Importers Plan a Supranational Agency', *International Herald Tribune*, October 3, 1974, page 2.

KNICKERBOCKER, F T, *Oligopolistic Reaction And Multinational Enterprise*, Harvard Business School, Boston, 1973.

KOBAYASHI, Noritake, 'Reactions of the Nation State to the Japanese Multinational Enterprise', Unpublished Ms, *Centre d'Études Industrielles* (CEI), Geneva, 1974.

KOCKA, Jürgen, *Unternehmensverwaltung und Angestelltenschaft am Beispiel Siemens 1847–1914*, Ernst Klett Verlag, Stuttgart, 1969.

KOEBNER, Richard and SCHMIDT, Helmut Dan, *Imperialism, The Story and Significance of a Political Word, 1840–1960*, Cambridge University Press, Cambridge, 1964.

KOKXHOORN, Nicoline, 'Das Fehlen einer konkurrenzfähigen westdeutschen Erdölindustrie', in EISENHANS, Hartmut, (Hrsg) *Erdöl Für Europa*, Hoffmann und Campe, Hamburg, 1974.

KRAUSE, Lawrence B, 'The International Economic System and the Multinational Corporation', *The Annals*, September 1972, p 97.

KRECH, D et al, *Individual in Society, A Text Book of Social Psychology*, McGraw-Hill, New York, 1962.

KUHN, LOEB & CO, *Aluminum Industry Review, 1967–1968*, New York, 1968.

KUHN, LOEB & CO, *The Aluminum Industry*, New York, 1971.

LANDES, D, *The Unbound Prometheus*, Cambridge University, Cambridge, 1969.

LANGRISH, J et al, *Wealth From Knowledge: A Study of Innovation in Industry*, Halsted Books, New York, 1972.

LAYTON, C, *European Advanced Technology*, Political and Economic Planning (PEP) London. 1969.

LEAGUE OF NATIONS, *International Cartels*, Lake Success, New York, 1947.

LEE, Pong S, 'Structural Change in Rumanian Industry', *Soviet Studies*, October 1968.

LENIN, V I, 'Imperialism, The Highest Stage of Capitalism', pp 707–815 in LENIN, V I, *Selected Works*, Foreign Language Publishing House, Moscow, 1960.

LEONTIADES, James, 'The Uprooted European Manager in America', *European Business*, No 36, Winter 1973.

LEWIS, Anthony, Editorial column in the *International Herald Tribune*, October 4, 1974.

LEWIS, W Arthur, *Economic Survey, 1919–1939*, George Allen and Unwin, London, 1949.

LIEPMANN, H, *Tariff Levels And The Economic Unity Of Europe*, George Allen and Unwin London, 1938.

LILLIENTHAL, David, 'The Multinational Corporation', in ANSHEN, M G and BACH, G C (eds), *Management And Corporations 1985*, McGraw-Hill, New York, 1961.

LINDER, S B, *An Essay On Trade And Transformation*, Almqvist and Wiksell, Stockholm, 1961.

LOMBARD, Andrew J, Jr, 'How European Companies Organize Their International Operations', *European Business*, July 1969.

LONGHURST, Henry, *Adventure in Oil*, *The Story of British Petroleum*, Sidgwick and Jackson, London, 1959.

LORENZ, Christopher, 'Brown Boveri: The Eccentric Multinational', *Financial Times*, September 19, 1973 (p 21).

MACK SMITH, D, *Italy*, The University of Michigan Press, Ann Arbor, 1969.

MAGDOFF, Harry, *The Age of Imperialism, The Economics of US Foreign Policy*, Monthly Review Press, New York, 1969.

MAILLET, P, *Quinze ans de politique communautaire*, Commission des Communautés Européennes, Direction Générale des Budgets, Document XIX/302/1/72-F, Brussels, December 5, 1972.

MANCHESTER, William, *The Arms of Krupp 1587–1968*, Michael Joseph Ltd, London, 1969.

MANNERS, G, *The Changing World Market for Iron Ore*, Johns Hopkins Press, Baltimore, 1971.

MANNESMANN, *75 Jahre Mannesmann, 1890–1965*, Mannesmann AG, Düsseldorf, 1965.

MASNATA, Albert, *L'émigration des industries suisses*, Etudes économiques, commerciales et financières, Lausanne, 1924.

MASON, E S, *Controlling World Trade: Cartels And Commodity Agreements*, McGraw-Hill, New York, 1946.

MAUTHNER, Robert, 'BP French chairman changed', *Financial Times*, January 20, 1975.

MAZZOLINI, Renato, *European Transnational Concentration: Top Management's Perspective on the Obstacles to International Consolidations in the EEC*, McGraw-Hill, New York, 1974.

McCLAIN, David Stanley, 'Foreign Investment in United States Manufacturing and the Theory of Direct Investment', Unpublished PhD Thesis, Massachusetts Institute of Technology, Cambridge, September 1974.

McKAY, J-P, *Pioneers for Profit, Foreign Entrepreneurship and Russian Industrialization, 1885–1913*, University of Chicago, Chicago, 1970.

McKERN, B, 'The US Automobile Industry in the World Market', in Vernon, R, *Manager in the International Economy*, Prentice-Hall, Englewood Cliffs, New Jersey, 1972.

MEADOWS, Donella, et al, *The Limits to Growth*, Earth Island Ltd, London, 1972.

MENNIS, B and SAUVANT, K P, 'Corporate Internationalization and German Enterprise', Manuscript, The Wharton School, Philadelphia, 1973.

MEYER, Fritz W, *Die Pläne der Wirtschaftsintegration in Europa und die Schweizerische Aluminiumindustrie*, University of Fribourg, (Switzerland) 1960.

MICHALET, Charles-Albert, 'France', in VERNON, Raymond (ed), *Big Business And The State, Changing Relations In Western Europe*, Harvard University Press, Cambridge, Mass, 1974.

MICHALET, C-A and DELAPIERRE, M, *La multinationalisation des entreprises françaises*, Gauthier-Villars, Paris, 1973.

MICHEL, A J, *Introduction To The Principal Patent Systems Of The World*, New York, 1936, page 15, as cited in PENROSE, E, *The Economics Of The International Patent Systems*, Johns Hopkins, Baltimore, 1951.

MIKDASHI, Zuhayr, 'The Scheme of Malmexport', from MIKDASHI, Z, *A Comparative Survey of Mineral Exporting Industries*, Organization of the Petroleum Exporting Countries, Vienna, 1971.

MIKDASHI, Zuhayr, *A Comparative Analysis of Selected Mineral Exporting Industries*, Organization of the Petroleum Exporting Countries, Vienna, 1971.

MIKDASHI, Zuhayr, 'Aluminum', in VERNON, R (ed), *Big Business and the State: Changing Relations in Western Europe*, Harvard University Press, Cambridge, 1974.

MILLER, Roger Emile, *Innovation, Organization and Environment: A Study of Sixteen American and West European Steel Firms*, Université Catholique de Louvain, Nouvelles Séries, No 86, Belgium.

MITCHELL, Wesley C and others, *Income in the United States: Its Amount and Distribution 1909–1919*, by the Staff of the National Bureau of Economic Research, Incorporated, Vol I – Summary, Harcourt, Brace and Co, New York, p 141.

MONOPOLIES COMMISSION, *Cholordiazepoxide and Diazepam*, Her Majesty's Stationery Office, London, 1973.

MORVAN, Y, *La concentration de l'industrie en France*, Armand Colin, Paris, 1972.

MOSLEY, L, *Power Play, Oil in the Middle East*, Weidenfeld and Nicolson, London, 1973.

NADOLNY, B and TREUE, W, *VARTA, Ein Unternehmen der Quandt-Gruppe, 1888–1963*, Verlag Mensch und Arbeit, München, 1964.

NATIONAL BUREAU OF ECONOMIC RESEARCH, *Income in the United States: Its Amount and Distribution, 1909–1919*, Vol I, Harcourt, Brace and Co, New York, 1921.

NEHRT, Lee Charles, *The Political Climate for Private Foreign Investment*, Praeger, New York, 1970.

NEUE ZURCHER ZEITUNG, 'Deutschlands Automobilproduktion auf tieferem Niveau', September 29, 1974.

NKRUMAH, Kwame, *Neo-Colonialism, The Last Stage of Imperialism*, Heinemann, London, 1965.

NOBEL, Peter 'Multinationale Unternehmen', in BUCHI, R and MATTER, K, *Schweiz-Dritte Welt, Solidarität oder Rentabilität*, Schulthess Polygraphischer Verlag, Zurich, 1973.

NORTHRUP, Herbert R and ROWAN, Richard L, 'Multinational Collective Bargaining Activity: The Factual Record in Chemicals, Glass and Rubber Tires', Part I, *Columbia Journal of World Business*, Spring 1974, pp 112–125: Part II, *Columbia Journal of World Business*, Summer 1974, pp 49–63.

NYE, Joseph S, 'Multinational Corporations in World Politics', *Foreign Affairs*, September 10 1974.

OECD, *Gaps in Technology, Electronic Components*, OECD, Paris, 1968.

OECD, *Gaps in Technology, Scientific Instruments*, OECD, Paris, 1968.

OECD, *Gaps in Technology, Plastics*, OECD, Paris, 1969.

OECD, *Gaps in Technology, Electronic Computers*, OECD, Paris, 1969.

OECD, *Gaps in Technology, Analytical Report*, OECD, Paris, 1971.

OECD, Development Assistance Directorate, *Stock of Private Direct Investments by DAC Countries in Developing Countries, End 1967*, OECD, Paris, 1972.

OECD, *Problems and Prospects of the Primary Aluminium industry*, OECD, Paris, 1973.

OECD, *The Non-Ferrous Metals Industry*, OECD, Paris, various issues, especially 1962 and 1972.

OGGER, G, *Friderich Flick der Grosse*, Scherz Verlag, Bern und München, 1971.

OIL PAINT AND DRUG REPORTER, 'Rhone Poulenc to Pull Out of Italian Joint Ventures', December 20, 1971.

OTTERBECK, Lars, HEDLUND, Gunnar, PERLMUTTER, Howard, 'The MNC, The Trade Union and the Nation State in the Next Ten Years – The Swedish Case', Unpublished Ms, The Swedish Institute of Management, Stockholm, 1973.

OXFORD ECONOMIC ATLAS, Oxford University Press, London, 1972.

PARKS, F Newton, 'Group Management, European Style', *Business Horizons*, Vol 9, No 3, 1966.

PARUSH, Y, 'The Order of Acquisition of Durable Goods', *Bank of Israel Bulletin*, February 1964.

PAVAN, Robert J, *Strategy and Structure of Italian Enterprise*, unpublished DBA thesis, Harvard Graduate School of Business Administration, Boston, 1972.

PAVITT, Keith, *The Conditions for Success in Technological Innovation*, OECD, Paris, 1971.

PÉCHINEY, S A, *Le groupe Péchiney aux États-Unis*, Groupe Péchiney, Service de l'Information, Paris, 1970.

PENROSE, E, *The Economics Of The International Patent Systems*, Johns Hopkins, Baltimore, 1951.

PENROSE, Edith, *The Large International Firm in Developing Countries: The International Petroleum Industry*, George Allen and Unwin Ltd, London, 1968.

PENROSE, Edith, 'The Multinational Oil Corporations in the Middle East and the "Oil Crisis",' *Mondes en Développement*, No 5, Editions techniques et économiques, Paris, 1974.

PETROLEUM ECONOMIST, THE, 'Shell Sale Boosts Italy's ENI', February 1964, page 65.

PETROLEUM ECONOMIST, THE, 'Labor Policy for UK North Sea', August 1974, page 284.

PETROLEUM PRESS SERVICE, 'Sonatrach's Oil Empire', February 1972.

PHILIPS, N V, *Facts About Philips*, Eindhoven, 1970.

PHILIPS, N V, 'Brief History of N V Philips Gloeilampenfabriken', Philips Press Office, Eindhoven, 1972.

PHILIPS, *Annual Report*, 1973.

PHILIPS, *Philips in the Developing Countries*, Philips, NV, Einhoven, 1974.

PRIOURET, R, *Les Managers Européens*, Denoël, Paris, 1970.

PIRELLI, Alberto, *La Pirelli, Vita di Una Azienda Industriale*, Milan, MCMXLVI.

PIRENNE, Henri, *Mohammed and Charlemagne*, tr MIALL, B, W W Norton, New York, 1939.

PITAVAL, R, *Histoire de l'Aluminium*, Publications Minières et Métallurgiques, Paris, 1946.

PLUMMER, A, *International Combines In Modern Industry*, Isaac Pitman, London, 1934.

POLITIKA, 'Multinacionais', Rio de Janeiro, April 14, 1974.

POOLEY-DYAS, Gareth, *Strategy and Structure of French Enterprise*, unpublished DBA thesis, Harvard Graduate School of Business Administration, Boston, 1972.

PRATTEN, C F, *Economies of Scale in Manufacturing Industry*, Cambridge University Press, Cambridge, UK, 1971.

PRODI, R, 'Italy', in VERNON, R (ed), *Big Business and The State: Changing Relations in Western Europe*, Harvard University Press, Cambridge, 1974.

RATHENAU, Walther, speech by, December 20, 1915, cited in POLLARD, S and HOLMES, C, *Documents of European Economic History, Vol III, The End of the Old Europe, 1914–1939*, St Martins, New York, 1972.

REEKIE, W D, 'Patent Data As A Guide To Industrial Activity', *Research Policy*, 2, 1973.

REID, Margaret, 'The Crown Agents Under New Management', *Financial Times*, October 2, 1974, p 17.

REUBER, Grant L, with CROOKELL, H, EMERSON, M and GALLAIS, Hamond, *Private Foreign Investment in Development*, Oxford University Press, London, 1973.

REVUE DE L'ALUMINIUM, 'Le vaste programme italien de développement de la production nationale d'aluminium', September 1972.

RHONE-POULENC, *Groupe Rhodia Brésil: Historique*, unpublished company document, 1969.

RHONE-POULENC, 'Histoire de nos sociétés', No 3, Rhône-Poulenc, SA, Paris.

ROBERTSON, Sir Dennis, *Britain in the World Economy*, London, 1954.

ROBINSON, H J, *The Motivation And Flow Of Foreign Private Investment*, Stanford Research Institute, 1961.

ROBOCK, Stefan, 'The Case for Home Country Controls Over Multinationals', *Columbia Journal of World Business*, Summer 1974.

ROLFE, Sidney, E, *The International Corporation*, The International Chamber of Commerce, Paris, 1969.

RONDOT, Jean, *La Compagnie Française des Pétroles*, Plon, Paris, 1962.

ROSENSTEIN-RODAN, P, 'Multinational Investment in the Framework of Latin American Integration', in Inter-American Development Bank, *Multinational Investment, Public and Private in the Economic Development and Integration of Latin America*, Bogota, Columbia, 1968.

ROYAL DUTCH-SHELL, *The Royal Dutch Petroleum Company, 1890–1950*, The Hague, 1950.

ROYAL INSTITUTE OF INTERNATIONAL AFFAIRS, THE, The Information Department, *South-Eastern Europe, A Political and Economic Survey*, Oxford University Press, London, 1939.

RUMELT, Richard, *Strategy, Structure and Financial Performance of the Fortune '500', 1950–1970*, Harvard University Press, Cambridge, 1974.

SALVEMENI, G, *Italy Under the Axe of Fascism*, Citadel Press, New York, 1971.

SANDOZ, A G, *75 ans d'activité*, Basel, 1961.

SASULY, Richard, *I G Farben*, Parish Press, New York, 1947.

SCAPERLANDA, A E and MAURER, L J, 'The Determinants Of US Direct Investment in the EEC', *American Economic Review*, September 1969.

SCHARRER, Hans-Eckart (ed), *Förderung privater Direkt-investitionen*, Hamburg, 1972.

SCHERER, F M, 'Economics of Scale and Industrial Concentration', unpublished Ms, International Institute of Management, Berlin, 1974.

SCHILDBERGER, Friedrich, 'The History of Industrial Automobile Production in the United States up to the Turn of the Century and the German Influence', Unpublished Ms, Daimler-Benz, AG, Stuttgart, undated.

SCHOLLHAMMER, Hans, 'Organization Structures of Multinational Corporations', *Academy of Management Journal*, Vol 14, No 3, September 1971.

SCHWAMM, Henry, 'Swiss Industrial Penetration in the Common Market', *Journal of World Trade Law*, No 5, pp 703–711, November–December 1971.

SCOTT, B and MACARTHUR, J, *Industrial Planning in France*, Harvard Business School, Boston, 1969.

SERVAN-SCHREIBER, J-J, *Le Défi Américain*, Denoël, Paris, 1967.

SHAPLEN, Robert, *Kreuger: Genius and Swindler*, Knopf, New York, 1960.

SHEAHAN, John, 'Government Competition and the Performance of the French Automobile Industry', *The Journal of Industrial Economics*, Vol 8, No 3, June 1960.

SHEAHAN, John, *Promotion and Control of Industry in Postwar France*, Harvard University Press, Cambridge, 1963.

SHIMONI, Y and LEVINE, E, *Political Dictionary of the Middle East in the 20th Century*, Jerusalem Publishing House, Ltd, Jerusalem, 1972.

SHIRER, W, *The Rise and Fall of the Third Reich*, Fawcett, Greenwich, 1960.

SHONFIELD, Andrew, *Modern Capitalism*, Oxford University Press, 1969.

SIEKMAN, Philip, 'Europe's Love Affair with Bigness', *Fortune*, March 1970.

SIEMENS, G, *History Of The House Of Siemens*, Vols I and II, Karl Alber Verlag, Freiburg/Munich, 1957.

SIDJANSKI, D and MEYNAUD, J, *L'Europe des affaires*, Payot, Paris, 1967.

SIMMONDS, Kenneth and ROBOCK, Stefan, 'International Business: How Big Is It?' *Columbia Journal of World Business*, May–June 1970.

SIMONDS, H R, *Source Book of New Plastics*, Vols I and II, Reinhold, New York, 1963.

SIMONET, Henri, 'Uneasy Bedfellows, A Diagnosis of USA—EEC Relations', Ms, 1974.

SKANDINAVISKA ENSKILDA BANKEN, *Quarterly Review*, No 2, 1972.

SKELTON, A, in ELLIOTT, W Y (ed), *International Control in the Non-Ferrous Metals Industry*, Macmillan, New York, 1937.

SKINNER, Jean Ross, 'Why Europeans Can't Control Their US Subsidiaries', *Dun's Review*, May 1973.

SKF, *SKF 1907–1957, A History in Pictures*, SFK, Sfären, 2, Gothenburg, 1957.

SMITH, Richard Austin, 'At St Gobain the First 300 Years Were the Easiest', *Fortune*, October 1965.

SOCIÉTÉ GÉNÉRALE DE BELGIQUE, *Société Générale de Belgique, 1822–1972*, Brussels, 1972.

SPILLMANN, Georges, *Napoléon III, prophète méconnu*, Presses de la Cité, Paris, 1972.

STALEY, E, *Raw Materials in Peace and War*, Council on Foreign Relations, New York, 1937.

STALEY, E, *War and the Private Investor*, Doubleday, New York, 1935.

STEPHENSON, Hugh, *The Coming Clash*, Weidenfeld and Nicolson, London, 1972.

STOCKING, G W and WATKINS, M W, *Cartels In Action*, Twentieth Century Fund, New York, 1946.

STONEHILL, Arthur, *Foreign Ownership in Norwegian Enterprise*, Central Bureau of Statistics of Norway, Oslo, 1965.

STOPFORD, John M, 'Organizing the Multinational Firm. Can the Americans Learn from the Europeans?' in BROOKE, Michael Z and REMMERS, H Lee (eds), *The Multinational Company in Europe*, Longman, London, 1972.

STOPFORD, John, 'The Evolution of UK-Based Multinational Enterprises', Manuscript for a Harvard Business School Conference on Multinational Enterprise, December 1972.

STOPFORD, John M, 'The Origins of British-Based Multinational Manufacturing Enterprises', *The Business History Review*, Autumn 1974.

STOPFORD, John M and WELLS, Louis T, Jr, *Managing the Multinational Enterprise*, Basic, Books, New York, 1972.

STORM, Baudouin, 'L'évolution du portefeuille de la Société Générale', *La revue nouvelle* No 11, November 1972.

STREHLER, Hermann, *Politique d'investissement à l'étranger des grandes enterprises industrielles suisses*, Zollikofer & Co, St Gall, 1969.

STUCKI, Lorenz, *L'empire occulte, les secrets de la puissance helvétique*, Robert Laffont, Paris, 1970.

SULZBERGER, Cyrus, 'The Enormous Unknown', *International Herald Tribune*, September 22–23, 1973.

SURREY, A J and CHESSHIRE, J H, *The World Market for Electric Power Generation Equipment*, Science Policy Research Institute, University of Sussex, Sussex, UK, 1972.

SUTTON, Antony C, *Western Technology and Soviet Economic Development, 1917 to 1930*, Hoover Institution, Stanford, 1968.

SWANN, D, *The Economics of the Common Market*, Penguin, London, 1972.

SWEDENBORG, Birgitta, *Den Svenska Industrins Investeringar i Utlandet*, Almqvist and Wiksell, Stockholm, 1973.

TECHNOMIC RESEARCH ASSOCIATES, *The Enlarged EEC and the American Technology Challenge*, Volume C, William D Witter, Inc, New York, 1973.

TEICHOVA, Alice, *An Economic Background To Munich: International Business And Czechoslovakia 1918–1938*, Cambridge University Press, London, 1974.

THANNHEISER, Heinz, *Strategy and Structure of German Enterprise*, unpublished DBA thesis, Harvard Graduate School of Business Administration, Boston, 1972.

THOMAS, D S, *Social and Economic Aspects of Swedish Population Movements, 1750–1933*, Macmillan, London, 1941.

TIGER, Michael, 'The Liberian-American-Swedish Mineral Company, (LAMCO): A Joint Venture in Africa', Photo-offset, Centre d'Études Industrielles, Geneva, April 1974.

TIGER, M and FRANKO, L G, *ENI*, Photo-offset, Centre d'Études Industrielles, Geneva, 1973.

TILTON, J E, *International Diffusion of Technology: The Case of Semiconductors*, The Brookings Institution, Washington, DC, 1971.

TO THE POINT INTERNATIONAL- 'What Gotland's Got', May 18, 1974, pages 33 and 34.

TO THE POINT INTERNATIONAL, 'Commercial Vikings', August 24, 1974, p 33.

TOYO KEIZAI, *Statistics Monthly*, Vol 32, June 1972.

TREUE, W and UEBBING, H, *Die Feuer verlöschen nie: August Thyssen-Hütte 1926–1966*, Econ Verlag, Düsseldorf, 1969.

TSURUMI, Y, 'Japanese Multinational Firms', *Journal of World Trade Law*, January–February 1973.

TSURUMI, Yoshihiro, 'Multinational Spread of Japanese Firms and Asian Neighbors' Reactions', Unpublished Ms, Conference on 'The Multinational Corporation as an Instrument of Development – Political Considerations', Yale University, New Haven, May 9–12, 1974.

TUDYKA, K P, *Multinational Corporations and Labor Unions*, Werkuitgave Sun, Nijmegan, 1973.

TUGENDHAT, C, *Oil: The Biggest Business*, Eyre and Spottiswoode, London, 1968.

TUMLIR, Jan, 'Oil Payments and Oil Debt in the World Economy', *Lloyds Bank Review*, July 1974, No 113, pages 1–14.

UNITED KINGDOM BOARD OF TRADE, *Board of Trade Journal*, January 26, 1968.

UNITED KINGDOM, *Board Of Trade Journal*, September 23, 1970.

UNION MINIERE, *Annual Reports*, various issues.

UNION MINIERE, Carte d'identité', Brussels, 1974.

UNITED NATIONS, *Statistical Yearbook*, various issues.

UNITED NATIONS, *Economic Survey of Europe in 1956*, United Nations Department of Economic and Social Affairs, prepared by the Research and Planning Division, Economic Commission for Europe, Geneva, Switzerland, Chapter IX, p 6, 1957.

UNITED NATIONS, *Patterns of Industrial Growth 1938–1958*, UN, New York, 1958.

UNITED NATIONS, *Long Term Trends in the European Steel Industry*, UN Economic Commission for Europe, 1959.

UNITED NATIONS ECONOMIC COMMISSION FOR EUROPE, *Incomes in Post-war Europe*, UN, Geneva, Vol I, 1957, and, Vol II, 1967.

UNITED NATIONS, *Statistical Yearbook*, United Nations, New York, 1971.

UNITED NATIONS, *Statistical Yearbook*, United Nations, New York, 1972.

UNITED NATIONS, *Multinational Corporations in World Development*, United Nations, New York, and Geneva, 1973.

UNITED NATIONS, *The Impact of Multinational Corporations on the Development Process and on the International Relations, Report of the Group of Eminent Persons*, US, ECOSOC, New York, No. E/5500/Add 1/Rev 1-ST/ESP/6, 1974.

UNITED NATIONS, General Assembly, *Permanent Sovereignty over Natural Resources*, Report of the Secretary General, UN, ECOSOC, New York, A/9716, September 1974.

UNITED STATES, *Statistical Abstract Of The United States*, various issues.

UNITED STATES, *Statistical Abstract of the United States, 1971*, Washington, DC, 1972, Table 504, p. 317.

UNITED STATES BUREAU OF MINES, *Mineral Facts and Problems*, Washington, DC, 1960.

UNITED STATES BUREAU OF MINES, *Minerals Yearbook, 1971*, Washington, DC, 1973.

UNITED STATES BUREAU OF THE CENSUS, *Historical Statistics Of The United States, 1798–1945*, Washington, DC, 1949.

UNITED STATES DEPARTMENT OF COMMERCE, *Survey of Current Business*, various issues.

US DEPARTMENT OF COMMERCE, *Foreign Long Term Investment in the United States, 1937–39*, Washington, DC, 1940.

UNITED STATES TARIFF COMMISSION, *The Rayon Industry*, Washington, DC, 1944.

UNITED STATES TARIFF COMMISSION, *Implications of Multinational Firms for World Trade and Investment and for US Trade and Labor*, Committee on Finance, United States Senate, Washington, DC, 1973.

URI, P (ed), *Trade and Investment Policies for the 1970's*, Praeger, New York, 1971.

VAITOS, Constantine, 'Foreign Investment Policies and Economic Development in Latin America', *Journal of World Trade Law*, Vol 7, No 6, November–December 1973.

VAITSOS, Constantine, 'Power, Knowledge and Development Policy: Relations between Transnational Enterprises and Developing Countries', Unpublished Ms, The Dag Hammarskjöld Foundation, Uppsala, Sweden, August 1974.

VAN DEN BULKE, D, *Les investissements industriels étrangers dans l'économie belge*, Université de Gand, Gand 1971.

VAN DER HAAS, Hans, *The Enterprise in Transition: An Analysis of European and American Practice*, Tavistock, London, 1967.

VAN DER WAL, S L, 'The Netherlands as an Imperial Power in South-East Asia in the 19th Century and After', in BROMLEY, J S and KOSSMANN, E H (eds), *Britain and the Netherlands in Europe and Asia*, Macmillan, London, 1968.

VANHEMELRYCK, Albert, 'John Cockerill', *Cockerill: Bulletin d'information pour le personnel de la S A Cockerill – Ougrée-Providence et Espérance-Longdoz*, No 164, 21ème année, troisième trimestre, 1970.

VAUPEL, James Walter, 'Characteristics and Motivations of the US Corporations That Manufacture Abroad', Unpublished Ms presented to the Agnelli Foundation Conference on Multinational Enterprise, Turin, June 1971.

VAUPEL, J and CURHAN, J, *The Making of Multinational Enterprise*, Harvard Business School, Boston, 1969.

VAUPEL, J and CURHAN, J, *The World's Multinational Enterprises, A Sourcebook Of Tables*, Harvard Business School, Boston, 1973 and CEI, Geneva, Switzerland, 1974.

VERNON, Raymond, Comparative Multinational Enterprise Study, *Annual Progress Reports*, 1966 through 1974.

VERNON, Raymond, 'International Trade and International Investment in the Product Cycle', *Quarterly Journal of Economics*, May 1966.

VERNON, Raymond, 'Organization as a Scale Factor in the Growth of Firms', in MARKHAM, Jesse W and PAPANEK, Gustav F, *Industrial Organization and Economic Development*, Houghton Mifflin, Boston, 1970.

VERNON, Raymond, *Sovereignty At Bay*, Basic Books, New York, 1971.

VERNON, Raymond, 'Some Tentative Hypotheses on the Behavior of European-Based and Japanese-Based Multinational Enterprises', Manuscript for a conference on Multinational Enterprises, Agnelli Foundation, Turin, Italy, June 1971.

VERNON, Raymond, 'Two-Ply, Inc', *Case in Manager in the International Economy*, Prentice-Hall, Englewood Cliffs, New York, 1972.

VERNON, Raymond, 'Influence Of National Origins On The Strategy Of Multinational Enterprise', *Revue économique*, July 1972.

VERNON, Raymond, 'Competition Policy Toward Multinational Corporations', *American Economic Review*, Vol 64, No 2, May 1974.

VERNON, R (ed), *Big Business and The State: Changing Relations in Western Europe*, Harvard University Press, Cambridge, 1974.

VICE, A, *Strategy of Takeovers*, McGraw-Hill, London, 1971.

VISION, 'Déplacer les ouvriers ou les usines', October 1971.

VISION, 'Multinationales: les européens sont à l'aise', October 1971, p 77.

VISION, Advertisement by L M Ericsson, December 15, 1972, p 126.

VISION, 'Well, Why Do Drug Prices Vary So Widely?' May 1973, p 97.

VISION, 'Ambroise Roux: Un manager sous forte tension', December 1973, p 58.

VISION, 'La vérité derrière les étiquettes', December 1973.

VISION, 'Ces matières redevenues premières', March 1974, page 40.

VON BERTRAB, H R, 'The Transfer of Technology: A Case Study of European Private Enterprises Having Operations in Latin America With Special Emphasis on Mexico', unpublished PhD Dissertation, University of Texas, Austin, 1968.

VON SALDERN, Sabine, *Internationaler Vergleich der Direkt-investitionen wichtiger Industrieländer*, HWWA-Institut für Wirtschafsforschung, Report No 15, Hamburg, February 1973.

WALLACE, D H, *Market Control in the Aluminum Industry*, Harvard University Press, Cambridge, Mass, 1937.

WANNER, Dr Gustaf Adolf, 'Fritz Hoffmann–La Roche (1868–1920)', *Schweizer Pioniere der Wirtschaft und Technik*, No 24, Verein für wirtschaftshistorische Studien, Zurich, 1971.

WARD, James, 'Product and Promotion Adaptation by European Firms in the US,' *Journal of International Business Studies*, Spring 1973.

WELLS, D A, *Recent Economic Changes and their Effects on the Production and Distribution of Wealth and Well Being of Society*, 1893, as cited in POLLARD, S and HOLMES, C, *Documents of European Economic History, Vol III, The End of the Old Europe, 1914–1939*, St Martins, New York, 1972.

WELLS, Louis T, Jr, 'The Evolution of Concession Agreements', Harvard University Development Advisory Service, Cambridge, June 1968.

WELLS, Louis T, Jr, 'Test of a Product Cycle Model of International Trade: US Exports of Consumer Durables', *Quarterly Journal of Economics*, February 1969.

WELLS, Louis T, Jr, 'The Multinational Business Enterprise: What Kind of International Organization?' *International Organization*, Vol XXV, No 3, Summer 1971.

WELLS, Louis T, Jr, (ed), *The Product Life Cycle and International Trade*, Harvard Business School, Boston, 1972.

WELLS, Louis, T, Jr, 'Economic Man and Engineering Man: Choice of Technology in a Low-Wage Country', *Public Policy*, Vol 21, No 3, Summer, 1973, pp 319–342.

WELLS, Louis T, Jr, 'Joint Ventures – Successful Handshake or Painful Headache?' *European Business*, No 38, Summer 1973.

WELLS, L T, Jr, 'Automobiles', in VERNON, R (ed), *Big Business and the State: Changing Relations in Western Europe*, Harvard University Press, Cambridge, Mass, 1974.

WHITEHEAD, Michael, 'The Multinationally-Owned Company: A Case Study', in DUNNING, John H (ed), *The Multinational Enterprise*, George Allen and Unwin, London, 1971.

WILKINS, Mira, *The Emergence Of Multinational Enterprise*, Harvard University Press, Cambridge, Mass, 1970.

WILKINS, Mira, *The Maturing Of Multinational Enterprise*, Harvard University Press, Cambridge, 1974.

WILKINS, Mira and HILL, F, *American Business Abroad: Ford On Six Continents*, Wayne State University Press, Detroit, 1964.

WILLATT, Norris, 'Hoffmann-La Roche: How Successful is a Secret', *Financial Times*, November 16, 1971.

WILSON, Charles, *The History of Unilever*, Volume II, Cassell, London, 1954.

WILSON, Charles, *Unilever 1945–1965*, Cassell, London, 1968.

WINNACKER, K, *Challenging Years*, Sidgwick and Jackson, London, 1972.

WINNACKER, Karl and KUCHER Leopold, *Chemische Technology*, Hansen, Munich, 1959.

WIPPLINGER, Günter, *Empresas Industriales con participación de capital alemán en la Argentina condiciones y actitudes en lo que se refiere a la exportación de productos manufacturados*, Instituto de Estudios Ibero americanos, Unpublished Ms, Hamburg, 1971.

WORTZEL, L, 'The Pharmaceutical Industry Study: An Overview', unpublished Ms, presented at a conference sponsored by the Agnelli Foundation in Turin, Italy on the Comparative Multinational Enterprise Project, June 1971.

WOYTINSKY, W S and WOYTINSKY, E S, *World Population and Production: Trends and Outlook*, The Twentieth Century Fund, New York, 1953, pp 409 and 407.

WOYTINSKY, W S and WOYTINSKY, E S *World Commerce and Governments*, The Twentieth Century Fund, New York, 1955.

YANAGA, C, *Big Business in Japanese Politics*, Yale, New Haven, 1971.

YOSHINO, M, *Japan's Managerial System*, MIT Press, Cambridge, 1968.

ZENOFF, David and ZWICK, Jack, 'LAMCO, (A) and (B)', in *International Financial Management*, Prentice Hall, Englewood Cliffs, New Jersey, 1969.

Index